本书出版得到《大中华文库》出版经费资助

大中华文库

LIBRARY OF CHINESE CLASSICS

大中华文库
汉英对照
LIBRARY OF CHINESE CLASSICS
Chinese-English

南柯记

A DREAM UNDER THE SOUTHERN BOUGH

（明朝）汤显祖　著
张光前　译

Written by Tang Xianzu
Translated by Zhang Guangqian

外文出版社
Foreign Languages Press

First Edition 2006
Second Printing 2020

ISBN 978-7-119-04165-0

Published by
Foreign Languages Press
24 Baiwanzhuang Road, Beijing 100037, China
http: // www.flp.com.cn

Printed in the People's Republic of China

总　　序

杨牧之

《大中华文库》终于出版了。我们为之高兴，为之鼓舞，但也倍感压力。

当此之际，我们愿将郁积在我们心底的话，向读者倾诉。

一

中华民族有着悠久的历史和灿烂的文化，系统、准确地将中华民族的文化经典翻译成外文，编辑出版，介绍给全世界，是几代中国人的愿望。早在几十年前，西方一位学者翻译《红楼梦》，将书名译成《一个红楼上的梦》，将林黛玉译为“黑色的玉”。我们一方面对外国学者将中国的名著介绍到世界上去表示由衷的感谢，一方面为祖国的名著还不被完全认识，甚而受到曲解，而感到深深的遗憾。还有西方学者翻译《金瓶梅》，专门摘选其中自然主义描述最为突出的篇章加以译介。一时间，西方学者好像发现了奇迹，掀起了《金瓶梅》热，说中国是“性开放的源头”，公开地在报刊上鼓吹中国要“发扬开放之传统”。还有许多资深、友善的汉学家译介中国古代的哲学著作，在把中华民族文化介绍给全世界的工作方面作出了重大贡献，但或囿于理解有误，或缘于对中国文字认识的局限，质量上乘的并不多，常常是隔靴搔痒，说不到点子上。大哲学家黑格尔曾经说过：中国有最完备的国史。但他认为中国古代没有真正意义上的哲学，还处在哲学史前状态。这么了不起的哲学家竟然作出这样大失水准的评论，何其不幸。正如任何哲学家都要受时间、地点、条件的制约一样，黑格尔也离不开这一规律。当时他也只能从上述水平的汉学家译过去的文字去分析、理解，所以，黑格尔先生对中国古代社会的认识水平是什么状态，也就不难想象了。

中国离不开世界，世界也缺少不了中国。中国文化摄取外域的新成分，丰富了自己，又以自己的新成就输送给别人，贡献于世界。从公元5世纪开始到公元15世纪，大约有一千年，中国走在世界的前列。在这一千多年的时间里，她的光辉照耀全世界。人类要前进，怎么能不全面认识中国，怎么能不认真研究中国的历史呢？

二

中华民族是伟大的，曾经辉煌过，蓝天、白云、阳光灿烂，和平而兴旺；也有过黑暗的、想起来就让人战栗的日子，但中华民族从来是充满理想，不断追求，不断学习，渴望和平与友谊的。

中国古代伟大的思想家孔子曾经说过：“三人行，必有我师焉。择其善者而从之，其不善者而改之。”孔子的话就是要人们向别人学习。这段话正是概括了整个中华民族与人交往的原则。人与人之间交往如此，在与周边的国家交往中也是如此。

秦始皇第一个统一了中国，可惜在位只有十几年，来不及做更多的事情。汉朝继秦而继续强大，便开始走出去，了解自己周边的世界。公元前139年，汉武帝派张骞出使西域。他带着一万头牛羊，总值一万万钱的金帛货物，作为礼物，开始西行，最远到过“安息”（即波斯）。公元73年，班超又率36人出使西域。36个人按今天的话说，也只有一个排的人数，显然是为了拜访未曾见过面的邻居，是去交朋友。到了西域，班超派遣甘英作为使者继续西行，往更远处的大秦国（即罗马）去访问，“乃抵条支而历安息，临西海以望大秦”(《后汉书·西域传》)。“条支”在“安息”以西，即今天的伊拉克、叙利亚一带，“西海”应是今天的地中海。也就是说甘英已经到达地中海边上，与罗马帝国隔海相望，“临大海欲渡”，却被人劝阻而未成行，这在历史上留下了遗恨。可以想见班超、甘英沟通友谊的无比勇气和强烈愿望。接下来是唐代的玄奘，历经千难万险，到“西天”印度取经，带回了南亚国家的古老文化。归国后，他把带回的佛教经典组织人翻译，到后来很多经典印度失传了，但中国却保存完好，以至于今天，没有玄奘的《大唐西域记》，印度人很难完整地编写印度古代史。明代郑和“七下西洋”，把中华文化传到东南亚一带。鸦片战争以后，一代又一代先进的中国人，为了振兴中华，又前赴后继，向西方国家学习先进的科学思想和文明成果。这中间有我们的领导人朱德、周恩来、邓小平；有许许多多大科学家、文学家、艺术家，如郭沫若、李四光、钱学森、冼星海、徐悲鸿等。他们的追求、奋斗，他们的博大胸怀、兼收并蓄的精神，为人类社会增添了光彩。

中国文化的形成和发展过程，就是一个以众为师、以各国人民为师，不断学习和创造的过程。中华民族曾经向周边国家和民族学习过许多东西，假如没有这些学习，中华民族绝不可能创造出昔日的辉煌。回顾历史，我们怎么能够不对伟大的古埃及文明、古希腊文明、古印度文明满怀深深的感激？怎么能够不对伟大的欧洲文明、非洲文明、美洲文明、澳洲文明，以及中国周围的亚洲文明充满温情与敬意？

中华民族为人类社会曾作出过独特的贡献。在15世纪以前，中国的科学技术一直处于世界遥遥领先的地位。英国科学家李约瑟说："中国在公元3世纪到13世纪之间，保持着一个西方所望尘莫及的科学知识水平。"美国耶鲁大学教授、《大国的兴衰》的作者保罗·肯尼迪坦言："在近代以前时期的所有文明中，没有一个国家的文明比中国更发达，更先进。"

世界各国的有识之士千里迢迢来中国观光、学习。在这个过程中，中国唐朝的长安城渐渐发展成为国际大都市。西方的波斯、东罗马，东亚的高丽、新罗、百济，南亚的南天竺、北天竺，频繁前来。外国的王侯、留学生及在长安供职的外国官员、商贾、乐工和舞士，总有几十个国家，几万人之多。日本派出"遣唐使"更是一批接一批。传为美谈的日本人阿倍仲麻吕（晁衡）在长安留学的故事，很能说明外国人与中国的交往。晁衡学成仕于唐朝，前后历时五十余年。晁衡与中国的知识分子结下了深厚的友情。他归国时，传说在海中遇难身亡。大诗人李白作诗哭悼："日本晁卿辞帝都，征帆一片远蓬壶。明月不归沉碧海，白云愁色满苍梧。"晁衡遇险是误传，但由此可见中外学者之间在中国长安交往的情谊。

后来，不断有外国人到中国来探寻秘密，所见所闻，常常让他们目瞪口呆。《希腊纪事》（希腊人波桑尼阿著）记载公元2世纪时，希腊人在中国的见闻。书中写道："赛里斯人用小米和青芦喂一种类似蜘蛛的昆虫，喂到第五年，虫肚子胀裂开，便从里面取出丝来。"从这段对中国古代养蚕技术的描述，可见当时欧洲人与中国人的差距。公元9世纪中叶，阿拉伯人来到中国。一位阿拉伯作家在他所著的《中国印度闻见录》中记载了曾旅居中国的阿拉伯商人的见闻：

——一天，一个外商去拜见驻守广州的中国官吏。会见时，外商总盯着官吏的胸部，官吏很奇怪，便问："你好像总盯着我的胸，这是怎么回事？"那位外商回答说："透过你穿的丝绸衣服，我隐约看到你胸口上长着一个黑痣，这是什么丝绸，我感到十分惊奇。"官吏听后，失声大笑，伸出胳膊，说："请你数数吧，看我穿了几件衣服？"那商人数过，竟然穿了五件之多，黑痣正是透过这五层丝绸衣服显现出来的。外商惊得目瞪口呆，官吏说："我穿的丝绸还不算是最好的，总督穿的要更精美。"

——书中关于茶（他们叫干草叶子）的记载，可见阿拉伯国家当时还没有喝茶的习惯。书中记述："中国国王本人的收入主要靠盐税和泡开水喝的一种干草税。在各个城市里，这种干草叶售价都很高，中国人称这种草叶叫'茶'，这种干草叶比苜蓿的叶子还多，也略比它香，稍有苦味，用开水冲喝，治百病。"

——他们对中国的医疗条件十分羡慕，书中记载道："中国人医疗条件很好，穷人可以从国库中得到药费。"还说："城市里，很多地方立一石碑，高10肘，上面刻有各种疾病和药物，写明某种病用某种药医治。"

——关于当时中国的京城，书中作了生动的描述：中国的京城很大，人口众多，一条宽阔的长街把全城分为两半，大街右边的东区，住着皇帝、宰相、禁军及皇家的总管、奴婢。在这个区域，沿街开凿了小河，流水潺潺；路旁，葱茏的树木整然有序，一幢幢宅邸鳞次栉比。大街左边的西区，住着庶民和商人。这里有货栈和商店，每当清晨，人们可以看到，皇室的总管、宫廷的仆役，或骑马或步行，到这里来采购。

此后的史籍对西人来华的记载，渐渐多了起来。13世纪意大利旅行家马可·波罗，尽管有人对他是否真的到过中国持怀疑态度，但他留下一部记述元代事件的《马可·波罗游记》却是确凿无疑的。这部游记中的一些关于当时中国的描述使得西方人认为是“天方夜谭”。总之，从中西文化交流史来说，这以前的时期还是一个想象和臆测的时代，相互之间充满了好奇与幻想。

从16世纪末开始，由于航海技术的发展，东西方航路的开通，随着一批批传教士来华，中国与西方开始了直接的交流。沟通中西的使命在意大利传教士利玛窦那里有了充分的体现。利玛窦于1582年来华，1610年病逝于北京，在华二十余年。除了传教以外，做了两件具有历史象征意义的事，一是1594年前后在韶州用拉丁文翻译《四书》，并作了注释；二是与明代学者徐光启合作，用中文翻译了《几何原本》。

西方传教士对《四书》等中国经典的粗略翻译，以及杜赫德的《中华帝国志》等书对中国的介绍，在西方读者的眼前展现了一个异域文明，在当时及稍后一段时期引起了一场“中国热”，许多西方大思想家的眼光都曾注目于中国文化。有的推崇中华文明，如莱布尼兹、伏尔泰、魁奈等，有的对中华文明持批评态度，如孟德斯鸠、黑格尔等。莱布尼兹认识到中国文化的某些思想与他的观念相近，如周易的卦象与他发明的二进制相契合，对中国文化给予了热情的礼赞；黑格尔则从他整个哲学体系的推演出发，认为中国没有真正意义上的哲学，还处在哲学史前的状态。但是，不论是推崇还是批评，是吸纳还是排斥，中西文化的交流产生了巨大的影响。随着先进的中国科学技术的西传，特别是中国的造纸、火药、印刷术和指南针四大发明的问世，大大改变了世界的面貌。马克思说："中国的火药把骑士阶层炸得粉碎，指南针打开了世界市场并建立了殖民地，而印刷术则变成了新教的工具，变成对精神发展创造必要前提的最强大的杠杆。"英国的哲学家培根说：中国的四大发明"改变了全世界的面貌和一切事物的状态"。

三

大千世界，潮起潮落。云散云聚，万象更新。中国古代产生了无数伟大的科学家：祖冲之、李时珍、孙思邈、张衡、沈括、毕昇……产生了无数科技成果：《齐民要术》、《九章算术》、《伤寒杂病论》、《本草纲目》……以及保存至今的世界奇迹：浑天仪、地动仪、都江堰、敦煌石窟、大运河、万里长城……但从15世纪下半叶起，风水似乎从东方转到了西方，落后的欧洲只经过400年便成为世界瞩目的文明中心。英国的牛顿、波兰的哥白尼、德国的伦琴、法国的居里、德国的爱因斯坦、意大利的伽利略、俄国的门捷列夫、美国的费米和爱迪生……光芒四射，令人敬仰。

中华民族开始思考了。潮起潮落究竟是什么原因？中国人发明的火药，传到欧洲，转眼之间反成为欧洲列强轰击中国大门的炮弹，又是因为什么？

鸦片战争终于催醒了中国人沉睡的迷梦，最先"睁眼看世界"的一代精英林则徐、魏源迈出了威武雄壮的一步。曾国藩、李鸿章搞起了洋务运动。中国的知识分子喊出"民主与科学”的口号。中国是落后了，中国的志士仁人在苦苦探索。但落后中饱含着变革的动力，探索中孕育着崛起的希望。“向科学进军”，中华民族终于又迎来了科学的春天。

今天，世界毕竟来到了21世纪的门槛。分散隔绝的世界，逐渐变成联系为一体的世界。现在，全球一体化趋势日益明显，人类历史也就在愈来愈大的程度上成为全世界的历史。当今，任何一种文化的发展都离不开对其他优秀文化的汲取，都以其他优秀文化的发展为前提。在近现代，西方文化汲取中国文化，不仅是中国文化的传播，更是西方文化自身的创新和发展；正如中国文化对西方文化的汲取一样，既是西方文化在中国的传播，同时也是中国文化在近代的转型和发展。地球上所有的人类文化，都是我们共同的宝贵遗产。既然我们生活的各个大陆，在地球史上曾经是连成一气的“泛大陆”，或者说是一个完整的“地球村”，那么，我们同样可以在这个以知识和学习为特征的网络时代，走上相互学习、共同发展的大路，建设和开拓我们人类崭新的“地球村”。

西学仍在东渐，中学也将西传。各国人民的优秀文化正日益迅速地为中国文化所汲取，而无论西方和东方，也都需要从中国文化中汲取养分。正是基于这一认识，我们组织出版汉英对照版《大中华文库》，全面系统地翻译介绍中国传统文化典籍。我们试图通过《大中华文库》，向全世界展示，中华民族五千年的追求、五千年的梦想，正在新的历史时期重放光芒。中国人民就像火后的凤凰，万众一心，迎接新世纪文明的太阳。

1999年8月　北京

FOREWORD TO THE *LIBRARY OF CHINESE CLASSICS*

Yang Muzhi

The publication of the *Library of Chinese Classics* is a matter of great satisfaction to all of us who have been involved in the production of this monumental work. At the same time, we feel a weighty sense of responsibility, and take this opportunity to explain to our readers the motivation for undertaking this cross-century task.

1

The Chinese nation has a long history and a glorious culture, and it has been the aspiration of several generations of Chinese scholars to translate, edit and publish the whole corpus of the Chinese literary classics so that the nation's greatest cultural achievements can be introduced to people all over the world. There have been many translations of the Chinese classics done by foreign scholars. A few dozen years ago, a Western scholar translated the title of *A Dream of Red Mansions* into "A Dream of Red Chambers" and Lin Daiyu, the heroine in the novel, into "Black Jade." But while their endeavours have been laudable, the results of their labours have been less than satisfactory. Lack of knowledge of Chinese culture and an inadequate grasp of the Chinese written language have led the translators into many errors. As a consequence, not only are Chinese classical writings widely misunderstood in the rest of the world, in some cases their content has actually been distorted. At one time, there was a "*Jin Ping Mei* craze" among Western scholars, who thought that they had uncovered a miraculous phenomenon, and published theories claiming that China was the "fountainhead of eroticism," and that a Chinese "tradition of permissiveness" was about to be laid bare. This distorted view came about due to the translators of the *Jin Ping Mei (The Golden Lotus)* putting one-sided stress on the raw elements in that novel, to the neglect of its overall literary value. Meanwhile, there have been many distinguished and well-intentioned Sinologists who have attempted to make the culture of the Chinese nation more widely known by translating works of ancient Chinese philosophy. However, the quality of such work, in many cases, is unsatisfactory, often missing the point entirely. The great philosopher Hegel considered that ancient China had no philosophy in the real sense of the word, being stuck in philosophical "prehistory." For such an eminent authority to make such a colossal error of judgment is truly regrettable. But, of course, Hegel was just as subject to the constraints of time, space and other objective conditions as anyone else, and since he had to rely for his knowledge of Chinese philosophy on inadequate translations it is not difficult to imagine why he went so far off the mark.

China cannot be separated from the rest of the world; and the rest of the world cannot ignore China. Throughout its history, Chinese civilization has enriched itself by absorbing new elements from the outside world, and in turn has contributed to the progress of world civilization as a whole by transmitting to other peoples its own cultural achievements. From the 5th to the 15th centuries, China marched in the front ranks of world civilization. If mankind wishes to advance, how can it afford to ignore China? How can it afford not to make a thoroughgoing study of its history?

2

Despite the ups and downs in their fortunes, the Chinese people have always been idealistic, and have never ceased to forge ahead and learn from others, eager to strengthen ties of peace and friendship.

The great ancient Chinese philosopher Confucius once said, "Wherever three persons come together, one of them will surely be able to teach me something. I will pick out his good points and emulate them; his bad points I will reform." Confucius meant by this that we should always be ready to learn from others. This maxim encapsulates the principle the Chinese people have always followed in their dealings with other peoples, not only on an individual basis but also at the level of state-to-state relations.

After generations of internecine strife, China was unified by Emperor

Qin Shi Huang (the First Emperor of the Qin Dynasty) in 221 BC The Han Dynasty, which succeeded that of the short-lived Qin, waxed powerful, and for the first time brought China into contact with the outside world. In 139 BC, Emperor Wu dispatched Zhang Qian to the western regions, i.e. Central Asia. Zhang, who traveled as far as what is now Iran, took with him as presents for the rulers he visited on the way 10,000 head of sheep and cattle, as well as gold and silks worth a fabulous amount. In 73 AD, Ban Chao headed a 36-man legation to the western regions. These were missions of friendship to visit neighbours the Chinese people had never met before and to learn from them. Ban Chao sent Gan Ying to explore further toward the west. According to the "Western Regions Section" in the *History of Later Han*, Gan Ying traveled across the territories of present-day Iraq and Syria, and reached the Mediterranean Sea, an expedition which brought him within the confines of the Roman Empire. Later, during the Tang Dynasty, the monk Xuan Zang made a journey fraught with danger to reach India and seek the knowledge of that land. Upon his return, he organized a team of scholars to translate the Buddhist scriptures, which he had brought back with him. As a result, many of these scriptural classics which were later lost in India have been preserved in China. In fact, it would have been difficult for the people of India to reconstruct their own ancient history if it had not been for Xuan Zang's *A Record of a Journey to the West in the Time of the Great Tang Dynasty*. In the Ming Dynasty, Zheng He transmitted Chinese culture to Southeast Asia during his seven voyages. Following the Opium Wars in the mid-19th century, progressive Chinese, generation after generation, went to study the advanced scientific thought and cultural achievements of the Western countries. Their aim was to revive the fortunes of their own country. Among them were people who were later to become leaders of China, including Zhu De, Zhou Enlai and Deng Xiaoping. In addition, there were people who were to become leading scientists, literary figures and artists, such as Guo Moruo, Li Siguang, Qian Xuesen, Xian Xinghai and Xu Beihong. Their spirit of ambition, their struggles and their breadth of vision were an inspiration not only to the Chinese people but to people all over the world.

Indeed, it is true that if the Chinese people had not learned many things from the surrounding countries they would never have been able to produce the splendid achievements of former days. When we look back upon history, how can we not feel profoundly grateful for the legacies of the civilizations of ancient Egypt, Greece and India? How can we not feel fondness and respect for the cultures of Europe, Africa, America and Oceania?

The Chinese nation, in turn, has made unique contributions to the community of mankind. Prior to the 15th century, China led the world in science and technology. The British scientist Joseph Needham once said, "From the third century AD to the 13th century AD China was far ahead of the West in the level of its scientific knowledge." Paul Kennedy, of Yale University in the U.S., author of *The Rise and Fall of the Great Powers*, said, "Of all the civilizations of the pre-modern period, none was as well-developed or as progressive as that of China."

Foreigners who came to China were often astonished at what they saw and heard. The Greek geographer Pausanias in the second century AD gave the first account in the West of the technique of silk production in China: "The Chinese feed a spider-like insect with millet and reeds. After five years the insect's stomach splits open, and silk is extracted therefrom." From this extract, we can see that the Europeans at that time did not know the art of silk manufacture. In the middle of the 9th century AD, an Arabian writer includes the following anecdote in his *Account of China and India*:

"One day, an Arabian merchant called upon the military governor of Guangzhou. Throughout the meeting, the visitor could not keep his eyes off the governor's chest. Noticing this, the latter asked the Arab merchant what he was staring at. The merchant replied, 'Through the silk robe you are wearing, I can faintly see a black mole on your chest. Your robe must be made out of very fine silk indeed!' The governor burst out laughing, and holding out his sleeve invited the merchant to count how many garments he was wearing. The merchant did so, and discovered that the governor was actually wearing five silk robes, one on top of the other, and they were made of such fine material that a tiny mole could be seen through them all! Moreover, the governor explained that the robes he was wearing were not made of the finest silk at all; silk of the highest grade was reserved for the garments worn by the provincial governor."

The references to tea in this book (the author calls it "dried grass") reveal that the custom of drinking tea was unknown in the Arab countries at that time: "The king of China's revenue comes mainly from taxes on salt and the dry leaves of a kind of grass which is drunk after boiled water is poured on it. This dried grass is sold at a high price in every city in the country. The Chinese call it 'cha.' The bush is like alfalfa, except that it bears more leaves, which are also more fragrant than alfalfa. It has a slightly bitter taste, and when it is infused in boiling water it is said to have medicinal properties."

Foreign visitors showed especial admiration for Chinese medicine. One wrote, "China has very good medical conditions. Poor people are given money to buy medicines by the government."

In this period, when Chinese culture was in full bloom, scholars flocked from all over the world to China for sightseeing and for study. Chang'an, the capital of the Tang Dynasty was host to visitors from as far away as the Byzantine Empire, not to mention the neighboring countries of Asia. Chang'an, at that time the world's greatest metropolis, was packed with thousands of foreign dignitaries, students, diplomats, merchants, artisans and entertainers. Japan especially sent contingent after contingent of envoys to the Tang court. Worthy of note are the accounts of life in Chang'an written by Abeno Nakamaro, a Japanese scholar who studied in China and had close friendships with ministers of the Tang court and many Chinese scholars in a period of over 50 years. The description throws light on the exchanges between Chinese and foreigners in this period. When Abeno was supposedly lost at sea on his way back home, the leading poet of the time, Li Bai, wrote a eulogy for him.

The following centuries saw a steady increase in the accounts of China written by Western visitors. The Italian Marco Polo described conditions in China during the Yuan Dynasty in his *Travels*. However, until advances in the science of navigation led to the opening of east-west shipping routes at the beginning of the 16th century Sino-Western cultural exchanges were coloured by fantasy and conjecture. Concrete progress was made when a contingent of religious missionaries, men well versed in Western science and technology, made their way to China, ushering in an era of direct contacts between China and the West. The experience of this era was embodied in the career of the Italian Jesuit Matteo Ricci. Arriving in China in 1582, Ricci died in Beijing in 1610. Apart from his missionary work, Ricci accomplished two historically symbolic tasks — one was the translation into Latin of the "Four Books," together with annotations, in 1594; the other was the translation into Chinese of Euclid's *Elements*.

The rough translations of the "Four Books" and other Chinese classical works by Western missionaries, and the publication of Père du Halde's *Description Geographique, Historique, Chronologique, Politique, et Physique de l'Empire de la Chine* revealed an exotic culture to Western readers, and sparked a "China fever," during which the eyes of many Western intellectuals were fixed on China. Some of these intellectuals, including Leibniz, held China in high esteem; others, such as Hegel, nursed a critical attitude toward Chinese culture. Leibniz considered that some aspects of Chinese thought were close to his own views, such as the philosophy of the *Book of Changes* and his own binary system. Hegel, on the other hand, as mentioned above, considered that China had developed no proper philosophy of its own. Nevertheless, no matter whether the reaction was one of admiration, criticism, acceptance or rejection, Sino-Western exchanges were of great significance. The transmission of advanced Chinese science and technology to the West, especially the Chinese inventions of paper-making, gunpowder, printing and the compass, greatly changed the face of the whole world. Karl Marx said, "Chinese gunpowder blew the feudal class of knights to smithereens; the compass opened up world markets and built colonies; and printing became an implement of Protestantism and the most powerful lever and necessary precondition for intellectual development and creation." The English philosopher Roger Bacon said that China's four great inventions had "changed the face of the whole world and the state of affairs of everything."

3

Ancient China gave birth to a large number of eminent scientists, such as Zu Chongzhi, Li Shizhen, Sun Simiao, Zhang Heng, Shen Kuo and Bi Sheng. They produced numerous treatises on scientific subjects, including *The Manual of Important Arts for the People's Welfare, Nine Chapters on the Art of Mathematics, Treatise on Febrile Disease Caused by Cold* and *Compendium of Materia Medica.* Their accomplishments included ones whose influence has been felt right down to modern times, such as the armillary sphere, seismograph, Dujiangyan water conservancy project, Dunhuang Grottoes, Grand Canal and Great Wall. But from the latter part of the 15th century, and for the next 400 years, Europe gradually became the cultural centre upon which the world's eyes were fixed. The world's most outstanding scientists then were England's Isaac Newton, Poland's Copernicus, France's Marie Curie, Germany's Rontgen and Einstein, Italy's Galileo, Russia's Mendelev and America's Edison.

The Chinese people then began to think: What is the cause of the rise and fall of nations? Moreover, how did it happen that gunpowder, invented in China and transmitted to the West, in no time at all made Europe powerful enough to batter down the gates of China herself?

It took the Opium War to wake China from its reverie. The first generation to make the bold step of "turning our eyes once again to the rest of the world" was represented by Lin Zexu and Wei Yuan. Zeng Guofan and Li Hongzhang started the Westernization Movement, and later intellectuals raised the slogan of "Democracy and Science." Noble-minded patriots, realizing that China had fallen behind in the race for modernization, set out on a painful quest. But in backwardness lay the motivation for change, and the quest produced the embryo of a towering hope, and the Chinese people finally gathered under a banner proclaiming a "March Toward Science."

On the threshold of the 21st century, the world is moving in the direction of becoming an integrated entity. This trend is becoming clearer by the day. In fact, the history of the various peoples of the world is also becoming the history of mankind as a whole. Today, it is impossible for any nation's culture to develop without absorbing the excellent aspects of the cultures of other peoples. When Western culture absorbs aspects of Chinese culture, this is not just because it has come into contact with Chinese culture, but also because of the active creativity and development of Western culture itself; and vice versa. The various cultures of the world's peoples are a precious heritage which we all share. Mankind no longer lives on different continents, but on one big continent, or in a "global village." And so, in this era characterized by an all-encompassing network of knowledge and information we should learn from each other and march in step along the highway of development to construct a brand-new "global village."

Western learning is still being transmitted to the East, and vice versa. China is accelerating its pace of absorption of the best parts of the cultures of other countries, and there is no doubt that both the West and the East need the nourishment of Chinese culture. Based on this recognition, we have edited and published the *Library of Chinese Classics* in a Chinese-English format as an introduction to the corpus of traditional Chinese culture in a comprehensive and systematic translation. Through this collection, our aim is to reveal to the world the aspirations and dreams of the Chinese people over the past 5,000 years and the splendour of the new historical era in China. Like a phoenix rising from the ashes, the Chinese people in unison are welcoming the cultural sunrise of the new century.

August 1999 Beijing

前　言

在中国戏剧文学的发展史上，汤显祖和他的代表作品“玉茗堂四梦”(《紫钗记》、《牡丹亭》、《南柯记》、《邯郸记》) 都具有举足轻重的地位。

汤显祖（1550—1616），明代江西临川人。同当时大多数读书人一样，他早年竞逐于科举和官场。万历二十六年（1598），从浙江遂昌任上弃官归里。此后，他在家乡临川度过了十八年漫长的乡居生活。在归隐乡居的最初两年，他完成了传奇《南柯记》的创作。《南柯记》与他稍后完成的《邯郸记》一起被称作“二梦”，是汤显祖在走过了坎坷的仕途，政治抱负和人生理想彻底破灭以后，痛定思痛、冷静反省的产物。它与其稍早完成的代表作《牡丹亭》同样具有惊世骇俗的力量，只是表现在不同的意义上。

汤显祖的“玉茗堂四梦”均取材于唐人传奇或《太平广记》所引录的笔记小说。《南柯记》的题材来源是唐人李公佐的传奇小说《南柯太守传》(见于《太平广记》卷四七五引《异闻录》，题《淳于棼》)。故事中的男主人公淳于棼曾以武艺任淮南军裨将，因使酒失主帅之心，弃官归里。他宅院里有一株古槐。一天，他在禅智桥边酒楼里喝醉，被僮仆扶归，卧于堂前东廊下。忽觉有人呼唤，原来是槐安国的使者，迎他去做驸马。数月后他任职于槐安国的南柯郡。任南柯太守的二十年中，他施德政，行教化，克己为民，兴利除弊，使得原先风气颓败、政事废弛的南柯郡，变成“雨顺风调”之地，呈现“民安国泰”的景象。因政绩卓著，淳于棼罢郡还朝，进居左丞相之职。公主死后，他身处的政治环境日趋险恶。右丞相妒他“威权太盛”，向国王进谗言。他自恃驸马的身份和治南柯郡的盛名，不再谨慎自律，以至放纵无度，终致被遣归家。淳于棼忽然醒来，环视四周，庭院、卧榻、持酒的僮仆、濯足的客人……一切如故；日正西沉，东窗下余酒尚温。美妻娇子，荣华富贵，赫赫政绩；世态炎凉，明争暗斗，恃宠骄纵……二十多年的欣喜悲哀，都留在南柯一梦中。他立即掘开古槐树根，见有大穴以及通往南枝的小穴，其中有形似城郭宫殿、土城楼台者，群蚁处其中，井然有序。淳于棼方悟所谓槐安国、南柯郡者，即在此中，至此幡然醒悟，顿感万象皆空，遂度脱众蚁升天，立地成佛。

“南柯一梦”故事的主旨不难理解，它生动地阐释了“人生如梦”这一中国文学史上古老的主题。在中国古代文人笔下，以梦境喻人生，其意旨是否定向来被崇尚、追逐的修身养性、克己治国的人生目标的意义。这常常表现为两层含义，一是对达到这一目标之可行度的怀疑，二是对追求这一目标的价值的否定。唐代李公佐写《南柯太守传》，就是“假实证幻”（见鲁迅《中国小说史略》第九篇），表达了对追逐高官厚禄的蝇营狗苟之徒的蔑视和嘲讽。有如《南柯太守传》结尾的“赞曰”：“贵极禄位，权倾国都，达人视此，蚁聚何殊。”汤显祖采用这一故事创作《南柯记》，基本意旨没有改变。他在《南柯梦记题词》中说：“嗟夫，人之视蚁，细碎营营，去不知所为，行不知所往，意之皆为居食事耳。见其怒而酣斗，岂不呋然而笑曰：‘何为者耶？’天上有人焉，其视下而笑也，亦若是而已矣。”应该说，共同的“人生如梦”的主题背后，是每个文学家极其个人化的人生感受和对现实的认识。《南柯记》以蚁国喻人世，剧中主人公最终断然唾弃尘世，是汤显祖弃绝仕途的决绝态度的写照。期望，奋争，碰壁，一而再，再而三……几经挫折，无能为力，汤显祖最终放弃了努力。汤显祖早年与当时的大多数文人士子一样，饱学诗书，对科举入仕充满热情，对政治清明有热忱的期望和宏大的抱负。所以，他几次三番赴考，直到万历十一年（1583）得中进士。万历十九年（1591），其时他已在南京任职近十年，对官场的种种弊病耳闻目睹，如鲠在喉，不吐不快。他向朝廷上了《论辅臣科臣疏》，历数时政的弊端，实际上对万历皇帝的一些决策也有所非议。这使他的从政生涯遭受了致命的打击，再也没能东山再起，被贬广东徐闻。两年后，迁任浙江遂昌县令。这期间他还没有改变积极的人生态度。任遂昌县令（1893—1898）的五年，是他一生中实践经世济国抱负的惟一机会。五年里，他实施以人为本的治理方针，创办学校，兴教劝学，扶持农耕，除夕纵囚，抑制豪强等等，赢得了遂昌人民的尊敬信任和长久爱戴。但是，他一己的自律奉公，忠于职责，影响、改变不了官场上钻营逢迎、倾轧构陷、营私舞弊、贪污腐败的风气。最终，他放弃了仕途竞逐，弃官回乡。所以，《南柯记》对人生如梦的慨叹，是痛切的人生经历带给他的，是以他一生的政治实践为沉重代价，表达的是看透世事后的愤懑、失望和无奈。长达四十四出戏的《南柯记》，其中对于作为现实影像的蝼蚁王国——槐安国及南柯郡，以及淳于棼在其中升迁沉沦的描写，无疑比仅近四千字的唐传奇细致真切。正如同时代的学者袁宏道（1568—1610）在《邯郸记总评》中所说："'一切世事俱属梦境'，此于《南柯》，可谓发泄殆尽矣。"

《南柯记》中寄寓丰富而深厚，很容易引起人们对现实社会的联想。虽然讲佛论禅贯穿全剧始终，以致明末人王思任（1575—1646）认为："《邯郸》，仙也；《南柯》，佛也；《紫钗》，侠也；《牡丹亭》，情也。"（见《批点玉茗堂牡丹亭词叙》）但是很明显，《南柯记》的内涵远不止一个"佛"字所能概括。如近代学者吴梅所说："所谓鬼、侠、仙、佛，竟是曲中之意，而非作者寄托之意。"（《四梦总跋》）剧中，第二十四出《《风谣》》中对南柯郡"征徭薄，米谷多，官民易亲风景和"、"仁风广被"的景象的描写，无疑是剧作家对美好和谐社会的怀想；第二十一出《录摄》》中对"大明律"讽刺，第二十五出《玩月》中对孔子之道教化功用的疑惑，第四十出《疑惧》中对君心莫测的感叹，体现剧作家对现实政治以及当时的主流意识形态的反省和批判。剧中描写淳于棼，无论是在人间的广陵郡，还是在虚幻的槐安国，他的所作所为，所思所想，都立足于尘世，立足于人之常情。直到最后一出戏《情尽》的前半部分，淳于棼也没有放下对父亲的怀念，对南柯郡百姓的牵挂，对妻子的思念，甚至还有对曾经善待他的槐安国的国王和王后的感戴。从剧中的描写看，淳于棼从世俗人情中退步抽身十分艰难，这都增强了剧作的现实色彩。再者，淳于棼在现实中就有由武将而免职、以至落魄纵酒的失意的经历。到槐安国，又经历了从太守升任左丞相、权势日盛到被罢官、失去恩宠、被遣回乡的落差很大的境遇。他自己的处世态度，有从勤谨治郡到恃宠放纵的巨大反差。这都表现出剧作者种种复杂的感受和意识：人生的不可预料，身不由己；人性的不可理喻，变化无常；世事的神秘莫测，不可抗拒，等等。总之，对人生难料的迷茫，对人性无常的困惑，对世事荒谬的义愤等，都包蕴在戏剧人物的命运中。在汤显祖的时代，他亲眼看到了太多惊心动魄的人间活剧。影响最大、最令人莫衷一是的，莫过于发生在当朝帝王和首相身上的变故。万历皇帝（1563—1620）从一个谨慎勤勉的君王变得荒淫懈怠，不理朝政；张居正（1525—1582）从国之栋梁，如日中天，到罪不容诛，累及满门。万历五年（1577）和万历八年（1580），汤显祖曾两度赴京会试，当时的首相张居正和其次子张懋修先后派人致意接纳，都被他谢绝，致使他自己名落孙山。而至万历八年，他已是四次会试落榜。他被贬谪到广东徐闻后，遇到流放此地的张懋修，当初的科场冤家穷途相见，前嫌尽释，“握语雷阳，风趣殊苦”（《寄江陵张幻君》）。现实的荒诞以至荒谬，都时隐时显、或浓或淡地折射在《南柯记》中。

但是无论怎样，契玄老僧的讲法在《南柯记》中前后呼应，是全剧的结构线索。剧的最后，借淳于棼之口，说出了全剧的题旨：“人间君臣眷属，蝼蚁何殊？一切苦乐兴衰，南柯无二。”《南柯记》在无情地揭示了人世间的一切均不可靠，人对功名利禄的追逐毫无意义以后，指出的精神出路是：出世成佛。这一点是唐传奇《南柯太守传》中所没有的。这个结局，彻底瓦解了那个时代人们普遍尊奉的以修身养性、高官厚禄、光宗耀祖为追求目标的人生观，也深刻质疑当时普遍崇尚的以修身治国为理想人生的价值观。人生的意义最终归于虚无。不可否认，“人生如梦”是《南柯记》的落脚点，只是我们不能忽视其中丰厚、深刻的现实内涵。

包括《南柯记》在内，汤显祖的“四梦”都是以梦境写人生，以虚幻写现实。一般说来，汤显祖的剧作以浪漫的艺术想象，绮丽的文笔和深邃的人文精神，在当时的剧坛超迈群伦，产生了震撼凡俗的冲击力。与汤显祖同时的曲论家王骥德（？—1623）评论他的剧作“婉丽妖冶，语动刺骨”（《曲律·杂论》），这是就汤显祖剧作的总体风格及语言特色而言。但是，《南柯记》在汤显祖的剧作中有鲜明的特色。“四梦”虽然都写梦，但惟有《南柯记》中的意象最为奇特。它以超现实的蝼蚁王国作为戏剧主人公活动的主要环境，作为剧作家言志抒怀的主要依托。但是，汤显祖在艺术形象的选择和塑造上，并不立足于形象的奇特，不强调蝼蚁的自然特性，而是着眼于蝼蚁王国深刻、形象的比喻意义。也就是说，《南柯记》并不通过艺术形象的夸张变形来显示其艺术力度和效果。剧作大部分篇幅描写梦境，但是对梦境的表现自然平实；虽然梦境中是蝼蚁王国，但其中的人和蚁，行为举动均依据人情之常。从艺术形象的塑造，也可以看出剧作家借寓言式故事的酒杯，浇胸中之块垒的初衷和匠心。

再者，《南柯记》一改汤显祖语言绮丽华美的风格，代之以本色淡雅的文笔。汤显祖在一封给友人的信中说：“二梦已完，绮语都尽”（见《答罗匡湖》），可见《南柯记》在艺术风格上的本色，是汤显祖有意的追求。《南柯记》中，即使是比较雅的曲词，也没有《牡丹亭》中许多曲文的那种华美和俏丽。以第二十五出《《玩月》中的两首曲词为例：【破齐阵】：“绕境全低玉宇，当窗半落银河。月影灵娟，天临贵婿，清夜暂回参佐。同移燕寝幽香远，并起鸾骖暮霭多，何处似南柯？”这段曲词之后，是一首【普天乐犯】：“踝光华，城一座，把温太真装砌的嵯峨。自王姬宝殿生来，配太守玉堂深坐。瑞烟微香百和，红云度花千朵。有甚的不朱颜笑呵？眼见的眉峰皱破。对清光满斟，一杯香糯。”这出戏写淳于棼陪公主离开南柯郡到瑶台避暑，正值月之十五，二人在玉石筑的高台上赏月。公主因身体欠佳，远离南柯，心生惆怅，淳于棼劝她对月开怀，尽享美景。曲词描写月夜景色和主人公的心情，虽然文词典雅，也用典，但意象明朗，抒情畅达，没有费解之处。《南柯记》中更多的曲文可谓明白如话。例如第二十四出《风谣》中有：【清江引】：“紫衣郎走马南柯下，一轴山如画。公主性柔佳，驸马官潇洒。俺且在这里整仪容权下马。”【孝白歌】：“征徭薄，米谷多，官民易亲风景和。老的醉颜酡，后生们鼓腹歌，你道俺捧灵香，因什么？”后一首曲词常被引用，是因为从中可以看到汤显祖憧憬的理想社会之一斑。从语言风格的角度看，《南柯记》中的这类曲文确是繁华落尽，尽显清淳，但又颇有情趣，不流入俗白，让人感受到汤显祖的清新淡雅的语言风格的特殊魅力。

另外，在剧作的结构上，《南柯记》虽然长达四十四出，而且描写尘世、佛界与蚁国三种戏剧情境，刻画了自然的、以及超自然的多重人物关系，剧情在佛界与俗世，人间与蚁国之间几度转换，人物在虚幻与真实之间交替出现，虚虚实实，真真假假，但不生枝蔓，不显延宕，松紧有致，一气呵成。正如王骥德所评论的："至《南柯》、《邯郸》二记，……其掇拾本色，参错丽语，境往神来，巧凑妙合，又视元人别一蹊径。技出天纵，匪由人造。"（《曲律·杂论》）一部长篇传奇，结构上可以给人以既"巧凑妙合"，又不显繁复、不觉人工斧凿、水到渠成的感觉，原因之一是这个剧的主体部分采用单线结构，不像当时许多才子佳人题材的传奇，离不开双线的套路；而且，许多出戏都很简洁，所以剧情进展利索、畅达。再者，剧作家注意运用暗示、铺垫、呼应等手法，所以，戏剧情境的转换不显突兀。例如从第二出《侠概》起到第十出《就征》，这九出戏依次循环写人间、蚁国和佛寺三界。《就征》开始，淳于棼入梦，直到第四十二出《寻寤》梦醒，三十多出戏全部写蚁国。第八出《情著》里，契玄老僧暗示了淳于棼的结局，到第四十三出《转情》中仍由契玄予以点破，与前面形成呼应。全剧结构十分严谨、紧凑。这些都显示出汤显祖作为戏剧大师的不凡功力。总之，《南柯记》用简约平实的笔法，将梦境的奇妙意境表现得出神入化，将梦境的深刻意义揭示得淋漓尽致。

《南柯记》问世后不久，有些单出就被选入当时刊刻的戏曲折子戏选集中。如万历年间刊刻的《月露音》中收录了《尚主》、《之郡》、《粲诱》、《生恣》等；明代崇祯年间（1628—1644）刻本《怡春锦》中收有《就征》和《玩月》，这说明这些折子戏一度在民间很受欢迎。另外，有些《南柯记》折子戏名目出现在清代宫廷演戏档案中，例如《穿戴题纲》、《内学昆弋戏目档》等剧目档案，录有《瑶台》、《花报》和《点将》三个单折，《昆弋腔杂戏目录册》录有《瑶台》等等，可见在清代宫廷里，《南柯记》中这三个折子戏演得最多。

明清两代，《南柯记》有不少版本流传。郑振铎（1898—1958）曾说，"玉茗堂四梦"中，"于《还魂》外，此曲刊本独多"。《南柯记》约有九种版本今存。本书英译所主要依据的钱南扬的校点本，就是以明代毛晋汲古阁校刻本为底本，与明万历刻本《南柯梦》等几种版本对校而成。

由此可见，《南柯记》诞生后，不仅剧本不断被重刻、复刻，是文人士大夫们案头的珍品，而且其中的一些折子戏经常在民间和清代宫廷里演出，这证明了《南柯记》历久不衰的文学魅力和艺术生命力。

20世纪30年代，日本汉学家青木正儿在他的著作《中国近世戏曲史》中，首先将汤显祖与英国戏剧家莎士比亚相提并论："显祖之诞生，先于英国莎士比亚十四年，后莎氏逝世一年而卒（笔者按：此说有误，实际二人系同一年去世），东西曲坛伟人，同出其时，亦一奇也。"确实，汤显祖的剧作无论是就其人文精神的深度和广度看，还是从其艺术上所达到的高度看，都无愧于世界性的声誉。但是，大概因为汤显祖的剧作篇幅长，曲词较为典雅华丽，被译成西方文字的时间较晚。而篇幅较短，文字相对质朴的元杂剧，在18世纪30年代就有剧本被译成西文。1735年出版的杜赫德（Jean Baptiste Du Halde）主编的《中华帝国全志》中，收入了法国传教士马若瑟（Fr. Joseph de Premare, 1666—1736）翻译的《赵氏孤儿》法文节译本，这是中国古典戏曲传入欧洲的起点。其后，《赵氏孤儿》才陆续有了德文和英文译本。而汤显祖的剧作，直至20世纪30年代，才有了《牡丹亭》的德文全译本，英文译本则只有《牡丹亭》中的单出《春香闹学》。而且，早期欧洲汉学家翻译中国古典戏曲剧本，常常删去曲辞，这从对中国古典戏曲介绍的角度看，十分不妥。因为中国古典戏曲剧本从结构组织到意蕴的传达，都是以曲辞为核心。剧曲与散曲一样，与源远流长的古典诗词一脉相承，继承了中国古代韵文的深厚传统。所以，在古代剧作家心目中，戏曲曲文是剧本的支柱和精华。1980年，美国汉学家白之（Cyril Birch）的《牡丹亭》英文全译本出版，近些年，国内学者和翻译家相继将汤显祖的这几个作品翻译出版，本书英译者张光前先生早在1994年就将《牡丹亭》全文英译出版面世，2003年继续完成了《南柯记》的全文英译并交由外文出版社出版。今天，这个英译本《南柯记》将再度纳入“大中华文库系列”出版，这对于促进汤显祖这位与莎士比亚同时代的伟大的中国戏剧家被更广大的世界认识和了解，让中国古代优秀的戏剧作品被世界更多的人接受和欣赏，无疑具有重要意义。

李　玫
中国社会科学院文学研究所

INTRODUCTION

A significant place in the history of traditional Chinese opera literature is occupied by the writer Tang Xianzu and his best-known work, the "Four Dreams of Camellia Hall," comprising *The Purple Hairpin, The Peony Pavilion, A Dream Under the Southern Bough* and *The Dream of Handan.*

Tang Xianzu (1550-1616) lived during the Ming Dynasty (1368-1644), hailing from Linchuan in south central China´s Jiangxi Province. Like most other scholars, Tang spent his early years taking the imperial civil examinations and working as an official, but in 1598, he resigned from office in Suichang, Zhejiang and returned to his hometown of Linchuan, where he spent the rest of his life in seclusion. During the first two years of his retirement, he wrote *A Dream Under the Southern Bough*, the first of his "Two Dreams" the later one being *The Dream of Handan*. The "Two Dreams" were the product of Tang Xianzu´s sober introspection and recollection of his ruined political ambitions and ideals after all the frustrations of his political career. It had the same powerful social impact as his earlier masterpiece *The Peony Pavilion*, but takes a different form of expression.

The plots of Tang´s "Four Dreams of Camellia Hall" were all based on Tang Dynasty short stories and sketches in *Records of the Taiping Era*. The source for the theme of *A Dream Under the Southern Bough* was the Tang Dynasty story *The Governor of the Southern Tributary* by Li Gongzuo (see "Chunyu Fen" in *Strange Stories*, Volume 475 of *Records of the Taiping Era*). In the story, the hero Chunyu Fen, a low-ranking officer in the Huainan army, resigns and returns home after losing favor with the Commander in

Chief because his fondness for alcohol. There is an old sophora tree in his courtyard. One day, taken home by a servant after getting drunk in a wineshop near the Chan Wisdom Bridge, he lies on the eastern porch in front of his main hall. Suddenly he becomes aware of someone calling him, and finds an envoy from the Great Sophora Kingdom fetching him to be married to their princess. Several months later he is appointed Prefect of the Southern Bough of the Great Sophora. During his 20 years in office here, Chenyu Fen introduces measures beneficial to the people´s well-being, promoting education and self-restraint in the public good, instituting good practice and weeding out graft; the result is that the previously corrupt and ill-governed Southern Bough Prefecture is transformed into a region of peace, prosperity and perfect weather. Because of his outstanding achievements, Chunyu Fen returns to court and is promoted to Vice Chief Minister of the Left in the central government but, after the princess dies his political situation deteriorates from day to day. Jealous of his power, the Vice Chief Minister of the Right brings false charges against him before the king; Chenyu Fen, relying on his status as the princess´s husband and the popularity he has won as Prefect of Southern Bough, abandons prudence and self-discipline, and gives way to debauchery. Finally he is dismissed from office and returns home. At this point Chunyu Fen wakes up, and, looking around, sees his courtyard, his bed, his servants holding wine vessels, his guests washing their feet. Everything is the same as before; the sun is setting, and the wine he left by the eastern window is still warm. The joys and sorrows of his 20 dream years are gone: his beautiful wife and children, his wealth and power, his outstanding achievements, the inconsistency of human relationships, rivalries overt and covert, his debauchery "licensed" by his imperial connection — all of them gone. He immediately digs out the root of the sophora tree, and finds a big cavity and a smaller hole extending towards a southern bough, where there are structures like city walls, palaces, castles and pavilions, all inhabited by a well-ordered population of ants. Chunyu Fen realizes that the "Great Sophora Kingdom" and

"Southern Bough Prefecture" are in fact these ant colonies. It dawns on him that everything in the material world is vanity. He asks a Buddhist monk to transmigrate the ants to heaven and becomes a Buddhist himself.

The theme is plain: the story a vivid illustration of the "life is but a dream" concept, an age-old subject in Chinese literature. Ancient Chinese scholars would often compare human life to a dream, representing a denial of any point to the life goals of self-cultivation and selfless devotion to state affairs, goals which had always been advocated and pursued. This denial often expresses two levels of meaning, namely, doubt that these goals can ever be attained, and denial of the value of pursuing them at all. The Tang Dynasty writer Li Gongzuo wrote his story to "prove the vanity with the reality" (See Chapter Nine, *A Brief History of Chinese Fiction* by Lu Xun), expressing his contempt and derision for those seeking high positions, fat emoluments and personal gain. As his conclusion says, "In the eyes of the wise, those who boast prominent positions, high salaries and great power and control in the capital are no different from a group of ants." In Tang Xianzu´s adaptation of the story, the theme remains unchanged. In his foreword to *A Dream Under the Southern Bough* Tang wrote: "Well, to human eyes, ants are always busy with trifling things, not knowing what they are doing or where they are going; dwelling and food are everything to them. When we see them fighting furiously, we laugh at them and say, ´What´s that all about?´ That is just how people in heaven look down on and laugh at us humans." We should note that, behind the common theme of "life is like a dream," each writer has an individual experience and perception of the reality of life. The hero in the play finally forsakes the world, which is compared to an ant colony. It is a portrait of Tang Xianzu´s determined abandonment of his political career which he finally gave up after repeated cycles of hope, struggle and frustration, realizing that he could do nothing. Like most scholars of his time, the young Tang Xianzu was well-read in the classics, eager to succeed in the imperial civil examinations and become a government official, full of enthusiastic expectations and lofty aspirations for good government. In 1583 he took the examinations again and won the title of metropolitan graduate. In 1591, after nearly 10 years of office in Nanjing, unable to suppress his resentment at all the malpractices of officialdom, he submitted a memorial to the emperor. This memorial, enumerating the ills of government and even condemning some of the emperor´s decisions, proved a heavy blow to his political career. It resulted in his demotion to Xuwen in Guangdong Province in south China and he was never re-promoted, being transferred two years later as county magistrate to Suichang in Zhejiang. He still maintained his positive attitude toward life, and this post was his one and only way to fullful his ambition of governing and improving the people´s lot. During his five years in office he adopted people-focused policies, founding schools and promoting education, supporting farming, paroling prisoners on the eve of the New Year, suppressing local despots and bullies. Although he had won the respect, trust, and love of the people of Suichang, Tang eventually resigned and returned home, knowing that his self-discipline, fairness and steadfastness in the performance of his duties could never change the prevailing ethos of toadyism, infighting, false charges, crooked deals and corruption. The play´s lament that "life is but a dream" is a conclusion drawn from the writer´s bitter life experience and political career, a lament expressing his indignation, disillusionment and frustration. The ant kingdom (the Great Sophora Kingdom and Southern Bough Prefecture), which is a reflection of reality and Chunyu Fen´s rise and fall within it, is indeed more finely and vividly depicted in the 44-scene play than in the Tang Dynasty story of only some 4,000 characters. As his contemporary scholar Yuan Hongdao (1568-1610) said in "A General Comment on *The Dream f Handan*": "´Everything in the world is but a dream´ and *A Dream Under the Southern Bough* gives complete expression to his feelings."

The play´s rich and deep analogy prompts associations with actual society. It is permeated by Buddhist thought, as Wang Siren (1575-1646) of the late Ming Dynasty observed: "*The Dream of Handan* is about immortals, *A Dream Under the Southern Bough* is about Buddhism, *The Purple Hairpin* is about chivalry, and *The Peony Pavilion* is about love." ("Introduction to Comments on *The Peony Pavilion* of Camellia Hall"). But it is obvious that the meaning of *A Dream Under the Southern Bough* is far more than Buddhism. The modern scholar Wu Mei commented: "The ghosts, knights, immortals and Buddhism are but superficial references, not the author´s true meaning." ("Postscript for ´The Four Dreams"´) In Scene 24, "Folk Lyrics," the portrayal of Southern Bough Prefecture as an area where "Light are the taxes; good is the harvest; the government and people live in harmony," and where "the moral code takes root in every home" is clearly the author´s yearning for a benign, harmonious society. His retrospection and criticism of the politics and the mainstream ideology of the times are evident in: the ridiculing of the "Laws of the Great Ming Dynasty" in Scene 21 "The Proxy;" the doubt about the educational function of Confucian thought in Scene 25 "Full-Moon Night," and the remark about the unfathomability of the emperor´s mind in Scene 40 "Pending Threat." The hero Chunyu Fen acts and thinks the same way as an ordinary citizen of real-world Guangling Prefecture and of the dream-world of the Great Sophora Kingdom. In the first half of the final scene "Love Ended," he is still missing his father, the people of Southern Bough Prefecture and his wife, and is even grateful to the king and queen of the Great Sophora Kingdom for their benevolence. The play describes realistically how hard it actually is for Chunyu Fen to withdraw from social conventions. In his real life Chunyu Fen experiences dismissal from the army and alcoholism; in the Sophora Kingdom first he is promoted from prefect to Vice Chief Minister of the Left, then is dismissed from office, falls from grace and returns home. His attitude also undergoes significant change, turning from diligence and prudence to self-indulgence under the emperor´s protection.

His experiences are an expression of the author Tang Xianzu´s own complex feelings and sensitivities: life´s unpredictability, individual powerlessness, the irrationality and inconsistency of human nature, and the world´s mystery and irresistibility. In a word, his own bafflement at the unpredictablity of life and human nature, his own indignation at the world´s absurdity are embodied in his hero´s fate. In his own time, Tang Xianzu witnessed too many human dramas, the most influential and controversial of which were those involving the emperor and his Chief Minister. The once diligent Emperor Wanli (1563-1620) had become self-indulgent and negligent; the former pillar of the state Chief Minister Zhang Juzheng (1525-1582) had been sentenced to execution for his crimes, along with his entire family. In 1577 and 1580, as a candidate for the imperial civil examinations in the capital, Tang Xianzu had declined overtures from the then Chief Minister Zhang Juzheng and his son Zhang Maoxiu. As a result, he failed both times. By 1580, he had failed the examination four times. Later, having been demoted to Xuwen in Guangdong, he met Zhang Maoxiu, who had been banished to the same area, and the two finally put aside their past grievances. The absurdity of reality is reflected in *A Dream Under the Southern Bough*, at times explicity, at times indistinctly.

Monk Qixuan´s remarks at the beginning of the play are echoed at the end and are its main thread. At the end the author expounds on the theme through the mouth of Chunyu Fen: "Isn´t the hierarchy of royalty and subjects the same as that of ants? The vicissitudes of life are no different than events in the Great Sophora Kingdom!" Having drummed in the idea that nothing in this world is to be counted on, and that pursuit of rank, fame and fortune is meaningless, the play indicates a spiritual way out, namely conversion to Buddhism. This message does not appear in the Tang Dynasty *The Governor of the Southern Tributary*. The ending completely demolishes the then prevailing ideology, whose goals were self-cultivation, attaining a powerful, highly-paid office, and bringing honor to one´s ancestors. It also poses a profound challenge to the commonly advocated values that make life ideals out of self-cultivation and becoming a good government administrator. At the end, the meaning of life is vanity. While it is true that the stand taken by *A Dream Under the Southern Bough*, is that "human life is like a dream," we should not ignore its rich and profound realistic content.

All of Tang Xianzu´s "Four Dreams" portray human life through dreams, reflecting reality through fantasy. Generally speaking, Tang Xianzu´s plays stood out from the dramatic repertoire of his day and had the power to shock, with their romantic artistic imagination, their flowery language and their profound and humanistic spirit. The contemporary critic Wang Jide (?-1623) once commented on the "graceful, bewitching style and piercing language" of his plays ("Miscellaneous Comments" in *Rules and Forms of Qu*). That said, of the "Four Dreams," *A Dream Under the Southern Bough* stands out by reason of its ingenious concept. The author expresses his own aspirations and emotions in the context of the surreal kingdom of ants, where the play´s hero lives in his dream. However, Tang Xianzu does not base his choice and creation of artistic images on oddity, nor does he emphasize the ants´ natural character; instead he focuses on the ant kingdom´s profound and clearcut metaphorical meaning. In other words, *A Dream Under the Southern Bough* does not exert its artistic power and effect through exaggeration of artistic imagery. The bulk of the play portrays the hero´s dream, but it is as natural as the real world. The hero and the ants behave like real people. From the artistic imagery he uses we can see the author´s intention and ingenuity in his attempt to drown his sorrows and frustrations with this allegorical tale.

A Dream Under the Southern Bough was written in quiet, elegant language, a clear departure from his usual flowery style. In a letter to a friend, Tang Xianzu wrote; "Having finished two dreams, I´ve exhausted all flowery language." ("Reply to Luo Kuanghu´) It is obvious that the artistic style of

A Dream Under the Southern Bough is what the author intended and aspired to. Even the more elegant lyrics in this play are not as elaborate as most of those of *The Peony Pavilion*. For example, in Scene 25, the lyric to the tune of "Smashing the Qis" goes: "The tower protrudes above surrounding roofs; / into its windows pours the Milky Stream. / Moonlight appeals, / heaven invites, / no other company is required. / We move our residence in fragrant night, / our horses canter through the dense twilight. / Nowhere can match our Southern Bough." This is followed by a lyric to the tune of "Everyone Happy": "The brilliant light / above the palace / makes its towers stand out in high relief. / It blends the grandeur of a royal home / and the solemnity of a Taishou´s hall. / Hundreds of incense sticks perfume the air; / thousands of blossoms burst into a cloud. / Why can´t all these evoke a smile from you / but you should knit your brows into a knot? / Let´s drink a toast to the moon, / with a cup of fragrant wine." The scene describes Chunyu Fen and the princess in a marble palace at summer retreat. As they admire the view of a full moon from the marble terrace, Chunyu Fen comforts the frail, unhappy princess, urging her to enjoy the beautiful scene around them. In elegant language scattered with literary allusions, producing distinct images and expressing emotions plainly, the lyrics describe the scenery of the moonlit night and the hero´s feelings. There are more lyrics written in vernacular language; in Scene 24 "Folk Lyrics" there is a lyric to the tune of "River Qing Interlude": "A purple officer gallops to the south; / the scenes spread like a painted scroll. / Amiable is the princess; / affable is the Taishou. / Let me dismount to dust and smooth my clothes." There is another to the tune of "White Filial Piety": "Light are the taxes; / good is the harvest; / the government and people live in harmony. / Elders enjoy a cup of wine; / youngsters sing songs on stomachs full. / Why do you think / wee are holding these incense sticks?" This lyric is often quoted, since it gives a glimpse of the ideal society for which Tang Xianzu longed. In terms of style, the lyrics in *A Dream Under the Southern Bough* are indeed much less luxuriant, but by no means common or less tasteful, exhbiting the special charm of the playwright´s fresh and elegant language.

In structure, the 44-scene play contains three dramatic settings, the human, Buddhist and ant worlds, and describes multiple layers of natural and supernatural relationships. Despite all the shifts of scene between the three worlds and the appearance of characters in both dream and reality, the plot is neither confusing nor over-long, but coherent and with tension and relaxation nicely balanced. Commenting on the play, Wang Jide wrote, "When he wrote *A Dream Under the Southern Bough* and *The Dream of Handan* ... he distinguished himself from Yuan-Dynasty writers by adopting a simple style with occasional ornate language, expressing feelings through the ambiance, and crafting the plot ingeniously. His techniques are superb." ("Miscellaneous Comments" in *Rules and Forms of Qu*) One reason that the ingenious structure of his long play is not over-elaborate is that its main body follows a single thread rather than two, unlike many romantic stories of the time. Moreover, as many of the scenes are short, the plot development is orderly and smooth. Such techniques as implication, foreshadowing and echoing prevent the shifts of scene being abrupt. For example, the nine scenes from Scene 2 "The Hero" to Scene 10 "Summoned to Court" present human, ant and Buddhist worlds in cycles. The 30-odd scenes between "Summon to Court" and Scene 42 "The Realization" describe the ant kingdom. In Scene 8 "Love Kindled" the elderly monk Qixuan hints how Chunyu Fen will finish up, and Qixuan expounds on it again in Scene 42 "Love Extended" in an echo of his earlier prediction. The well-knit structure of the whole play shows the outstanding talent of Tang Xianzu as a master playwright. In short, the play presents the spell-binding concept of the dream world and gives full expression to its profound meaning in simple and concise language.

Soon after *A Dream Under the Southern Bough* was published, certain of its scenes were selected for opera scene anthologies. For example, "Choosing a Son-in-law," "Reaching Town," "Inviting Lures" and "Reckless Abandon" were selected for the anthology *Yue Lu Yin*, block-printed in Wanli reign of the Ming Dynasty. "Summoned to the Court" and "Full-moon Night" were included in *Yi Chun Jin* block-printed during the reign of Ming Emperor Chongzhen (1628-1644). Obviously the scenes were popular with people. Some scenes from the play, notably "Princess Besieged," "The Enemy Roused" and "Selecting Staff," have been found in the Qing-dynasty imperial theater archives, a proof that they were the play´s most frequently staged scenes.

There were many versions of *A Dream Under the Southern Bough* in the Ming and Qing dynasties and nine of them are still extant. This English translation is based on the collated edition by Qian Nanyang.

The script has been reprinted time and again, and has become a treasure of literary scholarship. Certain scenes continued to be performed regularly in public and imperial theaters, evidence of the play´s never-fading literary appeal and artistic vitality.

In the 1930s, the Japanese Sinologist Aoki Masaru was the first to compare Tang Xianzu with the British playwright Shakespeare. In his work *The History of Chinese Theater of Modern Times*, he wrote: "Xianzu was born 14 years before Shakespeare, and died one year later than him. (In fact he died the same year as Shakespeare. — Author) What a wonder that the masters of Eastern and Western theater should live in the same age!" Indeed, Tang Xianzu´s plays deserve their worldwide fame because of their deep and broad humanistic spirit as well as for their artistic achievements. But his plays were translated into Western languages fairly late, perhaps because of their length and luxuriant language. The introduction of ancient Chinese opera into Europe began with the abridged translation into French of *The*

Orphan of the Zhao Family (a shorter Yuan Dynasty *zaju* (poetic drama set to music) written in less ornate language by the French missionary Joseph de Premare (1666-1736), which is contained in *Description de l'Empire de la Chine* compiled by Jean Baptiste Du Halde, published in 1735. It was later translated into German and English. Of the plays of Tang Xianzu, it was not until the 1930s that the full German translation of *The Peony Pavilion* and the English translation of one of its scenes, "Chunxiang Disturbs Class," were published. Early European sinologists often omitted the lyrics when translating ancient Chinese opera scripts; in terms of introducing ancient Chinese opera this was completely inappropriate, since the lyrics are the heart of the scripts in terms of structure and expressive content. Opera lyrics have the same origins as classical poetry, inheriting the rich legacy of ancient Chinese verse. To ancient Chinese playwrights, opera lyrics were both the pillar and essence of a script. In 1980, the American sinologist Cyril Birch published his full English translation of *The Peony Pavilion.* In recent years, Chinese scholars and translators have translated and published the works of Tang Xianzu. Mr. Zhang Guangqian, the translator of this book, published his full English translation of *The Peony Pavilion* in 1994. In 2003 Foreign Languages Press published his English translation of *A Dream Under the Southern Bough*, which is republished today as a part of the "Library of Chinese Classics." It is of great significance that this great Chinese playwright Tang Xianzu, a contemporary of Shakespeare, should be known and enjoyed by a wider world and that outstanding ancient Chinese plays be introduced to a wider international audience.

Li Mei
Research Fellow
Institute of Literature
Chinese Academy of Social Sciences

(Translated by Ouyang Weiping)

Scene 2 The Hero

Scene 3 The Sophora Kingdom

Scene 7 Chance Encounter

Scene 8 Love Kindled

Scene 11 Received in Audience

Scene 15 Royal Hunting Party

Scene 20 The Royal Send-off

Scene 25 Full-moon Night

Scene 27 Princess Besieged

Scene 29 Raising the Siege

Scene 34 Blocking the Road

Scene 39 Heavenly Signs

Scene 41 Sent Home

Scene 44 Love Ended

目　　录

CONTENTS

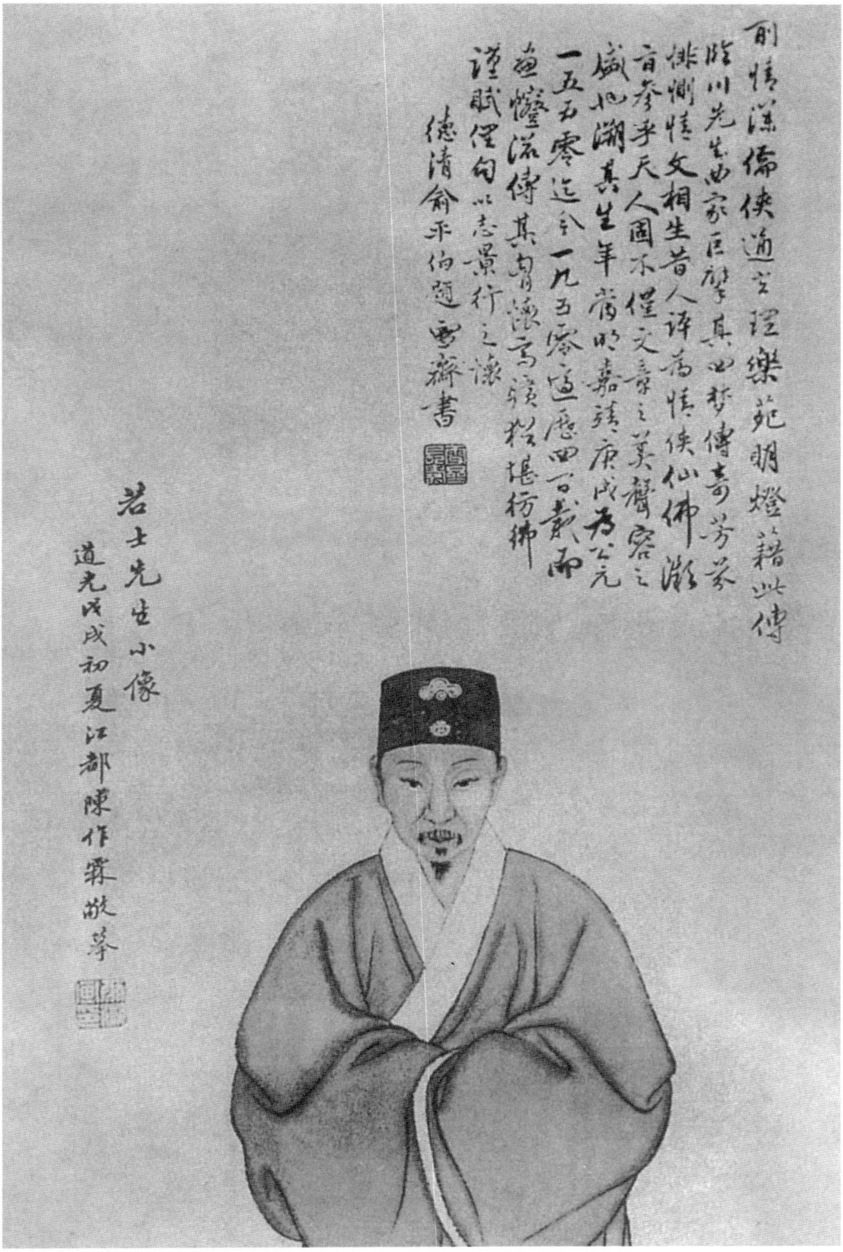

汤显祖（1550 — 1616）
Tang Xianzu (1550 — 1616)

第一出 提 世

【南柯子】

（末上）

玉茗新池雨，
金柅小阁晴。
有情歌酒莫教停，
看取无情虫蚁，
也关情。

国土阴中起，
风花眼角成。
契玄还有讲残经，
为问东风吹梦，
几时醒？

登宝位槐安国土，
随夫贵公主金枝。
有碑记南柯太守，
无虚诳甘露禅师。

Scene 1 Synopsis

(Enter MO[1])

【Southern Bough】

MO:

A shower has bathed Camellia Hall;[2]
sunshine now brightens Checkrein Bower.[3]
Let sensuous wine and songs forever flow,
and watch insensate insects busy themselves.
Their story might make sense.

A kingdom rises in the shades;
out of the corner of the eye
a romance unfolds as the preaching goes.
When will the eastern wind of spring
sweep away the dream?

He in Sophora Kingdom rises high,
With sturdy support from his princess wife.
Stelae at Southern Bough extol his feats;
The Master of Sweet Dew has insight deep.

第二出　侠　　概

【破齐阵】

（生佩剑上）

　　壮气直冲牛斗，
　　乡心倒挂扬州。
　　四海无家，
　　苍生没眼，
　　拄破了英雄笑口。
　　自小儿豪门惯使酒，
　　偌大的烟花不放愁，
　　庭槐吹暮秋。

〔蝶恋花〕

　　秋到空庭槐一树，
　　叶叶秋声，似诉流年去。
　　便有龙泉君莫舞，
　　一生在客飘吴楚。

　　那得胸怀长此住，
　　但酒千杯，便是留人处。
　　有个狂朋来共语，
　　未来先自愁人去。

小生东平人氏；复姓淳于，名棼。始祖淳于髡善饮，一斗亦醉，一石亦醉，颇留滑稽之名；次祖淳于意善医，一男不生，一女不死，

Scene 2 The Hero

(Enter Chunyu Fen,[1] with a sword at his waist)

【Smashing the Qis】

CHUNYU:

My ambition shoots at zenith heights;
in Yangzhou[2] though, my heart craves for home,
yet there's no home for me.
Those worldly folks with humble sights
can only make me laugh and sneer.
Since childhood I've been used to drinking bouts;
nothing can stop me from enjoying life.
Autumn ruffles the yard's Sophora tree.

Autumn arrives to find a lonely tree,
Each leaf hums the sound of fall,
As if lamenting the waning year.
A sword dance can't expel the woeful fact
That I have been a drifter all my life.

No intention have I to stay here long.
Where wine fills a thousand cups,
There I'll put up a transient home.
If a sportive friend comes to drink with me,
It grieves me more to think he has to leave.

I'm Chunyu Fen, a native of Dongping County.[3] The earliest known ancestor of the Chunyu clan was a man called Chunyu Kun,[4] a singular drinker. A pint would make him drunk, and a barrel would make no difference. That's how he earned a place in the history books as a man of good humor. Next in line came Chunyu Yi,[5] a practitioner who fathered

官拜仓公之号。传至先君，曾为边将，投荒久远，未知存亡。至于小生，精通武艺，不拘一节，累散千金；养江湖豪浪之徒，为吴楚游侠之士。曾补淮南军裨将，要取河北路功名。偶然使酒，失主帅之心；因而弃官，成落魄之像。家去广陵城十里，庭有古槐树一株；枝干广长，清阴数亩，小子每与群豪纵饮其下。偶此日间，群豪雨散。则有六合县两人：武举周弁，吾酒徒也；处士田子华，吾文友也。今乃唐贞元七年，暮秋之日，分付家僮山鹧儿，置酒槐庭，以款二友。山鹧可在？

（丑扮僮上）

腿似水牯子，

脸像山鹧儿。

禀告东人：置酒槐阴庭下，二客早到。

no son but was saved by a daughter. He was entitled Chief Custodian of the royal warehouse. So the line continued down to my father. He was a general garrisoned on the remote frontier. Since I haven't heard from him for many a long year, I doubt if he's still alive.

As for myself, I'm a master of martial arts with a generous heart. My large inheritance is spent on helping those ill-starred heroes like myself up and down the Yangtze valley. Earlier in life, I managed to secure the position of lieutenant with the Southern Huai army and was about to make a name for myself on the northern frontier when I lost my commander's favor by being, just once, a little heady with wine. Consequently, I had to give up that career, and here I am, without any aim in life.

At present, I live three miles outside the city of Yangzhou. In my courtyard there's an ancient Sophora tree. Its massive branches extend far and wide, and give acres of nice, cool shade in summer. There I often entertain my drinking pals. But now, the throng has dissolved like raindrops after rainfall. However, I still have two friends here from Liuhe County.[6] One is Zhou Bian, a martial arts graduate and my trusted drinking companion; the other is Tian Zihua, a lettered man whose learning I appreciate. I've invited them over for a drink on this late autumn day in the seventh year of the Zhenyuan reign,[7] and I've told Partridge, my houseboy, to lay out wine and viands in the shade of the tree. Partridge, where are you?

(Enter Partridge)

PARTRIDGE:

Oh, those legs of mine,
Were they not the buffalo's?
Oh, this face I have,
Resembling a partridge's!

My lord, wine and food are laid out under the tree. The two guests have arrived.

(Enter Zhou Bian and Tian Zihua)

【捣练子】

（净扮周、末扮田上）

花月晚，
海山秋。
人生只合醉扬州，
惯使酒的高阳吾至友。

（周）小子颍川周弁是也。
（田）小子冯翊田子华是也。
（周、田）我二人将归六合，去与淳于兄告别。
（丑）主人槐阴庭等候。
（见介）〔集唐〕

县古槐根出，
秋来朔吹高。
黄金犹未尽，
终日困香醪。

（生）数日门客萧条，令人困闷。
（周、田）连小弟二人，日晚归舟，竟来告别。
（生）二兄也要回去，好不闷人也！槐庭有酒，且与沉醉片时。（酒介）

【玉交枝】

（生）

风云识透，
破千金贤豪浪游。
十八般武艺吾家有，

【Pounding Raw Silk】

ZHOU, TIAN:

The moon lights the flowers;
autumn paints the hills.
Yangzhou is every drinker´s favored haunt;
the greatest drunkard is Chunyu, our bosom friend.

ZHOU: I´m Zhou Bian, a native of Yingchuan County.[8]

TIAN: I´m Tian Zihua, a native of Pingyi County.[9]

ZHOU, TIAN: We´re returning to Liuhe, so we´ve come to say goodbye to our friend Chunyu.

PARTRIDGE: My master is waiting for you both under the Sophora tree. (Zhou, Tian and Chunyu greet each other)

ZHOU, TIAN:

The ancient roots go deep;
The autumn skies are high.
When gold is plenty still,
Days float in wine´s fragrance.

CHUNYU: For days I haven´t had a single guest. You can imagine how tedious life is for me.

ZHOU, TIAN: We two are to set sail for home tonight, and we´ve come to bid you adieu.

CHUNYU: So you´re leaving too! I´ll be bored to death then. Anyway, wine is ready by the big Sophora tree. Let´s enjoy ourselves while we can. (They drink)

【Coral Branches】

CHUNYU:

I´ve seen through the fickle world;
so gold bars are lavished on feasting pals.
A master of the eighteen martial arts,

气冲天楚尾吴头。
一官半职懒踟蹰，
三言两语难生受。
闷嘈嘈尊前罢休，
恨叨叨君前诉休。

(周、田)槐庭下勾尊兄饮乐也。

【前腔】

(生)

把大槐根究，
鬼精灵庭空翠幽。
恨天涯摇落三杯酒，
似飘零落叶知秋。
怕雨中妆点的望中稠，
几年间马蹄终日因君骤。
论知心英雄对愁，
遇知音英雄散愁。

(周、田)二弟辞了。

(生)送贤弟一程。

【急板令】

道西归迎鸾镇头，
顺西风蔷薇玉沟。
送将归暮秋，
送将归暮秋。

I sought my fortune up and down the stream.
Minor positions I refused to hold;
reproof and scandal my ears couldn´t bear.
My mood is elated by cups of wine;
words bubbling, I pour out my heart to you.

ZHOU, TIAN: This good old tree can keep you merry company.

【Ditto】

CHUNYU:

What roots has this giant of a tree
that infuse life into the cryptic green?
When clouds inaptly shed three cups of wine
its fallen leaves announce summer´s end.
Heavy with blossom it has witnessed many men
who galloped by to capture an elusive chance.
Silent are comrades when misfortune calls;
lucky is he who finds sympathetic ears.

ZHOU, TIAN: We must be leaving now.

CHUNYU: Let me see you to the gate.

【Urgent Beats Minitune】

CHUNYU:

You say you must go westward back to home;
may a tailwind facilitate your trip.
In autumn´s twilight you set sail;
in autumn´s twilight you set sail.
Beneath the vastness of the sky,
your boat is but peach-leaf small.
Come again soon,
for much is left unsaid.

举眼天长，桃叶孤舟。
去了旋来，有话难周。

（合）

向晚霞江上销忧，
还送送怎迟留。

（周、田叹介）二弟此去，可能更来。

（生）兄弟怎出此话？

【前腔】

（周、田）

叹知交一时散休，
到家中急难再游。
猛然间泪流，
猛然间泪流。
可为甚携手相看，
两意悠悠？
肠断江南，
梦落扬州。（合前）

【尾声】

（生）

恨不和你落托江湖载酒游，
休道个酒中交难到头。

你二人去了呵，

我待要每日间睡昏昏长则是酒。

（周、田下）（生吊场介）他二人又去了，空庭寂静，好是无聊。山鹧儿，扬

(Refrain)

Toward the rosy skyline up the stream,

must you depart, lingering doesn´t help.

ZHOU, TIAN (sighing): After we leave this time, we may not be able to come again.

CHUNYU: Why not?

【Ditto】

ZHOU, TIAN:

We hate the separation of old pals!

Once home we´re unlikely to leave again.

Tears gush out at the doleful thought;

tears gush out at the doleful thought.

Why, behold, are our hands so tightly clasped,

as if we´re glued in one?

The river severs us;

only in dreams can we meet.

(Refrain)[10]

【Coda】

CHUNYU:

I wish I could sail with you with a load of wine.

It´s sheer nonsense to say that wine-friends never last.

After you two have left,

I´ll soak my solitary days in the besotting wine.

(Exeunt Zhou and Tian)

(Manet Chunyu)

CHUNYU: Now my last two friends are gone, this courtyard looks even more empty and desolate. How boring life is! Partridge, do you happen to know anyone in town with a good sense of humor?

州有甚么会耍子的人么？

(丑)那里讨？那则瓦子铺后有个溜二、沙三兄弟会耍。

(生)待去请来。

一生游侠在江淮，
未老芙蓉说剑才。
寥落酒醒人散后，
那堪秋色到庭槐。

PARTRIDGE: Where can we find someone with a good sense of humor? Well, there are two fellows living behind the mall called Liu Second and Sha Third. They´re said to be good fun.

CHUNYU: Go and invite them over.

Drifting between the Yangtze and the Huai,[11]
I boast about my sword and martial arts.
It´s cruel to wake up and find guests all gone,
And autumn has browned the Sophora leaves.

第三出　树　　国

【海棠春】

（蚁王引众上）

江山是处堪成立，
有精细出乎其类。
万户绕星宸，
一道通槐里。

（众）

绛阙朱衣，
丹台紫气，
别是一门天地。

（合）

把酒玉阶前，
且庆风云际。

（众行礼介）我王千岁！

〔清平乐〕

（王）

绿槐风下，
日影明窗罅。

Scene 3 The Sophora Kingdom

(Enter King, attended)

【Spring Crabapple】

KING:

A kingdom can be set up anywhere,
and wee are more refined than other breeds.
A million stars surround the Bear;
a throughway to Sophora leads.

ATTENDANTS:

Red coats and scarlet walls,
an air of purple grace,
ours is a world of different ways.

ALL:

Wee raise our cups on palace steps
to watch the heroes congregate.

ATTENDANTS (saluting King): May Your Majesty live a thousand years![1]

KING:

The verdant breeze sweeps;
The sun through skylights seeps.
Mighty palaces have been raised from soil;
A grain of dirt is worth a piece of gold.

A thousand years make animals human,
So here wee appear as king and subjects.
Within kingdoms, kingdoms exist;
Inferior to man, inferiors live.

I´m the king of the Great Sophora. Wee are of the Formicidae family,

宝界严城宫殿洒，
一粒土花金价。
千年动物生神，
端然气象君臣。
真是国中有国，
谁言人下无人？

自家大槐安国主是也。本为蝼蚁，别号蚍蜉。行磨周天，颇合星辰之度；存身大地，似蛰龙蛇之居。一生二，二生三，生之者众；万取千，千取百，众即成王。臭腐转为神奇，真乃是明则动，动则变，变则化；太山之于丘垤，故所谓均无贫，和无寡，安无倾。一年成聚，二年成邑，到三年而成都，寡人有些膻行；夏后以松，殷人以柏，及周人而以栗，敝国寄在槐安。火不能焚，寇不能伐。三槐如在，可成丰沛之邦；一木能支，将作酒泉之殿。列兰锜，造城郭，大壮重门；穿户牖，起楼台，同人栋宇。清阴锁院，分雨露于各科；翠盖黄扉，洒风云于数道。长安夹其鸾路，果然集集朱轮；吴都树以葱青，委是耽耽玄荫。北阙表三公之位，义取怀来；南柯分九月之官，理宜修备。右边宪狱司，比棘林而听讼；左侧司马府，倚大树以谈兵。丞相阁列在寝门，上卿蚤朝而坐；大学馆布成街市，诸生朔望而游。真乃天上灵星，国家乔木。树在王门之内，

otherwise known as ants. Just as all stars have their places in the sky, wee have our place in the universe, and wee take up residence in the bosom of mother earth like burrowing snakes and dormant dragons. One gives birth to two, two become three — thus millions are born. Out of the millions rise thousands, out of the thousands rise dozens, and then there arises a king. The despised can work miracles, for Confucius has put it clearly: "Knowledge brings about awareness; awareness brings about change; and change brings about transformation." So an ant hill and Mount Tai[2] are similar in nature. Accepting the philosophy that "equality ensures that no one will be poor; harmony guarantees no one will be forgotten, and hence the stability of state power," in one year I had a group, in the second year it became a colony, and in the third it grew into a monarchy. All this is achieved because I have a strong desire for putridity — I mean purity.

Each great dynasty has had a patron tree. The Xia Dynasty worshipped the pine tree, the Shang Dynasty the cypress tree, and the Zhou Dynasty the chestnut tree. My kingdom relies for protection on the Sophora tree — a sure guardian against fire and invaders.[3] As long as wee adhere to its basics, wee can look forward to establishing as great an empire as the Han Dynasty, for one good tree can support a magnificent palace. With our weapons laid aside, wee raise walled cities with many gates. Houses are built, with windows, doors and everything, for my people to live in. The extended branches of the crown of the tree redirect rainwater to the various departments, and channel air currents to the several regions. Thus, red coaches lumber along the capital´s boulevards, cranes flutter and domes shimmer in the verdant mist. To the north, high positions attract many loyal hearts; to the south, lower branches spread out their arms in hospitality. On the right is the courthouse, where verdicts are passed in its shade; on the left is the war department, where generals devise strategies leaning against its trunk. It is where the premier holds office and ministers make reports. All walks of learning gather into checkered blocks, where scholars debate at the new and full moons. So this tree is the pillar of the state, represented by a star in the celestial world.

待学周武王神禁，无益者去，有益者来；声闻邻国之间，要似齐景公号令，犯槐者刑，伤槐者死。此乃为君之法度，要全立国之根基。所喜内有中宫之贤，外有右相之助。今日政机多暇，且与君臣同游。筵宴已齐，右相早到。

【海棠春】

（右相上）

日晏下彤闱，
承诏又趋丹陛。

（行礼介）右丞相武成侯臣段功叩头，千岁！
（王）赐卿平身。今日召卿，知吾意乎？
（右）愚臣未知。
（王）国家所虑者，天地人三不同。且喜我国中天无阴雨之兆，地无行潦之侵。有礼有法，国中无漏网之鲸；无害无灾，境外有玄驹之马。便是檀萝无警，足知你槐棘有人。待与卿遨翔宫树之前，逍遥封壤之内，卿意云何？

I´ll follow the example of Emperor Wu of the Zhou Dynasty and have it planted by the palace gate to welcome the virtuous and repel the unworthy. I´ll learn from Prince Jinggong of the State of Qi, who had strict orders proclaimed that "Those who dare violate the tree shall be punished, and those who hurt it shall die." This is the way for a monarch to rule, and on this solid foundation a kingdom can be built. By good fortune, I have a virtuous wife assisting me within and a capable right-hand premier helping me without. Today as there´s some leisure at hand, I´ll enjoy the company of my ministers. A banquet is prepared, and here comes my right-hand premier.

(Enter Right-hand Premier)

【Spring Crabapple】

PREMIER:

I left Court[4] when the sun declined,
and am re-summoned to its steps.

PREMIER (kowtows to King): Your Majesty´s humble servant Duan Gong,[5] Right-hand Premier and Marquis of Martial Feats, kowtows. May Your Majesty live a thousand years!

KING: Please rise. Do you know why I´ve summoned you?

PREMIER: Your humble servant has no idea.

KING: The essential concern of a kingdom is harmony among heaven, earth, and the people. Fortunately, this part of heaven above our kingdom does not show signs of rain, our land is not subject to floods, and our laws and regulations are carefully woven so that no one, be he as big as a whale, can slip through. Thus causes for both natural disasters and human mistakes are weeded out. Though beyond our turf lies the Rattan Sandalwood, I know I have competent people in my Sophora cabinet as long as no border alarm is raised. Now I´m going to take a stroll in front of our patron tree and over the mound. Would you like to join me?

(右)君臣同游，太平盛事。但国家还有十八路国公，四门王亲，礼当侍驾。

(王)众国公、王亲别行赐宴，槐阶之下，但与卿同。(行介)

紫殿肃阴阴，
彤庭赫弘敞。
风动万年枝，
日华承露掌。

(众)酒到。

(右进酒介)愿我王进千秋万岁酒。

【惜奴娇】

(王)

大块无私，
费工夫点透了，
幽琐玄微。
谩道是帝虎人龙，
立定朝仪。
区区，
也教分取，
河山王气。

(合)

希奇，
今日风色晴和，
暂拥出宫庭游戏。

【前腔】

(右)

阶墀，

PREMIER: The sovereign and his subjects walking side by side, that´s the best show of peace and harmony. But, excuse me, what about the other nobles and members of the royal family? They should also be in Your Majesty´s company.

KING: They´ll be otherwise entertained. Under the Sophora, you come with me. (They walk)

The purple halls are bathed in shade;
Lofty and spacious is the court.
Her ancient branches comb the wind;
Her copper palms collect young dew.

ATTENDANTS: Here´s wine.

PREMIER (offers a cup of wine to King): May Your Majesty take a sip of this thousand-year brew and live as long!

【The Comely Singer】

KING:

Generous Providence!
It takes the trouble to enlighten
even the most minute.
Not only dragons or tigers or men
can rule a piece of land,
pee-wee,
wee too can have a share
of stately hills and rills.
(Refrain)
How rare!
It´s such a pleasant, balmy day!
Let´s swarm outdoors to stretch and play.

【Ditto】

PREMIER:

Up to the palace steps

新筑沙堤。
看高官贵种，
绛帻黄衣。
总千门万户，
烦星点缀。
依希，
太乙薇垣，
吾王端冕，
任意往来巡历。（合前）

【前腔】

（王）

须知，
秕粟能飞。
一星星体性，
谁无雄气？
恨些须封壤，
草朝粗立。
吾志，
要行天上磨，
还听海中雷。

（合）

且徘徊，
看地利天时，
再行移徙。

（右）臣启大王：敢嫌国土微小？

【前腔】

思之，

fresh sand was newly sprayed.[6]
Among the nobles and high bloods,
I sport a tawny robe and hat
and oversee all kith and kin,
numerous as stars in the sky.
And of course,
around Polaris wee all spin.
In crown and royal robe
His Majesty struts across the land.
(Refrain)

【Ditto】

KING:

You know
even grain chaff can soar.
In what tiny being isn´t there
a jot of virility?
Although my mound is yet modest,
because the state is young,
my goal
is to push the celestial millstone
and hear the thundering of the seas!
(Refrain)
Wee can wait
till both heaven and earth permit
us to make a further move.

PREMIER: Your Majesty, are you discontented with the smallness of our territory?

【Ditto】

Just think

蚍虱臣微。
共立成一国，
非同容易。
叹生灵日逐，
贫忙一粒。
何必，
平中堪取巧，
节外更生枝。(合前)

(王)久不曾槐阴下一游，今日尽与观赏。

【锦衣香】
荷浓阴，
叶儿翠；
映春光，
干儿碧。
来去瞻依，
纵横条直，
眼见参天百尺枝。
似楼桑村里，
殢柳丛祠。
一般儿重重遮盖，
到登基龙庭朝会。
但有分成些基业，
岂嫌微细?
人众成王，
排班做势。

how hard it already is
for us, the size of lice
to have chipped in to build a state.
See how wee labored every day
just for a single grain.
Why shall wee
attempt shortcuts on easy roads,
or let thorns crop up on smooth twigs?
(Refrain)

KING: It´s a long time since I last walked in the Sophora´s shade. Today I´ll have a good look around.

【Fragrant Silk Gown】

Its glossy leaves
provide a shade
of spring-light soft.
The trunk is sleek,
the branches overlap,
a scaffold of straight beams
that reach hundreds of feet into the sky.
Like the mulberry for Liu Bei,[7]
or the willow grove for Chen Sheng,[8]
its massive canopy with many folds
marks the location for a dragon court.
If only one can have a base to start,
trifling though it be!
A multitude produce a king
and all the pomp of royal rites.

【浆水令】

谢苍穹调匀风日，
承后土盘固根基。
九重深处殿巍巍，
一线之间，
九曲巡回。
穿巷陌，
列朝市，
土阶穴处今何世？
拜的拜，
跪的跪，
君臣有义。
走的走，
立的立，
赤子无知。

【尾声】

（王）

俺建邦起土登王位，
右相呵，
你入阁穿宫拜相奇。
但愿俺大槐安万万岁根儿蟠到底。

万物从来有一身，
一身还有一乾坤。
敢于世上明开眼，
肯把江山别立根？

【Starch Water Minitune】

Thank heaven for adjusting rain and shine,
and mother earth for such a solid base
that deep below my palace towers high.
A thread of winding trails
runs through a labyrinth,
from back lanes
to plazas.
What a substructure in the timeless caves!
Some are bowing,
some are kneeling,
the ruled and ruler know their place.
Some are walking,
some are standing,
ignorant are the rank and file.

【Coda】

I´ve heaped up a hill for my royal seat.
My right-hand premier,
you´ve bored your way into the cabinet.
May Great Sophora strike deep roots
and live tens of thousands of happy years!

In every worldly substance there´s a life,
Which in itself contains a world complete.
For those who dare to reach and look outward,
Will they give up their chance to mount the throne?

第四出　禅　　请

（净扮老禅师上）

〔集唐〕

老住西峰第几层，
琉璃为殿月为灯。
终年不语看如意，
长守林泉亦未能。

自家契玄禅师是也。自幼出家修行，今年九十一岁。参承佛祖，证取纲宗。从世尊法演于西天，到达摩心传于东土。无影树下，弄月嘲风；没缝塔中，安身立命。可以浮沤复水，明月归天；只为五百年前，有一业债。梁天监年中，前身曾为比丘，跟随达摩祖师渡江。比扬州有七佛以来毗婆宝塔，老僧一夕捧执莲花灯，上于七层塔上，忽然倾泻莲灯，热油注于蚁穴之内。彼时不知，当有守塔小沙弥颜色不快，问他敢是费他扫塔之劳？那沙弥说道，不为别的，以前圣僧天眼算过，此穴中流传有八万四千户蝼蚁，但是燃灯念佛

Scene 4 The Chan Master

(Enter Qixuan, an old Chan master)

QIXUAN:

Upon the summit of the Western Peak
The moon serves as lamp in my crystal hall.
There I've spent many silent years in thought,
But the mountains aren't an eternal home.

I'm a Chan master, Qixuan by name. I've been practicing Chan ever since early childhood, and now I'm ninety-one years old. Devoted body and soul to the holy Buddha, I'm studying hard to reach the truth worked out by Śākyamuni in the west, and brought to the orient by Bodhidharma. Under an illusory bodhi tree I played with the wind and moon; in the seamless stupa I found my own existence. Just as a bubble can easily return to its element, I could have ascended to heaven like the rising moon, if it hadn't been for a debt I ran up five hundred years ago. During Tianjian reign of the Liang Dynasty[1] my former self was then an ordinary monk, who had followed the great master Bodhidharma across the Yangtze River to Yangzhou. There was a pagoda there consecrated to Vipaśyin, the first of the seven Buddhas of the past. One night, I was climbing up the steep steps to the seventh floor of the pagoda with an oil lamp in one hand. Accidentally, I tilted the lamp and the hot oil spilled out and cascaded into an ant hole. I wasn't aware of the ant hole at all, but I noticed the unhappy expression on the face of the neophyte looking after the pagoda. Was he unhappy because the oil stain would be difficult to remove, I asked. He said, no. It was just because Mañjuśrī had observed with his heavenly eye that there were eighty-four thousand ant families living in that cavern to which the ant hole led. Every day, when it was time to light the lamps and chant the Buddhist scriptures, they would

之时，他便出来行走瞻听，小沙弥到彼时分，施散盏饭与他为戏。今日热油下注，坏了多生。老僧闻言，甚是忏悔，启参达摩老师父。老师父说道，不妨，不妨。他虫业将尽，五百年后，定有灵变，待汝生天。老僧记下此言，三生在耳，屈指到今，恰好五百来岁。欲往扬州，了此公案，老病因循。你看，这润州城对着金、焦，好不山川攒秀。禅堂幽静，我且入定片时，看做甚么境界也？

（众扮僧俗四人持书上）

有时鹤去愁冲锡，

何处龙来喜听经。

小僧和这居士们，是对江扬州孝感、禅智二寺住持。只因十方大众之发心，求契玄禅师而说法。此间是甘露寺方丈，捧书而进。呀！禅师入定，敲他云板三声。（敲介）

（净醒介）四众何为而来？

（众跪介）扬州合郡僧俗，敬选七月十五日大会盂兰，虔请大师升座。

swarm out to listen. On that occasion the neophyte would sprinkle a bowl of rice on the floor, and watch them scrabble about eating it. That hot oil might have killed many lives.

On hearing that, I deeply regretted having been so careless. In distress, I reported this incident to my master Bodhidharma. "Don´t worry," he replied. "Their incarnation as insects is almost over. In five hundred years a transmigration will take place, and you´ll be instrumental to their rebirth in heaven."

Those words were firmly planted in my memory through all the incarnations I´ve undergone. Now, as I bend my fingers to count, it´s exactly five hundred years since then. I´ve been thinking of crossing the river to Yangzhou to wind up this affair, but so far age and feeble health have delayed my trip.

Look, how beautiful Zhenjiang[2] is, with the twin islets Jin and Jiao floating on the Yangtze! Now it´s very quiet in the temple yard. I´ll go into meditation and see what will occur in my mind´s eye.

(Enter two monks, one holding a letter in his hand, and two lay devotees)

MONK:

Cranes may fly off as if to vex the monk;

Sometimes dragons drop in to hear him preach.

We´re the abbots and congregational representatives of Filial Force and Chan Wisdom Temples in Yangzhou, across the river. People from all walks of life there have a wish to invite Master Qixuan over to deliver a sermon. So here we are outside the master´s room at Sweet Dew Temple. We´ll go in and present this letter of invitation to him. Ah, he´s absorbed in meditation. I´ll knock thrice on this cloud-shaped chime-board to wake him up. (He knocks)

QIXUAN (roused from meditation): What has brought you four here?

THE FOUR (kneeling): The Buddhist believers throughout Yangzhou Prefecture have decided to hold a grand Ullambana ceremony on the fifteenth of the seventh month. With the greatest respects, we hope Your

十方善信书疏呈上。(呈书介)

(净)起来。将书表白一番。(展书念介)

窃以某等生维扬花月之区，岂无恶业；接古润金焦之境，亦有善缘。凡依玉蕊之花，尽抱香檀之树。恭维甘露山主契玄大师座下：性融朗月，德普慈云。中含三点之藏，带一转二；外示六爻之相，互五重三。钟鼓不交参，截断众流开觉路；风幡无动相，扫除尘翳落空华。见三世诸佛面目本来，入一切众生语言三昧。盂兰盆里，喝开朵朵金莲；宝月灯中，打破重重玉网。但见饮光微笑，普同大众归心。惟愿慈悲，和南摄受。

(净)贫僧老病将临，不奈过江也。(背介)才想起扬州蝼蚁因果，取在此行？

【正宫端正好】

我则是二文殊，
降下这三天竺，
渡江南一蚁菰芦。
金、焦摆列钟和鼓，
这寺里有名甘露。

Reverence will honor us with your presence and preside over the ceremony. Here's our letter of invitation. (They hand over the letter)

QIXUAN: Rise to your feet please. Let's see what it says. (He spreads open the letter and reads)

"As we are people born in the decadence of Yangzhou, it is unlikely that we have not sinned this way or that in our lives. On the other hand however, as we neighbor upon Zhenjiang where ancient temples thrive, we are not entirely devoid of goodness.[3] Therefore we now turn to your lotus seat with sandalwood incense. Our most reverend Master Qixuan, abbot of Sweet Dew Temple, your wisdom shines like the bright moon in the dark; your benevolence permeates like the cottony clouds. You have the penetrating sight of the third eye as is seen on Buddha's forehead; you are a master of *yin* and *yang* as is reflected in the changes of the eight diagrams.[4] Although the bell and the drum sound on different wavelengths, you can awaken new consciousness in the dumb and numb. Neither the wind nor the flag flutters but the heart — and you can whisk the dust off it. Since you've perceived the origin of the past, the present, and the future, please relate to us the essence of life in language we can easily understand. In the sacrificial bowl, you can command golden lotus to rise and bloom; by the lantern of the moon, you can cut the jade net trapping our souls. A benignant smile on Kāśyapa's face once converted the populace to Buddhism, so please give us your blessing. For that we plead with joined palms before our hearts."

I'm sorry. I'm too old and too sick to make it across the river. (Aside) Yet a moment ago I was thinking about the karma of those ants in Yangzhou. Shall I take this chance to have it settled?

【Base Tune Perfect】

Mañjuśrī and myself are one in two,
descending from the heartland of Buddha
to salvage lost ants on a drifting reed.
Isles Jin and Jiao are like the bell and drum[5]

(回介)不去罢。我看衲子们谈经说诵的，不在话下；一般努目扬眉，举处便喝，唱演宗门，有甚里交涉也？

【滚绣毬】

但说的是附雁传书有，
要还乡曲调无。
怎生是石人起舞？
怎生是新妇骑驴？
那里有笑拈花，
吃荔枝？
则许你单刀直入，
都怎生被箭逃虚？
我这里君臣位上宾和主，
水月光中我带渠，
世界如愚。

(众作请介)(净)既十方恳请，则待过江走一遭。

【倘秀才】

恁待要三千界楼台舌铺，
不消的十二部经坊印模。
禅门三下板，
你尘世一封书。
目前些子看何如？
我这里亲凭佛祖。

that flank the glorious Temple of Sweet Dew.

(Turning around) It seems hard to refuse your request, for I see you´ve been very enthusiastic about learning and preaching. You rolled your eyes, raised you brows, chanted the scriptures, and made the awakening shouts, but you simply missed the point.

【Rolling the Embroidered Ball】

Although you tried to put the message across,
you haven´t learned the proper tone.
Why did the rocky statues stir and dance?
How´s Buddha a new bride on donkeyback?
It isn´t as simple as plucking flowers,
for lychee´s taste can´t be described in words.
If you tend to make wild thrusts with a sword,
the audience will flee from the cutting edge.
Only I know how to bring out the hidden truth,
and lead them o´er the moonlight on the pond,
away from this world of fools.

(The four plead with Qixuan again)

QIXUAN: Since you´re so earnest, I suppose I must make a trip across the river.

【The Stupefied Scholar】

An eloquent tongue can sway three thousand worlds;
there is no need for printers to run stereotypes.
Enough are the three knocks at my door,
and that letter from the mortal world.
For the present, nothing else can be said.
In a few days I´ll come with Buddha´s aid.

四众先行，贫僧分付你：

【煞尾】

先在禅智院立一本
百千万亿投名簿，
后在孝感寺挂一轴
五十三参听讲图。
除了那戒坛上石点头，
则待看普诸天花下雨。

安排宝盖与幡幢，
方便乘杯一渡江。
地震海潮人施法，
管教蝼蚁尽归降。

You four may go back first. See to it that

【Coda】

Chan Wisdom Temple prepare an attendance book
for thousands of millions to sign their names,
and Filial Force unfold and hang up painted scrolls
of Sudhana taking lessons from fifty-three.
My preaching will not only make rocks nod their heads,
but also bring the world a shower of floral rain.

Array the canopy and flags for me;
I'll cross the river in a wooden cup.
Anon, the earth will quake, the tide will surge;
Upon the altar I'll convert the ants.

第五出　宫　　训

【夜游宫】

（老旦扮国母引宫娥上）

宫树槐根隐隐，
从地府学成坤顺。

（众）

画扇影随宫燕引，
听重门，
昼漏声，
花外尽。

（众叩头介）宫娥叩头，娘娘千岁。

〔清平乐〕

（老）

大槐秋色，
世外朱尘隔。
歌吹重重情脉脉，
怕道有人倾国？

孔雀扇影分行，
宫娥半袖通装。
却是洞门深杳，

Scene 5 The Princess′ Lesson

(Enter Queen with palace maids)

【Night Tour of the Palace】

QUEEN:

Among Sophora roots a kingdom spreads;
from nether world I learned a woman′s role.

MAIDS:

Behind the painted fans wee thread our way
through doors and doors,
which muffle out
the clepsydra′s drip.

MAIDS (kowtowing): Wee maids kowtow to Your Ladyship. May you live a thousand years!

QUEEN:

Sophora′s autumn tints
Fade out the hectic world beyond.
All tunes now seem to purr the theme of love.
Has a great beauty come of marriage age?

The column of peacock fans rolls apart
Revealing the bare forearms of the maids.
In the hidden depths of winding caves
Their swing and swirl can delight a king.

I′m the queen of the Great Sophora Kingdom. I was born a female ant and was lucky to have mated with a male. My waist is more slender than that of a flea′s wife, though my size is much larger than that of a mother mosquito. As it happened, my husband became the king, and I of course became the first lady. Wee have an only daughter named Yaofang, dubbed

折旋消得君王。

自家大槐安国母是也。初为牝蚁，配得雄蜉。细如虮虱之妻，大似蚊虻之母。偶尔称孤道寡，居然正位中宫。有女瑶芳一人，号作金枝公主。姿才冠世，婚嫁及期。受书史于上真仙姑，学刺绣于灵芝国嫂。昨承我王之命，要求人世之姻。必须有眼之人，方得有情之婿。我想起来，则有侄女琼英郡主，能会瞧人。待我先唤公主出来，示以此意，然后分付侄女依计而行。

(众)公主到。

【前腔】

(旦扮公主上)

幻质分灵蠢，
也会的施朱傅粉，
一般人物娇和嫩。
这芳心，
洞房中，
谁簇紧？

(见介)女儿瑶芳叩头，娘娘千岁千千岁。

(老)公主，你年已及笄，名方弄玉。今日依于国母，他日宜其家人。四德三从，可知端的？

(旦)孩儿年幼，望母亲指教。

(老)夫三从者：在家从父，出嫁从夫，老而从子。四德者：妇言，妇德，妇容，妇功。有此三从四德，可以为贤女子矣。听我道来：

【傍妆台】

(老)

一种寄灵根，

Princess of Golden Bough. She has attained marriage age, and her beauty and talent are beyond comparison. She has studied the Books and history[1] with the reverend Priestess Itty and learned embroidery from the royal elder sister, Lady Truffle.

Yesterday, the king decreed that her spouse should be a man from the upper world. He said that in order to find a son-in-law with a loving heart the matchmaker must have a shrewd eye. I´ve thought of the very person for this job: my niece Duchess Qiongying. She´s very good at judging people by sight. But before I have her carry out my plans, I should first send for the princess and tell her about the king´s intention.

MAIDS: Here comes the princess.

(Enter Princess Yaofang)

【Ditto】

PRINCESS:

Some beings have wits, some do not,
yet all know how to dab powder and rouge
to give themselves a sweet and lovely face.
But who will hug
my yearning heart
in the bridal cave?

(She greets Queen) Your daughter Yaofang kowtows to Your Ladyship. May you live thousands and thousands of years!

QUEEN: Daughter, you´ve reached womanhood, and should be ready for marriage. Up till now, you´ve been living with us, but soon you shall be living with your husband and his family. Do you know what the three obediences and the four virtues required of a woman are?[2]

PRINCESS: I´m still innocent. Please tell me, Mother.

QUEEN: The three obediences are obedience to father before marriage, to husband after marriage, and to eldest son should the husband die first. The four virtues are proper speech, diligent work, modest manner, and

依然楼阁贺生存。
论规模虽小可，
乘气化有人身。
中宫忝作吾王正，
下国凭称寡小君。
掌司阴教，
齐眉至尊。
你须知三贞七烈同是世间人。

【前腔】

（旦）

小小赘芳尘，
念瑶芳生长在王门。
虽不是人间世，
论相同掌上珍。
寒余窈窕深闺晚，
暖至丰茸别洞春。
父王庭训，
娘亲细论。
难道这三从四德微细的不如人。

【玩仙灯】

（贴扮琼英上）

踏绽鞋跟，
蚤向朱门步稳。

high morality. Observing these, you´ll become a graceful lady. Now, mind what I say:

【At the Dressing Table】

Though wee live at the very base,
wee enjoy the richness of palace life.
Diminutive as wee may seem,
time has granted us human forms.
Wee can be the mistress of a royal house
and win respect from vassal states.
Wee herd the female half,
an equal to the king.
Remember, wee, like humans, must defend our chastity.

【Ditto】

PRINCESS:

Born into a luxurious nest,
I have been raised within the purple walls.
Though this is not the human world,
I am no less a treasured child.
Winter sees me tucked in the warmest nook;
summer finds me moved to a shady cave.
Disciplined by Dad
and counseled by Mom,
my smallness won´t make me less virtuous than the humankind.

(Enter Duchess Qiongying)

【Celestial Lamp Dancers】

QIONGYING:

My tiny shoes burst their seams
as I hurry toward the purple steps.

自家蚁王侄女琼英便是。娘娘有召，敬入则个。(见叩头介)郡主琼英叩头，娘娘千岁。(见旦介)公主见礼。

(旦)尊姊到来。

(老)郡主听旨：近因瑶芳长成，堪招驸马。君王有命，若于本族内选婚，恐一时难得智勇之士，不堪扶持国家，要于人间招选驸马。闻得七月十五日，这扬州孝感寺，礼请契玄禅师讲经。人山人海，都往禅智寺天竺院报名。郡主可同灵芝夫人、上真子三人，同往听讲。但有英俊之士，便可留神。

(贴)谨遵懿旨。

【傍妆台】

(老)

女大急须婚，
不拘门户则待有良姻。
龙类中能煮海，
蝶梦里好移魂。

(贴)

知他同谁虰作夫妻分，
了你蚌亲父母恩？
俺抛眉晕，
忍笑痕，
可甚么人烟聚里看不出有情人？

(旦)琼英姐，俺便同你去听讲何如？

I´m Qiongying, the niece of the ant king. The queen has summoned me. Let me go in. (She kowtows to Queen) Duchess Qiongying kowtows to Your Ladyship. May you live a thousand years! (She greets Princess) My greetings, Princess.

PRINCESS: It´s so nice to see you, Cousin Qiongying.

QUEEN (to Qiongying): Now listen. The princess has attained woman´s estate, so it´s time to select a royal son-in-law. His Majesty has made it clear that if wee limit our choice to our own race, wee might not be able to find a man with both the administrative and military talents needed for the prosperity of our country. Therefore, wee are going to pick a human being. I hear that the Temple of Filial Force has invited Master Qixuan to preside over a grand ritual on the fifteenth day of the seventh month, and people are flocking to the Hindu Garden in Chan Wisdom Temple to sign up. Qiongying, you may go to attend the sermons, together with Lady Truffle and Priestess Itty, and be on the lookout for a handsome young man.

QIONGYING: Your wish is my command.

【At the Dressing Table】

QUEEN:

As soon as a girl comes of age
she should be married to the man destined.
A dragon maid can wed the man who boils the sea;[3]
a butterfly dream can transfer a soul.

QIONGYING:

Who knows which man she´ll sting to all her life,
whether she´ll *ant*knowledge your rearing pains.[4]
I´ll flash my catching eyes
and wear a coy smile.
Who said one can´t fish out a lover from a sea of men?

PRINCESS: Cousin Qiongying, can I go with you to the sermons?

(贴)公主体面，未宜出游。

(旦)这等，奴有金凤钗一对，文犀盒一枚，奉献禅师讲下，表我微情。

【前腔】

光景一时新，
待相同随喜终是女儿身。
献钗头金凤朵，
盛纳盒锦犀文。

(贴)

也知妹子无他敬，
如是观音着我闻。
我将为信，
去讲座陈。
管教他灵山会里直着个有缘人。

(老)郡主，此非小可之事。

【尾声】

到花宫不少的儿郎俊，
打叠起横波着人。

你去呵，

休得漏泄了机关
要老娘心上稳。

选佛场中去选郎，
禅床侧畔看东床。
疾去疾来须隐约，
好音先报与娘行。

QIONGYING: A girl of your status should keep away from crowds.

PRINCESS: I suppose you´re right. Here I have a pair of gold hairpins in the shape of flying phoenixes, and a small jewel case made out of rhino horn. Please place them before the altar as a token of my piety.

【Ditto】

That is a world I´d like to see,
yet as a virgin I can´t go with you.
To Buddha I donate my phoenix pins
and the rhino jewel case with pretty veins.

QIONGYING:

I know those are the things you treasure most.
Let Guanyin[5] be our witness from above.
I´ll take these tokens of your faith,
and lay them at the Master´s seat.
I promise you a matching spouse brought from the holy place.

QUEEN: Qiongying, this is no slight matter.

【Coda】

With no lack of handsome men at the temple fair,
you open your eyes to the very best.
Take care,
I do not want the purpose of your trip
to encourage a rumor all around.

Wee seek a groom where others look for God;
By the monk´s seat wee see a bridal bed.
Go and return unnoticed, quick and quiet;
You should report the good news first to me.

第六出　谩　　遣

【字字双】

（溜二上）

小生家住古扬州，
铺后。
祖宗七辈儿喜风流，
自幼。
衣衫破落帽儿彫，
狐臭。
能吹木屑惯扶头，
即溜。

自家扬州城中有名的一个溜二便是。一生浪荡，半世风流。但是晦气的人家，便请我撮科打哄；不管有趣的子弟，都与他钻懒帮闲。手策无多，口才绝妙。有那等吊眼子，敲他几下，叫做打草惊蛇；无过是脱稍儿，松他一筹，则是将虾吊鲤。着甚么南庄田，北庄地，有溜二便是衣食父母；难起动东邻邀，西邻请，则沙三是个酒肉弟兄。知音的，说是个妙人、好人、老成人；少趣的，叫我败子，倈子，光棍子。且自由他笑骂，只图自己风光。这几日不见沙

Scene 6 The Merrymakers

(Enter Liu Second)

【Coupled Words】

LIU:

In ancient Yangzhou I have made my home,
behind the mall.
Amour for seven generations reigns,
since swaddling clothes.
From foot to head in rags without a hat,
the body reeks.
I used to brag, and flatter just as well,
clever indeed.

I´m none other than the notorious Liu Second in the city of Yangzhou. I´ve never taken up any serious work in my life, and the major part of it has already been squandered. Families down on their luck send for me to conjure up some cheap laughter. I don´t care if they´re friendly or not. As long as I´m asked, I´m ready to help them kill time. There´s no secret to my craft, and what I pride myself on is my tongue. If I happen on a rich fool, I´ll fleece him. That´s called "beating the grass to warn the snake." All you need to do is pamper him with words and give his wish a whet. It´s like angling for a carp with a small shrimp. Neither does the location bother me. Whether it´s a farm to the south or a village to the north, as long as they can afford to be my benefactor, I´ll stick with them. But invitations from my immediate neighbors to the east or to the west are hard to come by. Only Sha Third is a sworn brother for free meals and wine. Those who like me say I´m a humorous guy, a good guy, an honest guy. Those who dislike me call me a bum, a scum, or a crumb. Let them laugh and scold. I only care about having a good time. That reminds me:

三，寻他闲串去。

【前腔】

(沙三上)

贱子姓沙行十三，
名滥。
就似水底月儿到十三，
圆泛。
六儿七儿巧十三，
胡蘸。
官司吊起打十三，
扯淡。

(溜)沙三，你犯夜了？

(沙)不犯夜，不是子弟也，哥。

(溜)兄弟，这几日嘴闲了。

(沙)和你大路头站去。

(丑上)白云在何处？明月落谁家？

(沙)小哥，落在这里。

(丑)大哥，我东人淳于家要请溜二、沙三官耍子，住在那门？

(溜、沙)我二人便是。你东人做甚么生意？

(丑)做裨将。

(沙)做皮匠，叫我去帮钻？

(丑)军营里副将哩。

I haven´t seen Sha Third for quite a few days. Let me go and find out what he´s up to.

(Enter Sha Third)

【Ditto】

SHA:

I am the Sha´s thirteenth ignoble son,
without a name,
like the moon on the thirteenth on the pond,
seemingly round.
Six and seven happens to be thirteen,
dull wit.
The judge usually metes out thirteen strokes,
bull shit.

LIU: Hi, Sha. Did you break the curfew again last night?

SHA: Hi, brother, you´re not a playboy if you don´t break the curfew.

LIU: Brother, my tongue has been out of business for quite some days.

SHA: Let´s go and wait by the crossroads.

(Enter Partridge)

PARTRIDGE:

O´er whose roof does the white cloud hang?
At whose room does the bright moon land?

SHA: Brother, it lands right here.

PARTRIDGE: Big brothers, my master, Mr. Chunyu, has sent me to invite a Liu Second and a Sha Third. Do you know where they live?

LIU, SHA: They´re right before your eyes. What kind of business does your master do?

PARTRIDGE: He´s a lieutenant.

SHA: What?! A left tenant has sent for us?

PARTRIDGE: An army lieutenant.

（溜）是那能饮酒的淳于公么？

（丑）着。

（溜、沙）便去，便去。

有酒旧倾盖，

无钱新白头。（下）

（生上）〔集唐〕

弃置复何道？

凄凄吴楚间。

相忆不相见，

秋风生近关。

我淳于棼休官落魄，赖酒消魂。争奈客散孟尝之门，独醉淮阴之市，想吾生直恁无聊也！

【锦缠道】

我本待，

学时流立奇功俊名，

谈笑朔风生。

怎如他，

苍生口说难凭？

便道你能奋发有期程，

则半盏河清，

挤了滴珠槽浸死刘伶。

道的个百无成，

只杜康祠蘸住了这穷三圣。

做个带帽儿堵酒瓶，

头直下酒淹衣裙。

难道普乾坤醉眼偏只许屈原醒？

LIU: Is he the famed drinker, Lord Chunyu?
PARTRIDGE: You bet!
LIU, SHA: We´ll go with you, right away.
Good wine can cement instant friends;
Poverty only breeds gray hair.

(Exeunt all)

(Enter Chunyu)

CHUNYU:
Once dropped out, you're forever lost,
Drifting as you may try to cling.
Friends meet, only in memory,
And a sharp wind will rise to kill.

Ah me! See how lost I am now. I´ve been thrown out of the army. Without wine I can´t live. And now even my friends have deserted me, leaving me in despair like Han Xin[1] before fortune smiled on him. How pointless life has become!

【A Silk-paved Street】

I had hoped
to establish a name in line with vogue,
and talk briskly among my peers.
But who could know
that fate could have been so unfair?
Even if you have the competence and the drive,
there´s only meager chance for you.
So I took solace in a trough of muddling wine
to forget I´d failed in a hundred ways.
Liquor relentlessly sucked down the underdog.
As I tried to plug my throat with the jar,
wine trickled down and soaked my garment flaps.
Why was Qu Yuan[2] the only man who kept a sober head?

（丑同溜、沙上）三家酒注子，一对色哥儿。

（丑报介）溜二、沙三官到。

（见介）（溜）小人名溜二，

（沙）贱子即沙三。

（生）久闻才识面，

（合）十个更酸咸。

（生）怎生十个更酸咸？

（溜）适闻老翁说把九文钱才吃个面，没盐醋的，因此小子加上一文。

（生笑介）敢问二位，在城在乡？

【好姐姐】

（溜、沙）

广陵郡中一城，
识溜二、沙三名姓，
玲珑剔透，
人前打眼睛。
随尊兴，
哩嗹花罗能堪听，
孤鲁子头嗑得精。

（溜做只脚跪、嗑连二头、叫爷介）

（沙唱哩罗嗹介）淳于兄，孤老院耍去。

（生）贫子行处，怎生好去？

（沙）不是。是婊子铺。

（生）扬州诸妓，我已尽知。可别有甚处消遣？

(Reenter Partridge, Liu and Sha)

PARTRIDGE, LIU, SHA:

We're a trio of wine funnels;
We're a pair of licentious twins.

PARTRIDGE (announces): Mr. Liu and Mr. Sha have arrived.

LIU (greeting Chunyu): I'm Liu Second.

SHA (greeting Chunyu): My humble name is Sha Third.

CHUNYU: Nice chance to meet you two.

LIU, SHA: A tenth for salt and vinegar.

CHUNYU: Pardon me?

LIU: Just now my venerable lord said "nine cents to eat noodle." I'll chip in a cent so you can have some salt and vinegar to go with it.

CHUNYU (laughs): May I venture to ask you your residence, in town or in the country?

【Kind Sister】

LIU, SHA:

In the downtown area of Yangzhou
Liu and Sha are a pair of well-known names.
Frisky and waggish,
we always draw a second glance.
Name what you wish.
Our lilting, lusty lyrics please the ear;
our tumbling kowtow is a work of art.

(Liu goes down on one knee and makes a succession of kowtows while muttering compliments. Sha sings a rustic tune)

LIU: Brother Chunyu, let's go to the bawdyhouse for some fun.

CHUNYU: What fun can we have at the baldies' place?

SHA: Not baldies. To the whorehouse.

CHUNYU: I'm afraid I'm already familiar with all the prostitutes in town. Can't you suggest somewhere else?

(沙)有，有。孝感寺中元盂兰大会，僧俗男女都去润州甘露寺，请契玄禅师讲经。

(生)便去听经如何?

(沙)那里吃素，淳于公贪酒哩!

(生)那有此话?

【前腔】

吾生，
醉乡酩酊，
饮中仙也有个逃禅中圣，
长斋绣佛到庄严得人世清。

山鹧儿，看马。

堪乘兴，
行随白马藏鞭影，
坐听黄龙喝棒声。

忽忽意不乐，
留人相伴闲。
上方随喜去，
秋色满盂兰。

SHA: Yes, yes. The Temple of Filial Force is holding a grand Ullambana ceremony on Ghosts´ Day. Both the monks and devotees have been to Zhenjiang´s Sweet Dew Temple to invite Master Qixuan over to preach.
CHUNYU: Then why don´t we go and listen to the sermons?
SHA: They only provide vegetarian food there. You´ll miss your bottle.
CHUNYU: I can do without wine for once.

【Ditto】

My life
is bogged in a swamp of wine.
Yet there are times when drunkards go to lecture halls.
Before the altar one may find a sober world.
Partridge, saddle my horse.
With spirits high,
I´ll get on my white steed and gallop off
to catch the awakening shouts of Chan.

Suddenly caught in moody tides,
I need someone to boost me up.
Setting out for a holy place,
I see a bowl of autumn bloom.

第七出　偶　　见

【普贤歌】

（僧上）

终朝顶拜如来，
人肉样的莲花业作台。
一家儿酒和色，
三分气命财，
领着个铁围山难布摆。

小僧扬州府禅智寺一个五戒是也。五戒，五戒，好些尴尬。近因孝感寺作中元盂兰大会，十方僧俗去请润州契玄禅师讲经。那禅师法旨威严，凡有听讲者，先于小寺投牒报名，方去听讲。却有西番一个婆罗门，名唤石延，客居小寺天竺院。此人善作西番《胡旋舞》，但有往来报名男女来此，他便施舞一回。俺寺中好不闹热也！目今天竺院水月观音座前点起香烛，看甚人报名？咱且回避。

正是：

此中留半偈，
别院演三车。（下）

Scene 7 Chance Encounter

(Enter a monk)

【Virtues Prevail】

MONK:

We worship Buddha day and night,
who sits aloft on a flesh-colored lotus seat.
Not averse to wine and women,
we´re subject to fortune, fate and face.
One can´t escape from the iron girdle round the world.

I´m a monk at Yangzhou´s Chan Wisdom Temple. My nickname is Five Don´ts. Five Don´ts, Five Don´ts, isn´t that name somewhat ironic? The Temple of Filial Force is planning to host a grand Ullambana ceremony on Ghosts´ Day, and people from all the eight bearings have been to Zhenjiang to invite Master Qixuan to come and preach on that occasion. That Master Qixuan is very particular about propriety. He ordered that all those who want to attend the sermons must first come to my temple to register.

At present, a Brahman from the west is staying at the Hindu Garden of my temple. His name is Shi Yan and he´s very good at doing the sema dance. Whenever a crowd gathers, he gives a performance, and the temple becomes abuzz with excitement.

Now, incense sticks and candles have been lit before the statue of Guanyin at the Hindu Garden. Let´s see who´s coming to sign up. For the moment I´ll step aside.

Withhold the couplet´s second half,
And watch the pageant rolling past.

(Exit)

【前腔】

（贴扮琼英、老旦扮灵芝、小旦道扮上真姑上）

天生微眇身材，
也逐天香过院来。
一尖红绣鞋，
双飞碧玉钗，
小玉纳汗巾儿长袖洒。

（贴）奴家琼英郡主，承国母之命，和这灵芝国嫂、上真仙姑同来禅智寺报名，孝感寺听经；就里将瑶芳妹子玉钗、犀盒施于禅师讲前；看有意气郎君，招与瑶芳为婿。这是禅智寺天竺院了，池边好座紫竹观音。那香案之上有报名疏簿，我们不免焚香拜了，佥名。

（三旦同拜介）

【黄莺儿】

一点注香沉，
礼南无观世音。
花根木艳低微甚，
趋跄宝林，
威光乍临，
今生打破前生荫。

（合）

拜深深，
姻缘和合，
虫蚁一般心。

(Enter Duchess Qiongying, Lady Truffle and Itty, a Taoist priestess)

【Ditto】

ALL:

Heavenly born in figures slim,
wee cross over, attracted by the fragrant scent,
in red embroidered pointed shoes,
with waving jade pins in the hair,
and flimsy kerchiefs tucked in lengthy sleeves.

QIONGYING: I´m Qiongying, the Duchess. At the Queen´s command, Lady Truffle, Priestess Itty and I have come to the Temple of Chan Wisdom to sign up for the sermons at the Temple of Filial Force. Wee are to place Cousin Yaofang´s hairpins and jewel case in front of the Master´s seat, and see if wee can find a promising young gentleman for her. Here wee are at the Hindu Garden of Chan Wisdom Temple. What a wonderful statue of Guanyin that is, beside the pond! The attendance book is laid out on the sacrificial table. Let´s offer incense and pay homage to Guanyin, and then sign our names. (They kowtow to the statue)

【The Yellow Oriole】

ALL:

The incense smoke carries up
our deepest respects to Guanyin.
From our abode beneath the lowly roots,
wee have crawled to your holy side.
Bathed in your golden light
wee wish for transformations to better lives.
(Refrain)
Deeply wee bow,
for a wedlock sealed in love
— insects and humans share one thought.

(贴)俺三人还将瑶芳妹子婚姻之事，密祷一番。(拜介)

【前腔】

槐殿欲成阴，
把金枝付瑟琴，
寻花配叶端详恁。
于中细任，
其间暗吟，
无明到处情儿沁。(合前)

(小旦)俺们池边消遣一会。呀！一个回回舞上来了。

【北点绛唇】

(扮回子上)

生小西番，
恭持佛赞，
朝炎汉。
蓦入禅关，
日影金刚灿。

自家婆罗门弟子石延的便是。行脚中华，寄食天竺禅院，好不奈烦，散心一会。呀！三位女菩萨从何而来？请看俺婆罗门《胡旋舞》一会也。

(三旦笑介)请了。(内鼓介)

【对玉环带过清江引】

QIONGYING: Let´s say a silent prayer to Guanyin for Cousin Yaofang´s marriage. (They kowtow)

【Ditto】

ALL:

The tree wants to expand its shade
by linking its golden bough with the harp
— the flower and leaf must be exactly matched.
What consideration!
What deliberation!
Love permeates throughout the pores of earth.
(Refrain)

ITTY: Let´s take a stroll by the pond. Ah, here comes a Brahman a-dancing!

(Enter a Brahman)

【Cherry Lips, Northern Style】

BRAHMAN:

Born in the western regions,
I practice Buddhism.
A pilgrim to central China,
I crossed the door to Chan,
where statues shine in the golden sun.

My name is Shi Yan, a Brahman. I´ve traveled to central China and have taken up lodgings at the Hindu Garden. Life is so boring that I need some relief. Ah, here come three charming patronesses. Please watch my sema dance.

THE THREE LADIES (smiling): Please. (Drums beat within[1])

【A Pair of Jade Bracelets, with River Qing Interlude】

（石舞介）

拍手天坛，
风飘长绣幡。
答剌兜绵，
腰身拴束的弯。
衫袖打斓斑，
西天俏锦阑。
燕尾翩翻，
观音座宝栏。
合掌开莲瓣，
散天香婆罗门回笑眼。（内喝采介）

（石）一个骑马官儿来，俺去了也。（下）

（贴众）有人来，我们且池边浣手去。（洗手介）

【缕缕金】

（生骑从上）

无聊赖，
不自怜，
特来禅智院，
打俄延。
花落苍苔面，
谁舞《胡旋》？
门前系马接了金鞭，
有人儿咱瞧见。

BRAHMAN (while dancing):

Clap, clap, I clap my hands;
in the cool breeze the banners flap.
Supple and soft,
my springy waist can bend and coil.
Of brightly colored western silk,
my long sleeves spin out rainbow hues.
In front of Guanyin´s railed-off throne,
I swivel up and down.
My fingers form a lotus bud;
my eyes cast smiling glances all around.
(Applause within)

A mounted officer is riding this way. Excuse me, please.

(Exit Brahman)

THE THREE LADIES: A man is approaching. Let´s move over to the pond to wash our hands. (They wash their hands in the pond)

(Enter Chunyu, riding)

【Every Strand Gold】

CHUNYU:

Lost and bored,
I loathe my life,
so I´ve come to the temple yard
to kill unwanted time.
Petals litter the mossy ground;
who did the sema dance?
Tying my horse to a post by the gate,
I´m sure I see a charming face!

(He walks in)

（到介）竹径通幽处，

禅房花木深。

观音座前，疏簿在此，我淳于棼就此拈香报名。（拈香拜介）

【江儿水】

淳于弟子，

愁情一片，

销愁无处去听闲经卷。

俺待佥名。（写介）

佥名自佥，

观音试观。

（作见贴介）

水竹池边，

因何活现。

（贴笑回身介）灵芝嫂，湿透这汗巾儿，挂在那处好？

（生背介）此女子秀入肌肤，香生笑语，世间有此天仙乎？（回介）小娘子的汗巾儿，待小生效劳，挂于竹枝之上。（贴笑递汗巾）（生接挂介）这汗巾儿粉香清婉，小生能勾似他，怀卿袖中，浥卿香汗？

（贴众笑不应介）池光花影，娟娟可人。

（生叹介）俺淳于棼可是遇仙也？他三回自语，一顾倾人，急节中间，难以相近。不如且自孝感寺听经去。山鹧，看马来。（上马介）

A trail leads through the bamboo grove
To temple halls concealed in green.

Ah, the attendance book is spread out in front of the statue of Guanyin. I´ll light a bunch of incense sticks and sign my name. (He plants incense sticks in the burner and kowtows)

【River Water】

A lost man named Chunyu,
mired in the thick of woe,
has rambled over to hear sermons for a change.

Let me sign up. (He writes)

At here I sign my name;
Guanyin must see the same.
(His eyes fall on Qiongying)
There by the bamboo pond,
is she a theophany?

QIONGYING (with a smile she turns her eyes away from Chunyu): Cousin Truffle, where do you think I can hang up this wet handkerchief to dry?

CHUNYU (aside): Gee! This woman´s beauty is certainly more than skin deep, and I can almost smell the sweetness of her smiles! Could she be anything but a fairy? (Turns around to face Qiongying) Miss, let me help you hang it on the bamboo stem. (Smilingly, Qiongying hands him the handkerchief. He hangs it up) This lucky kerchief has inhaled such fragrance from your body that I wish I could take its place in your sleeve and soak up your aromatic perspiration.

THE THREE LADIES (laugh, but ignore him): See the reflection of flowers on the pond? How lovely they look!

CHUNYU (sighs): Oh, have I ventured into the fairyland? It seems they have no desire to speak with an outsider. But, I simply can´t forget her looks! Well, if it´s impossible to strike up a quick friendship, I´d better move on to the Temple of Filial Force to listen to the sermons. Partridge,

紫骝嘶入落花去，
见此踟躇空断肠。(下)

(贴)此生，有情人也。他也去听讲，咱瞧他去来。

(老)咳，俺去不得。俺真是个信女，把水月观音倒做了。

(小旦)怎么说?

(老)月信来了。

(贴)罪过人。这等，咱和上真姑去便了。

【尾声】

过别院，
听谈禅。
老灵芝去也，
咱和这上真仙，
到讲堂呵，
把俺这觑郎君的眼稍儿再抛演。

为看婆罗舞，
相逢骑马郎。
寻荷终得藕，
池上白莲香。

bring my horse here. (He mounts)

My steed trotted into a field of flowers;
From there it couldn´t make out where to go.

(Exit Chunyu)

QIONGYING: This man has got some good sense. Since he too is going to attend the sermons, let´s follow him.
TRUFFLE: Sorry, I can´t go with you. I´m a most faithful woman — I´ve got the moon in the water.
ITTY: What do you mean?
TRUFFLE: I´m wet with my monthlies.
QIONGYING: Oh, Buddha forgive you. Well, if that´s the case, I´ll go with Itty.

【Coda】

To the other court
wee go to hear Chan talk.
Let Old Truffle return alone.
With Priestess Itty I will go
to the lecture hall
and once again cast my discerning eyes on nice young men.

Wee went to watch the Brahman dance,
And met as well a mounted youth.
Where lotus blooms there´re jointed roots;
A fragrance wavers on the pond.

第八出 情 著

（杂扮首座僧持钓竿上）

佛祖流传一盏灯，
至今无灭亦无增。
灯灯朗耀传今古，
法法皆如贯所能。

贫僧乃润州甘露寺中契玄禅师首座弟子是也。自幼出家，参承多腊。常只是朝阳缝破衲，对月了残经。近乃扬州孝感寺请师父说法，贫僧领着众僧，安排下香灯花果，禅床净几，待师父升座。大众动着法器者。（内鼓乐介）

（净扮老禅师拄杖拂子上升座介）

高临法座唱宗风，
翠竹黄花事不同。
但是众星都拱北，
果然无水不朝东。

（提拄杖介）

赛却须弥老古藤，
寒空一锡振飞腾。
拄开妙挟通宗路，

Scene 8 Love Kindled

(Enter Senior Monk, holding a fishing pole)

S. MONK:

The Great Buddha has left a lamp behind;
Its flames have burned steadily till this day,
Forwarding a legacy that still shines
Both in the inner self and outer world.

I´m the number one disciple of Master Qixuan at Sweet Dew Temple in Zhenjiang. I was given to the temple in my early childhood, and have studied the scriptures through many summers and winters. During the day I sit in the sunshine, mending my shabby gown; at night I sit under the moon, finishing off my daily lessons.

A few days ago, my master was invited to deliver a sermon at the Temple of Filial Force in Yangzhou. So here I am with the other monks to prepare the incense burners, lamps, flowers and fruits. Now the altar has been freshly cleaned, it´s time for my master to take the chair. You there, play your instruments! (Music strikes up within.)

(Enter Qixuan, the Chan Master, leaning on a walking stick and holding a horsetail whisk. He ascends the altar)

QIXUAN:

I ascend the seat to expound on Chan;
Bamboo and lily are of different stalks.
But all stars spin around the Polaris;
All watercourses run from west to east.
(He lifts his walking stick)
Tougher than old rattans on Sumeru,[1]
This stick can knock open your way to Chan.
When I throw it into the crystal air,
Even embattled troops will stop to stare.

打断交锋回避僧。

（执佛子介）

竖起清风洒白云，

河沙无地可容尘。

将军一事无巴鼻，

兔角龟毛拂着人。

取香来。（拈香介）此香：

不从千圣得，

岂向万机求？

虚空观不尽，

大地莫能收。

拈香指顶，透十方之法界，薰四大之神州；爇向炉心，祝皇王之万岁，愿太子之千秋。（垂钓介）

手把金钩月一痕，

乘槎独坐到河源。

悠悠泛泛经千载，

影落鱼龙不敢吞。

（首座）如何空即是色？

（净）

东沼初阳疑吐出，

南山晓翠若浮来。

（首座）如何色即是空？

（净）

细雨湿衣看不见，

闲花落地听无声。

（首座）如何非色非空？

（净）

归去岂知还向月，

(He lifts the horsetail whisk)

This whisk can sweep the air and brush the clouds,
For dust has no place in the holy land.
What are the generals there fighting for?
The horns of rabbits and the turtle's hair.

Hand me the joss sticks. (He holds them up in his hands) These joss sticks,

They come not from secular kings,
But from Buddha's generous hand.
The spacious sky can hold much more
Than what the massive earth can give.

Up I raise them to the sky, their smoke filters through all the ten worlds, and their fragrance embalms the four vast continents. Down I insert them into the burner, I wish His Majesty ten thousand years of life, and the crown prince a thousand. (He holds up the fishing pole as if fishing)

The hook is the gold crescent of the moon;
Up on the Milky Way I fish alone.
More than a millennium has floated by;
Neither fish nor dragon dare tempt the bait.

S. MONK: Master, why does the scripture say: "Śūnya is rūpa?"[2]

QIXUAN: Because

The red sun rises from the eastern void;
The greenness of southern peaks comes afloat.

S. MONK: Why say "Rūpa is śūnya?"[3]

QIXUAN:

Traceless is the drizzle that damps our clothes;
No sound is heard when petals drop to ground.

S. MONK: How can there be neither rūpa nor śūnya?

QIXUAN:

Won't you face a moon when you've lived this life?
Are not the clouds you dreamed of really clouds?

梦来何处更为云。

(首座)多谢我师！今日且归林下，来日问禅。(末下)

(净)大众，若有那门居士，禅苑高僧，参学未明，法有疑碍，今日稍伸问答。有么？

(外扮老僧上)有，有，有。敢问我师，如何是佛？

(净)

人间玉岭清霄月，

天上银河白昼风。

(外)如何是法？

(净)

绿蓑衣下携诗卷，

黄篾楼中挂酒篘。

(外)如何是僧？

(净)

数茎白发坐浮世，

一盏寒灯和故人。

(外)多谢我师！今日且归林下，来日问禅。(下)

(净垂钓介)

钓丝常在手中拿，

影得游鱼动晚霞。

海上半天留不住，

醒来依旧宿芦花。

大众，还有精通居士，俊秀禅郎，未悟宗机，再伸问答。有也是无？

S. MONK: Thank you, Master. I´ll go and ponder over this deep in the woods, and come back later with more questions.

(Exit Senior Monk)

QIXUAN: You lay devotees or veteran monks, if you have questions or doubts arising from your study of Chan, please raise them now. I´ll try to explain.

(Enter an old monk)

OLD MONK: I have some questions. May I beg to ask you, Reverend Master, what is Buddha?

QIXUAN: Buddha is

The beaming moon above the worldly peaks;
The wind descending from the Milky Way.

OLD MONK: What is dharma?[4]

QIXUAN: Dharma is

A poetry book under a rough man´s arm;
A filter hung by casks of turbid wine.

OLD MONK: What is saṅgha?[5]

QIXUAN: Saṅgha is

A few gray hairs in the temporal world;
A man consorting with a lonely lamp.

OLD MONK: Thank you, Master. I´ll go and ponder over this deep in the woods, and come back later with more questions.

(Exit Old Monk)

QIXUAN (continues fishing):

Holding the fishing pole I quietly watch
Fish shadows catch fire in the sunset glow.
But the waters cannot sustain this scene;
On a patch of reed catkins one awakes.

Do any of you, talented laymen or learned monks, still feel in the dark? You may pose more questions. Anyone?

【谒金门前】

(生上)

闲生活，
中酒嗔花如昨。
待近炉烟依法座，
听千偈澜番个。

小生淳于棼来此参禅，想起来落托无聊，终朝烦恼，有何禅机问对？就把烦恼因果，动问禅师。(见介)小生淳于棼稽首，特来问禅。如何是根本烦恼？

(净)

秋槐落尽空宫里，
凝碧池边奏管弦。

(生)如何是随烦恼？

(净)

双翅一开千万里，
止因栖隐恋乔柯。

(生)如何破除这烦恼？

(净)

惟有梦魂南去日，
故乡山水路依稀。(生沉吟)

(净背介)老僧以慧眼观看此人，外相虽痴，到可立地成佛。

(Enter Chunyu)

【The Golden Gate, first half】

CHUNYU:

My idle life
is spent day after day with wine and flowers.
Pushing my way toward the incensed seat
I want to relish the melodious hymns.

Here I am, to listen to the sermons. Alas! Look at my life! Dejected and distressed as I am, what intelligent questions can I come up with? Well, perhaps I can ask the master about the causes of all these miseries. (He steps forth to greet Qixuan) Chunyu Fen pays respects to Your Reverence. I´ve come with a question about the faith. May I beg to ask what causes mūlakleśa?[6]

QIXUAN:

Autumn leaves cast from the Sophora tree,
Pipe tunes beside a pond of jellied rouge.

CHUNYU: What causes upakleśa[7]

QIXUAN:

With wings that could have soared a thousand miles,
You stay fast wedlocked to an arbor branch.

CHUNYU: How can one get rid of all the kleśa?

QIXUAN:

When the sunny dream quits the southern bough,
You will return along the homebound route.

(Chunyu seems lost in thought)

QIXUAN (aside): To my old pair of penetrating eyes, this man is the type that can be converted to Buddha on the spot, though he appears to be dumb.

(Enter Duchess Qiongying and Priestess Itty)

【谒金门后】

（小旦道扮同贴上）

莲步天台踭蹉，
还似蚁儿旋磨。

上真仙，

竹院人儿情似可，
再与端详和。

（净笑）淳于生，你带着眷属来哩。

（生回介）是好两位女娘。

（背叹介）禅师，怎知我原无家室。

（贴见介）大师稽首。

（净）蚁子为何而来？

（贴）为五百年因果而来。

（净背笑介）是了，是了。叫侍者铺单。

（末铺座介）（响唱介）五十三单整齐。

（净）举来。

（贴响唱介）《妙法莲花经》、《观世音菩萨普门品》。

（净）

六万余言七轴装，
无边妙义广含藏。
白玉齿边流舍利，
红莲舌上放毫光。
喉中玉露涓涓润，
口内醍醐滴滴凉。
假饶造罪过山岳，
不须妙法两三行。

【The Golden Gate, second half】

QIONGYING:

Pushing our bound feet to celestial heights,
wee mill around like busy ants.

Priestess Itty,

the man we just met seems a likely choice.
This time wee must get a closer look.

QIXUAN (laughing): Mr. Chunyu, you´ve brought your family along.

CHUNYU (glances back): Ah, two beautiful ladies. (Aside, sighs) The master has no idea that I´m still a bachelor.

QIONGYING (greeting Qixuan): My respects to Your Reverence.

QIXUAN: What has brought you ants here?

QIONGYING: The karma arranged five hundred years ago.

QIXUAN (aside, laughing): That´s it. That´s it. Attendants, spread out the scroll paintings.

ATTENDANT (unrolling the scrolls and then sings out loudly): All the fifty-three paintings[8] are spread out.

QIXUAN: Hold them up!

QIONGYING (sings out loudly): *The Lotus Sutra:*[9] *The Book of Guanyin the Bodhisattva.*

QIXUAN:

Those sixty thousand words in seven scrolls
Hold a source of wisdom and boundless truth.
They pour out from between her pearl-white teeth;
Her tonic tongue radiates as she speaks.
From the perpetual fountain of her throat
Words gurgle out like cool elixir juice.
Mountain-colossal though your sins might be,
Two lines or three are to redeem your soul.

【Liangzhou Overture】

【梁州序】

人天金界，
普门开觉，
无尽意参承佛座。
以何因果，
得名观世音那？
佛告众生遇苦，
但唱其名，
即时显现无空过。
贪嗔痴应念总销磨，
求女求男智福多。

(合)

如是等威慈大，
是名观世音菩萨。
齐顶礼，
妙莲花。

(众)观世音菩萨云何游此世界？云何而为众生说法？方便之力，其事云何？

【前腔】

(净)

有如国土，
众生应度，
种种法身随化。
因缘说法，
以观世界婆娑。

The sutra opens up
the gate to golden sky.
The Ineffable asked Great Buddha
what virtues she has
that she is named Guanyin the Bodhisattva.
Buddha says whoever is suffering
need only enounce her name,
and she will never fail to show herself.
Greed, hate and foolish thoughts will be pardoned;
prayers for sons or daughters will be answered.
(Refrain)
For such benevolence and potency
she is called Guanyin the Bodhisattva.
We should prostrate ourselves
before her lotus seat.

THE AUDIENCE: Then how does she walk in this mortal world? How does she propagate Buddha´s teachings among living beings? And how is her power manifested?

【Ditto】

QIXUAN:

As if stepping on solid land
she travels to save the souls,
changing her form as fits the case.
She conveys her message
in ways each can best comprehend.
All beings, deva or human,
when in desperate need,
she´ll come to rescue them from fear and woe,
redeeming as many as river sands
in a twinkling, with no apparent strain.

一切天龙人等，
急难之中，
与他怖畏轻离脱。
十方齐现豁似河沙，
游戏神通一刹那。（合前）

（生）后来无尽意菩萨云何？

（净）尔时无尽意菩萨启过佛爷，叫世尊，我今当供养观世音菩萨了。当即解下颈上宝珠璎珞，价值紫金百千两，献于观世音菩萨，说道，愿仁者受此法施。那观世音菩萨不肯受。尔时佛告观世音，你可哀愍无尽意和这四众，权受下了这宝珠璎珞。那观世音菩萨因佛爷有言，受了璎珞，分作两分，一分奉释伽牟尼佛爷，一分奉多宝佛爷的塔。你众生们听讲这经，要知观世音菩萨有如是自在威神，普同发心供养。

（众）弟子们顶礼受持。

（生）谨参大师，小生曾居将帅，杀人饮酒，怕不能度脱也？

（净）经明说着，应以天大将军身度者，菩萨即现其身而度之，有甚分别？

（贴问介）禀参大师，妇女如何？

（净笑介）经明说应以人、非人等度者，即现其身而度之。

（贴作惊介）（对小旦背介）这大师神通广大，不说应以女身得度，到说个人、非人。你再问他。

（小旦问介）大师，似我作道姑的，也可度为弟子乎？

（净）你那道经中，已云“道在蝼蚁”，则看几粒饭，散作小沙弥。

(Refrain)

CHUNYU: What did The Ineffable say then?

QIXUAN: "Great Buddha," said The Ineffable Bodhisattva, "from now on I´ll worship Guanyin." So saying, he took off his necklace of precious jewels, which is worth hundreds of thousands of ounces of pure gold, and presented it to Guanyin. "Only the most benevolent deserves this," he insisted.

Guanyin declined the gift. Buddha then said to Guanyin, "You may accept it out of consideration for The Ineffable and the other monks." At Buddha´s bidding she accepted the necklace, but divided it into two parts. One part she contributed to Śākyamuni, the other to the pagoda of the Buddha of Many Treasures.

After you´ve learned this part of the sutra, you must have come to realize that Guanyin is such a powerful being herself that all of you should worship her wholeheartedly.

THE AUDIENCE: We´re all her disciples.

CHUNYU: Great Master, having been an army general, I´ve committed sins of killing and heavy drinking. Can I be redeemed?

QIXUAN: The sutra makes it clear: "If he ought to be converted to Buddha as a celestial general, Bodhisattva will appear in the theophany of a general to redeem his soul." So what difference does that make?

QIONGYING: Great Master, can women be saved as well?

QIXUAN (laughing): The sutra also clearly states: "If they are to be converted, be they human or non-human beings, Bodhisattva will appear in a theophany to redeem their souls."

QIONGYING (taken aback, aside to Itty): This master must have magic powers. He didn´t say women could be saved, but talked about human and non-human beings. You´d better ask him.

ITTY: Great Master, can a Taoist priestess like myself be her disciple?

QIXUAN: In your Taoist scripture it´s plainly stated: "The Way lies with crickets and ants." Since you´ve received many a grain of rice from the

怎度不的？

（贴、小旦跪介）大师真个天眼通。有个妹子瑶芳，深闺娇小，未克参承。附有金凤钗一双，通犀小盒一枚，愿施讲筵，望大师哀愍。（起唱介）

【前腔】

紫衣师天眼摩诃，
他颈莺娇几曾有璎珞？
待学尽形供养，
化身难脱。
待把宝珠抽献，
比龙女如何？
自笑身微末，
施的些儿个。
恨无多，
一分能分两分么？（合前）

（生背介）奇哉此女！（回介）大师，金钗、犀盒，愿一借观。（看介）（回眄小旦、贴介）人与物皆非世间所有。

【前腔】

巧金钗对凤飞斜，
赛暖金一枚犀盒。
（背介）
看他春生笑语，
媚翦层波，

neophyte, why can´t you be saved?

QIONGYING, ITTY (kneeling): Great Master, you have penetrating eyes! To be frank, wee have a young cousin called Yaofang, a budding girl raised in a sequestered boudoir. She´s still too young to come to hear your sermons, but she´s asked us to bring along a pair of gold phoenix hairpins and a small rhino-horn jewel case, and donate them at the altar. Please accept them. (They rise to their feet)

【Ditto】

Your Reverence has seen many priceless things,
but she doesn´t have a necklace of precious stones.
Although she wishes to devote herself,
she cannot shed her present form.
Though she´d prefer to give a jumbo pearl,
she isn´t the daughter of the dragon king.
Embarrassed by her humble size,
these trivial gifts are all she has.
Pitifully little,
how can they be divided into two?
(Refrain)

CHUNYU (aside): These two women are marvels! (To Qixuan) Great Master, may I have a look at the hairpins and jewel case? (Examining the gifts, he glances at Qiongying and Itty) These things and these women do not belong to this mortal world!

【Ditto】

A golden pair of flying phoenix pins;
a rhino case infused with body warmth.
(Aside)
See how her smiles sparkle like spring sunshine
rippling upon the lake.

把灵犀旧恨，
小凤新愁，
向无色天边惹。（净冷笑介）

（生回唱）

价值千百两，
未多些，
一笑拈花奉释伽。（合前）

（生）大师，此女子从何而来？

（净背介）此生痴情妄起，倩观音座前白鹦哥叫醒他。（内作鹦哥叫）蚁子转身，蚁子转身。（净）淳于生可听的么？

（生）道是女子转身，女子转身。

（净笑介）日中了，法众住参，咱入定去来。

大千界里闲窥掌，
不二门中暗点头。（下）

（生）禅师去了，到好絮那小娘子一会。敢问小娘子尊姓？（小旦、贴不应介）（生）贵里？（又不应介）（生）敢便是前日禅智寺看舞的小娘子么？

（小旦、贴笑介）是也。

（生）哎哟！

【节节高】

双飞影翠娥，
妙无过，

The legend of the rhino horn,
the secrets of the phoenix girl,
accost me at this holy land.
(Qixuan sneers)
(Chunyu turns around)
These gifts are worth a thousand taels
at the very least.
They´re tokens to lay before Buddha´s feet.
(Refrain)

Great Master, where did these women come from?

QIXUAN (aside): This man is smitten with love. I´ll make the white parrot by Guanyin´s seat wake him up. (A parrot squawks within: "Ants turned around! Ants turned around!") (To Chunyu) Did you hear that?

CHUNYU: It said, "Aunts, turn around! Aunts, turn around!"

QIXUAN (laughs): It´s noontime now. Let´s take a break, and I´ll go into meditation.

Reading my palm in this variety world,
I cannot but wonder at Buddha´s way.

(Exit Qixuan)

CHUNYU: The master is gone. I could take this chance to chitchat with the ladies. May I have the honor of knowing your names? (Qiongying and Itty ignore him) May I ask where you´re from? (Again they ignore him) Didn´t we meet the day before at Chan Wisdom Temple, watching the Brahman dance?

QIONGYING, ITTY (giggling): Yes, indeed.

CHUNYU: What surprise!

【Rising Ever Higher】

You are a pair of airy girls,
so charming

这人儿则合向莲花座。

(贴笑介)我有个妹子还妙哩。

(生笑介)才说那凤钗、犀盒，就是那妹子附寄的么？

他言轻可，

谁看破？

空提作。

世间人敢则有那人间货？

妹子，妹子，你有凤钗、犀盒，央他送在空门，

何不亲身同向佛前罗，

和我拈香订做金钿盒？

(小旦)啐！你也叫他妹子哩。

(生)呀，我淳于棼好是无聊！小娘子请了。

无语落花还自笑，

有情流水为谁弹？(下)

(贴)上真子，这生好不多情也。

(小旦)看来驸马，无过此人。

【前腔】

相逢笑脸涡，

太情多，

暮凉天他归去愁无那。

牙儿嗑，

影儿那，

心儿阁，

向人天结下这姻缘大。

(贴)这生我常见他来。

(小旦)你不知和我国里相近，淳于生名棼的便是。

that nowhere fits you better than the lotus throne.

QIONGYING (giggling): My young cousin is even more charming than wee are.

CHUNYU (smiling): Do you mean the one who asked you to donate the phoenix hairpins and rhino-horn jewel case?

Her words are vague.
No use guessing,
no use asking,
because the mortal world cannot boast such immortal things!

My dear sister, if you want to offer the hairpins and jewel case to Buddha,
why don´t you personally bring them here
and use them as betrothal gifts for you and me?

ITTY: Bah! Who are you to dare to call her sister?

CHUNYU: Sorry, that was imprudent of me. I beg your pardon.

The silent petals fall off with a sigh;
The dashing river doesn´t know my song.

(Exit Chunyu)

QIONGYING: Cousin Itty, this young man looks like a passionate lover.

ITTY: He seems to be the most suitable person for a royal son-in-law.

【Ditto】

Those smiling dimples in his cheeks
brim with love.
There he dolefully goes home in the chilling dusk,
his teeth clattering,
his feet shuffling,
his heart trembling,
because the union he aims at is out of bounds.

QIONGYING: Somehow, he looks familiar to me.

ITTY: Don´t you know he and wee are neighbors? He is the one called

（合）

大槐边宋玉旧东家，

做了罗浮梦断梅花卧。

我们归去来。

【尾声】

这一座会经堂高过似彩楼多，

是个人儿都不着科。

瑶芳，瑶芳，

我和你选这个人儿刚则可。

似蚁人中不可寻，

观音讲下遇知音。

有意栽花花不发，

无心插柳柳成阴。

Chunyu Fen.

BOTH:

So wee´re the eastern neighbor of Song Yu,[10]
and he had a fairy dream by a big plum tree.

Let´s go back.

【Coda】

The temple holds more than one sees upon a bridal stand,[11]
but among the vulgar crowd none can measure up.
Yaofang, Yaofang,
the man wee´ve chosen for you is your perfect match.

There is no groom amidst the antlike throng,
But near Guanyin wee find your other half.
The flower won´t bloom in spite of utmost care;
A willow stick will sprout when left alone.

第九出　决　　婿

【西江引前】

(老引众上)

蝼蚁也知春色，
宫槐夜合朝开。
生香一搦女娇孩，
少甚王孙帝子。

自家蚁王娘娘是也。为遣侄女琼英，参禅听讲；方便之中，因为公主瑶芳选取驸马。蚤晚到来，宫娥伺候。(宫娥应介)

【西江引后】

(贴上)

郎客青袍骏马，
女儿窄袖弓鞋。
他生未卜此生谐，
还则要宫闱听采。

(见叩头介)启娘娘：郡主琼英复命。

(老)讲座之中，可得其人？

(贴)有一伟秀人才，姓淳于，名棼；是这广陵人氏。同在讲筵，我和上真子于讲下献上公主的犀盒、金钗，此生顾盼有馀，赏叹不

Scene 9 Choosing a Son-in-law

(Enter Queen, with palace maids)

【Moon on West River, first half】

QUEEN:

The ants and crickets are aware of spring;
the Sophora leaves can tell day from night.
As wee have only one sweet little girl,
a throng of noble suitors cram our door.

I´m the ant queen. I´ve dispatched my niece Qiongying to attend the sermons, hoping that she can make use of the occasion to find my daughter Yaofang a bridegroom. She should be returning any moment now. You maids, be on the lookout. (The palace maids respond in chorus)

(Enter Qiongying)

【Moon on West River, second half】

QIONGYING:

Fine steeds and rich robes are a must for men;
women prize narrow sleeves and bow-arched shoes.[1]
No one can foretell this life´s pairing mate.
It´s yet to be decided by the queen.

(She kowtows to Queen) Your Ladyship, Duchess Qiongying begs to report on her mission.

QUEEN: Did you find a suitable person among the congregation?

QIONGYING: Yes. At the gathering wee ran into a brilliant and handsome young gentleman, named Chunyu Fen, a native of Yangzhou. When Priestess Itty and I presented the princess´ gold pins and jewel case at the altar, he was very attentive to us and very appreciative of the princess´

足。他既垂情于咱，咱堪留目于他。若婿此人，堪持咱国。

【黄莺儿】

天竺见他来，
顺梢儿到讲台，
眉来语去情儿在。
睃他外才，
瞟他内才，
风流一种生来带。

娘娘，你道此人住居那里？

（合）

畅奇哉！
槐阴不远，
连理就中开。

【前腔】

（老）

天与巧安排，
逗多情看宝钗，
向烧香院宇把人儿赛。
贪他俊才，
赔他个女才，
这姻缘一种前生债。（合前）

【尾声】

便奏知国王如意好宣差，
差的紫衣使者去相迎待，

待他睡梦了呵，

少不得做驸马吾家居上宰。

gifts. Since he thought highly of us, I eyed him closely. If wee can have him engaged to our princess, he may prove to be the mainstay of our country.

【The Yellow Oriole】

At the Hindu Garden he approached,
and wee followed him to the altar´s side.
An affection arose while wee conversed.
Wee judged his bearing
and fathomed his mind.
He carried himself with natural poise.
Your Ladyship, where do you think he lives?
(Refrain)
Believe it or not,
he lives in our Sophora´s shade;
his roots and ours are interlaced.

【Ditto】

QUEEN:

Heaven has had it so arranged
that the golden hairpins should catch his eye.
A secret contest was held in the temple yard.
For his brilliancy,
wee´ll barter a beauty.
This nuptial tie must have been predestined.
(Refrain)

【Coda】

Right away, I´ll report our findings to the king
so special envoys can be sent to fetch that man.
When Chunyu falls into a dream,
he will become the son-in-law and prime man of our house.

选郎须得有情人，
一似淳于好色身。
欲附玄驹为贵婿，
始知骐骥在东邻。

For a spouse, one must choose a man in love;
Man like Chunyu abounds in virile blood.
Only when wee look for an ant-in-law
Shall wee realize the dragon lies next door.

第十出　就　　征

【驻云飞】

（生作懒态上）

伶俐痴呆，
万事难消一字乖。
有的是年华大，
没的是心情奈。
咳！独自倚庭槐。
把日遮天矮，
听他唧嗗蚼蟧，
絮的我无聊赖。
死向扬州不醉咍？
记得谁家金凤钗。

我淳于棼，人才本领，不让于人。到今三十前后，名不成，婚不就，家徒四壁，守着这一株槐树，冷冷清清，淹淹闷闷。想人生如此，不如死休！前在孝感寺听了禅师讲经回来，一发无情无绪。我可甚打起头脑来？止有一醉而已。古人说的好："事大如山醉亦休。"罢了，独言独语，撇下了山鹧儿，我尽意街坊游去，但有高酒店铺，颠倒沉醉一番。正是：

Scene 10 Summoned to Court

(Enter Chunyu, slovenly)

【Scudding Clouds】

CHUNYU:

Whether clever or dull,
no person can escape from adverse turns.
All I possess is my advancing age;
what I find missing is a merry mood.
Ah, alone, I
lean against the Sophora tree;
its huge crown makes the sky hang low.
The cicadas humming among the leaves
drag the weary hours into empty days.
I cannot but drown myself in the cup.
My mind retains only a pair of pins.

If judged by talent, I, Chunyu Fen, am second to none, but reflecting on my thirty years of life, I´ve neither made a name for myself nor taken a wife. All I have is an empty house facing a solitary Sophora tree. It´s too quiet to endure and too depressive to tolerate. If life is like this, it´d be better to die! After returning from the sermons at the Temple of Filial Force, my mood ebbed even lower. What on earth can boost one´s spirits? Nothing but spirits! The ancients put it wisely: "Mountain-sized troubles dissolve in wine." Well, speaking from mouth to ear, I´ve lost sight of Partridge. I´ll follow my legs down the street and see if I can find a good liquor shop to buy myself an intoxicated moment. It´s said,

Don´t cry like Ruan Ji[1] *at a dead-end trail,*
But be buried like Liu Ling[2] *where you fall.*

(Exit)

不消阮籍穷途哭，

但学刘伶死便埋。（下）

（山鹧上）好笑，好笑，没烦恼，趁烦恼。我东人百般武艺，做了个淮扬裨将，使酒丢了这官，郁郁不乐。那酒友周弁、田子华，又散归六合去了。不禁萧索，请的个溜二、沙三，陪话解闷罢了。被那溜二、沙三劝我东人去孝感寺听讲甚么经，自那听经回来，一发痴了。不是醉，便是睡，没张没致的。恰才我溪边檀树下歇昼来，不知东人就往那里去了？怕他鬼迷一般，或是醉倒在街坊不雅相。待去寻他，又无人看家，怎生是好？（望介）好了，好了，溜二、沙三官正来哩。

（溜、沙上）

酒见酒，好朋友。

酒见茶，是冤家。

山鹧哥，主人在么？

（丑）正来央你二位看家，我寻主人去。

（溜、沙）恰好，恰好，你迎接主人去。

持将可怜意，

看取眼前人。（下）

【前腔】

（丑一手提酒壶、肩扶生醉上）

（丑）

落托摩陀，

烂醉如泥可奈何？

(Enter Partridge)

PARTRIDGE: It´s funny that a man should vex himself when there´s nothing to worry about. My master has admirable martial skills, and he once reached the position of lieutenant. He lost that position by letting wine loosen his temper. He´s down in the dumps now. Even his best wine-pals Zhou Bian and Tian Zihua have left him and gone home. To fill the vacancy, he invited a Liu Second and a Sha Third to entertain him. But who´d have thought that those two would induce him to go to the temple to listen to sermons. After he came back, he seemed more muddled than ever. If he isn´t asleep, he must be drunk. Nothing interests him nowadays.

Just now, I was taking a nap under the sandalwood tree by the brook. When I opened my eyes, he was nowhere in sight. I must go and look for him, in case he is bewitched by the devil or lying sprawled out drunk somewhere in the neighborhood. That would be most unseemly. But who´ll look after the house? (He looks around) Ah, here come Liu Second and Sha Third.

(Enter Liu Second and Sha Third)

LIU, SHA:

Wine and wine, friends combine;
Tea and wine, worse than brine.

Brother Partridge, is your master home?

PARTRIDGE: You´re just in time. Would you please look after the house while I go to search for my master?

LIU, SHA: All right. Go and bring him back.

Convey our best regards
To whom it may concern.

(Exeunt all)

(Reenter Partridge with a wine jar in one hand and Chunyu leaning drunk-

你噇的喉儿挫，
俺闪的肩儿那。
(内笑介)好醉也！
(丑)
哥，
醒眼看人多。
恁般低垛，
半落残尊，
又带去回家嗑。
万事无过一醉魔，
万醉无过打睡魔。

(溜、沙上)哎哟，这是怎的来？
(丑)好笑，好笑，再寻不见，可怜醉倒在禅智桥边酒楼上。扶的下楼，又舍不的这半瓶酒，可为甚来？东人，到家了，醒忪些。

【前腔】
(生)
这几日迷痴，(做跌介)
眼似瞢瞪脚似槌。
有个青儿背，
少个红儿睡。
(沙叫介)淳于兄，你何处来，醉的不寻常也。

enly on his shoulder)

【Ditto】

PARTRIDGE:

Down and out, licked and whipped,
you´ve drunk yourself into a muddy heap.
Liquor has burned and seared your throat,
and you´re wrenching my shoulder-blade.
(Laughter within and a voice: "What a state he´s in!")
Brother,
wakeful eyes have seen many types.
But have they seen a man so mean,
clutching half a cup of wine
he tries to take it home to drink?
All worries are resolved by getting drunk;
all drunkards take solace in snoring sleep.

(Reenter Liu and Sha)

LIU, SHA: Great heavens! What happened?

PARTRIDGE: Guess where I found him? You can´t believe it! He was dead drunk upstairs in a wineshop by the Chan Wisdom Bridge. When I carried him downstairs, he insisted on taking this half-emptied bottle. What´s so good of it? Master, we´re home. Wake up.

【Ditto】

CHUNYU:

These days I guess I am obsessed.
(He stumbles)
My eyes are gummed, my legs like drumsticks drag.
There is a man to lean upon,
but not a girl to take to bed.

SHA (loudly): Brother Chunyu, where have you been? You look unusually drunk.

(生作不知介)

谁?

道俺去何来?

寻常沾醉。

醉影柴门,

乱踏的斜阳碎,

老向霜红叶上催。

(吐介)(溜、沙)哎也!一肚子都倒在我两人腿脚上,好酒,好酒。山鹧哥,快取茶来。

【前腔】

你泛滥流琼,

倒玉山因一盏倾。

待把你衣冠正,

你好把跷儿定。(取茶进介)

兄,

靠着小围屏,

一杯清茗。

潇洒西风,

醒后留清兴,

和你待月乘凉看小萤。

(生倦介)扶俺东庑下睡去。那瓶酒好放着。

(丑)东人,你醉的这般,还记的这瓶酒。

CHUNYU (fails to recognize Sha):

Who are you
that ask me of my whereabouts?
I went my usual way,
by any rustic gate.
My wobbly steps disturb the evening rays;
frost enflames the leaves but has grayed my hair.
(He vomits)

LIU, SHA: Oh, my! He´s spilled his stomach onto our legs and feet. Fine wine that! Brother Partridge, hurry and fetch some tea.

【Ditto】

LIU, SHA:

You´ve let the sluice go.
See how a cup of wine can topple hills.
We´ll tidy up your clothes for you,
then you can stretch and rest your legs.
(They feed him tea)
Brother,
please sit against this painted screen,
and sip some fragrant tea.
Zephyr will softly soothe
the hangover from wine abuse.
Later, we can watch fireflies dance beneath the moon.

CHUNYU (wearily): Help me over to the eastern verandah. I need some sleep. Save that half bottle of wine for me.

PARTRIDGE: Master, as drunk as you are, you can still remember that half bottle of wine?

【Ditto】

【前腔】

　　好不惺忪，
　　似太白驴般压绣骢。
　　醉的那躯劳重，
　　枕席无人奉。
　　东，
　　江冷玉芙蓉，
　　水天秋弄，
　　门院萧条，
　　做不出繁华梦。

(扶睡介)

　　只落得枕上凉蝉诉晚风。

(丑)再煎茶去。

(溜、沙)我们洗脚去，随他睡觉。这是

　　人家堂上堪饮酒，
　　自家房里好安眠。(下)

(扮二黑巾紫衣、众引牛车上)

　　为筑王姬馆，
　　叨乘使者车。

俺两人，大槐安国使者便是。奉国王命，召请淳于公为驸马。他正睡在东廊，直入则个。(叫)淳于公。

(生惊醒介)是谁？

(紫衣跪介)

【锁南枝】

　　槐安国，
　　王者都，

So your mind stays alert,
while you´ve turned me into a burdened beast!
Your body weighs more than a soggy sack,
yet none is waiting in your bed.
Master,
like lotus leaves on chilly waves,
which water and wind molest,
you in this rundown yard
may fail to produce a luxurious dream.
(He places Chunyu on a couch)
You´ll only hear
shivering cicadas protest the evening breeze.

I´m going to brew more tea.

LIU, SHA: We´ll go wash our feet. Let him catch some sleep. It´s said:

When you drink better do so at friend´s place;
When you sleep better lie on your own couch.

(Exeunt Liu, Sha and Partridge)

(Enter two palace officers in purple robes and black headwear, followed by attendants escorting an ox cart)

OFFICERS:

To build a honey bower
Wee drive a bullock cart.

Wee two are special envoys from the Great Sophora Kingdom. By His Majesty´s decree, wee are to summon Lord Chunyu to Court to be the royal son-in-law. At this moment, he´s reposing on the eastern verandah. Wee shall go straight up to him. (They call out) Lord Chunyu!

CHUNYU (startled awake): Who´s calling me?

【Spring on the South Bough】

OFFICERS (kneeling):

吾王遣臣来奉书。

（生）因何而来？

（紫）

主命有些须，

微臣敢轻露！

（生）睡得正甜。

（紫扶生起介）

请下榻，

俺红袖扶。

俺那里有东床，

坦君腹。

【前腔】

（生）

从空下，

甚意儿？

正秋窗风剪槐叶初，

一枕黑甜余，

双星使临户。

咱朦胧醒，

申欠舒。

整衣行，

懒移步。（牛车上介）

【前腔】

（紫）

有青油障，

小壁车，

驾车白牛当步趋。

The Great Sophora
is where monarchs rule.
Here is an invitation from our king.

CHUNYU: What for?

OFFICERS:

A petty business is at hand,
something wee dare not disclose.

CHUNYU: You´re interrupting my sweet sleep.

OFFICERS (helping him up):

Please let our purple sleeves
help you out of bed.
In our east chamber wee too have a bed,[3]
where you can sleep.

【Ditto】

CHUNYU:

What do you want,
dropping from the blue
when the west wind begins to thin the leaves?
My head was snuggled in the pillow dent,
and you came to invade my home.
Drowsy still,
I stretch myself,
straighten my clothes
and lift my feet.
(The ox cart comes forward)

【Ditto】

OFFICERS:

This little cart
boasts an oil-paper tilt.
Just allow the white ox to save your feet.

（紫请生上车介）

左右有人俱，

扶君出门去。

（生）向那里去？

（紫）此古槐树穴下而去。

（生）怎生去得？

（紫）

古槐穴，

国所居。

若迟疑，

请前驱。（一紫衣先下）

（生向一紫衣介）槐树小穴中，何因得有国都乎？

（紫）淳于公，不记汉朝有个窦广国？他国土广大，也只在窦儿里。又有个孔安国，他国土安顿，也只在孔儿里。怎生槐穴中没有国土？

（唱前）

古槐穴，

国所居。

莫迟疑，

但前去。（下）

（右相上）

秋光满槐叶，

春色候夭桃。

自家槐安国右相武成侯段功便是。吾王传令，请东平淳于生为驸

(They beg Chunyu to board the cart)

With attendants on both your sides,

wee´ll take care of you on your trip.

CHUNYU: Where are we going?

OFFICERS: Into the hole at the foot of the ancient Sophora tree.

CHUNYU: How can we get in there?

OFFICER:

In the hollow

a kingdom lies.

If you have fears,

I´ll enter first.

(Exit one of the officers)

CHUNYU (to the other officer): How can there be a kingdom at the bottom of this tiny hole in the Sophora tree?

OFFICER: Lord Chunyu, don´t you remember that *The History of the Han Dynasty* tells of a Dou Guang-guo, whose vast country was built in a sinus, and a Kong An-guo, whose peaceful nation was established in a hole?[4] If those kingdoms were possible, why can´t there be a kingdom in a tree hole?

In the hollow

a kingdom lies.

Dismiss your fears

and enter first.

(Exeunt)

(Enter Right-hand Premier)

PREMIER:

Autumn rays leak through shriveled leaves;

Not far off is prolific spring.

I´m Duan Gong, Right-hand Premier of the Great Sophora Kingdom and Marquis of Martial Feats. His Majesty has decided on a Mr. Chunyu from Dongping County to be his son-in-law. Upon his arrival he shall be

马。请到时，东华馆中稍待，俺相见过，次后朝见。只驸马初到此中，精神恍惚，恐其不安。他平生有个酒友周弁，有个文友田子华，已奏过吾王，摄取他来，将周弁补司隶之官，领军吏数百，巡卫宫殿；请田子华替他宾馆中更衣赞礼。这不在话下。又，国母懿旨：着上真姑和灵芝夫人、琼英郡主，同去宾馆中探望驸马，调熟其心，方才请去修仪宫，与金枝公主成礼。我如今且待驸马到东华馆，拜望去。正是：

仙郎高馆下，

丞相小车来。（下）（前二紫衣同生车上介）

【前腔】

（生）

车箱路，

古穴隅，

豁然见山川风候殊。

（低语介）怎生有这一段所在？

不断的起城郛，

车舆和人物。

奇怪，奇怪，一路来但是见我的，都回避起立，何也？

附车者，

尽传呼。

为甚呵，

accommodated at Donghua Guesthouse. I´m to meet him there before he´s formally presented at Court. In case he is dazed by the change or feels uneasy in his new surroundings, I have, with permission from His Majesty, also fetched him his two best friends, Zhou Bian and Tian Zihua. Zhou Bian has been appointed commander of the capital´s garrison force, in charge of several hundred soldiers to guard the palace. And I´ve asked Tian Zihua to wait on him at the guesthouse. No problems about those matters.

On the other hand, Her Ladyship the queen has instructed Priestess Itty, Lady Truffle and Duchess Qiongying to go to the guesthouse to welcome the would-be son-in-law. Their task is to make him feel at home before he´s escorted to the Hall of Etiquette for the wedding with Princess of Golden Bough. I´m going to pay him a visit as soon as he arrives. It´s said:

A guest alights from hallowed heights;
The premier rides a tiny cart.

(Exit)

(Reenter Chunyu on an ox cart, accompanied by the two officers)

【Ditto】

CHUNYU:

The cart road leads
into an ancient cave.
All at once the landscape has changed its face.

(Muttering to himself) How can there be such a place?

One by one towns and cities have appeared,
various vehicles and attire.

Isn´t it strange that people along the path either avoid me or stand at attention?

Those attendants of mine
kept yelling at the crowd.

What on earth is going on

着行人，
都避路?

(紫跪介)已到国门。

(生)好一座大城!城上重楼朱户，中间金牌四个字，(念介)大槐安国。

(内扮一旗卒上)传令旨，传令旨：王以贵客远临，令且就东华馆暂停车驾。(卒叩头走起同向前道行介)

(生)城楼门东有这座下马牌。怎左边厢朱门洞开?

(紫)到东华馆了，请下车。

(生下车入门背笑介)这东华馆内，彩槛雕楹，华木珍果，列植于庭下；几案茵褥，帘帏肴膳，陈设于庭上。俺心里好不欢悦也！(内响道介)

(紫)右相到。

(右相见介)寡君不以敝国远僻，奉迎君子，托以姻亲。

(生)棼以贱劣之躯，岂敢是望!

(右)有紫衣官在此演礼，五鼓漏尽，相引见朝。

that people in the streets
should clear the way for me?

OFFICERS (kneeling): Here wee are at the gate of the capital.

CHUNYU: What a grand city! The multi-storied gate tower is freshly painted red. In the center there hangs a board inscribed with four huge characters in gold: The Great Sophora Kingdom.

(Enter a messenger holding a pennant)

MESSENGER: Hear His Majesty´s edict: Considering the fact that his distinguished guest has come from afar, His Majesty invites him to rest and recover at Donghua Guesthouse. (He kowtows, rises, and leads the way)

CHUNYU (to himself): We´ve turned east from the city gate and here´s a signboard that reads: RIDERS DISMOUNT HERE.[5] Why is the big red gate on the left thrown wide open?

OFFICERS: Here wee are at Donghua Guesthouse. Would you please alight from the cart?

CHUNYU (steps down from the cart and walks through the gate. Aside, beaming): Behold! The pillars and balustrades are beautifully carved and freshly painted; the courtyard is filled with exotic flowers and fruit trees; curtains, screens, cushions are all laid out neatly, and delicious food is ready on the table. What a delightful sight!

(Ceremonious shouts heard within)

OFFICERS: Here comes the right-hand premier.

(Reenter Premier)

PREMIER (greeting Chunyu): The king of my country, despite the great distance, has invited Your Lordship to our obscure land, wishing to engage you to his daughter.

CHUNYU: How could a humble person like myself expect such an honor?

PREMIER: The palace officers will stay with you and instruct you about the rituals. At the fifth drum[6] you´ll be received in audience by the king.

且就东华馆，
通宵习礼仪。
鸡鸣传漏晓，
驸马入朝时。

At Donghua Guesthouse you sojourn,
Practicing rituals through the night.
When cocks crow and the new day breaks,
It's time for you to go to Court.

第十一出　引　谒

【点绛唇】

（周弁领直殿同黄门官上）

古洞今朝，
一般笼罩，
山河小。
钟隐鸣梢，
绿满宫槐道。

请了。

绿槐根里侍朝班，
一点朱衣剑佩环。
尽道官除汉司隶，
此间那得似人间。

自家周弁是也。平生好酒使气，今日大槐安国中作一司隶之官，统领军吏数百，拥卫殿门。有故人淳于棼，新招驸马，初到朝见，不免和黄门官在此候驾。

【前腔】

（蚁王插花引众上）

素锦雪袍，
朱华玉导，
红云晓。

Scene 11 Received in Audience

(Enter Zhou Bian, leading officers on duty, together with a Yellow Gate Herald[1])

【Painting Cherry Lips】

ZHOU:

A new day in the ancient cave
comprises as of old
miniature hills and rills.
Here go the bells and cracking whips.[2]
A verdant carpet leads to Court.

(To Herald) You, please.

Serving the Court in the Sophora root,
I was given a red coat and a sword.
Although Commander is a lofty post,
This one is different from the human one.

I´m Zhou Bian. I´ve spent my life in liquor, and when I got drunk, I used to grow testy. Now I´m a commander in the Great Sophora Kingdom, in charge of several hundred soldiers guarding the palace. An old friend of mine, Mr. Chunyu, has been chosen to be the royal son-in-law, and today he´s going to make his first appearance at Court. So here I am together with the Yellow Gate Herald.

(Enter King with flowers stuck in the crown, attended)

【Ditto】

KING:

Clad in a snow-white robe,
I wear a floral crown
to greet the morning rays.

槐殿里根苗，
也引的红鸾到。

朱华一粒戴鳌鱼，
洞府深深小殿居。
开着五门遥北望，
外头还似此间无？

自家槐安国王，有女金枝公主，去请淳于棼为驸马，想已到来，不免升殿宣见。

（黄门跪介）奏知我王，驸马已到。

（王）着右丞相引他升殿。

（黄门应介）领旨。

【绛都春序】

（生随右相上）（生）

槐阴洞小，
怎千门万户，
九市三条？
猛然百步把朱门到，
段老先生呵，
怎生金殿上炉烟绕？

（右）

是吾王端严容貌。
看殿头左右，
金瓜玉斧，
明晃一周遭。

【前腔】

（生作怕介）

The seed of the Sophora house
brings a red phoenix to the tree.

Giant turtles carry hills, I raise a grain.
Deep in the hole I make a palace home.
Straining my eyes up north beyond the gates,
I wonder what it looks like there outside.

I´m the king of the Sophora Kingdom. I have an only daughter with the title Princess of Golden Bough, and wee have found her a husband called Chunyu Fen. I think he should have arrived by now. It´s time for me to ascend the throne and summon him.

HERALD (kneeling): Your Majesty, the prospective royal son-in-law is waiting outside.

KING: Tell Right-hand Premier to bring him in.

HERALD: Your Majesty´s wish shall be carried out.

(Enter Chunyu, following the Right-hand Premier)

【Spring in the Red Capital Overture】

CHUNYU:

How can a tiny hole
nest tens of thousands of households
and a network of streets and marts?
A hundred short steps lead me to the crimson gate.

Most respected Mr. Duan,

why is the palace veiled in incense smoke?

PREMIER:

That shows the solemnity of a king.
On both your left- and right-hand sides
menacing weapons
glitter alongside palace walls.

【Ditto】

CHUNYU (nervously):

猛然心跳，

便衣衫未整，

造次穿朝。

（周弁见介）驸马行动些，殿上等久。

（生）

呀！怎生将“驸马”来相叫？

（低语介）喜得周弁也在此。

向前欲问难亲靠。

（右）驸马近前，一同拜舞。

丹墀下扬尘舞蹈。（生同俯伏介）

（右）

微臣奏复，

天颜有喜，

驸马来朝。

（黄）右丞相起；驸马高声致词。（右相叩头呼千岁起立介）

（生跪高声奏介）前淮南军裨将臣东平淳于棼见。（黄门赞拜兴拜兴三叩头介）

（黄）驸马俯伏听令旨。

（王）寡人有女瑶芳，封为金枝公主，前奉贤婿令尊之命，不弃小国，许以金枝奉事君子。

（生俯伏介）千岁，千岁。

（王）驸马且就宾馆。

My heart sinks to realize
my casual attire scarcely fits
for an audience with a king.

ZHOU (stepping forth to greet Chunyu): His Majesty´s royal son-in-law, please hurry. His Majesty has been waiting a long time.

CHUNYU: Ah!

Why did he call me royal son-in-law?

(In a low voice) Good to find Zhou Bian here, too.

But now it seems inapt to speak to him.

PREMIER: Please step this way, His Majesty´s son-in-law. Let´s pay our respects.

Before the purple steps wee kneel and bow.
(Chunyu and Premier prostrate themselves)
Your servant here reports
glad news from heaven high:
a son-in-law has come to Court.

HERALD: Rise, please, His Majesty´s Right-hand Premier. Would-be royal son-in-law, present your compliments.

(Premier kowtows, shouts "Long live the king!" and rises from his knees)

CHUNYU (remains kneeling and speaks loudly): A former lieutenant with the Southern Huai Army, Your Majesty´s humble servant Chunyu Fen from Dongping County here pays his respects. (Herald conducts Chunyu through the procedure of three kowtows)

HERALD: Prospective royal son-in-law, bow deep and hearken to the royal edict.

KING: Wee have a daughter named Yaofang, entitled Princess of Golden Bough. Abiding by the wish of my dear son-in-law´s respectable father, who held my modest kingdom in no contempt, I´m offering you the hand of my golden bough.

CHUNYU (with head bent low): May Your Majesty live a thousand years!

KING: Dear son-in-law, for the time being please return to the guesthouse.

（黄门官唱驾还宫，内鼓响道，王还宫，生、右跪送介）

殿上初行叔孙礼，

宫里才成公主亲。（下）

(Herald announces the end of the court session. Drums beat within as King retires. Chunyu and Premier kneel and bow King out)

CHUNYU, PREMIER:

The first rituals have been performed in Court,
Paving the way to the conjugal day.

(Exeunt)

第十二出　贰　　馆

（听事官上）

出身馆伴使，
新升堂候官。
前程蝼蚁大，
礼数凤凰宽。

自家槐安国东华馆一个堂候便是。我王新招驸马见朝，暂停宾馆；今夕良时，往修仪宫与金枝公主成亲。你看：一路上摆列金羔银雁各二十对，鸾凤锦绣各百二十双，妓女丝竹之音，车骑灯烛之艳，无不齐备。真个天上牛女，地下蝼蚁也。远望驸马蚤到。

【上林春】

（生盛服上）

平步忽登天子堂，
尚兀自意迷心恍。

俺淳于棼，有何姻缘？得到此间，瞻天仰圣。说及成亲一事，“承贤婿令尊之命”，此话好不跷蹊！我父昔为边将，未知存亡。或是北

Scene 12 House Transfer

(Enter Receptionist)

RECEPTIONIST:

From a humble valet I rose
Of late to a receptionist.
My future looks fine as an ant´s;
I keep more rules than phoenix quills.

I´m the receptionist at the state´s Donghua Guesthouse. The king´s recently chosen son-in-law has arrived in the capital, and is sojourning at the guesthouse. At an auspicious hour tonight, he´ll go from here to the Hall of Etiquette for the wedding ceremony with Princess of Golden Bough. Look, spread out along the main street are twenty pairs of golden lambs, twenty pairs of silvery wild geese,[1] one hundred and twenty bolts of satin and as many bolts of brocade. Women singers, pipes and stringed instruments, carriages, horses, lanterns, candles, and what not! It´s true that "Altair and Vega herd the sky;[2] crickets and ants prevail on earth." Here comes the royal son-in-law.

(Enter Chunyu, richly dressed)

【Spring in Royal Garden】

CHUNYU:

I suddenly found myself near Heaven´s Son;[3]
my heart still flutters from the blinding leap.

What kind of fortune is destined for me that I, Chunyu Fen, should become so close to royalty?! When His Majesty spoke of the marriage, I remember he said, "abiding by the wish of my dear son-in-law´s respectable father." What does that mean? My father was an army general stationed on the frontier, and for years no one has heard from him. Perhaps

边番王，与这槐安国交好，家父往来其间，致成兹事，也未可知。呀！兀的三位女客来了。

【出队子】

（小旦道扮同老旦、贴上）

凤冠明漾，
凤冠明漾，
彩碧金钿珠翠香，
烟丝绣帔晚风飏。
谁在东华屋里张？

呀！恭喜淳于郎到此。（生羞避介）

（众）

却是淳郎，做了阮郎。

（众旦）淳于郎。（生作揖介）

（小旦）淳于郎比前兴了些。

（贴）瘦了些。

（老）向前摸摸他，是兴是瘦？（生作羞避介）

（小旦）淳于郎粗中有细。

（贴笑介）还是细中有粗。

（老）好一个赤琅当五寸长牛鼻子！（生作不奈烦介）

（老）中元之日，俺们禅智寺天竺院看舞《婆罗门》，足下与琼英娘子结水红汗巾，挂于竹枝之上，君独不忆念之乎？（生想叹介）

（贴）俺们曾于孝感寺听契玄师讲《观音经》，俺于讲下供养金钗、

the barbarian chieftain has good relations with this Sophora Kingdom so that my father has been able to travel between the two and have this affair arranged. Who knows? Ah! Here come three ladies.

(Enter Priestess Itty, Lady Truffle and Duchess Qiongying)

【Cheer Leaders】

THE THREE LADIES:

The phoenix coronet,
the coronet sparkles
with pearls and gems set in gold filigree;
our gossamery shawls float in the breeze.
Who is that man peeping out from Donghua?

Ah, congratulations, Mr. Chunyu. Welcome to our realm.

(Chunyu, embarrassed, turns aside)

So Mr. Chunyu has
become Bridegroom Ruan.[4]

Mr. Chunyu!

(Chunyu raises his clasped hands in salutation[5])

ITTY: He seems to have put on some weight since wee saw him last time.

QIONGYING: I´m afraid he has lost some weight.

TRUFFLE: Wee can give him a pinch to find out.

(Chunyu turns away bashfully)

ITTY: Mr. Chunyu feels stiff, but there is something soft.

QIONGYING (giggles): I should say he is soft, but there is something rather stiff.

TRUFFLE: What´s that five-inch thing dangling between his legs?! (Chunyu grows annoyed) Don´t you remember that on Ghosts´ Day wee watched the Brahman´s dance at the Hindu Garden in the Temple of Chan Wisdom together? Don´t you remember you helped Lady Qiongying wring her handkerchief and hang it up on a bamboo stem?

(Chunyu, remembering, sighs)

QIONGYING: Don´t you remember wee listened to Master Qixuan´s

犀盒，足下于筵中赏叹再三，顾盼良久，颇亦思念之乎？

（生想介）

中心藏之，

何日忘之！

（小旦）不意今日，与此君为眷属。俺们且去修仪宫相候。

却是淳郎，

做了阮郎。（下）

【前腔】

（田子华冠带引队子上）

彩楼宾相，

彩楼宾相，

不向天台向下方。

金枝公主字瑶芳，

得尚淳于一老郎。

他帽儿光光，

风流这场。

（见介）（田）

驸马请上，

别来无恙。

谨奉王命，

来为宾相。

（生）子非冯翊田子华乎？

（田）便是。

（生）子华，何以在此？

preaching about the Guanyin Scripture at the Temple of Filial Force? Don´t you remember that wee donated a pair of gold hairpins and a rhino-horn jewel case, which caught your attention and won your admiration?

CHUNYU (mutters, deep in thought):

In heart it buries;
for e´er there tarries.[6]

ITTY: Isn´t it marvelous that today wee are to become related to this man? Mr. Chunyu, wee´ll be expecting you at the Hall of Etiquette.

So Mr. Chunyu has
become Bridegroom Ruan.

(Exeunt the three ladies)

(Enter Tian Zihua, in full attire, leading a troupe)

【Ditto】

TIAN:

Best man at a wedding,
at the decked-out building,
goes down a cave, not up to heaven´s stage.
Princess Yaofang, known as the Golden Bough,
is to wed an old guy, my drinking pal.
See how his face beams, his hat gleams!
A lucky man is he!

(He greets Chunyu)

Here I pay my respects.
Really long time no see.
The king asked me to be
Your best man of selects.

CHUNYU: Aren´t you Tian Zihua, a native of Pingyi County?

TIAN: Who else?

CHUNYU: Zihua, how come you´re here, too?

(田)小弟闲游，受知于右相武成侯段公，因而栖托在此。

(生)周弁也在此，可知之乎？

(田)周弁，贵人也，职为司隶，权势甚盛，小弟数蒙其庇护矣。

(生笑介)三人俱聚于此，庶免羁孤之叹，可喜，可喜！

(紫上)驸马吉时，进宫成礼。

(田)不意今日睹此盛礼，愿无相忘。便请升车。(紫衣扶生升车介)(杂执灯上行介)

【前腔】

(众)

步围金障，

步围金障，

彩碧玲珑数里长，

花灯引道照成行。

(生)子华兄，

咱端坐车中意惚恍。

(田笑介)驸马享用，礼之当然。

且自安详，

何须悒怏！(下)

【前腔】

(贴众上、奏乐、戏笑介)

TIAN: I was idling around when His Excellency Lord Duan, Right-hand Premier and Marquis of Martial Feats, took a shine to me. So here I am.

CHUNYU: Do you know that Zhou Bian is also here?

TIAN: Yes. He´s a big shot now, commander of the capital´s garrison force! That´s a very authoritative position, and he has exerted his influence to help me on several occasions already.

CHUNYU (laughs): What a pleasant surprise it is that the three of us should gather here to keep each other company!

(Enter a palace officer in a purple robe)

OFFICER: It´s time now, royal son-in-law. Let´s set out for the palace ceremony.

TIAN: It´s an unexpected honor for me to be present at your grand wedding ceremony. I hope you won´t forget your old friends in your new position. Now please step aboard the carriage.

(Officer helps Chunyu board the carriage. An attendant enters holding a lantern, and leads the way)

【Ditto】

ALL:

Along the festooned streets,
along the festooned streets,
where rainbow colors stretch for many miles,
the lanes are lit up by the lantern lines.

CHUNYU: Brother Zihua,

I feel dazed sitting upright on this cart.

TIAN (smiles): That´s the privilege of the royal son-in-law. You should enjoy it.

Take it easy and relax;
there´s no cause to feel depressed.

(Exeunt all)

(Reenter the three ladies amid music, laughing and joking)

翠罗黄帐，
翠罗黄帐，
夜合宫槐覆苑墙。
偶然同向佛前香，
粉帕金钗惹梦长。（生众上介）

（合）

眼色相将，
迎归洞房。

（生众作引车避、看众旦下介）（生）子华兄，那群姑姊妹，各乘凤辇，往来此间。便是仙姬奏乐，宛转凄清，非人间之所闻听也。

（田）吉时将近，便好趱行。

【前腔】

（生）

仙音凄亮，
仙音凄亮，
来往仙姬辇凤凰。
似洞庭哀响隐潇湘，
使我心中感易伤。

（田）人生如寄，闻乐不乐，何也？

休忆人间，
相逢未央。

【Ditto】

THE THREE LADIES:

Behind the golden gauze,
behind the golden gauze,
the palace Sophora umbrellas all.
Wee accidentally met at Buddha´s seat;
the kerchief and pins have spun winding dreams.
(Reenter Chunyu and the troupe)

ALL:

Our eyes follow him
into the nuptial cave.
(Chunyu and the troupe step aside to let the ladies pass. Exeunt the three ladies)

CHUNYU: Brother Zihua, don´t you think those womenfolk are actually fairies riding phoenix carriages hither and thither? The music is so melodious that this must be some heavenly place.

TIAN: It´s almost time. Let´s hurry.

【Ditto】

CHUNYU:

Plangent and plaintive,
their music vibrates,
while fairies come and go on phoenix carts.
Like whining winds ruffling the troubled lake,
it sends quivers down my responsive heart.

TIAN: Life is but transient. Why don´t you let the music entertain you?

Forget the mortal past;
it´s here that we are.

前面修仪宫，请下车。群仙姊妹，纷然在旁，小弟告辞了。正是：

襄王赴神女，
宋玉转西家。（下）

Here we are at the Hall of Etiquette. Please alight from the carriage. Your fairy cousins are waiting in festive array. I must take leave of you now. It´s true to say

When the prince visits the mountain goddess,
It´s time Song Yu retreated to his side.[7]

(Exeunt)

第十三出　尚　　主

【清江引】

（贴众奏乐上）

仙家姊妹迎仙眷，
飞仙凤凰辇。
仙乐奏钧天，
仪从来仙苑。
教玉郎下车拜着修仪殿。

（老旦）请公主升殿。

【女冠子】

（扇遮公主上介）

彩云乍展，
下妆台回眸低盼。
才离月殿，
试临朱户，
知为谁绻缱？
教人腼腆。（贴众笑介）

（老）请驸马上殿开扇。

（生上）

天仙肯临见，

Scene 13 The Wedding

(Enter Qiongying, Itty and Truffle, with attendants playing music)

【River Qing Interlude】

THE THREE LADIES:

Fairy sisters receive a fairy guest,
cruising around on phoenix carts.
Celestial music fills the air,
escorting us to fairyland.
Let´s welcome the jade boy[1] into the wedding hall.

TRUFFLE (announces): Princess Yaofang, please enter the hall.

(Enter Princess Yaofang behind a fan)

【The Phoenix Hat】

PRINCESS:

Rosy clouds unroll,
as I back away from my dressing table
in the lunar palace
to the red-walled houses.
For whom am I going to stoop?
My face flushes at the thought.
(The ladies laugh at her coyness)

TRUFFLE (announces): Royal son-in-law, please enter the hall to remove the fan.

(Enter Chunyu)

CHUNYU:

Since you agreed to marry me,
why not reveal your lovely face?
Please draw the fan aside.

好略露花容，
暂回鸾扇。

（合）

这姻缘不浅，
金穴名姝，
绛台高选。

（老赞拜天地介）（转向拜国王、国母千岁介）（赞驸马拜见公主，公主答拜介）

（内使送酒介）

槐安国里春生酒，
花烛堂中夜合欢。

国主娘娘钦赐驸马、公主合卺之酒。（生、旦叩头谢恩介）

（老）驸马、公主，饮合欢之酒。（合卺介）

【锦堂月】

（生）

帽插金蝉，
钗簪宝凤，
英雄配合婵娟。
点染宫袍，
翠拂画眉轻线。
君王命即日承筐，
嫦娥面今宵却扇。

（合）

拈金盏，
看绿蚁香浮，
这翠槐宫院。

【前腔】

ALL:

Fate has arranged this wondrous match:
a belle from a golden cave,
a beau from the bridal stand.[2]

(Truffle conducts the bride and bridegroom through the ceremony. First they kowtow to heaven and earth, next to the king and queen, and then they bow to each other. A eunuch enters with wine)

EUNUCH:

Fragrant wine brewed in the Sophora spring
Best fills the nuptial cups in candlelight.

This is the conjugal wine bestowed by the king and queen.

(Chunyu and Princess kowtow in gratitude)

TRUFFLE (announces): The royal son-in-law and the princess will now drink the conjugal wine.[3] (They drink)

【Moon Over the Brocade Hall】

CHUNYU:

Gold flappers[4] adorn my hat;
phoenix pins fix your hair;
the hero and the beauty match.
Bedeck my palace robe,
and brush afresh your penciled brows.
By royal decree we marry tonight,
and now my goddess should remove her fan.
(Refrain)
Raise your golden cup
and sip the fermented juice.
Bliss fills Sophora´s palace yard.

【Ditto】

（旦）

羞言，
他将种情坚，
我瑶芳岁浅，
教人怎的支缠？
院宇修仪，
试学寿阳妆面。
号金枝旧种灵根，
倚玉树新连戚畹。（合前）

【前腔】

（老、小、贴背介）

姻缘，
向雨点花天，
香尘宝地，
无情种出金莲。

（回介）

偶语低回，
一笑凤钗微颤。
你百感生仙宅琼浆，
一捻就儿家禁脔。（合前）

【前腔】

（众）

天然，
主第亭园，
王家锦绣，
妆成一曲桃源。
窅窕幽微，

PRINCESS:

It shames me to say:
He, persistent as a soldier,
I, inexperienced as a babe,
how can I resist his advance?
In the Hall of Etiquette
I must learn to rouge and powder my face.
Being the golden bough of ancient roots,
I am to extend the Sophora crown.
(Refrain)

【Ditto】

THE THREE LADIES (aside):

What is fate?
It´s like flowers raining from the sky.
As they fall onto fragrant soil,
golden lotuses will sprout thereon.
(They turn around)
An accidental glance,
a smiling nod of phoenix pins,
provoked deep sentiments and heavy sighs,
not knowing the union is predestined.
(Refrain)

【Ditto】

Heaven gives us all.
Pavilions and gardens,
enhanced by regal pomp,
have created a perfect wonderland.
Petite and profound,
through the tunnels a sweet tune pipes.
(Aside)

乐奏洞天深远。

（背介）

西明讲士女喧坛，

东华漏王姬筑馆。（合前）

（众）月上了。

【醉翁子】

帘卷，

看明月秦楼正满。

（生）

把弄玉临风，

笑拈箫管。

今晚，

烟雾云鬟，

家近迷楼一笑看。

（合）

曾相见，

是那一种琼花，

种下槐安。

【前腔】

（生低介）

真罕，

一霎儿向宫闱腹坦。

想二十四桥，

玉人天远。

深浅，

只影孤寒，

怎便向重楼曲户眠？（合前）（行介）

Wee women attended a temple fair,
and brought a bridegroom to the Donghua lair.
(Refrain)

Look, the moon is up.

【The Old Sot】

Roll up the bamboo blinds
to let the round moon fill the nuptial hall.

CHUNYU:

I cuddle Nong Yu[5] in my arms,
who smiles into the flute.
Tonight,
in the fog of smoky light
I´ll merrily explore the maze of tracks.
(Refrain)
In times long past
a seed must have been unconsciously sown
beneath the Sophora tree.

【Ditto】

(Continues in a lowered voice)
How strange!
I´ve suddenly become a royal spouse.
When I stood on the moonlit bridge,
fairies seemed worlds away.
High and low,
I was on a lonely quest;
in a wink, I´m sleeping in the forbidden nest.
(Refrain)

【Colorful Flags Minitune】

【侥侥令】

槐余三洞暖，

花展一天宽。

记取斜月鸾回笑歌巘，

春压细腰难，

愁远山。

【前腔】

淳于沾醉晚，

灭烛且留残。

试取新红粗如人世显，

浑似遇仙还，

云雨间。

【尾声】

尽今宵略把红鸾蘸，

五鼓谢恩了，

蚤画蛾眉去鹓鹭班，

则怕你雨困云残新睡懒。

〔集唐〕

帝子吹箫逐凤凰，

断云残月共苍苍。

传声莫闭黄金屋，

好促朝珂入未央。

(He walks)
Deep in the warm Sophora hole
the bud made its first bloom of love.
Let´s print in mind the bright smile of the crescent moon.
Spring presses on her wispy waist,
knitting her distant hills.[6]

【Ditto】

Chunyu drinks late into the night,
and stays up till the lights are out.
Let me test my new red candle thick and hot.
It trembles to meet the fairy
in clouds and rain.[7]

【Coda】

Tonight there´s only time to make quick thrusts.
There goes the fifth drum, time to pay filial respects to the king and queen.
Quickly dab rouge and powder on the stains.
Don´t hug the bridal bed when rain and clouds are gone.

The flutist and Nong Yu have taken off;
The clouds are scattered and the moon has sunk.
It´s time we had to leave our nuptial bed,
And speed to the palace for morning Court.

第十四出　伏　　戎

【贺圣朝】

（檀萝王赤脸引队众上）

大地非常变化，
成团占住檀萝。
黄头赤脚瘦挼莎，
牛斗看成两下。

草昧成中国，
城池隔外边。
岂无刀画地？
仍有气冲天。

自家乃槐安国东檀萝国主是也。我国东尽白檀，西连紫逻；子孙分九溪八洞，门户有百孔千窗。滕薛同朝，山有木而谁能争长？槐檀一火，天有时而岂可钻先？止因他是玄驹，咱形赤驳；遂分中外，致有高低。恃他如赤象之雄，觑我如黍米之细。近日得他文书，于槐安国上加了一个大字，好不小视人也！隔江是他南柯郡，地方鱼

Scene 14 The Alien Tribe

(Enter the king of Rattan Sandalwood leading a group of soldiers, his face painted red)

【Praise the Dynasty】

RED KING:

Dramatically the world has changed;
in swarms wee took the sandalwood.
A brown head, wiry waist and auburn legs,
ferociously wee fight like bulls.

New states rise in chaotic times;
A trench becomes a borderline.
Is there no chance to cut a square?
Our aspirations reach the sky!

I´m the king of Rattan Sandalwood. My territory lies to the east of the Sophora Kingdom, circumscribed by a white sandalwood tree on the east and a red rattan bush on the west. My clan occupies nine gullies and eight caves, and our dwellings boast thousands of holes and gates. Both being trees on the same hill, why should one brag of being taller than the other? When chopped down for firewood, wee fall in the same season. Is it simply because they are black and wee are red that they should claim theirs is the central kingdom and wee are outlanders? And further consider themselves superior and us inferior? They flagrantly perceive themselves as elephants and look down upon us as chaff! Recently I received a note from them only to find that they have added the word "great" to the name of their kingdom, calling themselves the GREAT Sophora Kingdom! How dare they belittle us so? Bordering on our territory across the brook is their Southern Bough Prefecture, a land rich in rice and fish. I´ll muster my tribesmen and cross the river to do some plundering.

米，不免聚集部落，抢杀一番。（众演介）

【豹子令】

　　同是蚁儿能大多？
　　分土分兵等一窝。
　　欺负俺
　　国小空虚少粮食，不知俺
　　穿营蓦涧走如梭。
（合）
　　安排个个似喽罗。

【前腔】

　　隔江西畔有一郡南柯，
　　他聚积的膻香可奈何？
　　要那槐安安不的，
　　俺征西旗上也写着个大檀萝。（合前）

地接罗施鬼，
人称藤甲兵。
南柯堪一苇，
同去觅膻腥。

(The soldiers perform military exercises)

【The Leopard Minitune】

Ants alike, little bigger can they be;
into workers and soldiers both divide.
They despise us
because our land is small and harvest poor,
but they don´t know
wee excel at swimming and drilling holes.
(Refrain)
All of us can put up a stubborn fight.

【Ditto】

West of the river there´s a place named Southern Bough,
where piles of rice and mutton invite our greed.
Let the Sophora taste the sores of war;
"Great" will also be prefixed to my westward flag.
(Refrain)

Don´t settle near agents of hell
Who are known for their rattan shields.
Reed leaves ferry us to and fro,
To trace the source of mutton smell.

第十五出　侍　　猎

【宝鼎现】

（王引众上）

绿槐风小，
正绛台清暇，
日华低照。
巧江山略似人间，
立草昧暗凭天道。

（生同右相上）

且喜君臣游宴好，
南郡偶然边报。

（合）

看尺土拳山
寸人豆马，
一样打围花鸟。

（见介）

〔玉楼春〕

（王）

吴头楚尾吾家国，
台殿玲珑秋瑟瑟。

Scene 15 Royal Hunting Party

(Enter the king of Sophora, attended)

【Ancient Bronze Pot Unearthed】

KING:

The green Sophora soughs;
the purple house in leisure lies.
Morning sun rays slant low
o´er hills and rills that mimic human world.
By mere instinct wee obey heaven´s way.

(Enter Chunyu and Right-hand Premier)

CHUNYU, PREMIER:

Wee were enjoying a harmonious treat
when an alarm was raised in Southern Bough.

ALL:

Upon a foot of land with fist-big hills,
inch-high people on bean-sized steeds
go hunting just as humans do.

(Chunyu and Premier greet King)

KING:

My country flourishes from west to east;
Crisp autumn now hangs on the palace eaves.

CHUNYU:

Ten-thousand-year branches produce most sounds;
The dew drops on them foretell winter's steps.

PREMIER:

The sun is high and thin smoke streams up straight;
Our sky is no more than a foot away.

ALL:

(生)

万年枝上最声多，

报道蚤寒清露滴。

(右)

日高风细炉烟直，

洞壑朝天天咫尺。

(合)

诸邦蚁伏尽无虞，

惟有檀萝费裁划。

(王)昨日览奏，檀萝侵扰南柯郡界。国久无事，人不知兵，右相欲请寡人畋猎龟山，以讲武事。不知本朝先世，曾有征战之事乎？

(右)有祖宗朝的故事：汉乾封元年，曾在河内人家，千人万马，从朝至暮而往来；晋太元中，曾在桓谦之家，被甲持槊，沿几登灶而饮食；元魏天安元年，在兖州赤黑相斗，赤者断头而死；东魏武定四年，在邺都黄黑交战，黄者班师而薨；此我国征伐之故事也。

(王)先朝可有畋猎之事乎？

(右)南齐朝，曾在徐玄之家，武士数千，纵横于花毡之上，不止火猎，兼之水嬉，网罟数百，钓于砚山之池，获鱼数百千头；此我国畋猎之故事也。

(王)猎于龟山者，何也？

(右)天上星宿，龟为玄武，以此国家讲武，应向龟山。

(王)右相言之有理。陪从官员可已齐备？

All other ant tribes are submissive now;
Only the Sandalwood remains unbowed.

KING: I read in yesterday´s report that the Sandalwoods are harassing our Southern Bough Prefecture. Since my country hasn´t been involved in a war for a very long time, I´m afraid my people are out of practice when it comes to military affairs. Thereupon, my right-hand premier advised me to go hunting at Tortoise Hill and take it as a war game. I wonder if my predecessors had any experience of war at all.

PREMIER: Your Majesty, our dynasty has been through a good number of wars. In the first year of Qianfeng reign of the Han Dynasty, tens of thousands of foot soldiers and horsemen clashed from morning till night in a household in Henei Prefecture. During Taiyuan reign of the Jin Dynasty in Huan Qian´s house, armored soldiers carrying spears climbed up stool-legs onto the top of the kitchen range and feasted on the spoils. In the first year of Tian´an reign of the Northern Wei Dynasty, the blacks and reds fought in Yan Prefecture. The reds were slaughtered, and their heads were cut off. In the fourth year of Wuding reign of the Eastern Wei Dynasty, the blacks went to war with the yellows at Yedu. The yellows retreated, and their king expired. Those were the wars in our country´s history.

KING: Is there any precedent to go by for performing a grand royal hunt?

PREMIER: There is. During the Southern Qi Dynasty, at the home of Xu Xuanzhi, several thousand of our warriors combed the rug. They hunted not only for land game but water produce as well. With hundreds of nets, they fished the ink pool, and caught thousands and thousands of fish. That was the most famous hunt in our history.

KING: Then why did you suggest wee hunt at Tortoise Hill?

PREMIER: According to the celestial constellations, the Tortoise represents the guardian god of war. So when a country needs military inspiration, she should seek it at Tortoise Hill.

KING: That sounds convincing. Are the officers and officials ready?

CHUNYU: Yes, Your Majesty. Commander Zhou Bian will be in charge

（生）已着司隶校尉臣周弁掌武，处士臣田子华掌文，臣棼与右相段功护驾。

（王）这等，就此驾行。（行介）

【好事近】

游践海西郊，
摆鸾舆天开黄道。
阵旗花鸟，
闪开了兽喧禽噪。
连天金鼓，
山川草木惊飞跳。
拣良时，奏旨施行，
围子内听号头高叫。（到介）

（王）此所谓龟山乎？上隆法天，下平法地，背有盘文以法星宿，昔人九月登龟伐鼋，良有以也。且是丰草茂林，禽多兽广，长杨、上林，可以方矣。分付六军，大煞手打围。（众应领旨介）（擂鼓杀介）（射作擒虎介）（射雁介）

【千秋岁】

展弓刀，
便有翅飞难道，

of the troops, while Scholar Tian Zihua will oversee the civil servants. My humble self and Premier Duan will stay by Your Majesty´s side to guarantee your safety.

KING: Well, let´s set off now. (They march)

【Luck at Hand】

KING:

Wee toward the suburban west
march off according to the zodiac.
With waves of flags, a riot of hues,
our troops flush out big game and shrieking fowl.
The drums make thunderous booms
that shake the hills and startle trees and grass.
On my command at an auspicious hour,
trumpets will declare the enclosure done.

(The procession halts)

KING: Is this the Tortoise Hill? Look! The vault resembles heaven, the flat parallels the earth, and the veins correspond to the constellations above. That must be why the ancients claimed that the ninth month is the time to mount the tortoise for military action. See how luscious the grass is and how thick the woods are! There must be plenty of fowl and game out there. Such abundance may even surpass that of the most renowned gardens of the emperors, such as the Changyang and Shanglin gardens! Send my order to the troops: Commence! Let them exert themselves.

(Attendants respond in chorus, beat drums, and start hunting. Some aim and shoot at wild geese; some shoot a tiger and capture it)

【A Thousand Years】

KING:

Draw your bows and swords.
Let nothing escape, though wings they have.

看纷纷惊弹飞炮。
地网天牢，
地网天牢，
索撞着掘海爬山神道。
接着的剽，
踏着的捣，
骑和步，
横叉直钞。

（众喊介）拿倒穿山甲！

（王大笑介）此俺国世仇也。

（众）

任你穿山搅，
这风毛雨血，
天数难逃。

（田）处士臣田子华，文墨小臣，躬逢盛典，谨撰《大槐安国龟山大猎赋》奏上。

（王）奏来。

（田跪念介）幽哉！大槐安之为国也，前衿龙岭，后枕龟山。龟山者，玄武之精也。西望则有西王母之龟峰焉，东顾则有东诸侯之龟蒙焉。尔其为山也，其上穹窿，其中空同。形如巴丘之蜕骨，势似鳌山之顶蓬。草木生其背，禽兽穴其胸。文有河洛之数，武有介胄之容。驸马都尉臣淳于棼、右丞相臣段功等仰首叹曰：丕休哉！龟山郁郁

Slingstones and cannon balls crisscross the sky,
weaving a cage on land
and a net on high,
obstructing passages up and tunnels down.
Slash those that try to flee;
crush those beneath your feet.
On horseback or on foot,
wee scour the battlefield.

ATTENDANTS (yelling): Wee have caught a pangolin!

KING (laughing merrily): That's our most hated, inveterate enemy!

ATTENDANTS:

Despite its gifted drilling skills,
in such a storm of smelly blood
its doom is sealed.

TIAN: Your Majesty's humble civil servant Tian Zihua, who is good at nothing but letters, has composed a eulogy to commemorate this extraordinary occasion. The title is "A Eulogy to the Great Sophora Kingdom on the Occasion of the Grand Hunt on Tortoise Hill."

KING: Read it out for us.

TIAN (kneels and reads): Deep and serene is the Great Sophora Kingdom! It embraces Dragon Ridge and is backed by Tortoise Hill, which hosts the spirit of war. To the west is Turtle Peak where the Queen of the West presides; to the east is the Turtle Range that has cradled the eastern princedoms. What makes this tortoise mound a hill is its dome without and a hollow within. Shaped like the fossil of a giant cobra, it looms like an unsinkable island on the waves. Plants flourish on its back, and animals nestle in its chest. To scholars, its veins bear the puzzle of the eight diagrams; to warriors, it supplies the toughness of the shield.

"What a place of nature's profusion!" the royal son-in-law Chunyu Fen, the right-hand premier Duan Gong and the others raised their eyes and exclaimed in admiration. "If His Majesty does not harvest it, tigers would

葱葱。吾王不游，虎兕出于匣外；今日不乐，龟玉毁于椟中。君王感焉，武功其同。是月也，凉风至，草木陨，鹰击鸟，豺祭兽。君王乃冠通天之冠，被玄衮之袍，佩干将，登华芝。雨师洒道，风伯清尘。因是以左成侯、右淳侯，率其蚁附之属，若大若小，纷纷蛰蛰，乘玄驹而缀步趋者，殆以万计。金鼓震天，旌旗耀日，雷炮霜刀，风矰雨毕，周圆而阵于七十二钻之上。时至令起，人喧物华，挂飞猿，跐长蛇，碎熊掌，縻象牙，咀豹文，嘬犀花，髓天鸡，脑神鸦。至如雉兔数万，他他藉藉，君王未之顾也。最后得一甲兽，盖鲮鲤云。带穿山之甲，露浮水之嘴，舐啖至毒，不可胜纪。穴于山腹，火而献之。君王欣然，仰天而嘻曰：龟山有灵，此其当之矣。寡人鄙小，其敢朵颐？盖兹山以土石为玄壳，以草树为绿毛，今此之猎尽矣。乃遂收旗割鲜，鸣钟举酒，凯歌而旋。既醉既饱，

roam the area; if wee do not exploit it, the precious shell would be spoiled in its sarcophagus."

In accordance with the times, His Majesty decided to flex our military muscle. So, in the season when the cool breeze rises, grass and trees cease to grow, eagles prey on birds and jackals feed on fattened beasts, His Majesty, wearing the crown of heaven, donning a robe embroidered with royal patterns and with a sword hanging from his waist, mounted the regal chariot. The rain god had sprinkled the roads; the wind god had swept off the dust. With Lord Chunyu on his right and Lord Duan on his left, His Majesty sallied forth, leading *antre* legions of various sizes, scrambling and scurrying on foot and on horseback.

Drums made the sky shake and flags eclipsed the sun. Cannons roared like thunder and blades flashed like frost. Raining arrows and fire, the troops encircled the tortoise mound of seventy-two cracks and crags.

The hour came. At royal command, the troops dashed forth in war whoops. Flying apes were trapped, long snakes squashed, bear paws chopped off and elephant tusks pulled out. The spots of leopards were gnawed, the juice of rhino-horns was sucked, the marrow of golden pheasants was siphoned out, and the brains of magic ravens were extracted. The tens of thousands of hares and wild ducks that bumped into each other in panic were beneath royal notice. In the end, an armored animal was captured, known as the pangolin, which is armed with steely scales, gluey lips, a poisonous tongue, and what not! A pit was dug in the hillside and a bonfire was built, over which the pangolin was sacrificed. Its meat was offered to the sovereign, who addressed heaven with a pleased smile on his royal countenance, "It must be the spirit of Tortoise Hill blessing me to have this deadly enemy fall into my hand. But humble and small as I am, I must abstain from consuming this heavenly food!"

With a shell of rock and earth, with its green hair of grass and trees, Tortoise Hill that day had offered an overabundance of trophies. Therefore, at day´s end wee turned our banners homeward to celebrate our triumph amidst the chiming of bells and flowing cups of wine.

微臣授简作颂，献于座右。颂曰：

隆隆龟山，

龙冈所蔽。

玄玄我王，

卜猎斯至。

非虎非罴，

曰雨曰霁。

服猛示武，

遗膻去智。

愿以龟山，

卜年卜世。

蝼蚁微臣，

愿王千岁千千岁。

(王大笑介)妙哉!赋也。昔汉武皇见司马相如《子虚赋》，叹恨不得与他同时。今寡人与子同时，幸哉!

【好事近】

一声惊破紫霞毫，

赋就《上林》分晓。

堂堂一貌，

好个田郎京兆。

飘飘，

凌云气色争高。

驸马，这田子华才子之文，不可泯灭，可雕刻在金镶玉板之上，显的俺国中有人，

添故事与龟山荣耀。

赏他何官则好，

Sated with food and inspired by wine, His Majesty´s humble servant ventured to sum up the day´s historic feat in an ode and present it to the throne. It goes as follows:

Oh! Lofty Tortoise Hill,
Enclosed by Dragon Ridge!
Our king of birth divine
In person came to hunt,
Not for tigers or bears,
Not to disturb the folks,
But to display our strength,
And answer calls from sky.
Wee pray to the tortoise
For life´s eternity.
Wee ants diminutive
Wish our king a life of thousands of years!

KING (laughing merrily): How wonderful this eulogy is! It´s said that when Emperor Wudi of the Han Dynasty first read Sima Xiangru´s "A Eulogy to Mr. Zixu," he wished he had been born earlier. I´m more fortunate than he to have you as a contemporary.

【Luck at Hand】

Your brushpen has scribed an unusual piece,
a eulogy that will forever last.
With an air of nobleness
your talents shall win you a lasting name.
Soaring high,
the words echo in the ethereal heights.

Dear son-in-law, Mr. Tian´s marvelous eulogy should go down in history. Have it inscribed on a jade plate and encased in a gold frame to let all other nations know that our country is highly cultured.

This anecdote adds fame to Tortoise Hill.
What title should I award such a man?

笑子虚乌有，
寡人得侍同朝。

右侯，今日之猎乐乎？

（右）今日以南柯有警，讲武兹山，非乐也。臣已于国史之上书了一行。

（王）怎么书？

（右）大槐安国义成元年八月，大猎于龟山，讲武事也。

（王）这等，可传旨再讲武一番。（鼓吹演介）

【千秋岁】

演《龙韬》，
把猛兽似诛强暴，
密札札做势儿围绕。（演介）
一点旗摇，
看一点旗摇，
齐声杀上，
休教流落。
钯儿罩，
枪儿照。
前头跳，
后头扑着，
就里把兵机讨。
看这臂鹰老手，
汗马功劳。

（王）传旨众军，罢猎回朝。（众应介）（鼓吹介）

Pitiable are those empty names;
lucky is he who serves me in my Court.

Marquis Duan, what do you think of today´s hunt? Isn´t it a pleasant excursion?

PREMIER: In fact, this is no pleasure trip. It´s a war exercise due to the border alarm in Southern Bough. I´ve already entered this event in our national chronicles.

KING: How did you put it?

PREMIER: In the eighth month of the first year of Yicheng reign of the Great Sophora Kingdom, a hunting party gathered at Tortoise Hill to promote military awareness.

KING: In that case let´s do some more drilling.

(Trumpets and drums within. Soldiers perform military exercises)

【A Thousand Years】

KING:

Do combat moves
to tightly encircle the enemy
and decimate like foes the beasts of prey.
(The troops maneuver into various formations)
Watch my commanding flag
and act accordingly.
Advance in unison
and let no game escape.
Whack them with your rakes;
pierce them with your pikes.
Spring up in front;
pounce from behind.
Military arts are thus acquired.
See how veteran falconers
accomplish new exploits.

【越恁好】

大打围归去，

打围归去，

毕崩崩鼓细敲，

迸钲钲点铙。

齐悉索，

齐获铎。

唧喳喳玉箫，

玉箫，间着匹喇喇笛声儿，

哜嘈嘈唳嘹。

剪茸茸翠稍，

齐臻臻马道儿

立着队梢。

盔缨缴，

撒袋儿摇，

一个个把归鞭袅袅。

顺西风扬疾，

马上调笑。（传旨趱行介）

【前腔】

洒风尘故道，

风尘故道。

呆哈哈狡兽挑，

喘吁吁想逃。

狗儿载，

鹰儿套。

Hark my order: Stop hunting and return to Court.
(Attendants respond in chorus. Drums and trumpets within)

【Even Better】

KING:

Lift the siege and return,
lift the siege and return.
The waist-drums rattle in quick beats;
the cymbals crackle sharp and crisp.
They all chuckle;
they all rumble.
The vertical pipes tweedle,
mixed with the horizontal flutes´ tootle.
What sounds of clamor and jabber!
Holding halberds of equal length,
battalions march in perfect squares;
their ensigns flutter in the front.
Tassels twirl on helmets;
fodder bags bump on horse haunches;
triumphant whip cracks spur the homeward hooves.
Borne on the swift westerly breeze,
wee in the saddle jest and jerk.
(An order is issued for speeding up)

【Ditto】

Dust rises on the ancient road,
dust on the ancient road.
The trussed-up prey on shoulder-poles
are panting and struggling to escape.
Dogs help to pull,
eagles scout on high.

窣泠泠树梢，
蘸着湿漈漈兽巢儿
暂萧条这遭。
闹炒炒气淘，
打孩孩顺哨儿前喝后邀。
观禽貌，
揣兽膘，
猛说山川小。
有这些杀获，
不算穷暴。

(右侯)奏知俺王，已到都门了。

【红绣鞋】
听诸军肃静啰唣，
啰唣。
贺君王多得腥臊，
腥臊。
有分例，
大赏犒。
毛赤剥，
肉生烧。
沾老小，
祭枪刀。

【尾声】
倚长空秋色打围高，

The chilly treetops now
harbor nothing but damp and soggy nests;
let them be empty for a while.
A clamor of inviting noise
bounces across the columns and along the lines.
Judging by the fowls in hold
and the plumpness of the beasts,
no one can say the hill is small.
With such a bumper catch and kill,
it isn´t bad at all.

PREMIER: Your Majesty, wee have reached the city gate.

【Red Embroidered Shoes】

Pipe down, all of you in the rank and file,
pipe down.
Praise our king for reaping such smelly spoils,
smelly spoils.
Each will have
a lavish share.
Peal the skin,
cook the meat,
to feast our old and young,
and to anoint our knives.

【Coda】

Autumn hunting under the vast blue sky
fosters a hidden military plan.

ATTENDANTS:

May Tortoise Hill bless us for centuries on!

暗藏着观兵演哨。

(众)愿万万岁龟山镇国宝。

(王)国家大阅礼成，驸马中宫留宴。右相可陪众国公王亲以下，赐宴槐角楼，商议南柯一事。(众应介)

曾济齐师学阵图，
千人万马出郊墟。
吾王所馔能多少，
一猎归来满后车。

KING: So wee have accomplished a national defense exercise. Dear son-in-law, stay to have dinner with us. Mr. Premier, you host a banquet for the other royal relatives and high officials in the corner tower of the forbidden city, and discuss the Southern Bough emergency. (All respond in chorus)

Wee've drilled on various combat formations
With thousands of soldiers in the suburbs.
Despite the small appetite of our king
Our hunting booty fills a caravan.

第十六出　得　　翁

【蓦山溪】

（生）

人间此处，

有得神仙住。

春色锦桃源，

蚤流入秋光殿宇。

（旦）

细腰轻展，

渐觉水游鱼。

娇波潋滟横眉宇，

翠压巫山雨。

〔阮郎归〕

（生）

藕丝吹软碧罗衣，

缕金香穗飞。

（旦）

绿窗槐影翠依微，

出花宫漏迟。

（生）

穿玉境，

Scene 16 Lost Father Found

(Enter Chunyu and Princess)

【Tracing the Mountain Creek】

CHUNYU:

This place on earth
could even please the deities.
The peach garden in spring´s full bloom
joins autumn´s mellowness to fill the halls.

PRINCESS:

I twist my waist
like a fish swimming in the lake.
Sleek ripples sparkle in my lucid eyes;
supple rain sets in on Mount Wu.[1]

CHUNYU:

Soft as lotus-root fibers is my gown;
Fragrance floats from the golden rice.

PRINCESS:

Green shadows are glazing the windowpanes;
Outside it is already bright.

CHUNYU:

A trespass
On fairyland
Has transmuted my humble life.

PRINCESS: Oh, darling,

Don´t let our pleasures make you late for Court.
I´ll wait for you to paint my brows.

侍瑶姬，

微生遭际奇。

(旦)

驸马呵，

和你欢多怕忘却蚤朝时，

归来人画眉。

驸马到此月余，情义日深，荣华日盛；出入车服，宾御游宴，次于王者，意亦可矣。然窃观驸马，常有蹙眉之意，如闻嗟啧之声，含愁不语，却是为何？

(生)小生落魄多年，荣华一旦。不说倾宫罗绮，尽世膏粱；且说贵主娇姿，尽我受用；有何不足？致动尊怀。所以然者，遇贵主有天上之乐，想亡亲有地下之悲耳。

(旦)这等，公婆前过几年了？

(生)婆婆葬在家山，禅智桥边好墓田。则你公公可怜也。

(旦)驸马，试说其情。

【白练序】

(生)

心中事，

待说向妆台自叹吁。

吾先父为将佐，

边头失误……

(旦)原来老老爷用兵失利，可得生还？

(生叹介)身殁。

(旦)殁在何地？

(生)他殁在胡。

(旦)几年上有音信？

Darling, you´ve been here for a month already. With every passing day, our affection grows and royal favors increase. Look at the silk and satin you wear, the elegant coaches you ride in, the constant parties and banquets you attend. You´re treated almost like a king. That should have made anyone happy, yet why do I sometimes find you frowning and sighing as if something weighs heavily on your mind?

CHUNYU: I´d been down and out for many years when all of a sudden fortune smiled on me. With you at my side, I should be the happiest man in the world, not to mention the rich clothes that fill wardrobes and wardrobes, and the choicest viands from every nook of the earth. What can I have to complain about? However — I don´t want to arouse your concern — I can´t help thinking that while I´m enjoying such a heavenly life, my parents are suffering in the nether world.

PRINCESS: I see. How long has it been since my parents-in-law passed away?

CHUNYU: My mother was buried in the family graveyard by the Chan Wisdom Bridge, but my poor father...

PRINCESS: Darling, please tell me.

【White Silk Overture】

CHUNYU:

My heart is full;
a sigh wells up before a word is said.
My father was an officer.
He made a faulty move.

PRINCESS: So his troops were defeated. Was he able to return?

CHUNYU (sighs):

He in battle fell.

PRINCESS: Where was that?

CHUNYU:

Deep in barbarian land.

PRINCESS: When did you last hear from him?

（生）可十数年来无寄书。
近来却是古怪。
（旦）怎的来？
（生）前日成亲，蒙千岁亲口分付，系俺父亲之命，那时好不疑惑。
（旦）便好问俺父王所在了。
（生）以前未敢造次，直待龟山罢猎，留宴内庭，才敢动问："千岁既知臣父亲所在，臣请敬往问安。"那时千岁劈口应说："亲家翁职守北土，音问不绝。卿但具书相问，未可便去。"公主呵，

何缘故？
教人平白地，
暗生疑虑。

【醉太平】
（旦）

听语，
你少年孤露。
这遇妻所，
拾得亲父。

（生泣介）知他北土怎的？
（旦）

既然守土，
知他那里欢娱。

（生又泣介）俺待禀过公主，潜去北土，打听父亲消息。

CHUNYU:

That was more than a dozen years ago.
But something strange happened recently.

PRINCESS: What happened?

CHUNYU: The other day at our wedding, your father said our engagement was in accordance with the wish of my father. I just couldn´t figure out what that meant.

PRINCESS: Why didn´t you ask him directly?

CHUNYU: I didn´t want to be rude, so I held off asking him till after the royal hunt. At the celebration banquet last night I finally ventured to raise the question: "Since Your Majesty know the whereabouts of my father, your humble servant wishes to go there to pay his filial respects."

"Your father is faithfully guarding the northern territory," His Majesty replied offhandedly. "Wee often exchange correspondence. You may write to him, but you may not go there in person right now."

Dear Princess,
why can´t I go?
It only makes me suspect
there is something I shouldn´t know.

【Drink for Peace】

PRINCESS:

Your words disclose
that you suffered a lonely youth.
But where you found a wife,
you heard about your dad.

CHUNYU (weeping): I wonder how he´s faring up there in the north.

PRINCESS:

Since he´s still in command,
his life cannot be very bad.

CHUNYU (still weeping): With your permission, I want to slip out of the country and go north to look for him.

（旦）

模糊，
那胡沙如梦杳如无，
不明白怎寻归路？

（生）待俺再奏过千岁，分明而去。

（旦）

他眼前儿女，
几日成亲，
便教卿去？

【白练序】

（生）

难图，
怎教他在北土，
天寒草枯？
似俺这洞府，
比他何如？

（旦）且依父王旨，先寄问安书。

（生）

踟蹰空寄书，

（旦）也寄些礼物去。

（生泣介）

要报阳春寸草无。

（旦）这等，怎好？

（生泣介）

贤公主，
似这般有子，
等如无物。

【醉太平】

PRINCESS:

That´s crazy!

The desert is as empty as a dream.

How can you find your way there and return?

CHUNYU: Maybe I can beg a favor of His Majesty and win his support.

PRINCESS:

Do you think he´ll allow

his recently acquired

son-in-law to desert his bride?

【White Silk Overture】

CHUNYU:

Alas!

How can I yield him up

to withered grass beneath a frozen sky?

What a snug place this cavern is,

compared with his abode!

PRINCESS: Why don´t you do as my father advised, and first send him a letter?

CHUNYU:

How can a letter speak my mind?

PRINCESS: Wee can also send him a present.

CHUNYU (weeping):

But what do I have to repay his love?

PRINCESS: Well, what can wee do then?

CHUNYU (weeping):

Princess dear,

for him to have me as a son

is just like having none.

【Drink for Peace】

PRINCESS (aside):

（旦背介）

真苦，
他身为赘婿。
要高堂礼节，
内家区处。

（回介）驸马，想起来你在俺国中，岂可空书问候？奴家早已做下长生袜一双，福寿鞋一对，可同书寄去。

（生）这等，生受了。

（旦）

些微针指，也见俺一房儿妇。

（生）有谁将去？

（旦）

你修书，俺依然送与父王知，便千里一时将去。

（生）这等，俺即刻封了书礼，只烦公主入宫，转达下情。

（旦）使得。

奴便与，
系书胡雁，
怎教驸马不报慈乌？

（旦）还一件，请问驸马，你如今可想做个甚么官儿？

（生）俺酣荡之人，不习政务。

（旦）卿但应承，妾当赞相。

【尾声】

俺入宫闱取礼和你送家书，
见父王求一新除。

What a dilemma!
Besides the duties of a son,
he´s duty-bound as son-in-law,
and has a wife to care about.

(Turning around) Darling, since you´re now married, a mere letter certainly won´t do. I´ve already knitted a pair of longevity socks, and stitched a pair of propitious shoes. You can send them along with your letter.

CHUNYU: That´s most thoughtful of you.

PRINCESS:

The needlework may convey
the filial piety of a daughter-in-law.

CHUNYU: But who´s going to take the letter there?

PRINCESS:

You compose the letter,
and I´ll ask my father to forward it.
A thousand miles is traversed in a flash.

CHUNYU: If that´s the case, here´s my letter. I must trouble you to take it to His Majesty and tell him how anxious I am about my father.

PRINCESS: I will.

I´ll tie your mail
to the leg of a north-bound goose
and ask it to convey your filial love.

By the way, have you considered seeking public office? What kind of position would you like to have?

CHUNYU: I´m used to an uninhibited lifestyle. An official position may not suit me.

PRINCESS: Well, all you need to do is to accept it, and I´ll help you out.

【Coda】

I´ll go and hand your letter to Father,
and ask him to give you an office post.

(生)这等，做老婆官了。

(旦)便做老婆官，

有甚么辱没你淳于家七代祖。

骥子书犹隔，
鸾俦镜乍辉。
绿槐无限好，
能借一枝栖。

CHUNYU: But that would be a nepotic position.
PRINCESS: What if it´s a nepotic position?
Would that disgrace your ancestors and family name?

Father and son are torn apart,
While bride and bridegroom mirror match.
Snuggled in the Sophora shade,
Is there a branch to perch upon?

第十七出　议　　守

【绕池游】

（右相上）

金章紫绶，
独步三台宿，
正朝下日移花甃。
看簪发丝稠，
带腰围瘦，
无非为国机谋。

平明登紫阁，
日晏下彤闱。
未奉君王召，
高槐昼掩扉。

自家右相武成侯段功，忝掌朝纲，留心边计。昨因檀萝数为边患，我主赐宴槐角楼，与一众科道商议，奏选南柯太守，未知意属何人？紫衣官蚤到也。

（紫上）昼漏希传高阁报，君颜有喜近臣知。
（见介）段老先生，早朝辛苦。
（右）恰待文书房相问，奏补南柯郡太守一事，旨意可下了？

Scene 17 The Vacant Position

(Enter Right-hand Premier)

【Around the Pool】

PREMIER:

With a gold seal on purple sash,
I´m the chief of the cabinet.
Sunlight now pours into the water well.[1]
See how my hair turns thin and gray,
and how my belt hangs loose
due to my devotion to state affairs.

I come to Court before sunrise,
And do not go home till sunset.
If the king does not summon me,
The Sophora adjourns all day.

I´m Duan Gong, Right-hand Premier and Marquis of Martial Feats. Since I run the government, I must keep an eye on border affairs. The Sandalwood troops have made several intrusions. So yesterday His Majesty asked me and my cabinet to recommend candidates for the Taishou[2] of Southern Bough Prefecture during the banquet in the corner tower of the forbidden city. I wonder if His Majesty has made a decision yet. Ah, here comes a palace officer.

(Enter a palace officer in a purple robe)

OFFICER:

The bulletins are always slow and scant;
Only close courtiers perceive royal thoughts.

(Greeting Premier) Lord Duan, had a busy morning?

PREMIER: I was just thinking of going to the secretariat to check up on

(紫)右侯不得知，恰好此本上去，正直公主入宫，一来替驸马寄书令尊，二来替驸马求官外郡，则怕就点了南柯之缺，也未可知？

(右)这却难道。

【剔银灯】

论南柯跨踞雄州，
近檀萝要习边筹。
那淳于贵婿，
性豪杯酒，
怎生任得边州之守？

(合)

许否？
心中暗忧，
宫庭事又难执奏。

【前腔】

(紫)

论朝纲须问君侯，
大地方有得干求。

则一件，君侯疏不间亲了。

他与玉人金屋，
并肩交肘，
怎佩不得黄金如斗？(合前)

the nomination of the Taishou of Southern Bough Prefecture. Has a decree been issued concerning the appointment?

OFFICER: Well, there´s something Your Excellency may not know. It just happened that the princess was visiting her parents when your memorial was presented. She had gone to ask His Majesty to forward a letter from the royal son-in-law, and to seek a position for her husband in local government. I´m afraid His Majesty will give that vacancy to Chunyu out of hand.

PREMIER: That´s very likely.

【Shining the Silver Lamp】

The Southern Bough is a strategic place.
It borders Sandalwood, which threatens war.
But that royal in-law Chunyu
takes delight in his cups.
How can wee trust him with our border towns?
(Refrain)
Who will it be?
Although that worries me,
one can´t advise on family affairs.

【Ditto】

OFFICER:

The premier normally should have a say
in the appointment of the local chiefs.

But in this case, it´s advisable to shy away from the royal family´s domestic affairs.

He and the princess under one roof live,
and they walk hand in hand.
Why can´t he sport a gold seal of bushel size?
(Refrain)

（右）许他也索罢了，则怕此君权盛之后，于国反为不便。且自由他。

欲除新太守，
不少旧英豪。
且顺君王意，
相看儿女曹。

PREMIER: Well, let him have the post. What worries me is that, with his rise to power, he may jeopardize the fortunes of our country. For the moment, come what may.

To fill the recent vacancy,
Many old heads are pushed aside.
The king can do what pleases him;
Posterity's his first concern.

第十八出　拜　郡

【西江月】

（生上）

本自将门为将，
偶来王国扶王，
风流偏打内家香，
更有甚中情未讲？

〔集唐〕

秦地吹箫女，
盈盈在紫微。
可中才望见，
花月后门归。

几日前公主入宫，一来寄书礼于家尊，二来替我求一官职。这晚近一路纱灯，公主到来也。

【前腔】

（旦引女官灯笼上）

几夜宫闱宴赏，
爹娘爱惜瑶芳。
月高灯火照成行，
款蹙金莲步障。

Scene 18 The Appointment

(Enter Chunyu)

【Moon on West River】

CHUNYU:

Like my old man I was born an army man,
but was led to a kingdom to serve the king.
Once a loose guy ties himself to a wife
what romance is there left to talk about?

The princess of Qin plays the flute[1]
In the depths of ethereal void.
Just a mere glimpse I caught of her,
And through the back door she slipped in.

A few days ago, the princess went to the palace to pass on my letter and package to the king, and to seek an official position for me. Now I see a line of lanterns along the road. It must be my dear wife coming back.

(Enter Princess with palace maids holding lanterns)

【Ditto】

PRINCESS:

Regaling me with festive nights,
dad and mom dote on daughter Yaofang.
The moon is high, the lanterns sketch a line.
Their light illuminates my tiny steps.
(She greets Chunyu)

CHUNYU: These past few nights while you were away in the palace, I felt rather lonely and miserable. Have you handed my letter to His Majesty?

PRINCESS: Please listen:

(见介)(生)公主入宫数晚，小生殊觉凄凉。书奉家尊，可曾寄去？

(旦)听道来。

【玉胞肚】

将书传上，

父王言礼仪合当。

即时间人往边乡，

临付与叮咛停当。

(生)怕回书迟慢。

(旦)

粗将孝意表高堂，

但取平安要怎忙？

(丑扮小军上)

为人莫做军，

做军多苦辛。

俺小军，从北边来，取了驸马老老爷平安书，不免投上。(见叩头介)小人北边送书礼，老老爷十二分欢喜。回书呈上。

(生惊喜介)起来，起来。真个有了回书，我的亲爹呵！(捧书开看介)“平安报付男淳于棼”，呀，八个字分明老父手笔。

(旦)你且念书奴家听。

(生念书介)“伏承大槐安国王前示，欲汝尚主。得书、履、袜，知盛典成就，加以贵主有礼，喜慰发狂！别近廿载，朝夕忆念。儿以槐序，备国肺腑，百宜周慎。颇忆平生，亲戚里闾，存旺余几？宜详

【A Gem–Studded Belt】

I placed your letter in his hand,
and he endorsed your filial etiquette.
Immediately, he dispatched someone north,
and gave the man directions in detail.

CHUNYU: I wonder how long it´ll take to receive a reply from my father.

PRINCESS:

You are just doing what a son should do.
Why should you mind waiting a day or two?

(Enter a soldier)

SOLDIER:

Never be you a serviceman;
A serviceman is worked to death.

I´m a soldier returning from the north with a reply from the royal son-in-law´s father. Here I deliver it. (He kowtows to Chunyu) I carried your letter and gift far to the north, and Your Highness´ respectable father was extremely happy to receive them. Here´s his reply.

CHUNYU (thrilled): Please rise. Oh, dear father, can this be true? (He tears open the envelop and reads) "To my son Chunyu Fen." Ah, these words are indeed in my father´s handwriting.

PRINCESS: Why don´t you read it aloud?

CHUNYU (reads): The king of the Great Sophora Kingdom had kindly informed me of his wish to marry his daughter to you. Your letter and the shoes and socks you sent along attest to a successful marriage. And I am more than pleased to learn that His Majesty has been very kind to you.

It is nearly twenty years since I saw you last, and not a single day has passed without my thinking about you. Now that you have joined the royal house of the Sophora, you should learn to be more discreet in word and deed.

Your letter evoked many dormant thoughts in me. How are our relatives and neighbors? Are they still alive and well? Please tell me next time

再信，助展遐缱。欲往视儿，奈彼此路道乖远，风烟阻绝。父不见子，抱恨重深。汝且无便来观，岁在丁丑，当与汝相见。”(生拍书痛哭介)俺的爹相去十七八年，只道故了，何意今朝重见平安书迹，居然如在。不能勾往见他，要儿子何用也？(哭倒)

(旦扶介)驸马，休得过伤。

【前腔】

(生)

端然无恙，

如昔年教诲不忘。

问亲邻兴废存亡，

叙风烟悲楚哀伤。

(旦)约丁丑年相见好了。

(生)

知他后会可能相？

怎得温衾扇枕床。

【粉蝶儿】

(紫衣捧诏上)

诏选黄堂，

捧到秦楼开放。

令旨已到，跪听宣读。诏曰：“昔称华国，左戚右贤，文武并茂。吾

you write. That will be food for my dreams.

I would have liked to pay you a visit, but the sheer distance is insurmountable, and winds and weather forbid it. It is most regrettable that a father should be separated from his son. On the other hand, it is also inconvenient for you to come over at this time. We will not be able to meet again until the year of *ding-chou*.[2]

(He clutches the letter with trembling hands and wails) After seventeen or eighteen long years, my father is still alive, while we all thought him dead! And now I see his words in his own handwriting, as if he were talking directly to me! If I don´t go and see him in person, what´s the good of him having this son? (He collapses. Princess grabs hold of his arm and supports him)

PRINCESS: Darling, restrain your grief. Don´t cry so hard.

【Ditto】

CHUNYU:

He is still safe and sound,
and he worries about me as of old.
He asks about our neighbors, friends and all,
and he bemoans the space between us two.

PRINCESS: He said you´ll be reunited in the year of *ding-chou*.

CHUNYU:

Who knows if that prediction will come true?
Meanwhile I cannot help him weather storms.

(Enter a palace officer in a purple robe, holding an imperial edict)

【The Powdered Butterfly】

OFFICER:

To choose a new Taishou,
the edict goes straight to the daughter´s house.

Here comes His Majesty´s edict. Kneel and listen. It reads: "It is said that the country prospers and thrives when both talented people and relatives are appointed to high offices, and when liberal arts and martial arts are

南柯郡政事不理，太守废黜，欲藉卿才，可屈就之。便与小女同往。钦哉！谢恩。”（生、旦起，紫见叩头介）恭喜公主、驸马，黄堂之尊了。千岁还有别旨。

【玉胞肚】

叫有司停当，
把太守行装备详。
掌离珠感动娘娘，
出倾宫锦锈奁房。

（旦）还有？

（众）

车骑仆妾都列在广衢傍，
鸾驾亲身饯远行。

【前腔】

（生喜介）

敢前希望？
忆年时醉游侠场。
普人间没俺东床，
凑南柯饮着琼浆。

（合）

这是有缘千里路头长，
富贵荣华在此方。

【尾声】

（紫）

从来尚主有辉光，
你整朝衣五鼓朝廊，

balanced. The former Taishou of Southern Bough was demoted because he neglected his duties. I hope you will bend your talents to its administration by accepting this humble position. My daughter will go with you. That is my wish." Express your gratitude. (Chunyu and Princess kowtow, and then rise to their feet)

OFFICER (kowtows to Chunyu and Princess[3]): My congratulations on your appointment as Taishou. His Majesty has drawn up some other instructions as well.

【A Gem–Studded Belt】

He ordered bureaus in concern
to get ready the Taishou´s new outfit.
The queen is so reluctant to say goodbye
that she packed a whole wardrobe for princess.

PRINCESS: Any other news?

OFFICER:

Servants and carriages have filled the thoroughfare;
the king and queen will come to see you off.

【Ditto】

CHUNYU (exalted):

What else is in store for me?
Not long ago I was a drunken mess,
and no good girl would care to marry me.
In Southern Bough I´ll live in luxury.
No one can evade destiny´s magnetic pull,
and Southern Bough is where my fortune lies.

【Coda】

OFFICER:

To marry a princess procures good luck.
Get yourself ready for an early Court

谢恩了辞朝做一事讲。（众下）

（生）多谢公主抬举，有此地方。

（旦）惶愧，惶愧！

（生）还要请教。南柯大郡，难以独理；加以小生素性酣放；意下要奏请田子华、周弁二人，同典郡政，何如？

（旦）但凭尊裁。

新命守南柯，
恩光谢女萝。
明朝有封事，
数问夜如何？

to thank His Majesty and set out for the south.

(Exit Officer)

CHUNYU: My dear, I owe this position to you. Thank you for commending me to your father.

PRINCESS: Don´t mention that.

CHUNYU: The Southern Bough is a large prefecture, and you know, I used to be rather carefree. I´m afraid I can´t run it all by myself. So I wonder if I can make a further request and ask His Majesty for Tian Zihua and Zhou Bian to come and help me with the administration. What do you say?

PRINCESS: That´s all right.

His appointment to Southern Bough
Was due to ivy's clinging help.
As tomorrow will be the day,
He dreams about the crack of dawn.

第十九出　荐　　佐

【生查子】

（紫引队子上）

一掌瞰宫墀，
洞府晨光露。
万点正奔趋，
遍起了朱门户。

（众）将军上殿。俺大槐安国今日驸马辞朝，各官在此候驾。

【前腔】

（生朝服捧表上）

槐殿隐香炉，
禁幄承恩处。
五马更踟蹰，
御道里开贤路。

（紫）驸马请上御道。

（生跪介）新除南柯郡太守驸马都尉臣淳于棼谢恩，即日之任，敬此辞朝。（生三叩俯伏介）

（紫）驸马，谢恩表就此披宣。

Scene 19 Selecting Staff

(Enter a palace officer in a purple robe, leading a group of attendants)

【The Sour Pear】

OFFICER:

Looking down on a maze of halls,
the morning rays illume the caves.
A myriad of scurrying specks
pour out from behind the red dirt doors.

ATTENDANTS: Attention! The royal son-in-law of the Great Sophora Kingdom is leaving the Court today. Stand by for an audience with His Majesty.

(Enter Chunyu in an official robe, holding a scroll)

【Ditto】

CHUNYU:

Incense smoke fills the palace halls,
where royal favors issue forth.
I´m eager to assume my post;
the future unrolls from the royal walk.[1]

OFFICER: Royal son-in-law, please step onto the royal walk.

CHUNYU (kneels): The newly appointed Taishou of Southern Bough Prefecture, Your Majesty´s humble servant and son-in-law, Lieutenant Chunyu Fen here tenders his highest gratitude. He begs permission to leave Court this very day to take up his appointed office. (He makes three kowtows and remains in a kneeling position)

OFFICER: Royal son-in-law, you may now deliver your obligation oration.

(生)臣此表章，不止谢辞恩宠，兼之举荐贤才，伏望俺王听启：

【桂枝香】

念臣将门余子，
素无材术。
诚恐有败朝章，
至此心惭覆悚。
待广求贤士，
广求贤士，
备臣官属，
与臣咨助。

(紫)驸马所荐何人？

(生)伏见司隶颍川周弁，忠亮刚直，有毗佐之器；处士冯翊田子华，清慎通变，达政化之源；二人与臣有十年之旧，备知才用，可托政事。周弁请署南柯郡司宪，田子华请署南柯郡司农。庶使臣政绩有闻，宪章无紊。

念臣愚，
愿得从铨补，
南柯治有余。

(紫)驸马起候旨。

(生起介)想令旨必然俯从，周司隶、田秀才有此遭际也。

(内)令旨到。驸马荐贤为国，寡人嘉悦，依奏施行。

CHUNYU: In my oration I not only wish to express my gratitude, but also wish to recommend new talent. Now, with Your Majesty´s permission...

【Sweet Osmanthus Branch】

A rough son of an army man,
I ain´t the well-coached type.
For fear of my incompetence,
which may jeopardize state affairs,
I need talents of various kinds,
talents of various kinds,
to fill the office seats
and give me sound advice.

OFFICER: Whom do you wish to recommend?

CHUNYU: Commander Zhou Bian of the capital´s garrison force. He has a loyal heart and an upright bearing, and will be a staunch supporter. Scholar Tian Zihua from Pingyi County is a very cautious and learned man, and he has a thorough mastery of the principles of politics. Your humble servant has known both of them for more than ten years, and can attest to their qualifications. They can be trusted with responsibility. Zhou Bian could serve as the security minister of Southern Bough, and Tian Zihua as the prefectural finance minister. With their assistance, your humble servant would be able to bring law and order to Southern Bough and make some creditable achievements.

Please forgive my ineptitude,
and provide me with expert hands
so that Southern Bough can be managed well.

OFFICER: Please rise, and stand by for the imperial decree.

CHUNYU (rising to his feet): I believe His Majesty will grant my request. Mr. Zhou and Mr. Tian can look forward to bright careers.

VOICE WITHIN: Hark the imperial decree: Wee are very pleased with the royal son-in-law´s recommendation of capable people for the country.

（生叩头呼千岁起介）

【神仗儿】

（周、田上）

蒙恩点注，

蒙恩点注；

南柯太守，

淳郎推举。

做司宪司农前去，

来阙下叫山呼。

（跪介）新除南柯郡司宪前司隶臣周弁、新除南柯郡司农处士臣田子华叩头谢恩。（叩头叫千岁起介）（相见介）

（生）二君恭喜了。

（周、田）谢堂翁抬举之恩。

（紫）驸马便当起程，国王、国母蚤已关南有饯。

〔集唐〕

濯龙门外主家亲，

半岁迁腾依虎臣。

却羡二龙同汉代，

出门俱是看花人。

His request is granted.

(Chunyu kowtows and shouts "Long live the king!" and then rises to his feet)

(Enter Zhou Bian and Tian Zihua)

【Magic Weapons】

ZHOU, TIAN:

We thank His Majesty,
we thank His Majesty
and the new Taishou
for nominating us
as finance and security ministers.
Here we come to express our gratitude.

(They kneel) The newly appointed security minister of Southern Bough, former commander of the capital's garrison force, Your Majesty's humble servant Zhou Bian, and the newly appointed finance minister of Southern Bough, Your Majesty's humble servant Tian Zihua, here kowtow to express their gratitude. (They kowtow and shout "Long live the king!" Then they rise to their feet and greet Chunyu)

CHUNYU: Congratulations to you both.

ZHOU, TIAN: We're deeply indebted to our new superior for this advancement.

OFFICER: Royal son-in-law, you may like to move on now. The king and queen are holding a send-off banquet in your honor outside the city's south gate.

Marriage brings one into the royal house;
Soon he will rise up with a tiger pounce.
Don't admire the two dragons in the pond;
It's far wiser to be a looker-on.

第二十出　御　　饯

（二紫衣上）

玉楼银榜枕严城，

翠盖红旗列禁庭。

二圣忽排鸾路出，

双仙正下凤楼迎。

今日国王、国母饯送驸马、公主之任南柯，鸾舆蚤到。

【传言玉女】

（王同老旦引宫娥上）

玉洞烟霞，

一道晴光如画。

回首凤城宫院，

见琉璃碧瓦。

（众）

宫娥侍长，

半插貂蝉随驾。

（合）

送一对于飞，

凤娇鸾姹。

（紫衣见介）千岁千岁。

（王）筵宴齐备么？

Scene 20 The Royal Send-off

(Enter two palace officers in purple robes)

OFFICERS:

A silver moat surrounds the towering walls;
Red and green banners frame the palace halls.
The royal couple rides out in a coach
To see the pair of young swans taking off.

Today, the king and queen are to hold a grand banquet to send off the princess and her husband to Southern Bough. Here comes their train of coaches.

(Enter King and Queen, with palace maids)

【Message to the Daughter】

KING, QUEEN:

From our cave wee behold
a painted patch of rosy clouds.
Looking back at the palace halls
wee see a stretch of yellow tiles.

MAIDS:

Wee palace maids
follow with gold ornaments in our hair.

ALL:

Off wee send to yonder land
a pair of lovely swans.

OFFICERS (greeting King and Queen): Long live Your Majesty and Your Ladyship!

KING: Is the banquet ready?

(紫)俱已齐备。

(王)已敕有司，备办太守行李？

(紫)行李整齐。

(宫娥)娘娘传旨：房奁、金玉、锦绣、车马、人从，都要列于通衢之上，许万民纵观。

(紫)知道。

【疏影】

(生、旦上)

冠裳俊雅，
正瑶台镜里，
凤妆浓乍。

(旦)

好梦分明，
素情娇怯，
慢引香车随马。

(紫催介)

君王国母亲临饯，
快疾着绿槐幢下。

(合)

真乃是夫贵妻荣，
一对堪描堪画。

(紫衣报介)驸马公主见。

(生、旦俯伏介)微臣夫妇沾恩，远劳圣驾，无任诚欢诚忭！诚惶诚恐！

OFFICERS: Yes, Your Majesty.

KING: Have you told the relevant departments to get the Taishou´s outfit ready?

OFFICERS: Yes, Your Majesty.

MAIDS: Her Ladyship has decreed that the dowry, including jewelry and silk, coaches and horses, valets and serving maids, be displayed on the thoroughfare for all to view.

OFFICERS: Her wish shall be carried out.

(Enter Chunyu and Princess)

【Verdant Shadows】

CHUNYU:

How stylish is my hat and dress!
And yours so bright and rich,
a mirror image of heaven´s hues.

PRINCESS:

Jerked out of a pleasant dream,
my coyness lingers on;
I wish the horses would slow their pace.

OFFICERS (urgently):

The king and queen are already there;
please hurry to the verdant canopy.

ALL:

Such a noble husband and fabled wife
would be a painter´s true delight!

OFFICERS (announcing): Here come the royal son-in-law and the princess.

CHUNYU, PRINCESS (dropping to their knees and bent low): It´s an exceptional honor that Your Majesty and Ladyship should have taken the trouble to come so far to see us off. Such a distinction both overjoys and overawes us.

(王)本不忍处卿于外，南柯有卿，免劳寡人南顾之忧耳。

(老旦泣介)俺的公主儿，远行苦也！

(旦作泣介)俺的亲娘呵！

(王)在家为公主，出嫁为郡君，有何所苦而泣乎？

(生、旦叩头介)微臣忝受鸿私，愿大王、国母千岁千岁千千岁。

(王)愿汝夫妇同之。(生、旦进酒科)

【画眉序】

(王)

晴拂御沟花，
祖帐城南动杯斝。
尽关南一面，
借卿弹压。
凭仗你半壁门楣，
看觑俺一分天下。

(合)

南柯太守风流煞，
一路里威仪潇洒。

(老)公主呵，今日南柯，便是你家了。俺宫中宝藏，尽作陪奁。你看通衢之上呵：

【前腔】

KING (to Chunyu): Wee didn´t want to send you away from Court, but with you at Southern Bough, wee can put our mind at ease about the southern frontier.

QUEEN (to Princess, weeping): Oh, dear, it´s going to be a long and arduous journey!

PRINCESS (weeping): Oh, Mother!

KING: At home you´re a princess, and at Southern Bough you´ll be the first lady. What´s there to cry about?

CHUNYU, PRINCESS (kowtowing): Wee are deeply indebted for this royal favor. May Your Majesty and Ladyship live thousands and thousands of years!

KING: May you live a long and happy life too.

(Chunyu and Princess offer wine to King and Queen)

【The Thrush Overture】

KING:

The sun is caressing the flowers;
a feast is laid out at the south of town.
I´ll leave the entire southern front
up to you to defend.
As a half-son who joins this ancient house,
you should look after part of my estate.
(Refrain)
What dignity it is to be Taishou!
His procession offers a sumptuous show.

QUEEN: Daughter, from now on, Southern Bough will be your home. What I´ve hoarded up in the palace is now given to you as a dowry. Look at the splendor on the thoroughfare!

【Ditto】

QUEEN:

云树玉交花，
日影光辉度尘罅。
但闺房所要，
尽情相把。
摆天街色色珍奇，
出关外盈盈车马。（合前）

【前腔】

（生）
平地折宫花，
大郡猥当叹才乏。
便寻常饯送，
敢烦鸾驾。
祝太山太水千秋，
喜治国治家一法。（合前）

【前腔】

（旦）
生小正娇花，
酬谢东风许花发。
但随夫之任，
赐妆如嫁。
因夫主占了儿家，
为郡君将离膝下。（合前）

（生、旦跪介）微臣何德？烦动至尊。敢问南柯，以何而治？

Trees of coral and flowers of jade
flicker with shifting angles of the sun.
What domestically you may need
I have provided for.
Gems of the rarest nature fill the road;
they´ll by the carload all go south with you.
(Refrain)

【Ditto】
CHUNYU:
Unawares, I plucked a palace flower,
and reaped a stretch of earth too large to tend.
A simple send-off would suffice.
Why such a royal one!
May your royalty last a thousand years.
With the same ease we manage state and home.
(Refrain)

【Ditto】
PRINCESS:
I was merely a tiny bud.
Thanks to the east wind I have come to bloom.
To our new office in the south
I bring a marriage gift.
I must follow my husband from now on,
and forsake my parents and maiden home.
(Refrain)

(Chunyu and Princess kneel)
CHUNYU: It´s a shame that my humble self has not achieved anything that merits this royal send-off. Before we part, may I beg to ask in what way I am to rule Southern Bough?

(王)南柯，国之大郡，土地丰穰，民物豪盛，非惠政不能治之。况有周、田二卿赞治，卿其勉之，以副国念。

(生叩头介)微臣谨遵王命。

(老)公主行矣，听母亲一言：淳于郎性刚好酒，加之少年；为妇之道，贵乎柔顺，尔善事之，吾无忧矣。南柯虽封境不遥，晨昏有间，今日睽别，宁不沾巾？(老同旦泣介)

(旦)谨领慈命。(拜别介)

【滴溜子】

(王)

南柯郡，
南柯郡，
弗嫌低亚。
公案上，
公案上，
酒杯放下。
有脚的阳春五马，
休只管恋着衙，
长放假。
他那里地方，
人物稠杂。

(王)传旨：鼓吹旗帜，送过长亭。(行介)

KING: Southern Bough is one of my biggest prefectures. The land is rich and productive, the population dense. Rule humanely, otherwise you might run into trouble. Now you have Mr. Zhou and Mr. Tian to assist you, take care and don´t let me down.

CHUNYU (kowtows): Your humble servant shall abide by Your Majesty´s instructions.

QUEEN: My daughter, here´s a word for you. Chunyu has a fiery temper and drinks heavily. To overcome his youthful headiness, you must forbear from challenging him, but be sweet and tactful. That´s the way to be a good wife. Look after him, so that I won´t have to worry. Though Southern Bough isn´t very far away, wee will no longer be able to see each other from day to day. I can hardly hold back my tears when I think of that. (They weep together)

PRINCESS: I´ll bear your words in mind. (She bids adieu)

【Glassy Slippy】

KING:

The Southern Bough,
the Southern Bough,
don´t consider it low.
Remove the cup,
remove the cup,
from your office desk.
Don´t in the office plant yourself,
nor take long days off;
you need to ride out to inspect your land.
People of different walks of life
may harbor various thoughts.

Hark my order: Sound the bugles and spread the banners. Wee shall see them to the boundary pavilion. (They all walk)

【鲍老催】

（众）

街衢闹杂，
街衢闹杂，
鸾舆直送仙郎发。
秦箫吹彻鸾同跨，
看乘龙，
乘的是，
五花马。
君王驸马多欢哈，
则娘娘公主凄惶煞，
留不住双头踏。

（众）千岁爷，过长亭了。

（王）终须一别，驸马、公主勉之。

（生、旦俯伏介）微臣夫妇，不敢有忘。愿我王、娘娘千岁千岁千千岁。

（生、旦下）

（王）传旨回宫。

【双声子】

（众）

力力喇，力力喇，
都是些人和马。
哜哜咋，哜哜咋，
两下里吹和打。
嘻嘻哈，嘻嘻哈。
去了价，去了价。

【Old Bao in Haste】

OFFICERS, MAIDS:

A hubbub in the street,
a hubbub in the street!
The old couple sends off the younger one;
jade flutes accompany their phoenix ride.
The son-in-law
is riding on
a fine tall steed.
The king and half-son are engrossed in talk;
the queen and daughter gawk through tear-filled eyes.
All the while the procession marches on.

Your Majesty, wee have reached the boundary pavilion.

KING: However far wee may go, wee will have to say goodbye eventually. Take care of yourselves.

CHUNYU, PRINCESS (dropping to their knees and bent low): Wee, your humble servants, will always remember what you´ve said. May Your Majesty and Ladyship live thousands and thousands of years!

(Exeunt Chunyu and Princess)

KING: Hark my order: Return to the palace.

【Alliterated Pairs】

OFFICERS, MAIDS:

Di di da, di di da,
horses and people fill the road.
Chi chi cha, chi chi cha,
cymbals and flutes commingle notes.
Gi gi ga, gi gi ga,
away they go, away they go.

向槐阴路转，
数点宫鸦。

【尾声】

看他们时至气化，
一鞭行色透京华。
似这样夫妻人世上寡。

〔集唐〕

双凤衔书次第飞，
骎骎羽骑历城池。
琼箫暂下《钧天乐》，
今日河南胜昔时。

Toward the palace wee return
to count the palace crows.

【Coda】

You see how time and tide can make a man.
A whip cracks and the town is left behind.
Such a nice pair of man and wife are rare to find!

A pair of phoenixes are flying south;
A line of horsemen speeds through town and town.
The flute pipes up the tune of Happy Times;
The south may prove to have a better clime.

第二十一出　录　　摄

【字字双】

（丑扮府幕官上）

为官只是赌身强，
板障。
文书批点不成行，
混帐。
权官掌印坐黄堂，
旺相。
勾他纸赎与钱粮，
一抢。

自家南柯郡幕录事官是也。阙下正堂，小子权时署印。日高三丈，还不见六房站班，可恶，可恶！

【前腔】

（扮吏上）

山妻叫俺外郎郎，
猾浪。
吏巾儿糊得翅帮帮，
官样。
飞天过海儿桩桩，
蛮放。

Scene 21 The Proxy

(Enter Chief of Staff)

【Coupled Words】

CHIEF:

I sought public office to make a name,
but failed.
I can´t write one good line without mistakes,
too bad.
Now the official seal is in my charge,
very promising,
I can get grain and money by my pen,
like robbing.

I´m the chief of staff of Southern Bough Prefecture. As the Taishou was dismissed from office, the official seal was placed in my hand. I´m in charge of things here — for the moment at least. The sun is already three rods high. Why isn´t there a single member of my staff in the offices? Damn it! Damn it!

(Enter a clerk)

【Ditto】

CLERK:

My old lady nicknamed me clerk-o´-quack,
a trickster.
I starched my hat to make it stiff and tall,
a bureaucrat!
I´ve wheedled and duped my boss more than once,
brazen facedly.

下乡油得嘴光光，

（揖介）销旷。

（丑恼介）咄！

几时不上公堂望，

摇摇摆摆来销旷。

莫非欺负俺老权官？

教你乞拷在眉毛上。

（吏跪介）

恩官兴头忒莽撞，

百事该房识方向。

（作送鸡介）

下乡袖得小鸡公，

送与恩官五更唱。

（丑）好个鸡鸡儿。

（吏）听得老爷好睡觉，出堂忒迟，因此告状的候久都散了。小的想起来，老爷寸金日子，不可错过，下乡捞的两只小鸡，母的宰了，公的送爷报晓。一日之计，全在于寅。

（丑）有意思，有意思。我的都公，请起。（丑跪扶吏起介）我从来衙里没有本《大明律》，可要他不要？

（吏）可有可无。

（丑）问词讼，可要银子不要？

（吏）可有可无。

（丑恼介）不要银子做官么？

（吏）爷既要银子，怎不买本《大明律》看，书底有黄金。

Every village trip oils my smacking lips.
Reporting back.

CHIEF (angrily): Bah!

How long haven't you in your office stopped?
And now you swing and swag to make reports.
Are you testing the power I just assumed?
I can have you beaten up on the spot.

CLERK (kneels):

My lord, you too easily take offense.
I know the rules of conduct well enough.

(He presents a rooster)

In the village I snatched a rooster young.
That's a gift to you to make morning songs.

CHIEF: What a fine cock!

CLERK: I hear my lord likes to sleep late. And you often come so late to the office that those who had been waiting to file lawsuits have lost patience and left. As I understand it, Your Excellency's time is money, and you can't afford to let it slip away like that. So while I was in the country I seized a couple of chickens. I butchered the hen and left the rooster to wake you up in the morning. A proverb says, "A day's work depends on an early start in the morning."

CHIEF: That's an interesting saying — a very interesting saying. My benefactor, please rise to your feet. (He kneels down to help Clerk up) In my office there isn't even a copy of *The Laws of the Ming Dynasty*.[1] Do you think it's necessary to have one?

CLERK: You can do with or without it.

CHIEF: When judging a lawsuit, should I accept silver or not?

CLERK: With or without.

CHIEF (angrily): Without silver, what's the good of being an officer?

CLERK: If my lord really wants silver, why don't you buy a copy of *The Laws of the Ming Dynasty*? There's gold in that book.

(扮报子上、见介)飞报送上。

(丑看报介)右相府一本,"南柯缺官事,奉令旨,驸马淳于棼有点。"呀,新官到了,寸金日子丢在那里?

(报)驸马爷马牌到。

(丑)叫各房打理迎接。

(吏)都有旧规。

(丑)旧规不同:要起驸马府、公主殿;要珍珠轿、销金伞,女户扛抬。

(吏)小的知道。如今事体迫了,爷两只手标票儿才好。(丑作两手标票介)

(吏)一票,叫吏房知会官吏;一票,户房支放钱粮;一票,兵房差点吹手、皂快、轿马勘合;一票,礼房知会生儒、耆老、僧道,又要几个尖嘴的教坊。

(丑)要他怎的?

(吏)会吹。一票,刑房查点囚簿,解送刑具;一票,工房修理府第、家火,第一要个马子、线香。

(丑)这缓得些。

(吏)奶奶下了轿,满地跳。一票,架阁库整顿宗卷交代;一票,承

(Enter a messenger)

MESSENGER (greets Chief): Here comes the latest issue of the official bulletin.

CHIEF (reads): An announcement from the right-hand premier's office: As Southern Bough is in want of a Taishou, His Majesty decrees that Chunyu Fen, the royal son-in-law, be appointed to the position. Ah! A new Taishou is on his way. What will happen to my time-is-money days?

MESSENGER: And here's the itinerary of the royal son-in-law.

CHIEF: Tell each and every office to get prepared for the new Taishou.

CLERK: Wee can follow the old practices.

CHIEF: The usual practices won't work this time. Wee need to build a new official mansion for the royal son-in-law and a palace for the princess. Wee also need a stringed-pearl sedan-chair with a gold-threaded umbrella, and women chair-bearers.

CLERK: Yes, sir. Since time is pressing, you'd better use both hands to draft the directives.

(Chief writes with a brushpen in each hand)

CLERK: One to the Personnel Department to notify all officers and staff members; one to the Finance Department to allot funds; one to the Army Department to arrange a band, footmen, and sedan-chair bearers; one to the Protocol Department to notify the Confucian scholars, country elders, Buddhist monks and Taoist priests, and to send for a couple of sweet-mouthed singers from the opera house.

CHIEF: What are they for?

CLERK: They know how to please the ear. Another one to the Penitentiary Department to head-count the prisoners in the jail and put them in the stocks; one to the Construction Department to renovate the houses and repair the furniture. First and foremost is to prepare a chamber stool and incense cords.

CHIEF: Those are not urgent, are they?

CLERK: Once off the sedan-chair, Her Ladyship needs must relieve herself. One more to the Archives to clear up the files; one to the Secretariat

发科写理脚色、宪纲；一票，杂办吏铺毡结彩；一票，带办吏送心红纸张；一票，各马驿下程中火；一票，各社总选门子，要一丈二尺长。

(丑)太长么?

(吏)新太爷还长一丈八。一票，娘娘庙借珍珠八角轿伞；一票，表子铺借铺陈、胭粉、馨香。

(丑)这个使不得，要星夜制造才是。

【亭前柳】

此郡镇南方，
前任总寻常。
缘何差驸马?
甚样有辉光!

(合)

宪纲，
前件开停当。
分付该房，
须急切要端详。

【前腔】

珠翠缕金装，
怕没现钱粮?

(吏)没钱粮，有处。

因公且科派，
事后再商量。(合前)

to make a copy of everyone´s resume; one to the Odd-job Office to spread out carpets and hang up streamers; one to the Couriers Office to deliver the invitations written on bright-red paper; one to the posthouses along the main road to have the meals ready; one to the various guilds to recommend footmen twelve feet tall.

CHIEF: Isn´t that a bit too tall?

CLERK: The new Taishou could be beyond our measure. One more to the Temple of Mothers to borrow their pearl sedan-chair and octagonal umbrella; one to the brothels to borrow their decorations, powder, rouge and perfume.

CHIEF: No, no. Whorehouse things won´t do. Wee must have them produced overnight.

【Willow by the Pavilion】

As this prefecture lies far south,
the previous chiefs were common knaves.
Why a royal kinsman this time?
What a distinction wee have gained!
(Refrain)
In line with the law
everything has been well arranged.
Tell offices all
to make haste and take the utmost care.

【Ditto】

For all the need of gold and pearls,
I fear wee don´t have ready cash.

CLERK: Don´t worry. There´s always a way out.

Levy it from whatever source.
Paying is but an afterthought.
(Refrain)

权官才打劫，
正官便交摄。
支分各色人，
远远去迎接。

The proxy has just fleeced the folks
When the chief follows on his heels.
Every office is mobilized
To welcome in the latest boss.

第二十二出　之　　郡

〔集唐〕（队子上）

结束征车换黑貂，
行人芳草马声娇。
紫云新苑移花处，
洞里神仙碧玉箫。

请了。俺们驾上差来，护送公主、驸马爷南柯赴任去，迤逦数程，公主、驸马起早也。

【满庭芳】

（生、旦、众上）

紫陌尘闲，
画桥风浅，
鸾旗影动星躔。

（旦）

朝云浓淡，
行色映花钿。
为问夕阳亭饯，
下鸾舆惨动离筵。

（合）

关南路，
春晖绿草，
何日再朝天。

Scene 22 Reaching Town

(Enter a troop of soldiers)

SOLDIERS:

The carts packed, the Taishou has changed his hat;
The horses canter through the sweet fresh grass.
When transplanting a flower from virgin land,
Celestial music fills the fairy caves.

Wee were dispatched by His Majesty to escort the princess and her husband to their new office at Southern Bough. Wee have already covered several days′ distance. The princess and the royal son-in-law are up early.

(Enter Chunyu and Princess, with attendants)

【Sweet Garden】

CHUNYU:

Red dust has settled down,
and playfully the wind
nuzzles the star-embroidered flags.

PRINCESS:

Flushed with the changing hues,
my face reflects the morning dew.
The farewell party in the setting sun,
has faded into a distant memory.

ALL:

The south-bound road,
though lush and sappy green,
will it lead back to heaven′s side?

PRINCESS:

The palace blossom bade the warbler stay,

〔木兰花令〕

宫花欲唤流莺住，
恰是南柯迁莺处。
绣帘娇马出都城，
宝盖斜盘金凤缕。
华年得意频相顾，
笑问卿卿来几许？
绿槐风软度行云，
回首沁园东畔路。

（生）公主，自拜辞了君王、国母，不觉数程，此去南柯相近了。左右趱行。（行介）

【甘州歌】

宫闱别饯，
摆五花头踏，
迤逦而前。
都人凝望，
十里绣帘高卷。
四方宦游谁得选，
一对夫妻俨若仙。

（合）

青袍旧，
绿鬓鲜，
大槐宫里着貂蝉。
香车进，
宝马连，
一时携手笑嫣然。

But it said it's migrating to the south.
Out of the capital in tasseled carts,
Gold phoenixes fly with the canopy.

In the bloom of life I was often asked:
How many years do I intend to stay?
The soft wind puffs away the floating clouds;
On the horizon lies my maiden home.

CHUNYU: Dear princess, since we parted from your parents we've been on the road for several days. Southern Bough can't be far off. Let's set off immediately. (They walk)

【Song from Ganzhou】
CHUNYU:
Soon as the banquet closed,
my guard of honor led the way
from one post to the next.
The townsfolk stopped to stare,
and modest maidens raised the blinds to ask:
who, of all men, is that selected groom
with a wife gorgeous as a fairy queen?
ALL:
His old gray gown,
her jet-black bangs,
a striking match in the Sophora realm.
Rumbling carts,
harnessed steeds,
how sweetly smiles the couple hand in hand!

(Enter an officer)
OFFICER: The chief of staff of Southern Bough Prefecture has sent me to deliver a copy of his directives for your approval and to welcome Your Excellency.

（扮官吏上）南柯郡录事，差官吏投批，迎接爷爷。

（生取看介）发批回；前去伺候。（官吏应介）

【前腔】

（生）

宫花压帽偏，
问有何能德，
紫绶腰悬？
玉楼人并，
翠盖绿油轻展。
指挥风景迟去辇，
为惜流光懒下鞭。

（合）

携琴瑟，
坐锦鞯，
一条官路直如弦。
游春样，
尽世缘，
秦楼箫史弄云烟。

（众）禀爷，南柯郡界了。

（丑）南柯郡录事参军迎接老大人。

（生）远劳了。

（丑）不敢。有新轿伞、兵卫、男女轿夫，齐站下班迎接。

（生）知道了，就回。（丑应下）

CHUNYU (accepting and glancing through them): Tell him it´s appreciated. Go and get everything prepared. (Officer makes a response and exits)

【Ditto】

CHUNYU:

Royal favors adorn my hat.
What have I achieved to deserve
the gold seal at my waist,
the jade girl by my side,
the leafy canopy above my head?
The charming scenery arrests my coach;
my whip hates to disturb this precious time.

ALL:

The zithers sound;
the saddles bound;
the broad official road is bowstring straight.
On a vernal jaunt,
wee savor life;
the clouds are dancing to the master´s flute.

ATTENDANTS: Your Excellency, wee have reached the border of Southern Bough.

(Enter Chief of Staff)

CHIEF: The chief of staff of Southern Bough welcomes Your Excellency.

CHUNYU: Thank you for coming so far out to meet me.

CHIEF: You´re welcome. I´ve brought with me a brand-new sedan-chair and umbrella. Male and female chair-bearers and guards are waiting over there for your orders.

CHUNYU: I see. You can go back now.

(Chief makes a response and exits)

（内介）合郡官吏迎接爷爷。

（生）起去，伺候。

（内介）生儒迎接老大人。

（生）请起，郡中相见。（应介）

（内介）僧道耆老迎接爷爷。

（生）都起去。

（内介）教坊女乐们迎接爷爷。

（生）趱行。（众妓鼓吹引介）

【前腔】

鸾铃动翠钿，
看满前旗影，
冠佩翩联。
争来迎跪，
陌上红尘深浅。
邦君夫人鸾凤侣，
父老儿童竹马年。

（合）

军民闹，
士女喧，
妓衣时杂紫衣禅。
弹筝觑，
击鼓传，
锦车催怕日华偏。

VOICE WITHIN: All the officials and staff of Southern Bough are here to welcome Your Excellency.

CHUNYU: To your feet, and wait for orders.

VOICE WITHIN: The Confucian scholars are here to welcome Your Excellency.

CHUNYU: Please rise. I´ll receive you in town. (Response in chorus)

VOICE WITHIN: The Buddhist monks, Taoist priests, and country elders are here to welcome Your Excellency.

CHUNYU: To your feet.

VOICE WITHIN: Singers from the opera house are here to welcome Your Excellency.

CHUNYU: Let´s move on.

(The singers lead the way, playing instruments)[1]

【Ditto】

CHUNYU:

Bells jingle on the horses´ necks,
flags stretch as far as one can see
and long sleeves flow like waves.
People have thronged the streets,
tramping the road into red powdered dust.
The Taishou and wife make a perfect match;
the old and young turn out to pay respects.

ALL:

Men´s husky throats,
girls´ chirping tongues,
the singers´ colors mix with monks´ drab gowns.
The harps vibrate,
the drums resound,
the convoy has driven the sun down west.

（生）远远望见如烟如雾、郁郁葱葱者，是何地方？
（众）十里之近，南柯郡城。
（生）公主，真好一座城台。

【前腔】

遥遥十里前，
见葱葱佳气，
非雾非烟。
雉飞鸾舞，
台观叠来苍远。
似兰亭景幽围翠岭，
春谷泉鸣浸玉田。

（合）

山如画，
水似缠，
自怜难见此山川。
重门拥，
旌旆悬，
玉楼金榜洞中天。

（内灯笼接上介）（众）禀太爷，进城。
（生）今夕公馆休息，五鼓升任。

【尾声】

闪纱灯一道星毬转，
曜街衢棨戟森然。

CHUNYU: I see in the distance a verdant blur like haze or fog. What place is that?

ATTENDANTS: That´s the prefectural seat of Southern Bough. It´s less than three miles from here.

CHUNYU: Princess dear, isn´t it a wonderful place!

【Ditto】

There, waiting three miles right ahead
is our city in vernal green.
It´s neither haze nor dream.
Behind the parapets
extend the roofs of towers and halls.
It is surrounded by the lushest hills;
bubbling springs irrigate the richest fields.

ALL:

The landscape hills,
the ribbon streams,
one can hardly imagine such a scene!
Gate after gate,
flags upon flags,
the cave boasts a heaven of gold and jade.

(Enter lantern-bearers)

BEARERS: Welcome Your Excellency to the city.

CHUNYU: Tonight we´ll stay in the official mansion. At daybreak tomorrow I´ll hold my first audience.

【Coda】

The stars have appeared with the lanterns´ dance;
frosty light sparkles from the weapons´ blades.
Dear princess,

公主，

　　和你且把下马公堂笑铺展。

〔集唐〕

露冕新承明主恩，
山城别是武陵源。
笙歌锦绣云霄里，
南北东西拱至尊。

let´s enjoy our first night in our new official home.

Royal favors shower on me from above;
The hilly town conceals a lovely nest.
Pipes and flutes compose a heavenly tune;
All four corners buttress the central throne.

第二十三出　念　　女

【夜游湖】

（老旦引众上）

窣地荣华开内苑，
紫云袍花胜朝天。

（众）

扇影斜分，
宫娥慢拥，
望南柯阿娇仙眷。

〔忆秦娥〕

（老）

屏山列，
香风暗展青槐叶。

（众）

青槐叶，
洞天深处，
彩云明灭。

（老）

女儿十五辞宫阙，
南柯婉瞰西楼月。

Scene 23 Motherly Concern

(Enter Queen, with maids)

【Night Tour on the Lake】

QUEEN:

The garden erupts in a riot of blooms;
embroidered robes fulfill ambitious dreams.

MAIDS:

Wee palace maids
fan out behind the queen,
who fixes her gaze toward Southern Bough.

QUEEN:

The mountains spread;
A scented breeze unfurls Sophora leaves.

MAIDS:

Sophora leaves,
Above our cavern depths,
Obscure the rosy clouds.

QUEEN:

At fifteen Daughter left home for the south,
Where she often ascends the western tower.

MAIDS:

The western tower,
Over which wild geese race,
Grieves separated souls.

QUEEN: I´m the queen of the Great Sophora Kingdom. My daughter has been in Southern Bough for nearly twenty years. Yesterday I received a letter from her, saying that she feels somewhat exhausted by the burden of raising many children. She´s emaciated and can´t stand the hot climate,

（合）

西楼月，

南飞鹊影，

照人离别。

自家大槐安国母，一女远在南柯，将二十年。昨有书来，说他儿女累多，肌瘦怕热，近于堑江城清凉地面，筑一座瑶台城避暑，要请佛王经千卷供养。已着郡主去禅智寺请问契玄师父，还未到来。

【玩仙灯】

（贴持经上）

禅智谈玄，

又请下的法王经卷。

（见叩头介）郡主琼英叩头，千岁。

（老）平身。手中所进，是何经卷？

（贴）到问契玄禅师，他说，凡生产过多，定有触污地神天圣之处。可请一部《血盆经》去，叫他母子们长斋三年，总行忏悔，自然灾消福长，减病延年。娘娘听启：

【玉山颓】

这《血盆经》卷，

大慈悲孩儿目连。

（老）因何？

（贴）目连尊者为救母走西天，经过羽州追阳县，旷野之中，见一座血盆池地狱，有多少女人，散发被枷，饮其池中污血。目连尊者动问狱主，此是因何？狱主言道，这妇人呵，

so they recently built a marble palace at the cooler riverside resort of Gorgeville. She said she would like to have a thousand volumes of Buddhist scriptures in her palace. So I asked Duchess Qiongying to make a trip to Chan Wisdom Temple to consult Master Qixuan. I wonder if she´s back yet.

(Enter Duchess Qiongying, holding Buddhist scriptures)

【Celestial Lamp Dancers】

QIONGYING:

To Chan Wisdom for wise talk,
and here are scriptures from the Great Buddha.

(She kowtows to Queen) Duchess Qiongying prostrates herself at your feet. May Your Ladyship live a thousand years!

QUEEN: Please rise. Which sutra is that in your hand?

QIONGYING: In answer to my request, Master Qixuan said that those who have too profusely reproduced must have profaned either the earthly gods or the heavenly deities. Therefore, it would be most appropriate to copy and chant the *Blood Pool Sutra*. Both mother and children should stick to a vegetarian diet for three years and repent of their misdeeds. In that way, they may turn misfortune into fortune, and live long and healthy lives. This is what he said:

【Jade Mountain Collapses】

The *Blood Pool Sutra* talks about
Maudgalya,[1] the most filial child of all.

QUEEN: Why say so?

QIONGYING: He was trekking in the west to save his mother from hell when in the wilderness of Zhuiyang County, Yu Prefecture, he came upon a hellish pool of blood. Immersed in the pool were many disheveled women in shackles, drinking the dirty blood. He asked the warden why they were so treated. The warden replied that their

生产时血污了溪河，

煎茶供厌污了良善。

(老)是了，供奉三宝的茶水，被血水污，因此果报。后来?

(贴)目连尊者听见，大哭起来:“俺母亲也应受此苦楚了。”竟以神通，走向佛所，致心顶礼:“惟愿世尊为我等开示，云何报答慈亲，脱离此苦?”佛言，善哉!

待酬恩眷，

则三年内长斋拜忏，

声声把弥陀念。

(老)念了怎的?

(贴)有好处。

渡河船，

便是血盆池上产金莲。

【前腔】

(老)

佛爷方便，

向诸天把真言示宣。

想来则有妇女苦，生男种女大家的；便是产时昏闷，倾污水于溪河，也是丈夫之罪。怎那经文呵，

明写着外面无干，

偏则是女人之谴?

便宣紫衣官一员，分付马上捧持此经一千部，星夜前去。

parturient blood had defiled the rivers and streams,
the water from which they used to make tea for gods.

QUEEN: That explains it. It´s retribution for the contaminated tea they offered to Buddha. What did Maudgalya do then?

QIONGYING: When he heard that, he burst into tears and cried, "My mother must be suffering this very same punishment!" Then he used his magic powers and came before the Great Buddha. Prostrating himself, he pleaded, "May Great Buddha show me how I can redeem my mother and repay her for raising me." The Great Buddha said, "You raised a good question."

To repay her kindness,
keep a vegetarian diet for three years,
and keep praying from day to day.

QUEEN: What will that bring about?

QIONGYING: You´ll certainly benefit.

A golden lotus will appear on the bloody pool
to ferry you across.

【Ditto】

QUEEN:

Wee thank the Great Buddha
for revealing the truth to all the worlds!

But, now that I come to think of it, how is it that only women suffer? It takes both a man and a woman to produce a child. In our postnatal faintness, how were wee able to throw bloody water into the river? It was the husband who did that! But why does the sutra

proclaim it has nothing to do with man,
and woman alone is to take the blame?

Now summon a palace officer, and tell him to leave immediately for Southern Bough with one thousand copies of the sutra.

紫衣乘传，
直赍到瑶台宫院，
免到追阳县。
说与公主呵，
教他广流传，
把俺老娘三世也带生天。

古来儿女得娘怜，
女病娘愁各一天。
惟有受经勤忏悔，
南柯应产玉池莲。

The officer must take
the tomes to the steps of her summer home
to spare her a trip to Zhuiyang.
Please tell the princess
to propagate the Buddha's word
so that my old self may also ascend to sky.

A mother always cares about her child,
More so with a sick daughter far from home.
With constant prayer and repentance deep
A lotus flower should sprout in Southern Bough.

第二十四出　风　谣

【清江引】

（紫衣走马捧经背敕上）

紫衣郎走马南柯下，
一轴山如画。
公主性柔佳，
驸马官潇洒。
俺且在这里整仪容权下马。

事有足差，
理有故然。

自家紫衣官是也。承国王、国母之命，送佛经与公主供养，并加升驸马官爵门荫。才入这南柯郡境，则见青山浓翠，绿水渊环；草树光辉，鸟兽肥润。但有人家所在，园池整洁，檐宇森齐。何止苟美苟完，且是兴仁兴让。街衢平直，男女分行。但是田野相逢，老少交头一揖。曾游几处，近见此邦。且住，待俺借问公主平安，看百姓怎生议论？前面几个父老来了。

【孝白歌】

（众扮父老捧香上）

Scene 24 Folk Lyrics

(Enter a palace officer in a purple robe, riding, with a scroll slung over his shoulders and scriptures in his hand)

【River Qing Interlude】

OFFICER:

A purple officer gallops to the south;
the scenes spread like a painted scroll.
Amiable is the princess;
affable is the Taishou.
Let me dismount to dust and smooth my clothes.

However puzzling things may seem,
A reason always lurks behind.

I´m a palace officer. The king and queen have ordered me to take these Buddhist scriptures to the princess, and to announce the promotion of the royal son-in-law. As soon as I set foot in Southern Bough, it seemed that the mountains had become greener, the waters clearer and the trees lusher. Even the animals look plumper! Around every spruce little cottage, I find well-tended fields and gardens. It´s more than idyllic or idealistic; it´s a place where ethical codes and propriety prevail. Look! The streets and avenues are smooth and straight, men and women do not mingle. When people meet, even in the fields, they bow to each other. I´ve been to many places but nowhere comes near this one. Well, just to make sure I´ve got the right impression, let me inquire after the princess to see how people respond. Here come some elders.

(Enter elders holding joss sticks in their hands)

【White Filial Piety】

ELDERS:

征徭薄，
米谷多，
官民易亲风景和。
老的醉颜酡，
后生们鼓腹歌。
你道俺捧灵香，
因甚么？
(紫前问介)敢问老官人，公主好么？
(父老叹介)(唱前)
你道俺捧灵香，
因甚么？(下)

(紫)这些父老们，欢欢喜喜，唱个甚的？又邀的几个秀才来了。

【前腔】
(众扮秀才捧香上)
行乡约，
制雅歌，
家尊五伦人四科。
因他俺切磋，
他将俺琢磨。
你道俺捧灵香，
因甚么？
(紫)敢问秀才，公主好么？
(秀叹介)(唱前)
你道俺捧灵香，
因甚么？(下)

Light are the taxes;
good is the harvest;
the government and people live in harmony.
Elders enjoy a cup of wine;
youngsters sing songs on stomachs full.
Why do you think
wee are holding these incense sticks?

OFFICER (greeting them): May I ask you seniors how the princess is?

ELDERS (passionately):

Why do you think
wee are holding these incense sticks?

(Exeunt Elders)

OFFICER: Fancy seeing old men sing like that! What makes them so happy? Ah, here come some Confucian scholars.

(Enter scholars holding joss sticks in their hands)

【Ditto】

SCHOLARS:

The village-bond works;
classical music rings;
the moral code takes root in every home.
Wee study the code carefully,
the code carefully guides our way.
Why do you think
wee are holding these incense sticks?

OFFICER: May I ask you scholars how the princess is?

SCHOLARS (passionately):

Why do you think
wee are holding these incense sticks?

(Exeunt Scholars)

【前腔】

（扮村妇女捧香上）

多风化，
无暴苛，
俺婚姻以时歌《伐柯》。
家家老小和，
家家男女多。
你道俺捧灵香，
因甚么？

（紫）敢问女娘们，公主好么？

（妇叹介）（唱前）

你道俺捧灵香，
因甚么？（下）

【前腔】

（扮商人捧香上）

平税课，
不起科，
商人离家来安乐窝。
关津任你过，
昼夜总无他。
你道俺捧灵香，
因甚么？

（紫）大哥几分面善。

（商）俺是京师人，在此生意。

（紫）正是，听见公主可好？

（商）俺们正去太爷生祠进香，保祝驸马、公主二人千岁千岁。

(Enter village women holding joss sticks in their hands)

【Ditto】

WOMEN:

Nice manners are in;
savage laws are out;
decency governs the lasses and lads.
All generations live in peace;
the population has increased.
Why do you think
wee are holding these incense sticks?

OFFICER: May I ask you womenfolk how the princess is?

WOMEN (passionately):

Why do you think
wee are holding these incense sticks?

(Exeunt Women)

(Enter merchants holding joss sticks in their hands)

【Ditto】

MERCHANTS:

Taxes have been reduced,
and taxed items few.
To this place merchants flock to lay their base.
No toll booths block the roads or fords;
traffic is open day and night.
Why do you think
wee are holding these incense sticks?

OFFICER: Big brothers, it seems wee have met somewhere before.

MERCHANTS: That´s quite likely, for wee too are from the capital. Wee are doing business here.

OFFICER: I see. How´s the princess? Is she doing well?

MERCHANTS: Wee are on our way to offer joss sticks at the shrine of Taishou Chunyu. Wee wish him and the princess a thousand years of life.

(紫)你又不是这境内人民，保他则甚？

(商)淳于爷到任二十年，人间夜户不闭，狗足生毛。便是俺们商旅，也往来安乐，知恩报恩。

(紫)前面一伙老的，一伙秀才，一伙妇女，都捧着香往那里去？唱些甚么？

(商)你是不知。这南柯郡，自这太爷到任以来，雨顺风调，民安国泰，终年则是游嬉过日，口里都是德政歌谣。各乡村都写着太爷牌位儿供养，则这是大生祠，祠宇前后九进，堂高三丈，立有一丈五尺高的几座德政碑，碑上记他行过德政，二十年中，便一日行一件，也有七千二百多条，言之不尽。

(紫)想是学霸刁民胡弄的。

(商作恼介)(唱前)咳，

　　你道俺捧灵香，

　　因甚么？(下)

(紫)奇哉！奇哉！真个有这等得民心的官府。

OFFICER: You aren´t natives of this region. Why are you praying for them?

MERCHANTS: During the twenty years of Lord Chunyu´s reign, people have found no need to lock their doors at night, and even the dogs have lost their vigilance. This peacefulness has encouraged many people like us to start business here. It´s only natural for us to show our gratitude.

OFFICER: Just now I met a group of elders, some scholars, and some women. They were all holding joss sticks too. Where were they heading? And what were they singing about?

MERCHANTS: Wee would be glad to tell you. Since Lord Chunyu took office, Southern Bough has been blessed with the most agreeable weather. Life is prosperous and people are content. Every day is a holiday, and lyrics abound in praise of his humane rule. Every village has erected a shrine to worship him. And the temple wee are going to is the biggest one. Its compound consists of nine courtyards in a row. The main hall is more than thirty feet high, housing several fifteen-feet-high stelae, on which records of his good deeds are inscribed. Even if he did only one good thing a day, during the past twenty years that would have amounted to more than seventy-two hundred entries. In fact, his bounty is inexhaustible.

OFFICER: Maybe those so-called good deeds were invented by a handful of crooks or toady scholars.

MERCHANTS (angrily): Bah!

Why do you think
wee are holding these incense sticks?

(Exeunt Merchants)

OFFICER: Amazing! Can there really be a government so loved by its people?

二十年事事循良，
遍歌谣处处焚香。
立生祠字字纪实，
诏书中一一端详。

Twenty years has taken a thriving course;
Folk lyrics and incense smoke fill the place.
The stelae bear witness in solid rock.
Good truth will be reported to the king.

第二十五出　玩　　月

（录事官上）

官居录事尊崇，
放支帐历粗通。
再不遇缺官看印，
教我录事衙门嗑风。
新近一场诧事：
公主生长深宫。
二十年南柯地方怕热，
访知堑江城西北凉风；
筑一座瑶台城子，
单单一个公主避暑其中；
周、田二公督造，
果然不日成功。
怎生唤做瑶台城子？
四门有高台玉石玲珑。
驸马、公主新来便待赏月，
那头行的正是周、田二公。（虚下）

【绕池游】

（扮周、田上）

人间怎么？

Scene 25 Full-moon Night

(Enter Chief of Staff)

CHIEF:

The chief of staff is a personage,
And a moneymonger of lineage.
Were there always a Taishou in the chair,
I'd have nothing to eat but empty air.
A weird thing happened recently:
The princess in the palace deep
Can no more bear the twenty years of southern heat.
Somehow she learned Gorgeville enjoys a northwest breeze
And promptly raised a palace in its lee,
Where she alone takes shelter from the sweltry sun.
Zhou and Tian oversaw the project,
And in no time it became perfect.
For what is it called a marble palace?
Because delicate jade towers rise above the gates.
Princess and husband will arrive to watch the moon;
Zhou and Tian are coming to join their party soon.

(He steps aside)

(Enter Zhou Bian and Tian Zihua)

【Around the Pool】

ZHOU, TIAN:

What's good to be human?
Better be nether ministers,
with feasts to attend in our leisure hour.
Up rises the silver dish,

地下为参佐，
乘公暇得从深座。
玉镜台移，
绛桥星度，
下秦楼双鸣玉珂。

（周）下官司宪周弁。
（田）下官司农田子华。
（周）蒙太老先生提挈，赞相有年。近因公主避暑于堑江西畔，筑了座瑶台城。今夕驸马、公主驾临，正当明月三五，良可贺也。
（田）以下官所言，瑶台虽则壮丽，江外切近檀萝，公主移居，深所未便。
（周）有堑江城一卫兵马，可保无危。（内响道介）
（田）驸马、公主蚤来，我们且须回避。（虚下）

【破齐阵】

（生、旦引众上）

绕境全低玉宇，
当窗半落银河。
月影灵娟，
天临贵婿，
清夜暂回参佐。
同移燕寝幽香远，
并起鸾骖暮霭多，
何处似南柯？

ferrying stars across the vault.
A phoenix couple will ascend the tower.

ZHOU: I´m Zhou Bian, the security chief.

TIAN: I´m Tian Zihua, the finance minister.

ZHOU: Thanks to the favor of His Excellency Mr. Chunyu, we two have enjoyed prominence for many years. As the princess wishes to escape from the summer heat, we recently constructed a marble palace on the west bank of the gorge. Today is the fifteenth of the month, the full-moon night. The royal son-in-law and the princess are coming to celebrate the occasion.

TIAN: In my opinion, though the palace is magnificent, it´s unwise for the princess to live here all by herself. Rattan Sandalwood lies on the other side of the river.

ZHOU: A division of soldiers is stationed in Gorgeville. Her safety is guaranteed.

(Shouts heard within clearing pedestrians from the street)

TIAN: The royal son-in-law and princess have arrived. We´d better get out of the way.

(Exeunt Zhou and Tian)

(Enter Chunyu and Princess, attended)

【Smashing the Qis】

CHUNYU, PRINCESS:

The tower protrudes above surrounding roofs;
into its windows pours the Milky Stream.
Moonlight appeals,
heaven invites,
no other company is required.
We move our residence in fragrant night;
our horses canter through the dense twilight.
Nowhere can match our Southern Bough.

(周、田上)(吏进禀介)司宪司农禀见。

(生)叫该吏禀知，公主在此，不便请见，请二位老爷先回。(吏应禀)(周、田下)

(生)我为公主造此一城，都是白玉砌裹，五门十二楼，真乃神仙境界也。今夜月明如洗，倾倒一杯。

(老贴酒上)

金屋人双美，
瑶台月一轮。

酒到。

【普天乐犯】

(生)

蹍光华，
城一座，
把温太真装砌的嵯峨。
自王姬宝殿生来，
配太守玉堂深坐。
瑞烟微香百和，
红云度花千朵。
有甚的不朱颜笑呵？
眼见的眉峰皱破。
对清光满斟，一杯香糯。

(Reenter Zhou and Tian)

CLERK (enters to announce): The chief of security and the finance minister are waiting outside.

CHUNYU: Tell them their company is not requested tonight. The princess wants to make it a family occasion. So they´re dismissed. (Clerk makes a response and exits)

(Exeunt Zhou and Tian)

CHUNYU: I´ve designed and built this palace especially for you. Its outside walls are made of pure white marble, and it has five gates and twelve towers like those in fairyland. Tonight, the moon looks as if it were freshly washed. Let´s have a toast.

(Enter a maid with wine)

MAID:

A charming couple beam like gold;
A bright moon shines on silver towers.

Here´s wine.

【Everyone Happy】

CHUNYU:

The brilliant light
above the palace
makes its towers stand out in high relief.
It blends the grandeur of a royal home
and the solemnity of a Taishou´s hall.
Hundreds of incense sticks perfume the air;
thousands of blossoms burst into a cloud.
Why can´t all these evoke a smile from you
but you should knit your brows into a knot?
Let´s drink a toast to the moon,
with a cup of fragrant wine.

(旦叹介)甚般好景，苦没心情，奈何？奈何？

(生)是了，你饮兴欠佳，叫孩子们劝你。请王孙、贵女出来。

(杂扮二小男小女上)

　　月儿光，月儿光，

　　娑婆树下好烧香。

老爷，亲娘，吃一杯酒儿么？

(灌旦酒、旦笑介)我吃，我吃。

【雁过沙犯】

(旦)

　　姮娥，

　　自在争多，

　　养孩儿恁个那些儿不病过？

　　念载光阴一掷梭，

　　大的儿攻书课；

　　次的儿敢聪明似哥，

　　小丫头也会梳裹。

　　霎儿间，

　　眼前提着，

　　又校得心头活。

【倾杯犯】

(生)

　　娇波，倚瑶台，

　　新镜磨，

　　嵌青天人负荷。

PRINCESS (sighs): No matter how beautiful the night is, I´m not in the mood to drink. I can´t help it. I just can´t help it.

CHUNYU: I see. You´re in low spirits. I´ll get our children to cheer you up. Call the children here.

(Enter two boys and two girls)

CHILDREN:

The moon is round, the moon is bright,
Let´s offer incense in the night.

Dad and Mom, please have a cup of wine. (They press wine on Princess)

PRINCESS (smiling): All right, I´ll drink.

【Wild Geese Honking】

PRINCESS:

Dear Chang Er,[1]
how I envy your carefree life!
Bearing so many babies simply ruins one´s health.
Twenty years of days and nights have shuttled past:
The eldest son is now at school;
my second son seems to be brighter still;
even the youngest girl knows how to comb.
In a flash,
as they appear before my eyes,
old memories come back to life.

【Three Cheers Overture】

CHUNYU:

Oh, the bright moon!
It hangs like a bronze mirror freshly ground
on welkin´s backdrop just above our heads.

CHILDREN:

Just add

（杂）

消多儿阵微风，
一茎清露，
半缕残霞，
淡写明抹。
称道你洞府仙人，
清凉无暑，
爱弄娑婆。

（合）

好大槐安，
团圆桂影今夜满南柯。

（旦）夫妻儿女，真是团圞，只为哥儿们长成，亲事未定，热我心怀。

（杂）娘住这瑶台之上，怕忒高寒些儿？

【山桃红犯】

（旦）

一些些思量过，
闷哟哟怎题破？
看这座瑶台是不比其他，
界断银河冷淡些儿个。
便似背儿夫窃药向寒宫躲，
念瑶芳怎学的嫦娥。

（内介）报，报，报，令旨到。

（紫衣上宣旨介）令旨到，跪听宣读。制曰："寡人闻之，治国之法，一曰贤贤，二曰亲亲。恩礼之施，用此为准。咨汝公主瑶芳、厥配南柯

an occasional puff of wind,
a string of dewdrops on grass blades,
and a faint strip of rosy cloud
across the canvas of the sky.
Such life is promised in a fairy cave,
cool in the summer heat,
reading the Buddhist text.

ALL:

Oh, the Great Sophora!
A full moon pours its light all over Southern Bough.

PRINCESS: Husband and wife, parents and children, it´s really a happy union of the family. However, it makes me agitated to think that our sons have grown up and yet they´re not engaged.

CHILDREN: Mom, isn´t it a bit chilly living in this lofty tower?

【Mountain Peach Red】

PRINCESS:

I´ve given that considerable thought.
And yet I´d rather keep it to myself.
I like this marble palace mainly for its height,
though it´s chilling to stay aloft on Milky Way.
It seems I´m secretly seeking the longevity drug,
but I doubt if I can make it like Chang Er.[2]

VOICE WITHIN: Report, report, report. Here comes an imperial decree. (Enter Palace Officer)

OFFICER (announces): Here´s His Majesty´s decree. Kneel and listen. It reads: I, your sovereign, hear that the way to rule a country is to respect the respectable ones and to love the loved ones. With respect and love as guidelines, everything falls into place. Twenty years ago, I married my

郡太守驸马都尉淳于棼，自下车以来，将二十载，仁风广被，比屋歌谣，寡人心甚重之。兹特进封食邑三千户，爵上柱国、集议院大学士、开府仪同三司，仍行南柯郡事。二男二女，俱以门荫授官，许聘王属，与国咸休。钦哉！谢恩。”

(生、旦叩头)千岁千岁千千岁。

(紫衣叩头见生、旦介)恭喜公主、驸马高升。

(生扯紫介)劳了。

(紫)娘娘还有懿旨：请下《血盆经》千卷，送与公主供养流传，消灾长福。

(生)齐家治国，只用孔夫子之道，这佛教全然不用。

(旦)奴家一向不知，怎生是孔夫子之道？

(生)孔子之道，君臣有义，父子有亲，夫妇有别，长幼有序，朋友有信。

(旦)依你说，俺国里从来没有孔子之道，一般立了君臣之义，俺和驸马一般夫妇有别，孩子们一样与你父子有亲，他兄妹们依然行走

daughter Princess Yaofang to Lieutenant Chunyu Fen, who was later appointed Taishou of Southern Bough Prefecture. During his term of office there, benevolence has prevailed and the people sing his praises. Wee appreciate what he has done, and therefore have decided to confer on him the highest honorary title of *Shangzhuguo*, together with a fief of three thousand households. He is also appointed member of the consultative academy. With regard to official residence and guard of honor he is entitled to those of a cabinet member while he shall still exercise the duties of Taishou of Southern Bough. His two sons and two daughters shall enjoy inheritable titles and they are allowed to marry members of the royal family, thus binding their fate to that of the reign. That is my wish. Express your gratitude.

CHUNYU, PRINCESS (kowtowing): May His Majesty live thousands and thousands of years!

OFFICER (kowtowing to Chunyu and Princess): Congratulations to you both on the promotion.

CHUNYU (helping Officer to his feet): We´re most indebted to you.

OFFICER: Her Ladyship the Queen has a message as well. She has begged from Buddha one thousand copies of the *Blood Pool Sutra*, and here they are for the princess to read and propagate. It will help turn misfortune into fortune.

CHUNYU: We only need Confucius´ teachings to guide family and state affairs. What´s the use of Buddhist scriptures?

PRINCESS: I´ve never learned anything about Confucius´ teachings. What are they?

CHUNYU: Confucius teaches us that fealty should govern the relations between the subjects and their sovereign, love between son and father, respect between wife and man, order between the younger and the older, and trust between friends.

PRINCESS: Well, my country has never heard of Confucius´ teachings. So how would you explain the fact that wee subjects also do fealty to the sovereign, you and I respect each other, our children love their father, and

有序，这却因何?

(生笑介)说是这等说，便与公主流传这经卷罢了。

公主瑶台养病身，
一天恩诏满门新。
但愿福随长命女，
相依佛度有缘人。

the siblings march in good order?

CHUNYU (laughing): Never mind. That´s what the books say. But, if you wish it, we´ll spread the teachings of Buddha.

The princess recuperates in the tower
When royal favors rain down from the sky.
May she enjoy a long and healthy life;
Buddha will help those who believe in him.

第二十六出　启　　寇

【梨花儿】

（丑扮贼太子上）

小小的檀萝生下咱，
生下咱太子好那查。
没有了老婆较子傻，
嗏，
但婆娘好把咱檀郎打。

自家檀萝国王位下四太子是也。小名檀郎，性格风洒。父王分下咱三千赤驳军，镇守全萝西道。日昨丧了房下，急切要寻个填房。恰好一场天大姻缘，那大槐安国金枝公主，嫁了南柯郡守，随夫之任，怕府里地方燥热，单作瑶台城一座，在堑江地面，与俺国相近。老天，老天，他那里是怕热，是不耐烦，要撇开汉子，自由自在，分明天赐我姻缘也。我待点精兵一千，打破瑶台城，抢了公主。则未知他意思如何？早已差小卒儿扮作卖花郎打看去，早晚到来。

（贴扮报子花鼓上）报，报，报，好事到。

（丑）快说来。

Scene 26 The Enemy Roused

(Enter Prince of Rattan Sandalwood)

【Pear Blossoms】

PRINCE:

The peewee Sandalwood has given birth
to a young prince of admirable looks.
One manages poorly without a wife.
Oops!
But the old hag was fond of beating me.

I´m the fourth son of the king of Rattan Sandalwood, nicknamed Sandalson. I´m a gallant young man, and my father has allotted me three thousand red-breasted soldiers to defend the Western Province of my country.

Yesterday my old wife died, so I have a burning need to find a new bride to fill my bed. It just happens that there´s a gigantic chance for me. The Sophora´s Golden Bough Princess, who was married to the Taishou of Southern Bough, has built a marble palace in Gorgeville to escape the intolerable heat in the official mansion. Gorgeville borders on my country. Great heavens! To escape the heat can be no more than an excuse. She´s simply bored with her old man and is trying to escape from him — to have some liberty! Isn´t heaven offering me a chance in a lifetime? With just one thousand soldiers, I can storm the palace and have her carried off. But it might be wiser to figure out her mind first. So I had a soldier disguise himself as a flower-peddler, and dispatched him across the gorge to sniff out her intentions. He should be back by now.

(Enter a soldier with flowers and a rattle-drum[1])

SOLDIER: Report, report, report! Good news coming!

PRINCE: Speak up!

【北调脱布衫】

（报）

小番儿蚤离了檀萝，
无明夜打听南柯。
做探子的精细无过，
横直着货郎儿那些货。

好一座瑶台城。

（丑）怎见的？

【中吕小梁州】

（报）

真乃是玉砌金装巧毵罗，
绕殿宫娥，
珍珠垒就翠银河，
无弹破，
一曲锦云窝。

（丑）可到得公主跟前？

（报）小的卖花，宫娥引见。

【幺】

卖花声斜抹着宫墙过，
那穿宫引见俺妆标垛。

（丑）公主可要了些花儿？

（报）便叫货郎，有甚妆花名数？小的应说，有，有，有。绒线花，通草花，缕金花，攒翠花，数上百十样，他府中都有，则留下两种儿。

（丑）那两种？

（报）

是宝檀丝粟点香和，

【Removing the Shirt, Northern Style】

SOLDIER:

In the wee hours I left our Sandalwood,
and worked day after night in Southern Bough.
Carrying trifles on a shoulder-pole,
I took in every tiny bit of news.

The marble palace is really magnificent!

PRINCE: Tell me more.

【Liangzhou Minor】

SOLDIER:

It´s an architectural wonder of jade and gold,
teeming with palace maids
and encircled by a moat of pearls.
No bragging,
it´s heaven on this very earth.

PRINCE: Were you able to meet the princess in person?

SOLDIER: I was hawking flowers when a palace maid beckoned me in.

【Ditto】

My hawking cries scaled and vaulted the palace walls;
my disguise helped me into the forbidden halls.

PRINCE: Did the princess buy any flowers?

SOLDIER: She asked me if I had any rare species. I told her I had many, such as the floss flower, the rice-paper flower, the golden thread, the aster ball, and so on and so forth. Although I named more than one hundred kinds, she said she had them all. She only bought two.

PRINCE: Which two?

SOLDIER:

One was the fragrant yellow sandal flower,

小装窝那翠剪萝，
春纤两朵，
斜插笑镜儿睃。

(丑作昏跌介)妙也！妙也！宝檀花，翠萝花，正是"檀萝"二字，公主接下这花，天缘也。报子，还则怕他汉子守着？

(报)一个驸马，回南柯管事去了。

(丑)有这等一个松驸马。

【耍孩儿三煞】

(报)

驸马呵，
他守着个闹喳喳的画卯堂着甚科？
倒把个翠臻臻画眉台脱了窝。
俺偷风斫砦寻闲货，
则要俺蛇皮鼓再打向花廊过。
少不的会温存的飞虎把河桥坐，
少不的怕聒炒的昭君出塞和。
是惹起风流祸，
为一个观音菩萨，
起三千拼命喽罗。

【尾声】

太子呵，
你先把撞门羊宰了大犒贺，
把拖地锦做征旗尾后拖。
抢到公主呵，

the other was the starry rattan bloom.
With a smile at the looking glass
she inserted them in her hair.

PRINCE (stumbles and falls backward as if overpowered by exhilaration): Fancy that! Fancy that! The two flowers clearly signal her preference for Rattan Sandalwood! It must have been heaven´s design that she picked out those two. By the way, was her husband with her?

SOLDIER: The Taishou has gone back to his office in the prefectural capital.

PRINCE: What an impotent coward he must be!

【Playing with Children】

SOLDIER: Oh, that royal son-in-law!
What´s the use of running a mighty office full of bustling bees,
while the doll-house beauty has slipped out of the honey-comb?
I´m good at pilfering and burglary.
When again my snake-skin drum rattles through her corridor,
our virile young commander will besiege her maiden bed,
and the new bride must cross the border to appease the foe.
The beauty of a princess thus invites
the catastrophe of connubial war.
Three thousand braves are therefore mobilized.

【Coda】

Oh, Prince,
why not cook the betrothal lamb to feast the troops
and trail as banners shreds of moss behind our ass?
When you´ve captured the princess,
let that feather-brained old Chunyu sit there to puff and huff,
while you smart chap will be the one who steals the final laugh.

(Exit Soldier)

偏背那扑楞生老淳于干别煞了他，

成就这悄不剌小檀郎快活煞了我。（下）

（丑吊场介）好称心的事儿也！就分一枝兵，蘸住堑江城，俺亲自抢公主去。正是：

他要伐檀来不得，

咱自无媒去伐柯。

(Manet Prince)

PRINCE: What an ideal situation! I´ll send a detachment to pin down their garrison force in Gorgeville while I personally lead a regiment to catch the princess.

They lack the means to chop the Sandalwood,
But wee´ve the ax to lop the Sophora.

第二十七出 闺 警

【好事近前】

（老旦贴扮宫娥上）

秋影动湘荷，
风定瑞炉香过。
帘外呢喃归燕，
怪琐窗人卧。

我们公主位下宫娥是也。公主贵体，原自娇柔；加以儿女累多，心烦怕热；因此避暑瑶台。这早还睡也。

【好事近后】

（旦上）

弄凉微雨隐秋河，
残暑殢人些个。
好梦暗随团扇，
再朱颜来么？

〔清平乐〕

（旦）

阴阴院宇，
枕上昏凉雨。

Scene 27 Princess Besieged

(Enter two palace maids, one old, one young)

【Luck at Hand, first half】

MAIDS:

Autumn sparkles on lotus leaves;
wisps of smoke drift out from the incense pot.
Beyond the curtains the swallows debate:
How can a person sleep so late?

Wee are maids serving the princess. The princess´ already delicate health is further impaired by the burden of numerous children, and the hot weather makes her all the more edgy. That´s why she´s taking shelter in this marble palace. It´s late in the morning, and she isn´t up yet.

(Enter Princess)

【Luck at Hand, second half】

PRINCESS:

A shower brought on only a wrapping haze;
the lingering summer drives me mad.
A nice dream flipped and flapped with the fan.
Will my younger looks reappear?

Clouds press down on the yard;
The pillow muffles dripping rain.

OLD MAID:

The green Sophora´s branches wave and dance;
The sun has climbed above the painted walls.

PRINCESS:

What a curtain of pageant dreams
And a potful of incense ash!

（老）

风动槐柯交翠舞，

恰恰画墙低午。

（旦）

一帘幽梦悠扬，

金炉旋注沉香。

（合）

风吹几年都尉，

病慵休殢宫妆。

（旦）宫娥，这瑶台风景，比南柯郡凉些。

（老）也是新秋了。

（旦）你知我有病在身么？

（老）便是，驸马爷在南柯，这些时不来相看。

（旦）他政事羁身，何暇到此？好闷呵！

【六犯宫词】

落红凝院，

暮云沉阁，

秋动绣帘犹卧。

起来无力，

金钗半坠云窝。

（老）瑶台城过了一夏哩。

（旦）

俺汗减了湘文簟，

萤低了扇影罗。

（老）公主也忒娇怯。

（旦）

多娇处，

BOTH:

How long will last the phoenix song?
Poor health can't bear the palace gowns.

PRINCESS: Isn't the weather here cooler than that in the prefectural capital?

OLD MAID: Well, it could be because it's already autumn.

PRINCESS: Do you think he knows I'm so ill?

OLD MAID: He should. But why does he remain in town? He hasn't been here for quite a while.

PRINCESS: He's tied down by his administrative duties. How can he find time to come over? My life has never been so boring!

【Six Combined Palace Tunes】

PRINCESS:

Red petals stain the yard;
dark clouds hang on the eaves.
The wind keeps lifting the drapes of my bed,
but I feel too weak to care.
My gold hairpins are tangled in my hair.

OLD MAID: You've spent the whole summer in this marble palace.

PRINCESS:

Constant sweating has brined my bed's bamboo mat;
even fireflies seem to be burning hot.

OLD MAID: You're really too fragile, Madam.

PRINCESS:

Fragile indeed!
Illness preys on me,
while sleep has been elusive through the year.

OLD MAID: The weather is much cooler now.

PRINCESS:

A slight chill will send me burrowing under heavy quilts;
yet in another moment I'll feel hot and want a bath.

忒病多，

年来无奈睡情何？

(老)天气早凉些。

(旦)

我一时间如凉便得沾罗幙，

一会间似热又寻思浴翠波。

(老)午膳哩。

(旦)

没些时个，

花阴午殛，

蚤氳人的茶饭沾唇过。

(老)公主有了王孙、贵女，还闷甚么？

(旦)

你休波，

眼前儿女，

风月暗消磨。

(老)整办酒筵解闷，公主只是想驸马爷。

【前腔】

蚤则是琐窗人唤，

梦云初弹，

一线枕痕无那。

迟迟媚妩，

还留人画双蛾。(宫娥送酒介)

(老)

一盏心头过，

OLD MAID: It´s lunchtime now.

PRINCESS:

I´ve lost my sense of time.
Flower shadows now contract.
The sustaining food has no more than touched my lips.

OLD MAID: With so many lovely sons and daughters, how can you still feel bored?

PRINCESS:

Don´t mention them.
It´s they who call me Mom
that have eroded my younger looks.

OLD MAID: A banquet may boost your spirit and divert your thoughts from the royal son-in-law.

【Ditto】

Although aroused from her curtained bed,
she still hugs a cloud of dream,
with pillow patterns printed on her face.
She walks in trancelike peace,
her crescent brows retaining last night´s paint.
(A maid enters with wine)
A cup of wine goes down the throat
and rises again to flush the cheeks.
(Princess declines, while Old Maid kneels to plead. Princess takes a sip)
I pleaded thrice
and she took half a sip.
How can I make her crack a sunny smile?

I know. I´ll order the maids to sing and dance.

(Enter maids singing and playing musical instruments)

PRINCESS: What noise!

OLD MAID:

胭脂晕脸涡。(旦怕饮、老跪劝、旦略饮介)

(老)

三回劝，

半口多，

朱颜怎得个笑微酡？

(老)有方法，叫小宫娥吹弹歌舞。(内吹弹上介)

(旦)聒人那！

(老)

怎人偏喜处生嫌涡？

再有消愁似舞和歌？

(背唱介)

他凤腮微托，

长裙半拖，

病梢儿剪不的愁痕破。(旦照镜叹介)(老回身)

事多磨，

淹淹镜里，

有得气儿呵。

(末扮大儿子上)

秦楼通戍火，

汉苑入边愁。

报知母亲，檀萝兵起，逼近瑶台，如何是好？

(旦泣介)这等，怎好？我的儿那，你星夜往南柯，报知父亲；我一边督率城中男女，守城防备。

【风入松】

原来只合住南柯，

有甚么清凉不过？

How can one in luxury feel so glum?
Singing and dancing are the best of cures.
(Aside)
See how she barely holds her chin,
and limply drapes her skirt.
There seems no way for her to shed her ills and woes.
(Princess looks into the mirror and sighs)
(Old Maid turns around)
Fickle health!
Her frail mirror image
only displays a breath of life.

(Enter Princess´ eldest son)

SON:

Beacon-fire flames the palace hall;
A border alarm shakes the throne.

Mother, Rattan Sandalwood has started a war against us. Their troops are advancing toward our marble palace. What shall wee do?

PRINCESS (weeps): What can wee do? You must go immediately to the prefectural capital to inform your father. Meanwhile, I´ll organize the men and women in the palace into a defense.

【Wind Through Pine Trees】

So, I should have stayed in the central town,
and not been tempted by the cooler clime.
To have come to this end is all my fault,
and now it has caused an aggressive war.
What goal is the foe trying to achieve?
(Refrain)
Women as well as men must guard the walls.

【Ditto】

下场头都是俺之错。
到如今惹下了干戈，
知他那意儿怎么？

（合）

男共女守台坡。

【前腔】

（末）

喜的是亲娘身子减沉痾，
儿去也俺娘挣挫，
急忙间打不的这瑶台破。
怕你这娘子军没得张罗，
俺那父子兵登时救活。（合前）

（旦、末哭别介）

【尾声】

从来不说有干戈，
俺小胆儿登时吓破。
别将领兵不济事，
须则是驸马亲来才救的我。（旦众下）

（末吊场急马走上）手下趱行。

【滴溜子】

边报急，边报急，
怎生煞和？
流星去，流星去，
尘飞不过。

SON:

It´s good to see that Mom looks eager and refreshed.
Do keep your spirits up while I´m away.
It won´t be easy for them to pierce the walls
as long as you women warriors panic not.
An army of fathers and sons will rescue you.
(Refrain)
(Princess and Son part in tears)

【Coda】

PRINCESS:

Until now war has been a distant thought,
and its eruption frightens me to death.
No other general can save me
except that your father in person leads the troops.

(Exeunt)

(Reenter Son immediately, galloping)

SON: You soldiers, hurry up!

【Glassy Slippy】

Border alarm, border alarm,
what is in store for us?
Spur your horse, spur your horse!
Clouds of dust hide the road.
The more you hurry, the slower the horse.
Three hundred miles to the prefectural seat,
I wish to cover in a flash.
If rescue comes too late,
what would happen to Mom?
What would happen to Mom?

(Exit)

心急马行迟，
那把三百里老南柯，
做一会子抹。
迟误兵机，
教娘怎么？
教娘怎么？（下）

【前腔】

（杂扮妇女插旗守城上）

边报急，边报急，
怎生煞和？
轮班去，轮班去，
挨查不过。
心急步行迟，
那把三百个锦城窝，
做一会子逻。
失误城池，
教娘怎么？
教娘怎么？

（丑笑介）奇怪，奇怪，一座瑶台城，砌的蚁子缝也没一个，甚鸟报道，有甚钻城贼。公主下令：瑶台一卫老军丁男，出吊桥迎贼；军妻守垛四门，每门一个女小旗总领。奴家是王大姐，平日有些手面，领了东门女小旗。哎哟，陈姥姥，赵姨姨，你也来了。

（老）老身领了西门。

（小旦）奴家领了北门。只南门小总不到。

（贴扮小厮插旗上）列位大娘拜揖。

(Enter women with pennons stuck to their shoulders)

【Ditto】

WOMEN:

Border alarm, border alarm,
what is in store for us?
Let´s take shifts, let´s take shifts.
Wee are forced out of home.
The more you hurry, the slower the steps.
Three hundred sentry nests atop the wall,
wee wish to patrol in a flash.
If the castle should fall,
what would happen to us?
What would happen to us?

SISTER WANG (laughing): Unbelievable! Some nitwit is thinking of boring into the palace! Who made that damned report? Even ants can´t find a crack in this seamless palace wall! The princess, however, has issued an order that males go out to meet the enemy beyond the drawbridge, while their wives defend the four palace gates. A woman captain has therefore been appointed for every gate. I´m Sister Wang. As I know a little about fighting, I was appointed captain of the east gate. Aha! Granny Chen, Auntie Zhao, you´re here too!

GRANNY CHEN: My old self is in charge of the west gate.

AUNTIE ZHAO: I´m appointed captain of the north gate. So where is the captain of the south gate?

(Enter a lad with pennons stuck to his shoulders)

LAD: My respects to you, grannies and aunties.

SISTER WANG: What a handsome young man!

LAD: My mom has been appointed captain of the south gate. She´s ill, and has asked me to come in her stead.

SISTER WANG: The south wind makes a fortune![1] Well, the princess has

(丑)一个俊哥儿。

(贴)我母亲是南关女小旗，病了，小子替领。

(丑)南风发了。也罢，公主号令，旗婆们都要演习武艺。咄!陈姥姥看把势。(踢老跌介)

(老)哎，我老人家了。

(丑)赵姨姨看跌。

(小跌介)哎，王大姐，饶了罢那。

(丑)小哥看飞尖。(贴放丑倒介)

(丑)不信老娘倒了架。(再三打，丑跌介)

(丑)我的哥，跌打你不过，和你耍枪。(枪杀，贴胜，丑怕介)

(贴)王大姐，这等手面，怎么防贼?

(丑)奴家有计，贼上城，热屎热尿淋头撒下去。我连马子、煮粥锅都搬上城来了。

(老、小)休罗唣，我们绕城走一遭，回报公主去。

【醉罗歌】

一朵两朵城台座，
一个两个铺团窝。
密札札穿针缝没过，
枪和炮成堆垛。
军妻姥姥，
这些老婆；
军余舍舍，
这些小哥；
斗儿东唱到参儿趖。(内锣鼓马嘶介)
把尘头望，
路脚那，

ordered us women captains to practice martial arts. Duh! Granny Chen, look out! (She kicks out and knocks Granny Chen to the floor)

GRANNY CHEN: Don´t bully me. I´m too old to fight you.

SISTER WANG: Auntie Zhao, look out! (Auntie Zhao falls to the floor)

AUNTIE ZHAO: Ouch! Sister Wang, please spare me.

SISTER WANG: Young man, watch my leg. (She kicks out but is thrown to the floor by Lad) I can´t let you get the upper hand. (She wrestles with Lad and is once more thrown to the floor) Oh, brother, I can´t throw you off your feet. Let´s try the spears. (They engage in a spear fight. Lad wins and she cowers)

LAD: Sister Wang, how can you defend the palace with such poor skills?

SISTER WANG: I´ve already thought out a wonderful defense tactic: When our enemies try to climb the wall, wee will pour heated shit and piss down on their heads. Look, I´ve brought my family chamber pot and even our porridge pot to the wall.

GRANNY CHEN, AUNTIE ZHAO: Let´s not stand here talking. Wee should make the rounds and then report back to the princess.

【The Drunkard´s Song】

Wee count merlons and crenels one by one,
and every padded bunker step by step.
Even a needle couldn´t find a crack;
spears and cannons are stored in piles.
The soldiers´ aged grans,
together with their wives,
and other relatives,
such as this handsome lad,
from dusk to dawn wee chant and walk around.
(Drums and gongs beat and horses neigh within)
Wee look up;
wee look down.
Patrolling the parapet wee strike gongs.

傍城墙走马那数声锣。

(内紧鼓报介)檀萝贼兵来了。

(贴)边报来紧，且催集各家老小上城。

瑶台城四面，
炮眼枪头箭。
但有贼星儿，
女兵先绰战。

(Drums beat faster within)

VOICE WITHIN: The Sandalwoods are attacking!

LAD: They´re upon us! Let every family member gather on the wall.

The marble palace has four sides.
Cannon balls, spear and arrow heads.
If any foe should come in sight,
The women are the first to fight.

第二十八出　雨　　阵

【逍遥乐】

（生引众上）

池上秋声响，
还把彩鸾双扇掌。
老槐阴新雨碧油幢，
独坐黄堂，
闲燕寝，
凝幽香。

吾在南柯有岁华，
丽谯清昼卷高牙。
刑书日省三千牍，
民版秋登百万家。

自家出守南柯，物阜民安，辞清盗寡，皆周、田二君赞相之力。杯酒为欢，缺然未举。近因公主避暑瑶台城，衙内孤寂，此中旧有一所审雨堂，审的地气湿热将雨之候，果然微雨，应此新秋。分付置酒，与二君听雨。左右伺候。

Scene 28 The Forewarning Rain

(Enter Chunyu, attended)

【Happily Free】

CHUNYU:

Rain splatters on the autumn pond,
while I lazily wave my painted fan.
Behind the turquoise screen I sit and watch,
alone in my office,
the napping swallows,
the curdling fragrance.

Many a year I've spent in Southern Bough;
My standard flies high on the city tower.
A peaceful era has made lawsuits rare;
An autumn census counts a million homes.

Since I took office as Taishou of Southern Bough, prosperity and peace have reigned over the place. There have been few lawsuits or cases of theft and robbery. I owe this to the help of Mr. Zhou and Mr. Tian. For this, we've long forsaken the pleasure of the cup.

As my wife, the princess, is recuperating at the marble palace, the official mansion seems empty and deserted. There's an old pavilion in the compound named The Rain Observatory. It's very sensitive to the sultry humidity from the earth, and when it starts to drip, rain will soon follow. Here comes the first autumn shower.

I've ordered a wine table to be laid out in the pavilion, and have invited my two colleagues over to listen to the falling rain. Attendants, get the things ready.

(Enter Zhou Bian and Tian Zihua)

（周、田上）

大府威容盛，

同官礼数亲。

祗候的，通禀。

（丑）田爷、周爷见。（见介）

（生）

三匝南枝总旧游，

（田）

双攀玉树此庭幽。

（周）

偏因听雨承恩泽，

（合）

共看郊原作好秋。（看酒介）

（生）今夕之酒，专为听雨而设。

【啼莺儿】

偶然西风吟素商，

霎煞几般疏响。

悉阑珊玉马叮当，

忽弄的冰壶溜亮。

倒檐花碎影琳琅，

敲鸳瓦跳珠儿定荡。

猛端相，

断魂何处，

环佩赴高堂？

【前腔】

银河湿云流素光，

点滴翠荷盘上。

ZHOU, TIAN:

Imposing is the Taishou's house;

We colleagues are the best of friends.

Attendant, please announce our arrival.

ATTENDANT: Lord Tian and Lord Zhou are at the gate.

(Chunyu and Zhou, Tian greet each other)

CHUNYU:

Birds circle around their familiar branch.

TIAN:

Vines cling to the huge tree that offers shade.

ZHOU:

More favors drop from heaven with the rain.

CHUNYU, ZHOU, TIAN:

Together we observe the autumn scene.

(They pick up wine cups)

CHUNYU: Today's wine treat is especially for listening to the first autumn rain.

【Singing Orioles】

The west wind suddenly pipes up a song;
sporadic sharp gusts shriek along.
Ding-dong ding-dong the iron eave-bells clink,
glistening like translucent icicles.
The painted eaves flicker in little pools;
marble balls hop and skip on glazy tiles.
All at once,
it makes one think:
Are they pearl eardrops at a ball?

【Ditto】

The wet clouds flash an opalescent light,
and shed drops on the lotus leaves.

吉琤琤打鸭银塘，
撒喇喇破萍分浪。
清切在梧桐井床，
飒答在芭蕉翠幌。
隐垂堂，
珠帘暮卷，长似对潇湘。

【啄木鹂】
华堂静，好对觞，
细语纱厨今夜凉。
怕搅他蝴蝶飞双，
聒醒我鸳鸯睡两。
更那画船眠处沙鸥望，
屏山醉后余香漾。
弄悠扬，
人间此际，别有好思量。

【前腔】
催花紧，钞燕的忙，
一阵阵黄昏愁雁行。
偏有他侧耳空房，
闪窗纱半灭银釭。
一般儿天涯薄宦穷途况，
洞庭归客孤篷上。
数天长，
十年心事，和泪隔秋窗。

They lash and splash against the silver pond,
slice and split lanes amidst the duckweed mead.
The well-side parasol tree sings on high;
the glossy palm leaves sway and purr nearby.
In this pavilion,
pearl curtains drawn aside,
we´re peering out from the cyclone´s eye.

【The Woodpecker】

Cool and quiet,
a toast to friends.
We lower our voice behind the dusking screen,
not to fluster the mating butterflies,
nor disturb the nap of mandarin ducks.
Beyond, the gulls sentry the sleep of painted boats;
the sodden hills emit a verdant scent.
A flute pipes.
In this place, at this time,
one´s thoughts are carried up to sky.

【Ditto】

Autumn comes on.
Swallows are packing up;
lines of wild geese honk through the darkening eve.
A vacant bedroom at this time of year,
a dim lamplight fluttering in the night,
add to the chagrin of a wandering career,
like a lonely traveler on Dongting Lake.
Long, empty days,
a decade of waning hope,
flows past with tears behind the window panes.

(生)司农，我昼寝忽然一梦，大儿子诵《毛诗》二句：“鹳鸣于垤，妇叹于室。”是何祥也？

(田想介)依下官愚见，诗云：天将雨而蚁出于垤，鹳喜食蚁，故飞舞而鸣。妇叹于室，似是公主有难，要与老堂尊相见。此乃《东山》之诗，主有征战之事。

(生)多谢指教，当谨防之。(内鼓介)

(生)问报鼓为甚而忙？

(末打马急走上)

风传流贼起，
火速报君知。

报爹爹，檀萝兵起，一半攻打堑江城，一半向瑶台城来了。

(生慌介)怎了？怎了？瑶台，公主所居；堑江，边城要路；贼兵两路而进，其意难量。我与田司农领兵去解公主之围；别遣周司宪守御堑江城一带；孩儿把守南柯，暂且休息去。

(末)

要活娘儿命，
无过子父兵。(下)

(生)司农，司农，梦之响应如此。

(周、田)便是。公主在围，须得星夜前进。

Mr. Tian, I had a dream when I was taking a nap that my eldest son cited two lines from *The Book of Poetry*. They are "Stork cries on anthill; wife sighs at home." What does that prophesy?

TIAN (pondering): The book says when it´s going to rain, ants will crawl out of their hole, and because the stork likes to eat ants, it hovers above them and cries. In my humble opinion, that the wife sighs at home is a hint that the princess is in danger and she wants to see you. Since these two lines are from "The East Hill," it may suggest that a war is imminent.[1]

CHUNYU: Thank you for your analysis. I´ll be alert to that. (Drums beat within) Why are they beating the drums?

(Enter Chunyu´s eldest son, galloping)

SON:

The wind breathes word that bandits rise;
It´s urgent to report to you.

Daddy, Rattan Sandalwood is waging war on us! Half of them are attacking Gorgeville, while the other half are advancing toward the marble palace.

CHUNYU (in a flurry): What shall I do? What shall I do? The marble palace is where my dear wife is residing now, and Gorgeville is a border town of strategic importance. It´s hard to guess their objective in attacking the two places simultaneously. Minister Tian and I will lead an army to rescue the princess. Minister Zhou will take a division to reinforce the defense of Gorgeville. My child, you stay here and guard the prefectural capital. For the moment, you may go and have a rest.

SON:

To save the threatened life of mom,
Naught works better than dad and son.

(Exit Son)

CHUNYU: Mr. Tian, the dream´s prophecy proves to be true!

ZHOU, TIAN: Indeed! Now the princess is besieged, we must set out

(众军上)

瑶台先救月，

别骑见临江。

(生)听我号令：五千兵跟周爷救堑江城；选锋三千名，跟我星夜前救公主。

(众)禀太爷：演阵。

(田)禀堂尊：救堑江只排个寻常蚁阵；救公主的，要依诗云，排一个老鹳阵。

(众应排阵走介)蚁阵完。(排阵舞叫介)老鹳阵完。

(生)我与周司宪分兵而去。

(周)禀堂尊：三军鼓气，全在于酒；周弁一生，全仗酒力；望主公大赐恩波。

(生)五千名军，赏他五千个泥头酒去。则一句话，司宪在心：小生昔为淮西裨将，使酒误事，二君所知。自拜郡以来，戒了这酒。司宪平日颇有酒名，既掌兵机，记吾嘱付，酒要少饮，事要多知。就此起行了。

【刮鼓令】

(生、田)

冲星一剑忙，

向瑶台相对当。

immediately.

(Enter soldiers)

SOLDIERS:

To save the moon all must hurry;
To the gorge dash the cavalry.

CHUNYU: Hark my orders: Five thousand of you go with Minister Zhou to reinforce Gorgeville. Three thousand will go with me in the vanguard to save the princess.

SOLDIERS: Your Excellency, wee are ready to do the formation exercises.

TIAN: Your Excellency, an ordinary ant formation will do for the Gorgeville division, but according to the book those going to save the princess need to exercise the stork formation.

(Soldiers respond in chorus and maneuver into battle formations)

SOLDIERS: The ant formation is done. (Dancing and shouting, they change into another formation) The stork formation is done.

CHUNYU: Minister Zhou and I will now go our separate ways.

ZHOU: Your Excellency, the spirit of the troops is buoyed up by wine, and my strength depends on the strength of wine too. We all hope Your Excellency won´t begrudge us a generous gift.

CHUNYU: For the five thousand soldiers, I´ll give you five thousand clay jars of wine, but there´s one thing I want you to bear in mind: Years ago I lost my position as a lieutenant with the Western Huai army just because of drinking too much. I think both of you know that story well. So I´ve abstained from drinking ever since I took office here as Taishou. Mr. Zhou, you have a reputation for being a heavy drinker. Now you have military responsibilities, remember my words — drink less and think more. Let´s set off without further delay.

【Drum Scratch Minitune】

CHUNYU, TIAN:

The constellations are disturbed,
and we dash forth to meet the foe.

公主呵，

他烟花阵怎生围向？
那檀萝真掘强。
筑下个粉坛场，
良时吉方阵头安上。

（合）

听楚天秋雨过残阳，
倒做了金镫响丁当。（生、田下）

【前腔】

（周）

孤城号堑江，
敢囊沙聚米粮。
看仔细檀萝模样，
望江乡策应忙。
杯酒衬戎装，
他居中主量，
我从傍儿赶上。（合前）

瑶台城傍月儿边，
为惹兵戈破镜悬。
此日相逢洗兵雨，
一天长堑凯歌旋。

Oh, princess,
how is she to survive this carnal war?
Damn those audacious Sandalwoods,
who have laid a lascivious siege
by their choice of time and place,
on horseback and on foot.
(Refrain)
We were listening to the sunset autumn rain
when the stirrups summoned us to the battleground.

(Exeunt Chunyu and Tian)

【Ditto】

ZHOU:

A cut-off town known as Gorgeville
can´t require much tactics and strategy.
I will stare the enemy in the eye
to relieve the imperiled town.
Rough wine inflames my coat of mail.
With him taking central command,
I´ll quickly catch up via bypaths.
(Refrain)

The marble palace stands beside the moon,
And it has attracted a warring horde.
Today a fresh shower has just washed my troops;
Tomorrow I´ll return with triumphant whoops.

第二十九出　围　　释

【金钱花】

(贼太子引众行上)

俺们太子是檀萝，
檀萝。
日夜寻思要老婆，
老婆。
瑶台城子里有一个，
咱编桥渡过小银河，
要抢也波，
抢得么？
赤剥剥的笑呵呵。

好了，好了，围了瑶台城。你看城子，高接广寒，明如阆苑，便待一鼓破了瑶台，何难之有？又怕惊了公主，不成其事。昨日打了战书入城，他那里敢回话？想只等驸马来救。我别遣一枝兵马，攻取堑江城，直逼南柯，看那驸马怎生来得？公主，公主，眼见的到手也。今日故意再把城子紧围，他问时，叫公主亲自上城打话，待小子饱瞧一会。众把都，紧围，紧围。

(内鼓噪介)紧围了。

(内使女官忙泣上)哎哟！檀萝兵紧上来了，眼见得无活的也。快请公主

Scene 29 Raising the Siege

(Enter Prince of Rattan Sandalwood with troops, marching)

【Gold–coin Flowers】

PRINCE:

I am the prince of Rattan Sandalwood,
Sandalwood.
I dream day and night of getting a wife,
a wife.
In the marble tower there´s a lovely one.
I´ll build a bridge to cross the silver stream,
and take her in my arms.
Can I do that?
I giggle gaggle my whole body red.

Good, good. I´ve got the marble palace encircled. Look, the palace almost touches the moon, and it virtually gleams! It´ll fall at the first strike of my forces, there isn´t the least doubt about that. But I´m afraid that might frighten the princess and ruin my chances. So yesterday I sent them a letter of challenge, and of course they didn´t have the guts to reply. I guess they´re trying to hold out till the royal son-in-law comes to rescue them. That´s why I´ve dispatched a detachment to take Gorgeville, and then push toward the prefectural seat itself. In that way the royal son-in-law won´t be able to come over here. Oh, princess, you can´t escape from my hands. Now I´ll press the siege. If they beg to negotiate, I´ll ask for a direct talk with the princess on the gate tower, so that I can have a good look at her. You badurs,[1] press forward!

(Drums beat within and the troops shout "Advance!")

(Enter a weeping woman palace officer in haste)

OFFICER: Oh, my! The Sandalwoods are attacking! Wee are all doomed!

升帐。

(旦引队子上)天呵，天呵，怎了也？

瑶台试一临，
贼子逼城阴。
胆破青鸾色，
情伤驸马心。
女墙边月近，
孤枕阵云深。
怎得南柯去，
高楼横笛音？(内鼓介)

(旦众哭介)如何是好？

【南吕一枝花】

(旦)

冷落凤箫楼，
吹彻胡笳塞。
是甚男心多，
偏算计这女乔才。
避暑迎凉，
甚月殿清虚界？
倒惹他西施兵火到苏台。
遭劳扰两月幽闲，
养病患又一天惊骇。

(内鼓介)(旦)天，天，天，怎生来？这瑶台城内，钱粮不多，贼子因何图此？昨日打下战书，思量起来，男女不交手，怎生轻敌而战？专等驸马到来。如今着人问他，或是要些小财物，舍些他去，免得搅

Please ask the princess to take command.

(Enter Princess with attendants)

PRINCESS: Oh, heavens! Heavens! What next?

I to the marble palace came,
And bandits followed on my heels.
My face has turned as pale as ash,
And that would break my loved one´s heart.
The parapet adjoins the moon;
Evil clouds press down thick and dark.
How can I laugh away the siege
and flee to the prefectural seat?

(Drums beat within)

PRINCESS, ATTENDANTS (weeping): What can wee do?

【A Spray of Flowers】

PRINCESS:

The frosty height of phoenix tower
is filled with tunes from nomad flutes.
What man bears such a crafty heart
that he schemes against the softer sex?
Away from summer heat,
in the coolness of lunar quiet,
how could I still have attracted the flames of war?
A recuperation of two short months
didn´t cure my illness but caused a fright.

(Drums beat within) Oh, heavens! What´s the matter now? There isn´t much grain or money stored in this palace. What could they be coveting? They sent us a letter of challenge yesterday, but as I understand it, women shouldn´t mingle with men. So it´s best to avoid any engagement, and wait till my husband comes. However, I think I can have someone ask them what their demands are. If grain and goods can satisfy them, I´ll give

扰一番。叫通事问他，此来主何意思？（内问介）

（太应介）要问俺起兵主意，请公主自来打话。

（通回禀介）他要请公主打话。

（旦叹介）我乃一国之贵主，这些毛贼，怎敢对话？

（通回太介）公主乃一国之贵主，怎与你们打话？

（太）俺非以下将佐，乃是本国四太子，叫你公主就是姐姐一般，请来打话。

（通回旦介）他说是本国四太子，叫公主就是姐姐一般，可以打话。

（旦）这等，只得扶病而去，倘然三两句言词，退了他兵，也未可知？

（众）贼意难知，公主须得戎装，城楼一望。

（旦）然也。（旦换戎装弓箭介）

【梁州第七】

怎便把颤嵬嵬兜鍪平戴？
且先脱下这软设设的绣袜弓鞋，
小靴尖忒逼的金莲窄。
把盔缨一拍，
臂鞲双抬。
宫罗细揣，
这绣甲松裁。
明晃晃护心镜月偃分排，
齐臻臻茜血裙风影吹开。

them some and send them away without further harassment. Tell the interpreter to ask them what they´re after.

(Interpreter asks within)

PRINCE (answering): If you want to know the objective of this raid, tell the princess to show herself and talk with me in person.

VOICE WITHIN (to Princess): He asks to talk with you in person.

PRINCESS (sighs): I´m a princess! Those bandits are not in a position to talk with me!

VOICE WITHIN (to Prince): Her Ladyship is of a noble strain. She won´t talk to you.

PRINCE: Tell her I´m not any ordinary general. I´m the fourth prince of Sandalwood. So she can be as good as my sister. Just ask her to come.

VOICE WITHIN (to Princess): He said he´s the fourth prince of his kingdom, so a talk between you is just like that between a brother and a sister.

PRINCESS: Well, I think I´ll have to resign myself to talking to him. Maybe a few words can make him withdraw his troops. Who knows?

ATTENDANTS: The bandits are cunning. You´d better put on a coat of mail before you ascend the gate tower.

PRINCESS: All right.

【Seventh Tune from Liangzhou】

(Putting on a coat of mail, together with a bow and arrows)
It´s no easy task to balance this heavy casque.
Let me first remove my embroidered socks and bow-arched shoes
to pull on a tight pair of pointed leather boots.
Giving the tassel one more shake,
I raise my arms for the rerebrace.
Tug in my silken blouse.
Over it comes the coat of mail
and the silvery breastplate of a half-moon shape;
the hem of my scarlet skirt streams out from beneath.

少不得女天魔摆阵势，
撒连连金锁枪垒；
女由基扣雕弓，
厮琅琅金泥箭袋；
女孙膑施号令，
明朗朗的金字旗牌。（众喝采介）
奇哉！
你待喝采。
小宫腰控着狮蛮带，
粉将军把旗势摆。
你看我一朵红云上将台，
他望眼孩台。

（内鼓噪）（旦惊介）来的好不怔忡也！权请他太子打话。

（太笑介）妙也！妙也！真乃是月殿姮娥，云端里观世音。姐姐请了。

（旦）太子请了。太子，君处江北，妾处江南，风马牛不相及也，不意太子之涉吾境也，何故？

（太）公主，你把我的主意，猜一猜来。

【牧羊关】

（旦）

看他蚁阵纷然摆，
风雹乱下筛，
他待碗儿般打破这瑶台。
我好看不上他嘴脚儿，
赤体精骸。

Like a heavenly warrior I appear to be,
above the endless rows of abatis.
Like an expert archer I draw my bow
and notch an arrow from a gilded hold.
Like the mastermind of the other sex
my orders are issued on slabs of gold.
(Attendants cheer in chorus)
What a sight!
Give me a rousing cheer.
See the lion belt around my tiny waist.
A fair general waves the signal flag.
A flaming cloud, I mount the tower to take command.
Let him in blank amazement gawk.

(Drumbeats and shouts within)

PRINCESS (startled): The clamor makes my heart race. Let the prince come forth to speak.

PRINCE (laughing): How beautiful she looks! Beautiful! She´s either Chang Er from the moon or Guanyin from above the clouds. Greetings, Sister.

PRINCESS: Greetings, Your Highness. You live north of the river, I on the south side. Except for the wind, there has been no contact whatever between us. And now you´ve crossed over to our side. Is there a good reason for that?

PRINCE: Princess, you can make a guess.

【Shepherd Pass】

PRINCESS:

Look at his regiments of restless ants,
poised like hailstones about to fall
against this palace fragile as a porcelain bowl.
How ugly and distasteful are his looks,
naked and without shame!

小则小心肠儿多大，
则不过领些须鱼肉块，
觅些小米头柴。
怎做作过水兴营砦？
太子，
你敢拚残生来触槐？

（通）四太子，我公主说，你止要些米头鱼骨，犒赏你些去便了。
（太笑介）小子非为哺啜而来，好不欺负人也！只擂鼓紧围罢了。
（旦）通事，你说与他：

【四块玉】
逐些儿打话来，
则把你虚脾卖。
敢要牲口？
（太）不要。
（旦）要些金银？
（太）不要。
（旦）
为甚么钱粮牲口都不在怀？
（太）你不知，俺那国里，少些女人，故此而来。
（旦）
原来女人国不近你那檀萝界。
（太）不是以次女人，近来小子亲自断了弦。
（旦）
则道少甚么粉丕丕女将材，
原来要帽光光你个令四太。（内鼓噪介）

So small a body can´t contain a giant heart.
What he wants could not exceed specks of fish and lamb,
or flecks of firewood and coarse grain.
Is that worth an invasion across the gorge?
Oh, Prince,
don´t bang your head against the Sophora tree.

VOICE WITHIN: Fourth Prince, Her Ladyship the Princess says if what you hanker after is grain flecks and fish bones, she´ll gladly give you some and send you away.

PRINCE (laughing): Don´t belittle me. I didn´t come to beg for food. My braves, beat the drums and press ahead with the siege.

PRINCESS: Interpreter, tell him:

【Four Pieces of Jade】

Come to the point if he intends to talk.
Don´t prattle on and beat around the bush.
Does he want draft animals?

PRINCE: No.

PRINCESS: Gold and silver?

PRINCE: No.

PRINCESS:
How´s it that beasts and money are not to your taste?

PRINCE: Though it may sound incredible, my country is in want of women. That´s why I came here.

PRINCESS:
So Sandalwood is deprived of the female half.

PRINCE: No, my country has no lack of ordinary females. It´s me myself. My wife has just passed away.

PRINCESS:
I just wondered how your camp could be so denied.
So it´s Your Highness who is looking for a bride!

（太）快回将话来，俺要媳妇儿紧。

（旦）

奇哉这贼！

忒急色。

（旦）说与他，待我奏知国王，选个女儿送他，着他休了兵去。

（太）吾乃太子，要与国王为女婿哩。

（旦）他是不知。

【骂玉郎】

说知他我国王位下无了尊爱。

（太）公主是他尊爱。

（旦）禁声，

蚤有了驸马

养下了婴孩。

（太）公主还嫩嫩的。

（旦）

便做你看不出也三十外。

（太）驸马在那里？

（旦）

他，他，他，去南柯选将材。

来，来，来，那时节替你担利害。

（太）管驸马来不来，公主会了俺的人，插了俺的花，难道不容我做夫妻一夜儿？

【哭皇天】

（旦）

呀，呀，呀，这风魔也似九伯，

使村沙恶茶白赖。

(Drumbeats and shouts within)

PRINCE: Tell me yes or no. I´m badly in need of a wife.

PRINCESS:

How can there be a man
as famished as this one?

Interpreter, tell him I´ll ask my father the king to select a good girl for him. Let him withdraw his troops.

PRINCE: I´m a prince. My wife must be a princess.

PRINCESS: He doesn´t seem to understand.

【Scolding the Jade Boy】

Tell him our king does not have a daughter to marry off.

PRINCE: You´re his daughter.

PRINCESS: Nonsense!

I have been married many years,
and became a mother long ago.

PRINCE: You still look young and charming.

PRINCESS:

Believe it or not, I am thirty and beyond.

PRINCE: Then, where is your husband?

PRINCESS:

He? He´s in town assembling seasoned troops.
Then, then he´ll come to show you what is strength.

PRINCE: I don´t care a bit if he comes or not. Since you´ve received my go-between and accepted my flowers, you´re going to be my wife, even if it´s for no more than one night.

【Crying to Heaven】

PRINCESS:

Oh, my! He must be deranged by the moon
that he could have made such a loutish claim!

宫娥，问他那里会他的人？插了他的花？

(太)前日宝檀丝、翠剪萝，都是俺送你公主插戴的，你接下了约我来。

(旦恼介)哎哟！原来到为此贼所算了。宫娥，快取花来，碎了撒下城去。(旦碎花介)哎！

原来土查儿生扭做檀郎卖，
女丝萝到被你臭缠歪，
小觑我玉叶金枝胡揣。

(掷花着太恼介)你俺一般金枝玉叶，作践我的花，气死俺也！一枝冷箭，去吓死花娘。(射介)公主看箭！(箭响介)

(旦作袖闪半跌介)哎也！

扑琅生射中了八宝攒盔金凤钗，
险些儿翎拴了凤髻，
钩挂住莲腮。

(内鼓响介)(太慌问虚下介)(内呼)驸马兵到。

(卒报旦介)贼兵纷纷解散，鼓声震天，驸马救兵到也。(旦喜介)

【赚尾】

纷纷蚁队重围解，
冉冉尘飞杀气开。
驸马征西大元帅，

Attendants, ask him when and where I met his man and accepted his flowers.

PRINCE: The yellow sandal flower and the starry rattan bloom are what I sent you the other day. You accepted them and invited me to visit you.

PRINCESS (enraged): Aha! So wee have fallen into his trap! Attendants, go and fetch the flowers. I´ll tear them to pieces and throw them in his face. (She tears the flowers up) Bosh!

So they were nothing but kneaded figures of sandal dirt!
Wee were entangled in the rattan´s putrid vines,
and yet the golden bough is not for you to climb!
(She throws the flower fragments at Prince)

PRINCE (angrily): I´m from as noble a branch as you are. How can you crush my flowers? That´s most insulting! I´ll shoot an arrow and teach that silly girl a lesson. (He shoots) Watch your head! (Sound of a flying arrow)

PRINCESS (waves her sleeve, dodges and slips): Oh, my!

It hit my jewel-studded helmet´s golden phoenix clip.
Its feathers nearly caught my bun of hair
and hung my soft cheek in the air.

(Drums beat within. Prince, alarmed, makes inquiries and withdraws with his troops toward the exit)

VOICE WITHIN: The royal son-in-law has brought his troops here!

SOLDIER (enters to report to Princess): The bandits are scattering. Hear the heaven-shaking drums. That´s the royal son-in-law with the rescue force.

【Pre-coda】

PRINCESS (happily):

Our formic columns slice the hostile ranks;
dust clouds explode above the battleground.
The royal son-in-law leads the way,

马践征埃，

花攒战铠。

我呵，

城台上助鼓三咚与他大喝采。(下)

(生领众上)

将军不战他人地，

杀伐虚悲公主亲。(太子众上介)

(生)檀萝小贼，何不蚤降？

(太)俺乃檀萝四太子，才与公主打话片时，你便吃醋怎的？(战介)

(生问介)他是蚁阵，我三军飞舞作老鹳阵，方可破他。(再战，太败走介)

(旦众上)谢天谢地！驸马得胜而回，众三军，开城迎接。(见介)

(生)好不吓杀我也！

(旦)真个吓死人也！

【乌夜啼】

奴本是怯生生病容娇态，

蚤战兢兢破胆惊骸。

怎虞姬独困在楚心垓，

为莺莺把定了河桥外。

射中金钗，

吓破莲腮。

咱瞭高台是做望夫台，

his stallion crushing foes,
his armor stained with blood.
I´ll beat the drum atop the wall to give him three loud cheers.

(Exeunt Princess and attendants)

(Enter Chunyu with soldiers)

CHUNYU:

No motive better justifies a fight
Than saving the life of one´s loving wife.

(Prince and troops turn around) You petty bandit from Sandalwood, why don´t you surrender?

PRINCE: I´m none other than the fourth prince of Rattan Sandalwood. I´ve just had an interesting talk with the princess. Are you jealous?
(They fight)

CHUNYU: They´re arrayed in the ant formation. To defeat them, we must take to the air and deploy the stork formation.
(They fight again. Prince and his troops are routed)
(Reenter Princess and attendants)

PRINCESS: Thank heaven and earth that the royal son-in-law has won the battle. Attendants, throw open the gates to welcome them.
(She and Chunyu greet each other)

CHUNYU: The alarm gave me a real fright.

PRINCESS: It was frightening indeed!

【Ravens Croaking in the Night】

My delicate health was on the verge of collapse
when the attack further scared me out of my wits.
How was it that I fell into the eye of storm
and became the one to defend the angel´s nook?
His arrow hit my helmet clip
and scratched my lily cheeks.
Onto the gate tower I climbed to look out for you;

他连环砦打烟花砦。
争些儿一时半刻，
五裂三开。

(生)三军城外犒赏。酒来，与公主压惊。
(旦)瑶台新破，不可久居，星夜起程往南柯郡去。

【尾煞】
卧番羊拜告了辕门宰，
听金鼓喧传拜将台，
抵多少笙歌接至珠帘外。
不是你亲身自来，
红云阵摆，
险些儿把这座小瑶台做乐昌家镜儿摔。

脚踹鸳鸯阵，
头顶凤凰盔。
马敲金镫响，
人唱凯歌回。

his iron hoops almost cracked my rouge defense.
If you had been delayed a minute more,
wee would be smashed and slashed!

CHUNYU: Throw a victory-celebration banquet for the army outside the palace. Now fetch me some wine to calm down the princess.

PRINCESS: Since this marble palace has caught the enemy´s attention, I won´t want to live here any longer. Let´s return to the prefectural capital tonight.

【Coda】

After the lamb was released from the slaughterhouse,
the deafening camp drums summoning rescue troops
became more agreeable than the gentle flutes.
If you had not in person led a force
and come to our relief,
this palace would fate like a broken glass with pieces scattered far and wide.

I had to don a pair of boots,
And wear a casque before the brutes.
Then came the clatter of relief;
Victory songs extol the feat.

第三十出　帅　北

【六么令】

（贼大众上）

檀萝饥渴，
出山来觅食为活。
藤编铁甲树兵戈，
穿东涧，
抢南柯。
堑江城堑的住江儿么？

把都们，好了，好了。俺檀萝太子去抢瑶台城，着咱这一枝径抢堑江城，望南柯征进。前面便是，快抢上去。

【前腔】

（守城军上）

南来烽火，
一星星报去南柯。
府堂中备御计如何？
呀！
那前来的，
是檀萝。
堑江楼那位将军坐？

俺们是把守这堑江城小军。兄弟，檀萝来得这般紧急，还不见守御

Scene 30 The Thwarted Commander

(Enter Rattan Sandalwood troops)

【Emerald Waist Minitune】

TROOPS:

When thirst and hunger urge,
wee swarm out of the hills to hunt for food,
equipped with rattan shields and spears of twigs.
Across the eastern brook,
toward the southern bough,
the gorge can neither stop the river nor our troops.

Fellow badurs, wee are now on the other side. Our prince himself went to capture the marble palace, and he ordered us to take Gorgeville and then push toward the seat of Southern Bough. Gorgeville lies just ahead. Let´s rush forward.

(Exeunt)

(Enter Gorgeville militia)

【Ditto】

MILITIA:

The beacon fires stretch north
to report an invasion to the chief.
What are our headquarters´ defensive plans?

Ah!

Those swiftly approaching
are the Sandalwoods.
Who´s to take command on our city tower?

Wee are the militiamen of Gorgeville. Brothers, the Sandalwoods will

官来，俺们只得上城巡警。

【前腔】

（扮周弁领众上）

一番兵火，
一些些唤做檀萝。
俺兵半万出南柯，
走饥渴，
转林坡。
堑江城有得酒儿嗑。（守城军接介）
（周）盼的这座城到了。
（众）堑江城要得酒儿嗑。

（周）渴了，渴了。
（众）是渴了，爷。
（周）叫守城军，司农爷运的犒赏酒可到哩？
（守军应介）到了。但一名军一个泥头酒，五千军五千个泥头。大河清，小河清，配着南京真正一寸三分高堆花老烧酒。禀爷：起用那一号？
（周）便取一半水酒，一半烧酒，取名水火既济，都堆上这城门首来。
（众军取酒上介）算泥头：一百一百又一百，二三而五五个百，五个五百两个百，两个五百五个百。
（周）五千个酒勾了尽着吃。泥头都丢在战场上去。众军吃水酒，俺

soon be upon us, but it seems nobody´s coming to take command. For the present, all wee can do is man the walls and stand guard.

(Enter Zhou Bian with soldiers)

【Ditto】

ZHOU:

The fire of war was set
by such measly creatures called Sandalwoods.
My five thousand valiants will smash their troops,
but we´re parched by the march.
Around that woody hill,
Gorgeville will offer us abundant booze.
(They are received by the militia)

So we´ve finally reached Gorgeville.

SOLDIERS:

Gorgeville must offer us abundant booze.

ZHOU: I´m thirsty, very thirsty!

SOLDIERS: My lord, wee are thirsty, too.

ZHOU: You militiamen, the finance minister has promised to send us a reward of wine. Has it arrived?

MILITIA: It´s already here. There´s one clay jar of wine for each soldier. So there are five thousand jars in all for the five thousand soldiers. Fiery brew, watery brew, all in one-and-three-tenths-inches-tall genuine Nanking[1] cut-clay liquor jars. My lord, which do you prefer?

ZHOU: Make it half watery and half fiery to mean a good balance of the elements, and stack them all on the gate tower.

MILITIA (bringing wine): Let´s count. One hundred, one hundred, and another hundred; two and three makes five, and that´s five hundred; five five-hundred and two more hundred; two five-hundred and five more hundred.

ZHOU: Five thousand jars are plenty. Drink your fill, and throw the empty jars down the wall onto the battlefield. You drink the watery stuff, I´ll

吃烧酒，不论量，以渴止为度。

（众作饮介）渴哩，渴哩。（丢泥头介）

（周）俺从来好酒，则因府主相拘，怕官箴有玷。这才是俺显量时节也。（饮酒，众醉介）

（内鼓介）报！报！檀萝贼到城下了。

（周）由他，且饮酒。

（内急鼓介）报！报！报！檀萝贼先锋挑战。

（周作恼介）这贼好无礼，酒刚吃到一半，则管冲席。众军，乘酒兴杀出城去。

（众应介）

　　脸从醉后如关将，

　　酒尚温时斩华雄。（下）

（贼唱介前上）把都们抢进堑江去。

（周领众上）来者莫非檀萝贼乎？（战介）（周众作醉不敌，贼赶下介）

（周急上）众军，再取一大觥烧酒来，战的渴也。（众取酒上饮介）

（贼上）那边厢好不香的烧酒哩，抢上去！（又战，周众又败介）

drink the fiery stuff. Drink as much as you can till you´ve quenched your thirst.

SOLDIERS (drinking): Wee are thirsty. Wee are thirsty. (They throw the empty jars down the wall)

ZHOU: I can never do without wine, but my boss has kept a close eye on me, and I didn´t dare to incur his displeasure. Now it´s time to show my capacity. (He drinks. All get drunk)

(Drums beat within)

VOICE WITHIN: Report! Report! The Sandalwoods have reached the foot of our city wall!

ZHOU: Never mind them. Let´s drink.

(Rapid drumbeats within)

VOICE WITHIN: Report! Report! Report! The commander of their vanguard is challenging you.

ZHOU (angrily): That thug hasn´t learned any manners! I ain´t nearly slaked and here he comes to annoy me! Now, fired up with wine, let´s charge the enemy! (Soldiers respond in chorus)

My drunken face is red as Lord Guan Yu´s,
Who slew Hua Xiong before his wine got cold.[2]

(Exeunt)

(Reenter Sandalwood troops, chanting "Across the eastern brook ...")

TROOPS: Fellow badurs, let´s charge into the town.

(Reenter Zhou with soldiers)

ZHOU: So you´re the bandits from Sandalwood?

(They fight, Drunk, Zhou and his soldiers fight poorly and are chased offstage)

(Reenter Zhou hastily)

ZHOU: Men, get me another big bowl of hard liquor. Fighting makes me real thirsty. (Soldiers reenter with wine and he gulps it down)

(Reenter Sandalwood troops)

TROOPS: There´s such a sweet smell of wine over there! Let´s lick him and

(周独身上)哎也，贼好无礼，便认输了这一阵。天气炎热，日势已晚，且卸下征袍，月下单骑回去也。(下)

(贼上)好，好，好，趁这番抢入南柯去。(跌介)哎也，为甚跌了也？则见酒气薰天，流涎满地。呀，原来城门首堆着几千个泥头塞路也。(作看天介)看此天气，必然大雨涨江，妨俺归路。俺们且搬了这几个余酒，唱个得胜歌，回去也。

【前腔】

旗幡摇播，
拥回军擂鼓筛锣。
肴山酒海笑呵呵，
哩罗哇，
哩哇罗。
抢南柯得胜回齐声贺。

南柯败损数千军，
剩得泥头扑鼻醺。
遇饮酒时须饮酒，
得饶人处且饶人。

the wine.

(They fight again. Zhou and his soldiers are defeated and driven off)

ZHOU (reenters alone): Oh, my! Those bandits are impertinent! Well, let them count it their victory. It´s so hot, and the day is getting late. Let me cast aside this coat of mail and slip back to the prefectural capital in the moonlight.

(Exit)

(Reenter Sandalwood troops)

TROOPS: Hurrah! Hurrah! Hurrah! Let´s take this opportunity to seize the town. (They stumble and fall) Ah-hah? What caught our feet? What a stifling smell of wine! And what a slimy mess! Oh, my! So there are several thousand clay jars blocking the entrance. (They look up at the sky) It looks like rain. That´ll flood the river and block our retreat. Let´s carry the remaining jars and go home in triumphant songs.

【Ditto】

Our banners flutter on high.
Wee sing our way home beating gongs and drums,
with mountains of food and a sea of wine.
La-li-la,
la-li-la,
wee have made a triumphant sack of Southern Bough.

Southern Bough has lost several thousand males.
All that remains is a lingering smell.
When you can drink make sure you drink your fill;
When you can let someone go let him go.

第三十一出　系　　帅

【三台令】

（生引众上）

长年坐策兵机，
这几日有些狐疑。
檀萝欲剪快如飞，
怎不见捷旌旗？

〔集唐〕

才到城门打鼓声，
《武陵》一曲想南征。
谁知一夜秦楼客，
白发新添四五茎。

俺淳于棼，久镇南柯，威名颇重。近乃公主避暑瑶台，幸解檀萝之困；只愁堑江一带，别遣周弁救援，颙伺捷音。蚤已分付司农，整排筵宴，十里长亭与周弁接喜，可蚤到也。

【前腔】

（田上）

太平筵上花枝，
酒旗风偃征旗。
喜气欲淋漓，
这胜算兵家怎拟？

Scene 31 Commander Imprisoned

(Enter Chunyu, attended)

【Three Terraces Minitune】

CHUNYU:

I´m a veteran at deploying troops,
but lately queer doubts have begun to sprout.
One quick assault should have subdued the foe.
Why so far is there no news of success?

At last the first drum sends the long day off;
A southern song reminds me of our troops.
Even if one hides in the pleasure house,
Patches of gray hair may occur at dawn.

I, Chunyu Fen, have been governing Southern Bough for a long time and have earned a high reputation. Recently, my wife the princess was besieged by the Sandalwoods in the marble palace, where she was spending the summer. Luckily, no harm was done. Only the situation at the gorge front remains uncertain. I´ve dispatched Zhou Bian there with a large detachment, and news of victory can be expected any moment. So I´ve told the finance minister to prepare a celebration banquet in his honor at the boundary pavilion. Ah, here comes the finance minister himself!

(Enter Tian Zihua)

【Ditto】

TIAN:

The banquet tables are bedecked with flowers;
wine pennons have replaced battalion flags.
We can look forward to a feast,
but how can the war´s outcome be foretold?

（见介）（田）

妙算老堂翁，

（生）

协赞是司农。

（田）

准备花前酒，

（生）

来听塞上风。

司农，战期已数日了，还不见捷报，俺心下忧疑。

（田）一来国主洪福，二来府主威光，三来司宪英勇，定然得胜而回。

（报上）

江山看是堑，

草木怕成兵。

报，报，报，周将军单马回城来了。

（生）司宪先回，多应得胜，叫乐工们响动。（内鼓吹介）

【北醉花阴】

（周弁幅巾白袍带剑走马上）

俺这里匹马单鞭怕提起，

即渐的一家儿这里。

头直上滚尘飞，

(He greets Chunyu)

Your tactics are the best designed.

CHUNYU:

You are the one who gave advice.

TIAN:

Wine and flowers are in abundance.

CHUNYU:

All we need is the border news.

Mr. Tian, it´s already several days since Commander Zhou left for the front, but so far we haven´t got a single word from him. That somewhat puzzles me.

TIAN: Don´t worry. He´ll come back with flying colors, for he´s an intrepid soldier, not to speak of the heavenly blessings our king enjoys and Your Excellency´s military prestige.

(Enter a messenger)

MESSENGER:

A natural barrier is the gorge,
But what if the trees turn hostiles?[1]

Report! Report! Report! Commander Zhou is returning to town on horseback all by himself.

CHUNYU: I guess he´s coming back ahead of his troops to personally announce his victory. Tell the musicians to strike up.

(Music within)

(Enter Zhou Bian galloping, hatless and in a plain white gown, a sword at his side)

【Drunk Under Flowers, Northern Style】[2]

ZHOU:

Conspicuousness is the last thing a lone man seeks;
finally, there´s only my horse and me,
with rolling dust above my head.

一边厢擂鼓扬旗，
那唱贺的欢天地。
(望介)原来是太老先生与司农寮长，置酒在长亭之上，咳，
他只道俺敲镫凯歌回，
曲恭恭来压喜。

(见介)请了。
(生)呀，周司宪得胜回来，俺同寮们安排喜酒。
(周)好了，好了，快讨酒来。

【南画眉序】
(生)
花柳散金杯，
一片惊心在眼儿里。
当初去，有黄金锁子甲，
怎全身赤体，
卸甲投盔？
睹形模事体堪疑，
得胜了怎单骑而至？
(田)不瞒堂尊大人说，周司宪此来，真个可疑。
(合)
怎的意头儿没张致？
还责取后来消息。

【北喜迁莺】
(周)
为甚俺裸肩扬臂？

Yonder, banners flutter and music blares;
a jolly crowd is chanting victory songs.

(Looks ahead) So, it´s my boss and my colleague the finance minister waiting there! They´ve spread a banquet for me at the boundary pavilion. Ah!

They think I´m bringing home a triumphant force,
and have come to applaud my feat.

(They greet each other)

ZHOU: Thanks for coming to meet me.

CHUNYU: Your colleagues and I have prepared a banquet to celebrate your triumphant return.

ZHOU: Thank you for taking so much trouble. Please pass me some wine.

【The Thrush Overture, Southern Style】

CHUNYU:

As if trees had blossomed in gold,
my eyes are shocked and filled with dazzling stars.

When he set out, he was wearing a gold chain-mail coat.

What happened to his armor suit?
And the helmet on his head?
His appearance can´t but suspicions raise.
How can a triumphant army be one man?

TIAN: Your Excellency, frankly speaking, Commander Zhou´s return seems rather strange.

BOTH (refrain):

How´s it he acts as if he´s lost his head?
We certainly should further question him.

【Nesting Orioles, Northern Style】

ZHOU:

You ask why I´m swinging my naked arms.

热天头助喊扬威。
颓也么颓，
没个儿帮闲取势，
激的俺赤甲山前被虏围。

（生）呀！被围了，怎的出得来？

（周）

冲围退，
不是俺使些精细，
险些儿头利无归。

快讨酒来。

（生）这等是兵败了，还说酒哩。且问你：

【南画眉序】

当日摆兵齐，
半万个选锋尽跟你。
一个个枪来会躲，
箭去能挥。

如何通不见一个回来？

你一家儿人马平安，
那些儿何方使费？（合前）

（周）那五千个人去时，俺是见他来。

【北出队子】

给千兵果然编配，

Because it was hot and I cheered the troops.
Damn my luck!
None was there to lend me a helping hand,
so my brave self was surrounded at Red Rock Cliff.[3]

CHUNYU: What! You were surrounded?! How did you manage to escape?

ZHOU:

By slipping out, of course.
If I did not have a resourceful head,
I´d have lost both interest and capital.

Pour me some more wine.

CHUNYU: So you mean you were defeated. Stop drinking for a moment. Let me ask you:

【The Thrush Overture, Southern Style】

CHUNYU:

The other day we reviewed the troops.
Five thousand best were then assigned to you.
All of them know how to avoid the blade,
and how to fend off arrows.
How is it not a single one of them came back?
But you alone made it back safe and sound?
What happened to those fifty hundred men?
(Refrain)

ZHOU: I remember seeing them when I set out.

【Cheer Leaders, Northern Style】

ZHOU:

No doubt I was assigned five thousand men.

点兵单个个齐。

(生)战场上可有呢?

(周)战时还有，战了后，俺通不知那里去了?

(田)司宪公，敢是尽被檀萝杀了?

(周)这也难道。

(生)则问他半万个人头。

(周)

划单鞭投至一身亏，

甚半万个人头要俺赔?

呀，

你便是半万个泥头俺也赔不起。

(生)我说人头，他说泥头，是怎的?通不听他，只以军法从事，先斩后奏了。

(周)谁敢无理!

(生恼介)败军之将，还敢倔强!

【南滴溜子】

败军的，

败军的，

全生误国。

论军法，

论军法，

难容恕你。

叫正典刑是理。

诸人听指挥：

将他捆执，

量决一刀，

做个旁州之例。

They were there when I called the roll.

CHUNYU: Didn´t they follow you to the battleground?

ZHOU: They were with me when we engaged the enemy, but after the battle I don´t know where they went.

TIAN: Sir, do you mean they were all slaughtered by the Sandalwoods?

ZHOU: Maybe.

CHUNYU: You´re responsible for those five thousand lives!

ZHOU:

Can´t you see how much I´ve already lost?
Are you charging me for those fifty hundred heads?
I can´t even pay for the fifty hundred liquor jars.

CHUNYU: I´m talking about human lives, and you keep talking about wine jars. Are you nuts? No more of your nonsense! I´ll have you court-martialed and executed on the spot without preapproval by His Majesty.

ZHOU: You wouldn´t dare!

CHUNYU (angrily): You´re a loser! What face do you have to talk back!

【Glassy Slippy, Southern Style】

CHUNYU:

You lost the war,
you lost our land.
You only saved your skin.
By military law,
by military law,
you cannot be pardoned.
An execution is what you deserve.
All you there, now I order you:
Tie him up tight and fast,
and cut off his head
to set an example for other men.

(众持刀绑，周不伏介)

【北刮地风】

(周)呀，

忽地波怒吽吽坏脸皮，
那些儿刘备、张飞？
大槐安国内君王婿，
谁不知倚势施为？
便做着你正堂尊贵，
俺可也不性命低微。

(生)快取首级哩。

(周笑介)

俺怎生般透贼围，
挣得这首级归，
你划口儿闲胡戏。
你便申军法，
俺怎遵依？
“斩”字儿你可也再休题。

(生)俺是掌印官，施行你不得？叫刽子手，一齐向前绑了。

(田)禀堂尊：此事未可造次。

【南滴滴金】

(田)

念周郎至友同乡籍，
地拆里相逢忒遭际。
横枝儿住札南柯地，
是堂尊荐及，

(Zhou struggles as attendants, broadsword in hand, try to tie him up)

【The Sweeping Winds, Northern Style】

ZHOU: What´s this?

All at once you put on another face.
What of the brotherhood of Liu and Zhang?[4]
As Son-in-law of the Sophora king,
you used to bully your subordinates.
You may be the noble prefectural chief,
but my life is in no way dirtlike cheap!

CHUNYU: Behead him immediately!

ZHOU (laughing scornfully):

How valiantly through the enemy lines
I fought my way back just to save my neck!
And now with a flip of your ready tongue,
invoking military law,
you expect me to obey?
Never again pronounce the word "behead"!

CHUNYU: I´m the person in charge here. Why can´t I punish you? You headsmen, get him tied up!

TIAN: Your Excellency, don´t push too hard.

【Every Drop Gold, Southern Style】

TIAN:

Please consider: He´s a friend from our native place.
How shall we face him in the netherworld?
The fact that he came to our Southern Bough,
and was appointed security chief,
was by your recommendation.
Think of the merry moments we shared in the past.
Think twice.
This is not an occasion to make haste.

荐及他为元帅。
他平生也为人今怎的?
堪详细,
便消停到底争迟疾。

(生)依说便再问他。周弁,你因何犯此失机之罪?

(周)非关小将之事,也非关五千个军人之事,都是你堂尊半万个泥头酒。诸人走渴之时,一鼓而醉,忽报檀萝索战,一个个手觯脚软。只小将一人,酒量颇高,向前迎战,独力难加,只得弃甲丢枪,乘夜而走。你不信,有诗为证:

暑往寒来春复秋,
夕阳西下水东流。
将军战马今何在?
野草闲花满地愁。

这都是你半万个泥头酒之过也。

【北四门子】

千不合万不合伊把半万个泥头兑,
烧不是水不是蒙汗药酘的醅。
却怎生软兀剌烧葱腿难跳踢?
急麻查扶泥臂刀怎提?

(生)这等怎生战的来?

(周)还说战哩。

(生)这等,则怕檀萝军杀过堑江城这边来了?

(周)这到不要慌。俺留下一计,正待抢杀进城,被俺将酒泥头尽数

CHUNYU: All right. Let´s question him further. Zhou Bian, how could you possibly have lost the war?

ZHOU: It was not my fault, nor was it the fault of the five thousand soldiers. It was your fault for giving us the five thousand jars of wine. A forced march made us thirsty, and we drank and became drunk. Just at that time, the Sandalwoods challenged us to a fight. Our hands and feet were all limp and numb. All were drunk except me, because I have an insatiable capacity. I dashed forth to meet the enemy, but a single man couldn´t defeat so many. So I had to dump my armor and spear, and slip away under cover of night. If you don´t believe me, a poem can prove my words. It goes:

Summer and winter take their endless turns;
The sun goes west, the rivers always east.[5]
Where is the hero who once made his fame?
Wild grass has reclaimed the historic site.

It was all the fault of your five thousand jars of wine.

【Four Janitors, Northern Style】

You shouldn´t have made good your promise of five thousand jars.
Neither wine nor water, it must have been a mickey brew,
otherwise, how could our legs have been weak as string beans
boiled,
our arms as limp as mud that couldn´t lift a sword?

CHUNYU: The way you put it, probably no one could have put up a good fight.

ZHOU: Fight? No way!

CHUNYU: Well, I´m afraid by now the Sandalwoods have swarmed past Gorgeville and are on their way here.

ZHOU: Don´t worry. I had an ace up my sleeve. I had the clay jars strewn all over the battlefield. When the enemy tried to charge the town, their

丢在战场之上，把他战马一个个都绊倒了，不曾抢的城来。此又半万个泥头酒之功也。

那酒瓶儿似山，
泥头似堆，
党沙场滑剌叉酬退了贼。
你记他一功，
赎他一罪，
道的个君当恕、
人之醉。

(生)周弁，你去时俺怎生说来？酒要少吃，事要多知，你都不在意。一定要正军法。

(周)哎！从古来谁不饮酒？天若不爱酒，天应无酒星；地若不爱酒，地应无酒泉。天地都爱酒，俺饮酒是兵权。汉樊哙，三国周公瑾、关云长，都也贪杯，希罕于俺一人？

【南鲍老催】

(生)

你攀今比昔，
那樊将军他殢酒把鸿门碎；
关大王面赤非干醉；
比周瑜，
饮醇醪，
量难及。

也罢，俺念你一是同乡，二是同寮，停了军法，且把你牢固监候，

horses tripped over the jars. So Gorgeville is safe. You see, the wine jars turned out to be useful after all.

The empty jars piled up mountain-high,
the clay turned into hills,
and the slippery slime on the ground bogged them down.
Give him merit
to set off his crime.
It´s said a gentleman should pardon
a drunken slip.

CHUNYU: Zhou Bian, what did I tell you when we parted? "Drink less and think more." And you didn´t pay any attention. I should have you court-martialed!

ZHOU: Bosh! If you read history, was there ever a man who didn´t drink? If heaven didn´t like wine, there wouldn´t be a wine star up there. If earth didn´t like wine, there wouldn´t be a place called Wine Spring down here. Given that both heaven and earth like wine, my drinking is nothing but a show of military might. Fan Kuai[6] of the Han Dynasty, and Zhou Yu[7] and Guan Yu of the Three Kingdoms Period were all heavy drinkers. Why must I alone be blamed?

【Old Bao in Haste, Southern Style】

CHUNYU:

Historical references will not help,
for General Fan drank to foil the Hongmen Plot;
and Guan Yu´s red face was not due to wine.
Compared with Zhou Yu,
his degree of charm
is beyond your match.

Well, considering the fact that we´re from the same native place and we´ve been colleagues for so long, I´ll suspend the execution and simply put you

奏请定夺。

　　把你贪杯子反的头权寄，
　　上丹青于禁身牢系，
　　忙奏请随宽急。

(生)兵快们，拿周弁监了。(众绑周不伏介)

【北水仙子】

(周)

　　呀，呀，呀，
　　放你的呸！

(生恼介)拿也！

(周取剑舞介)

　　拿，拿，拿，
　　拿的俺怒气冲天舞剑晖。

(生)住了！你道俺拿不的你么？挂起令旨旗牌来。(挂起旗牌介)

(田)司宪公，酒放醒些，抬眼哩。

(周看作怕背介)

　　他，他，他，
　　他叫俺挣着眯瞁。

(抹眼介)

　　我，我，我，
　　打些儿抹昧。

(回斜看介)

　　可，可，可，
　　可怎生挂起了老君王令旨旗？
　　你，你，你，
　　你敢有甚么密切钦依？

(众)周司宪，挂了令旨不跪，是何道理？

behind bars, pending His Majesty´s judgment.

You may retain your sottish head a few more days
to reflect on the shame of your defeat,
while I submit a report to the king.

Attendants, throw him in jail.

(Zhou puts up a struggle as attendants try to tie him up)

【The Narcissus Flower, Northern Style】

ZHOU:

Shit! Shit! Shit!
Bullshit of you!

CHUNYU (enraged): Hold him!

ZHOU (draws and wields his sword):

Hold! Hold! Hold!
I can no longer hold my anger nor myself.

CHUNYU: Stop that! You think I don´t have the authority to penalize you? Attendants, raise His Majesty´s personal flag.

(Attendants raise the flag)

TIAN: Commander Zhou, you´d better sober up. Look up there.

ZHOU (looks up and then looks away, intimidated):

He, he, he,
he told me to open my gummy eyes.
(He wipes his eyes)
I, I, I,
I´d rather stay boozy woozy.
(He glances over his shoulder)
But, but, but,
but why did they raise His Majesty´s personal flag?
You, you, you,
do you possess a secret warrant from the king?

ATTENDANTS: Commander Zhou, how is it you don´t prostrate yourself before His Majesty´s personal flag?

（周反手介）

火，火，火，
火的俺阃外将军向阃内归。
少，少，少，
少不的拖番硬腿随朝跪。（跪介）

（生）周司宪，可伏绑了？
（周）周弁不是伏别人，

这，这，这，
这是俺为臣子识高低。

（生）这等，送你收监去。（行介）

【南双生子】

前日里，
前日里，
曾劝你酒休吃。
全不记，
全不记，
鬼弄送胡支对。
输到底，
输到底。
倒了嘴，
倒了嘴。
看君王发落，
权时监里。

（丑上）司狱官接爷。
（生）周司宪败军，暂请此中宽坐数日。
（周恼介）咳，周弁何等英雄，今日到此。

ZHOU (putting his hands behind him):
Why, why, why,
why must a general surrender to a bureaucrat?
Well, well, well,
I might as well bend my knees before the royal flag.
(He kneels)
CHUNYU: Commander Zhou, are you ready to surrender now?
ZHOU: I´m not surrendering to anyone, but
this, this, this,
this is what a subject should do before the crown.

CHUNYU: Now I´ll personally see you to the prison. (They walk)

【Twin Lines, Southern Style】
The other day,
the other day
I advised you not to drink.
In one ear,
out the other,
you made a vague promise to fob me off.
Defeated now,
defeated now,
you brag no more,
you brag no more.
Wait in your cell
to be sentenced by the king.

(Enter a jailer)
JAILER: The jailer greets Your Excellency.
CHUNYU: You guilty man, please take a few days´ rest in here.
ZHOU (sighs): Ah! What a hero I was, and now I have fallen so low!

【北尾】

俺透重围

透不出这牢墙内。

背膊上好不疼也！好歹和俺瞧一瞧哩。

（众看笑介）一个酒刺儿，大红疙疸。

（周）罢了，罢了。

敢气的俺周亚夫疽生背。

俺气死不怨别的，则怨着半万个酒堆儿也。

悔不当初，

悔不当初枕着个破泥头，

做一个醉卧沙场征战鬼。（下）

（生）

三军斩首为贪杯，

（田）

一面权收寄剑才。

（合）

今朝酒醒知寒色，

悔不当初奏凯回。

【Coda, Northern Style】

I can break through a heavy siege,
but I can´t break out of this cell!

Ouch! There´s a pain in my back. Please take a look and tell me what´s wrong.

ATTENDANTS (looking and laughing): It´s nothing but a big red wine pimple.

ZHOU: What a shame! What a shame!

Is my fury blowing out as an ulcer on my back?

If I should die of remorse, those five thousand jars of wine are to blame.

How I regret
I didn´t die with my head pillowed on the earth
and become a drunken ghost haunting the battleground!

(Exit Zhou)

CHUNYU:

He lost his head because he loved the cup.

TIAN:

A reprieve was granted the gifted man.

BOTH:

Sobering up he grew aware of dread.
How he regrets he didn´t win the war!

第三十二出　朝　　议

【小蓬莱】

（王引众上）

世界于今几变，
精灵自古如常。
槐国为王，
柯庭遣将，
近事堪惆怅。

〔集唐〕

隋朝杨柳映堤稀，
台殿云凉秋色微。
闻道王师犹转战，
黄龙戍卒几时归。

寡人槐安大国，素与檀萝小仇。近乃公主困围，侥幸驸马救解。别遣周弁往援堑江，捷书未见飞传，右相必知消息。

【前腔】

（右相持表文上）

俨尔尊为右相，
居然翼戴君王。

咳，

Scene 32 A Court Session

(Enter King, attended)

【Little Penglai】

KING:

The world has gone through many a change,
all the while insects remain the same.
I, the Sophora king,
command the nation´s troops,
but recent events worry me.

Willows on the old dike are thinning fast,
As palace autumn chills the paling clouds.
The royal troops are still engaged in war.
When can the expedition make it back?

Big as my Sophora kingdom is, wee have long held a little grudge against Rattan Sandalwood. Recently, they besieged the princess. Fortunately, my son-in-law was able to rescue her. At the same time, he dispatched Zhou Bian to reinforce Gorgeville, but since then wee have lost track of events. My right-hand premier might have the latest news.

(Enter Right-hand Premier, holding a scroll)

【Ditto】

PREMIER:

Eminent as a premier is,
staunchly I still support the king.
Rules have been established,
yet borders neglected.
A new report speeds me to Court.

立下朝纲，

坏了边防，

奏到星忙上。

吾为右相，每念南柯重地，驸马王亲，在郡二十余年，威权太盛。常愁他根深不剪，尾大难摇。偶值公主困围，堑江失事，得他威名少损，此亦不幸中之幸也。星夜驸马奏来，请正将军周弁之罪。俺将表文带进，相机而行。(见介)臣右相段功见。

(王)右相外来，颇知檀萝用兵胜算乎？

(右)驸马飞传表文，臣谨奏上。

【琐窗郎】

(右)

念臣棼诚恐诚惶，

堑江城遭寇与拦当。

(王)有周弁领兵去。

(右)

谁料三军出境，

止得一将还乡。

(王)这等，大败了。

(右)

臣棼肺腑，

理难欺诳。

望我王

将臣削职随钦降，

还议罪

周弁将。

As the right-hand premier, the strategically important Southern Bough always sits on my mind. His Majesty´s son-in-law has been governing that place for twenty-odd years, and has gained too much prestige. It often worries me to think that his roots are striking ever deeper into the soil, and, as a proverb has it, one cannot comfortably control a heavy tail. Happily, the princess´ plight and the loss at Gorgeville have more or less marred his reputation. Here´s an urgent report he has just sent in, asking His Majesty to punish Zhou Bian. I´ll hand it in and bide my time. (Greets King) Your Majesty´s humble servant and Right-hand Premier, Duan Gong, seeks an audience.

KING: Since you just came in, do you happen to have any news about our war against the Sandalwoods?

PREMIER: The royal son-in-law has just sent in an urgent report. This is what it says:

【Man at the Window】

With reverence and awe Chunyu reports:
Gorgeville was attacked and we reinforced.

KING: Yes, Zhou Bian led a force there.

PREMIER:

The three services were dispatched,
but only one man reemerged.

KING: Does that mean wee suffered a heavy defeat?

PREMIER:

Chunyu must tell the truth,
for cheating is no use.
I beg Your Majesty
to demote or discharge my humble self,
and pass sentence on
Commander Zhou.

KING: A country´s fortune is a reflection of the times. When the time is

(王)论我国家气势，得时而羽翼能飞，失水则蛟龙可制。瑣瑣檀萝，遭其挫败。咳！驸马好不老成也。

【前腔】

倚南柯锁钥疆场，
那檀萝多大势难当。
怎提兵数万，
战死残伤？
这风声外敌，
把吾轻相。

可恼！可恼！

驸马在中军帐，
怎的用周弁将？

【前腔】

(右)

论边机失误非常，
则二十年为驸马也星霜。

(王)正是，俺也念驸马在边年久，加以公主屡请还朝，止为南柯太守难得其人，因此暂止。

(右)驸马取回，还有田子华在彼。

看田生知略，
可代淳郎。
堪取回公主，
到京调养。

(王)春秋丧师，责在大夫，今日驸马之过也。

right, wee can put on wings and soar. On the other hand, even the dragon can be grounded when it´s out of its element. And now wee have been defeated by that teeny weeny Sandalwood! Ah! My son-in-law should have acted more discreetly!

【Ditto】

Upon our home ground of the southern bough,
how could Sandalwood get the upper hand?
Why have tens of thousands of our braves
all been mangled and maimed?
Should other countries learn of that,
they´d surely belittle us.
What a shame! What a shame!
Since he had full authority,
why did he select
that Commander Zhou?!

【Ditto】

PREMIER:

No doubt this event is a serious blow,
but his twenty years at the front was quite a feat.

KING: That´s right. I know it must have been hard for him to serve on the frontiers for so long, not to mention that the princess has asked many times for permission to return to the capital. But the problem is that I haven´t been able to find a more suitable person to replace him.

PREMIER: Mr. Tian can take over if the royal son-in-law is recalled.

If by his talents wee judge him,
Tian can succeed Chunyu,
so that the princess may come home
to recover her health.

KING: According to long-established tradition, the chief executive must take the blame for a military defeat. In this case, the royal son-in-law is

（右）

妨亲碍贵宜包奖，
权坐罪
周弁将。

（王）这等，周弁失机应斩。

（右）周弁乃驸马至交，两次荐举，斩周弁恐伤驸马之心，不如免死，立功赎罪。

（王）依奏。

周弁免死且饶他，
接管南柯田子华。
公主惊伤同驸马，
即时钦取到京华。

responsible.

PREMIER:

Kinfolk and lords should always be exempt.
If someone is to blame,
let it be Commander Zhou.

KING: You´re right. Zhou Bian failed in his mission. He should be beheaded.

PREMIER: Zhou Bian and Your Majesty´s son-in-law are very close friends, and he was twice recommended by Chunyu. If you´re to have him executed, you may hurt the other´s feelings. Why not spare his life and let him atone for his crime with some future exploits?

KING: Very well.

While Zhou Bian is spared from the headsman´s ax,
Southern Bough is handed to Tian Zihua.
Both the exhausted princess and her spouse
Should to the capital be summoned back.

第三十三出　召　还

【意迟迟】

（贴扶病旦上）

一自瑶台耽怕恐，
愁绝多娇种。
泪湿枕痕红，
秋槐落叶时惊梦。

（贴）

倚妆台掠鬓玉梳慵，
盼宫闱不断眉山耸。

〔古调笑〕

（旦）

魂去，
魂去，
梦到瑶台秋意。
醒来依旧南柯，
折抹娇多病多。
多病，
多病，
富贵丛中薄命。

Scene 33 Recalled to Court

(Enter Princess, sick, and supported by a maid)

【A Languid Mind】

PRINCESS:

The siege has left me in relentless fear
— a sharp blow to my feeble health.
Tears seep into my pillow case;
a falling leaf would devastate my dream.

MAID:

Her combing often pauses in the midst;
her eyes would go moist at the thought of home.

PRINCESS:

My soul roams,
My soul roams,
To the autumn palace it floats,
Only to wake up at Southern Bough,
Torturing my weak self sicker still.
Sicker still,
Sicker still,
A hard fate in a luxurious home.

I was born weak and delicate. The trauma of the recent siege, Zhou Bian's defeat, and my husband's consequent humiliation have all added to the burden of my heavy heart. I've therefore submitted several petitions asking for permission to return to Court so as to be with my parents and regain my health. A private consideration is that my husband has stayed too long at Southern Bough and attained too much prestige, and so I'm afraid the courtiers will very likely feel jealous and threatened. If I'm back

自家生成弱体，加以围困惊伤；又听周弁败兵，驸马惶愧，奴家一发伤心。曾经几度启请回朝，图见父王、母亲，一来奴家得以养息；二来驸马久在南柯，威名太重，朝臣岂无妒忌之心？待俺归去，替他牢固根基；三来替儿女完成恩荫之事：未知令旨蚤晚何如？

【步蟾宫】

（生上）

一片愁云低画栋，
挂暮雨珠帘微动。
倚雕栏和泪折残红，
消受得玉人情重。

（见介）公主，贵体若何？

（旦）多分是不好了。且问驸马，来此多年？

（生）整整二十年了。

（旦叹介）淳郎夫，听奴一言：奴家生长王宫，不想有你姻缘，成其匹配。俺助你南柯政事，颇有威名。近日檀萝败兵，你威名顿损；兼之廿年太守，不可再留。俺死为你先驱蝼蚁耳。（泣介）

（内作树声清亮、生问介）此声何也？

（儿上介）禀爹娘：是槐树作声。

（旦笑介）驸马，这树声清亮，可喜。

（生）难得公主这一喜。

（旦）你不知，此中槐树，号为声音木，我国中但有拜相者，此树即

in the capital I can help him consolidate his base. And I can also make marriage arrangements for my sons and daughters. But, so far, no royal response has been issued.

(Enter Chunyu)

【Strolling in Lunar Palace】

CHUNYU:

A heavy cloud hangs from the painted eaves;
raindrops weave into a curtain of beads.
By the balustrade she picks up fallen red;
her deep affection is immeasurable!

(Greets Princess) My dear, how do you feel today?

PRINCESS: Not very well. Let me ask you: How long have wee lived here?

CHUNYU: It´s exactly twenty years.

PRINCESS (sighs): Darling, there´s something I must impart to you. I was born and raised in the seclusion of the palace, and had never imagined that fate would bring us together and make us man and wife. With my assistance, you´ve established an eminent reputation, but the recent defeat by the Sandalwoods has all of a sudden tarnished your name. Besides, twenty years is really too long for one to govern the same jurisdiction. Take my advice and quit immediately. After my death, I´ll be a cricket or an ant, and wait for you underground. (She cries)

(A rustle of leaves within)

CHUNYU: What´s that sound?

SON (enters): It´s the Sophora singing.

PRINCESS (breaking into a smile): Darling, the sound seems so light-hearted and merry.

CHUNYU: Oh, how nice to see you smile!

PRINCESS: You probably don´t know that the Sophora is also called the music wood. It produces a pleasant sound whenever a new premier is to be appointed in my country. I guess this is a good omen that you´ll soon

吐清音。看此佳兆，驸马蚤晚入为丞相矣。则恐我去之后，你千难万难那！

【集贤宾】

（旦）

　　论人生到头难悔恐，

　　寻常儿女情钟，

　　有恩爱的夫妻情事冗。

奴家并不曾亏了驸马，则我去之后，驸马不得再娶呵，

　　累你影凄凄被冷房空。

淳于郎，你回朝去不比以前了。

　　看人情自懂，

　　俺死后百凡尊重。

（合）

　　心疼痛，

　　只愿的凤楼人永。

【前腔】

（生泣介）公主呵，

　　听一声声惨然词未终，

　　对杜宇啼红。

　　你去后俺甘心受唧哝，

　　则这些儿女难同。

公主呵，

　　你的恩深爱重，

　　二十载南柯护从。（合前）

be promoted to that post. What worries me is that after I´m gone things may get very, very difficult for you.

【Honored Guests】

At life´s end one tends to review its course.
In youth, love was a straight affair;
an older couple, however, have much more cares.

I never did anything unworthy of your love. After my death, I hope you won´t take another wife.

I hate to leave you with a cold bed and empty room.

Darling, when you return to Court, it won´t be the same as it was.

Learn to handle relations well;
be cautious and uphold your self-respect.
(Refrain)
My heart aches.
How I wish wee could both forever live!

【Ditto】

CHUNYU (weeping): Dear princess,
every word you said was torn from a bleeding heart,
like a cuckoo dripping blood.[1]
They´ll echo in my ears through my remaining days,
something our children may not understand.
Oh, dear,
your unreserved love has buoyed me
through twenty long years in Southern Bough.
(Refrain)

【Amber Cat´s Eye】

PRINCESS (weeping):
Fits of cold and fever
have bleached the rosy color from my cheeks.

【琥珀猫儿坠】

(旦泣介)

如寒似热，
消尽了脸霞红。
那宫女开函俺奏几封，
蚤些儿飞入大槐宫。

(生拜介)

天公，
前程紧处，
略放轻松。

(旦)病到此际，也则索罢了。

(生)怎说这话？

【前腔】

(生)

香肌弱体，
须护好帘栊。
裙带留仙怕倚风，
把异香烧取明月中。

(旦)

惺忪，
断魂一缕，
分付乘龙。

(儿上)报，报，报，令旨到。爹爹，娘病了，怎生接旨？

(生)儿子，扶着母亲拜便了。

(紫读诏介)令旨已到，跪听宣读。大槐国王令旨：公主瑶芳同驸马淳

Please ask the maid to prepare paper, ink and pen,
for I must write to the Sophora Court.

CHUNYU (bows):

Heaven above!
At the tight turns of life,
please relax yourself.

PRINCESS: Considering my condition, maybe I do need to let go.

CHUNYU: Don´t say that.

【Ditto】

As for your delicate health,
just keep the curtains tightly drawn
in case admiring winds carry you off,
while I burn magic incense toward the moon.

PRINCESS:

Faint and frail,
a hanging thread of life,
I´ve disclosed my mind to you.

(Reenter Son, followed by a palace officer in a purple robe holding an edict)

SON: Report! Report! Report! Here comes an imperial edict. Dad, Mom is so sick, how can she receive the edict?

CHUNYU: You can lend her a hand.

OFFICER: Here comes His Majesty´s decree. Kneel and listen. (Reads) By edict of the king of the Great Sophora, Princess Yaofang and Chunyu Fen the royal son-in-law are recalled to Court. For his years of excellent service in Southern Bough, Chunyu Fen is promoted to the position of the left-hand premier. The Taishou´s office of Southern Bough is to be taken over by Tian Zihua, the present prefectural finance minister. That is my wish. Express your gratitude.

于梦，南柯功高岁久，钦取回朝，进居左丞相之职。其南柯郡事，着司农田子华代之。钦哉！谢恩。

（众呼千岁起介）

（旦）恭喜驸马，拜相当朝。槐树清音，果成佳兆。

（生）多谢公主抬举。（紫叩头介）

（生）周弁作何处置？

（紫）有旨了，驸马分上，免死立功。

（生）天恩浩大哩！且请皇华馆筵宴。

（紫）

诏许王人会，

恩催上相归。（下）

（生）公主，我在此多年，一朝离去，应有数日周详善后之事。待着孩儿送你先行，到朝门之外，候俺一齐朝见。

（旦）正是。则这二十年南柯郡舍，一旦抛离，好感伤人也！

（生）人生如传舍，何况官衙？则你将息贵体。孩儿看酒。（酒上介）

【皂莺儿】

（生）

杯酒散愁容，

病宫花小桂丛。

我儿呵，

(All shout "May His Majesty live a thousand years!" and then rise to their feet)

PRINCESS: Congratulations on your promotion to premier. The prophecy of the Sophora tree has come true.

CHUNYU: I should thank you for all you´ve done for me.

(Officer kowtows to Chunyu)

CHUNYU: What sentence is pronounced on Zhou Bian?

OFFICER: His Majesty decreed that for the sake of your friendship with him he is exempted from the death penalty, and is permitted to atone for his defeat by future victories.

CHUNYU: How merciful His Majesty is! Please attend a banquet at the guesthouse.

OFFICER:

When the king assembles his Court,
It´s time the premier was recalled.

(Exit Officer)

CHUNYU: My dear, after so many years here I think I need a few days to clear up the loose ends in order to hand my position over properly. You and our children may go first. I´ll catch up with you in the capital, and we´ll make our appearance at Court together.

PRINCESS: All right. In fact, I also feel that it´s very hard to tear myself away from this home. Wee have lived for twenty years in this house!

CHUNYU: One´s life is just a journey, going from one station to another. What of this official mansion? The most important thing is your health. Children, bring us some wine. (Wine is brought in)

【The Black Oriole】

CHUNYU:

A cup of wine expels your woes,
and helps to flame a pallid rose.

Son,

你长途细把亲娘奉，
调和进供，
温凉酌中。
你乌纱绰鬓非无用。

(末)

承爹厚命，
叮咛在胸；
奉娘前进，
寒温必躬；
管平安遇有人传送。

(合)

靠苍穹，
一家美满，
排备御筵红。

(贴报介)启公主、驸马：外间官属、百姓等，闻的公主回朝，都在府门外求见。

(旦)宫婢，你说公主分付，生受你南柯百姓二十年，今日公主扶病而回，则除是来生补报了。(内哭介)

(生)叫不要感伤了公主。看轿来。

金枝玉叶病委蕤，
廿载南柯寄一枝。
不是大家随子去，
争看贵主入宫时。

take care of Mother on the distant road.
Keep her diet balanced;
make her warm and snug.
To shoulder responsibilities you´re old enough.

SON:

I´ll bear in mind
your very words.
I´ll see to it
that Mom is fine,
and send you a message from time to time.

BOTH:

Heaven show mercy!
And make us happy.
A royal feast is ready.

MAID (reports): Your Ladyship and Your Excellency, the officials and peasants are grieved to learn that the princess is leaving. They´ve gathered outside the gate to say goodbye.

PRINCESS: Go and tell them that I´m most grateful to them for their twenty years of support. Since my health doesn´t permit it now, I´ll repay their kindness in my next life.

(Crying and wailing within)

CHUNYU: Tell them not to cry. That distresses the princess even more. Bring in a sedan chair.

The golden bough has become indisposed
After a score of years transplanted south.
It´s not a sick branch leaving with its scions;
It´s the princess returning with éclat.

第三十四出　卧　辙

【浪淘沙】

（老录事上）

狗命带酸寒，
不做高官，
白头纱帽保平安。
职掌批行和带管，
有的钱钻。

自家南柯府录事官便是。南柯府堂风水，单好出些老官。你不信？驸马爷二十年，田司农二十年，俺录事也二十余年。来时油光嘴脸，如今胡子皓白了。天恩钦取公主、驸马还朝，三日前公主起行，驸马将府事交盘与田司农，今日起程。司农爷长亭饯别，蚤分付了。驸马爷来时是太守，今回朝去是个左丞相了。车路欠平，着人堆沙，填起一堤，约有三十里长，两头结彩为门，题着四个大字："新筑沙堤"，好些小百姓来看也。

Scene 34 Blocking the Road

(Enter Chief of Staff, advanced in years)

【Washing off Sand】

CHIEF:

My life is cheaper than a dog´s,
so I can´t expect to rise;
my only hope is to live long and safe.
Now my signature is of consequence,
I have a lot to reap.

I´m the chief of staff of Southern Bough Prefecture. The *fengshui*[1] of this official mansion seems to favor lengthy terms of office. You don´t believe it? Take for example the royal son-in-law. He was Taishou for twenty years. Lord Tian, the finance minister, has also held that office for twenty years, and I myself have been the chief of staff for twenty-odd years. When I first took this job, my cheeks were smooth and ruddy. But now, even my beard is stubbly and gray. By heaven´s grace, the princess and royal son-in-law have finally been recalled to Court. The princess set out three days ago, and the royal son-in-law, having handed over his office to Lord Tian, is leaving today. A grand farewell banquet has been ordered by Lord Tian at the boundary pavilion. He said it´s a remarkable accomplishment of Lord Chunyu that he came as Taishou and is leaving as left-hand premier. The road is rough, and so fresh sand was spread over it for ten miles.[2] A gate was erected at each end, decorated with silk flowers and a board inscribed with four big characters: "Newly Built Sand Causeway." Many locals have gathered to watch the festivities.

(Enter village elders holding a petition)

【Ditto】

【前腔】

（扮父老持奏上）

少壮老平安，
一郡清官。
贤哉太守被征还，
百姓保留天又远，
要打通关。

（见丑跪介）参军爷，小的们有下情。

（丑）甚么事？

（父老）淳于爷管府事二十年，百姓家安户乐，海阔春深。一旦钦取回朝，百姓怎生舍得？

（丑）这不干俺事。

（父老）众父老商量，尽南柯府城士民男妇，签名上本，保留淳于爷再住十年。京师窎远，敢央及参军爷，拨下快马十数匹，一日一夜三百里，飞将本去，万一令旨着驸马爷中路而转，重镇南柯。但凭百姓们亲赍，恐不济事了。

（丑惊介）你们要留太爷，怕上本迟了，央俺拨快马十数匹，一日一夜飞将本去，万一令旨着驸马爷中路而转，重镇南柯。罢了，列位父老哥，免照顾。

（父老泣介）参军爷不准，央田爷去。

（丑）央田爷么？你去，你去。（众起介）（丑）回来，讲与你听：便是田爷知南柯府事了，不好意思得。

ELDERS:

Both the old and young live in peace
under a clean government.
Now our beloved Taishou is recalled,
wee want to make him stay, but heaven´s far
— many passes block our way.[3]

(They kneel before Chief of Staff) Your Honor, wee have a favor to ask.

CHIEF: What is it?

ELDERS: Under Lord Chunyu´s twenty-year rule wee peasants enjoyed a peace as vast as the sea and a happiness as warm as springtime. Wee simply can´t bear to let him go.

CHIEF: That´s none of my business.

ELDERS: Wee have discussed the matter among ourselves, and here is a petition signed by every man and woman in Southern Bough requesting that Lord Chunyu be retained as Taishou for another ten years. Since the capital is far away, wee beg Your Honor to arrange for a dozen fast horses that can cover one hundred miles a day to take this petition to Court. By good luck, it may bring about a new decree so as to intercept the royal son-in-law halfway and send him back to Southern Bough. If wee have to carry it to the capital ourselves, it may be too late.

CHIEF (surprised): You want to have His Excellency retained? You´re afraid that your petition may be too late, so you´re asking me to arrange for a dozen fast horses to relay your petition day and night to Court in the hope that a decree will intercept His Excellency midway and send him back to govern Southern Bough once again? Forget it! Respected elders, please spare me.

ELDERS (weeping): If you won´t help us, wee will go and ask Lord Tian.

CHIEF: Ask Lord Tian? Do as you please. Do as you please. (Elders rise to their feet and are about to leave) Just a minute! Let me tell you, it´s Lord Tian who´ll replace Lord Chunyu. You´d embarrass him.

（父老）原来新太爷就是田爷，不便央他了，还是百姓们蚁行而去罢。

（丑）着了。田爷将到。（众避介）

【一落索】

（田上）

　　廿载府堂签判，

　　奉旨超阶正转。

　　长亭相送旧堂还，

呀！

　　塞路的人千万。

（丑参见介）禀老大人：酒筵齐备。

（田）红尘拥路，想都是送太爷的么？好百姓！好百姓！

（丑）鼓吹声喧，太爷蚤到。（田、丑走接介）

【懒画眉】

（生引众上）

　　一鞭行色晓云残，

　　五马归朝百姓看。

（内作喊哭）俺的太爷呵！

（生）拥路者数千人，因何如此？

（丑）都是攀留太爷的。

（生）

　　原来是衔恩赤子要追攀，

　　俺有何功德沾名宦？

知道了，是百姓们厚意，

ELDERS: So Lord Tian is the new Taishou. In that case it´s certainly improper to ask him. Wee have to crawl all the way to the capital ourselves.
CHIEF: Do as you please. Ah, here comes Lord Tian.
(Elders withdraw to one side)

(Enter Tian Zihua)

【A String of Pearls】

TIAN:

For twenty years a subordinate,
then I became the superordinate.
This morning I´ll see off my former boss.
Wow!
A multitude have jammed the road!

CHIEF (greets Tian): Your Excellency, the farewell banquet is ready.
TIAN: What a big crowd of people! Have they all come to see Lord Chunyu off? How nice of them! How nice of them!
CHIEF: The fanfare is up. It must be Lord Chunyu coming.
(They walk over to meet Chunyu)

(Enter Chunyu with attendants)

【The Lazy Thrush】

CHUNYU:

A file of horses through the morning mist,
the whole town has turned out to bid farewell.
(Wailing within: "Our dear lord!")
Why are thousands of people blocking the road?

CHIEF: They´re begging Your Excellency to remain with them.
CHUNYU:

So they´re my people who wish to have me retained.
What could I´ve done for them to be so esteemed?
I´m much obliged to them for their fidelity.

他替俺点缀春风好面颜。

(田跪接介)司农田子华迎接公相。

(生)司农请起，下车相揖。(下介)(揖介)司农，这条官路几时修好了？呀，彩门金字："新筑沙堤"。

(田)是，新筑沙堤宰相行。

(生笑介)愿与足下同之。(同行介)

【前腔】

(生)

俺承恩初入五云端。

(田)

这新筑沙堤宰相还。

(生)

重重树色隐鸣銮。

(田)前面长亭了，下官备有一杯酒。

便停骖只觉的长亭短。

(生)

恰正是取次新官对旧官。

(做到介)(田参见介)

(生)蚤间别过了周司宪，便到贵衙，未得相见。借此官亭之便，拜谢司农。

(田)不敢。(拜介)

(生)

廿载劳君作股肱，

Their devotion adds golden glory to my face.

TIAN (kneeling in greeting): Tian Zihua, the prefectural finance minister is here to welcome Your Excellency the new premier.

CHUNYU: Please rise. First, let me alight from this carriage. (He steps down. They raise their clasped hands in greeting) Mr. Tian, when did you have this road repaired? Ah! What a decorative gate, bedecked with colorful silk! And there are four golden characters inscribed on it: "Newly Built Sand Causeway."

TIAN: This sand causeway was especially built for the new premier.

CHUNYU (smiling): Let´s walk on it together. (They walk)

【Ditto】

CHUNYU:

Royal favors have lifted me above the clouds,

TIAN:

over a sand path to the premier´s post.

CHUNYU:

The palace waits in the Sophora shade.

TIAN: Ahead is the boundary pavilion. I´ve presumed to prepare a cup of wine in your honor.

The roadside pavilion makes the long distance short;

CHUNYU:

here the new officer sees off the former one.

(They arrive at the pavilion. Tian pays his formal respects to Chunyu)

CHUNYU: Before I left town, I went to the jail to say goodbye to Commander Zhou. Then I paid a visit to your office, but you were not in. So, let me take advantage of this occasion to express my thanks.

TIAN: I haven´t done anything worthy of that. (He bows)

CHUNYU:

For twenty years you were my right-hand man;

(田)

　　堂尊恩德重难胜。

(生)

　　公私去后烦遮盖，

(田)

　　还望提携接后程。

(丑参见介)录事官叩头。

(生)起来。二十年的参军清苦，俺去后，司农好看觑他。(丑叩头谢介)

(田)看酒。

(吏持酒上)

　　竹映司农酒，

　　花催上相车。

酒到。

【山花子】

(田送酒介)

　　喜南柯一郡棠阴满，

　　公归故国槐安。

　　二十载家宁户安，

　　到今朝行满功完。

(生)印务俱已交盘了。

　　看黄金印文边角全，

　　文书查交仓库盘。

　　筵席上金杯满前离恨端。

(合)

　　归去朝廷，

　　跨凤骖鸾。

TIAN:

Your favors outweighed all that I have done.

CHUNYU:

Please cover up for me after I leave;

TIAN:

Please continue to help and favor me.

CHIEF (paying formal respects to Chunyu): The chief of staff kowtows to Your Excellency.

CHUNYU: Please rise. It must have been very taxing to be the chief of staff for twenty years. Mr. Tian, please take good care of him. (Chief kowtows in gratitude)

TIAN: Bring us wine.

CLERK (enters with wine):

Good wine reflects the green bamboo;
Sweet blossoms speed the premier's steed.

Here is wine.

【Mountain Flowers】

TIAN (offering Chunyu wine):

Southern Bough was bathed in your sunny shine;
now you return to the Sophora Court.
For twenty years families have lived in peace;
so wondrously you completed your term.

CHUNYU: I've handed over the official seal to you and made a smooth transfer.

The seal's golden edges remain intact;
documents are filed and warehouses checked.
Though gold cups fill the table top I hate to leave.
(Refrain)
Back to the royal Court
to take a phoenix ride.

【前腔】

（生）

俺旧黄堂政事新人管，

有一言听俺同官：

休看得一官等闲，

也须知百姓艰难。

（田）

喜明公教条金石刊，

下官遵承无别端。

二十载故人依依离别颜。（合前）

（生）公主久行，本爵难以羁迟，告辞了。（生起行介）

【大和佛】

（众父老上）

脑顶香盆天也么天，

天留住俺恩官。

（跪泣介）老爷呵，

你暂留几日待借寇长安，

舍的便抛残。

（生泣介）父老呵，难道我舍的？

朝廷怎敢违钦限？

俺二十年在此教我好不回还。

（父老）

俺男女们思量，

二十载恩无算，

怎下的去心离眼。

【Ditto】

A new officer enters the official house.
Here is a word of advice for my peer:
Don´t assume it´s easy to take this chair;
one must know the hardship of peasants´ life.

TIAN:

I´ll carve your golden teaching in my mind,
and to the very letter follow it.
It´s doleful to part with a friend of twenty years.
(Refrain)

CHUNYU: I must say goodbye now, for the princess is several days ahead, and I must hurry to catch up with her. (He sets out)

(Elders step forth)

【Harmonious Buddha】

ELDERS:

Wee raise the incense burners to the sky
and pray for the retention of our lord.
(Kneeling and weeping) Your Excellency,
just give us a few days to petition the throne.
You don´t wish to abandon us?

CHUNYU (weeping): Oh, respected elders, how can I bring myself to go away!

But no one dares to defy a decree.
Twenty years has tied my heart to this very place.

ELDERS:

When wee chitchat among ourselves,
it´s always about your benevolence.
How can the limbs survive without the head?
(Weeping, some cling to the carriage, some throw themselves before it)

（泣攀卧介）老爷呵，
俺只得，
倒卧车前
泪斓斑手攀阑。

（生）少不的去了，起来，起来。（行介）

【舞霓裳】

（众）
众父老拥住骏雕鞍，
众男女拽住绣罗襕。
（生泣介）
车衣带断情难断，
这样好民风留着与后贤看。
司农呵，
为俺把苍生垂盼。
（众泣介）
留不得，
只蚤晚生祠中跪祝赞。

（生）父老，我去也。

【红绣鞋】

（众）
扶轮满路遮拦，
遮拦。
东风回首泪弹，
泪弹。
长亭外，
画桥湾。
齐叩首，

Your Excellency,
with blurry eyes,
wee will use our bodies to block the way
just to make you stay.

CHUNYU: I have to go now. Please get up. Please get up. (He moves forward)

【Rainbow Skirt Dance】
ELDERS:
Fellow elders, go grab and hold the reins;
you youngsters, cling to his embroidered robe.
CHUNYU (weeping):
Ribbons may snap but friendship will endure.
Such genuine feelings shall go down to posterity.
Mr. Tian,
take good care of them after I have left.
ELDERS (sobbing):
Since wee have to part,
wee will pray for you and burn incense at your shrine.

CHUNYU: Goodbye to you all.

【Red Embroidered Shoes】
ELDERS:
Wee tried to block the carriage wheels,
carriage wheels,
with rolling tears on every face,
every face.
Beyond the pavilion,
across the bridge you go.
Here wee kneel

捧慈颜。
贤太守，
锦衣还。

(生)众父老子弟们，请回了。

(众)百里内都是南柯百姓送行。

(生)生受了。

【尾声】

(众)

官民感动去留难。

(生)

二十年消受你百姓家茶饭，
则愿的你雨顺风调我长在眼。(下)

(父老吊场)好老爷，好老爷。俺们一面拜见田爷，一面保留驸马爷，还是驸马爷管的百姓稳。俺们权坐一坐，每都派一名赴京。(做派数)

(内响道介)

(丑上)

天有不测风云，
人有无常祸福。

呀，你们父老还在这里。

(众)老爷，还待赶送一程。

(丑)你们都不知，太爷行到五十里之程，前路飞报，公主不幸了。

and wish you well.
Our worshipped man
in glory leaves.

CHUNYU: Thank you all, elders and friends, for coming. Please return.
ELDERS: People from all over the prefecture have turned out to see you off, and they line the road for miles upon miles.
CHUNYU: I´m most indebted to them.

【Coda】
ELDERS:
Such a sentiment makes the parting hard.
CHUNYU:
For twenty years I have been nourished by your food and tea.
May you enjoy the best of weather and a prosperous life.
(Exeunt Chunyu and attendants)

(Manent Elders)
ELDERS: What a good lord! What a good lord! Now let´s go and pay our respects to Lord Tian. At the same time, wee shall petition the Court to allow Lord Chunyu to stay. Life is more secure under the royal son-in-law. Sit down, everybody. Each district shall appoint one representative to go to the capital. (They select people)
(Fanfare within. Reenter Chief of Staff)
CHIEF:
Dark clouds appear from nowhere in the sky
Like fickle fortune changing by the hour.
Oh! How is it you elders are still lingering?
ELDERS: Your Honor, wee are thinking of accompanying His Excellency a little further.
CHIEF: Haven´t you heard? His Excellency hadn´t gone a score of miles when he received a report from the advance party that the princess has

(众)怎么说?

(丑)公主薨了。

(众哭介)怎么好?天也!当真么?

(丑)不真哩!田爷分付俺回来,取白绫、素绢、檀香去行礼,还说不真?

(众)这等,驸马爷不能勾回郡了。打听是真,俺们合众进香去。

贤哉太守有遗恩,
去郡伤哉好郡君。
自是感恩穷百姓,
千年泪眼不生尘。

passed on.

ELDERS: What?!

CHIEF: The princess died.

ELDERS (howling): Oh, heavens! How come? You´re kidding!

CHIEF: No kidding. Lord Tian ordered me to come back to fetch pure white silk and sandalwood joss sticks for mourning. It´s no joking matter.

ELDERS: Well, in that case, the royal son-in-law won´t be able to return to Southern Bough. If the news is confirmed, wee must go and offer incense too.

The Taishou has left behind many gifts;
The loss of the good princess grieves our hearts.
People here will always remember them,
Their eyes forever washed with cleansing tears.

第三十五出　芳　　陨

【绕红楼】

（老旦引宫娥上）

生长金枝岁月深，
南柯上结子成阴。
怕病损红妆，
归迟紫禁，
槐殿暗伤心。

〔清平乐〕

玉阶秋草，
绿遍长秋道。
礓石宫前红泪悄，
人在楼台暗老。
淑女南柯，
病损多娇娇若何？
极目倚门无奈，
休遮小扇红罗。

老身贵处深宫，自闻女孩儿瑶台惊战，日夕忧惶。喜的千岁有旨，取他夫妇还朝。昨日报来，公主带病先行数日，知他路上如何？老身好不挂怀也！（泣介）

Scene 35 The Wilted Flower

(Enter Queen with maids)

【Around the Red Mansion】

QUEEN:

It took long years to nurse my Golden Bough;
at Southern Bough abundant fruit were borne.
It worries me in the palace deep
that the illness may blanch her cheeks.
Better rush her back to Court.

Autumn grass by the stoop
Has spilled onto the pebble walks.
Suppressed tears trickle in the palace nook;
Up on the silent tower my hair turns gray.

My girl at Southern Bough,
How is she faring with her weakened health?
Leaning against the door I stare straight south;
The silk fan cannot hide my anxious gaze.

Although my old self lives in the luxury of the palace, I can´t help worrying about my daughter ever since I heard of her close call at the marble palace. To my relief, the king issued a decree to recall her and her husband back to the capital. Yesterday, news came that she had set out from Southern Bough several days ahead of her husband because of her worsening condition. I wonder how she´s doing on that long and arduous journey.

(She weeps)

(Enter a woman palace officer)

OFFICER:

The blue bird carries joyful news.

（旦扮女官走上）

　　青鸟能传喜，

　　慈乌怎报凶？

启娘娘：宫娥今日掌门，听的宫门外人说，公主病重，千岁与大小近侍哭泣喧天，不知怎的？

（老惊介）这等，怎了也？（泣介）（内响道介）

【哭相思】

（王引内史上）

　　钦取太迟临，

　　问天天你断送我女孩儿忒甚！

（见介）梓童，梓童，淳于家的主儿不幸了。

（老）怎么说？

（王）公主先行数日离南柯，卒于皇华公馆。

（老哭介）俺的儿呵！（闷倒、宫娥扶醒介）

（王）你且休为死伤生也。

【红衲袄】

（老）

　　俺儿度护娇花一寸心。

（王）

　　俺则道他美前程一片锦。

（老）

　　止知他娇多好昵鸳鸯枕，

（王）

　　也怪他病浅长依翡翠衾。

（老）

　　当日个凤将雏你巧笑禁。

Why should the crow pronounce a dirge?

Your Ladyship, just now I was on duty at the gate. I heard people outside say that the princess was failing fast. Wee even heard loud wailings from His Majesty and his courtiers. I´m not sure what was going on.

QUEEN (alarmed): Oh, heavens! No! (She sobs)

(Fanfare within. Enter King with palace officers)

【Crying Over Lost Love】

KING:

Too belated was my decree!
Heaven above!
How can you so ruthlessly snatch my daughter off?

(He greets Queen) My dear, Chunyu´s better half is no more!

QUEEN: How can that be?

KING: She left Southern Bough a few days in advance of him, and died at the posthouse.

QUEEN (wailing): Oh, my daughter! (She swoons. Maids support and comfort her)

KING: Please restrain your grief. It´s no use to torment yourself for the dead.

【Red Padded Coat】

QUEEN:

I always tried to shield the flower from wind and rain;

KING:

I thought a splendid future was in store for her.

QUEEN:

I fancied she was spoiled and liked to stay in bed;

KING:

I imputed that to the frailty of a girl.

QUEEN:

Remember how you beamed when her first child was born?

（王）

今日呵掌离珠我成气喑。

（老）天呵，

俺曾写下了目连经卷也，

谁知道佛也无灵被鬼侵。

【前腔】

（王）梓童呵，

俺则道他在凤箫楼不挂心。

（老）

谁想他瑶台城生害了恁？

（王）

又不是全无少女风先凛，

（老）

可甚的为有姮娥月易沉？

（王）

还记的饯双飞俺御酒斟，

（老）

谁想道酒归旌把红泪饮？

（王）

这是前生注定了今生也，

则苦了他嫩女雏男我也怕哭临。

（老）千岁只有这一女，凡丧葬礼仪必须从厚。

（王）闻得公主灵车先到，俺与梓童素服哭于郊外；将半副鸾驾迎丧于修仪宫里；其谥赠一应礼节，着右相武成侯议之。

KING:

And now I sob to think the pearl no longer shines.

QUEEN: Oh heavens!

I had Maudgalya´s scripture copied and intoned,
but who knew Buddha could be cheated by the ghost!

【Ditto】

KING: My dear,

well married as she was I´d put her out of mind.

QUEEN:

Who knew the marble palace could have harbored ill.

KING:

It´s not a rule that beauties should be snapped by wind;

QUEEN:

the moon, however, sinks because there Chang Er lives.

KING:

I still remember proposing a farewell toast.

QUEEN:

Who thought wee would be gulping tears at her return.

KING:

All that must have been destined in her previous life.
It´ll break my heart to face her weeping boys and girls.

QUEEN: Since she was your only child, she should be accorded a stately funeral.

KING: Her hearse will soon arrive. Let´s change into mourning white and go to receive her at the city boundary. From there, her hearse shall be accompanied by half my honor guard to the Hall of Etiquette. The right-hand premier shall work out the details of the obsequies.

满拟南柯共百年，
谁知公主即生天？
国家礼节都从厚，
要得慈恩照九泉。

Wee thought they'd share a long and happy life.
Who knew heaven could interrupt the course.
The services should be the grandest one,
To comfort her afterlife underground.

第三十六出 还 朝

【绕池游】

（右相上）

多人何用？

一个为梁栋。

咳，

道南柯乘龙骖凤。

廿载恩深，

一方权重，

恰好是到头如梦。

节去蜂愁蝶不知，

晓庭还绕折残枝。

自缘今日人心别，

未必花香一夜衰。

俺看淳于驸马，依倚至亲，久处南柯，贪收人望。俺为国长虑，请旨召回，尊以左相之权，防其遥制之害。谁知事不可测，公主丧亡。国王、国母郊迎其丧，举朝哭临三日，谥为顺义公主，礼节有加。昨奉旨议其葬地，只有龟山可葬，欲待奏知，听的驸马今日见

Scene 36 Returning to Court

(Enter Right-hand Premier)

【Around the Pool】

PREMIER:

No use for more!
One pillar surely is enough.[1]

Ah!

Southern Bough boasts a royal son-in-law.
He over twenty years
has built up a power base,
but all´s a dream when things come to a head.

The bees are conscious of the season change,
While butterflies still haunt the flowerless stems.
Though sentiments will shift from time to time,
Flowers may not lose their fragrance overnight.

That royal son-in-law Chunyu! In my opinion, he simply profits from his royal relations, and used his protracted stay in Southern Bough to buy popular support. For the long-term good of the kingdom, I advised His Majesty to have him recalled and honor him with the title of Left-hand Premier. The uprooting, I had hoped, would prevent him from becoming too unruly. But who could have guessed that the princess would die at that juncture. The king and queen went as far as the city boundary to receive her hearse, and declared three days of national mourning. She was posthumously titled Princess of Righteousness and accorded many other honors. Yesterday, His Majesty instructed me to select a burial site for her. No other place seems more fitting than Tortoise Hill. I was just going to make a report on that matter when I learned that the royal son-in-law was coming for a royal reception today. So I´m waiting for him here, in case

朝，在此伺候，倘令旨着他面议葬地，亦未可知。道犹未了，驸马蚤到。

【前腔】

(生朝服执笏上)

断弦难弄，
蚤被秋风送，
生打散玉楼么凤。

(顿足泣介)

合郡悲啼，
举朝哀痛，
痛煞俺无门诉控。(见右介)

(右)驸马见朝，且休啼哭。(内响鼓)

(生舞蹈拜介)前南柯郡太守、今升左丞相、驸马都尉臣淳于棼朝见叩头，千岁千岁千千岁。

(内)令旨到来：驸马新失公主，寡人不胜悲悼。已着尚膳监设宴后宫。其顺义公主葬地，可与右相武成侯朝门外酌议回奏。

(生叩头介)千岁千岁千千岁。

(起介)右相请了。

(右)驸马请了。

(生)久不到朝门之外了。昨日远劳迎接，缘未朝见，故此谢迟。

His Majesty should seek his opinion about the burial site. Who knows? While I´m saying this, here comes the royal son-in-law.

(Enter Chunyu, in a ceremonial robe and holding a court-tablet[2])

【Ditto】

CHUNYU:

A string snaps, the instrument chokes,
made worse by the autumn blasts
that blow apart the loving phoenix pair.
(He wails and stamps his feet)
The whole prefecture is in tears;
The entire nation moans in pain;
but I can find no one to speak my mind.
(He greets Right-hand Premier)

PREMIER: Please control yourself when you meet His Majesty. (Drums beat within)

CHUNYU (makes a ceremonial kowtow): The former Taishou of Southern Bough and recently appointed Left-hand Premier, Your Majesty´s humble servant Lieutenant Chunyu Fen kowtows. May Your Majesty live thousands and thousands of years!

VOICE WITHIN: Hark His Majesty´s decree: I, your sovereign, am extremely grieved by my son-in-law´s recent loss of his spouse. Therefore, I have ordered the royal kitchen to prepare a reception banquet at the inner palace. As to the burial site for the princess, he may discuss it with the right-hand premier outside the palace gate, and then report back to me.

CHUNYU (kowtows): May Your Majesty live thousands and thousands of years! (Rises to his feet) Right-hand Premier, I´ll follow you.

PREMIER: You first, Royal Son-in-law.

CHUNYU: It´s a very long time since I was at Court. I owe a debt of gratitude to you for having gone so far to receive me yesterday. And I´m

(右)不敢。

(生)请问公主葬地，择于何方？

(右)龟山一穴甚佳。

(生)龟山乃国家后门，何谓之吉？俺曾看见国东十里外蟠龙冈，气脉甚好，何不请葬此地？

(右)蟠龙冈是国家来脉，还是龟山。

(生)右相不知，点龟者恐伤其壳。

(右)驸马，便龙冈好，则枕龙鼻者，也恐伤于唇。

(生)便是龟山，也要灵龟顾子，子在何方？

(右)便是龙冈，也要蟠龙戏珠，珠在那里？

(生)俺只要子孙旺相。

(右)驸马子女俱有门荫，何在龙山？

(生)右相怎说此话？生男定要为将相，生女兼须配王侯，少不的与国咸休，此乃子孙万年之计。

(右背笑介)好一个万年之计。

sorry that I didn´t have a proper chance to pay my personal respects to you then.

PREMIER: Don´t mention it.

CHUNYU: So, which place have you selected for the princess´ tomb?

PREMIER: There´s a good pit in Tortoise Hill.

CHUNYU: Tortoise Hill lies in the rear of the country. How can that be propitious? I remember seeing a hill that looks like a curling dragon three miles to the east of the capital. Its geographical location seems most auspicious. Why can´t she be buried there?

PREMIER: That´s Dragon Hill. It holds the incoming entryway of the country. Better entomb her at Tortoise Hill.

CHUNYU: Your Excellency must be aware that it would be most unfortunate if one should damage the tortoise shell.

PREMIER: Your Excellency the royal son-in-law, though Dragon Hill may be auspicious, he who tries to lie on the dragon´s nose may actually damage its lips.[3]

CHUNYU: Well, if you recommend Tortoise Hill, in order to be propitious the tortoise must have a son in sight. Is there any landmark representing the son there?

PREMIER: Well, if you insist on Dragon Hill, the dragon must have a pearl in its mouth. Where is the pearl?

CHUNYU: All I want is to have good fortune attend my posterity.

PREMIER: Your children are all granted inheritable titles. Whether we choose Dragon Hill or not doesn´t matter at all.

CHUNYU: How can Your Excellency say that?! It´s said a worthy son should grow up to be either a premier or a general; a worthy daughter should be married to either a king or a prince. That´s exactly what we mean by "sharing one´s fate with the country." So the princess´ burial site will affect the fortunes of the tens of thousands of years of my descendants.

PREMIER (turns aside and laughs): Tens of thousands of years of his descendants! (Turns around) Well, as you please. But, I´m afraid that the

(回介)这也罢了。只是龙冈星峰太高，怕有风蚁之患。

(生)右相于此道欠精了。虎踞龙盘，不拘远近大小；蜂屯蚁聚，但取圆净低回。何怕风蚁？

(右笑介)驸马不怕蚁伤，再向丹墀回奏。

(右奏介)臣右相武成侯段功谨奏：

【马蹄花】

　　问祖寻宗，

　　妙在龟山鼻穴中。

(内介)龟山有何好处？

(右)

　　他有蛾眉对案，

　　金诰生花，

　　罗带临风。

(内介)龟山可似龙山？

(右)

　　世人只知龙虎峰上更生峰，

　　怎知道龟蛇洞里方成洞？

　　肯教他玄武低藏，

　　不做了蚁垤高封。

(生奏介)驸马臣棼谨奏：

【前腔】

那龟山呵，

　　拭泪捶胸，

stars over Dragon Hill are too high and that it may be plagued by ants.

CHUNYU: It seems Your Excellency isn´t steeped in this profession. Provided that it has the configuration of a crouching tiger or a curling dragon, it doesn´t matter whether it´s big or small, near or far. As for infestation by bees or ants, as long as the pit is smooth and clean, deep and seamless, you don´t have to worry about that.

PREMIER (laughing): If you, the royal son-in-law, aren´t worried about ants, wee can now make a report to the throne. (Reporting) Your Majesty´s humble servant Duan Gong, Right-hand Premier and Marquis of Martial Feats, respectfully reports:

【The Calla Lily】

To extend the family tree,
in the tortoise´s nostril lies the key.

VOICE WITHIN: What are the advantages of Tortoise Hill?

PREMIER:

It balances a pair of beauties´ brows,
and sports a floral gown
with ribbons stretching far.

VOICE WITHIN: How do you compare Tortoise Hill with Dragon Hill?

PREMIER:

People like the dragon hill merely for its higher peaks;
they have no idea it´s in tortoise hole where fortune smiles.
Better lie low like a tortoise´s drooping head[4]
than stand conspicuous on an anthill crest.

CHUNYU (reporting): Your Majesty´s son-in-law and humble servant Chunyu Fen respectfully reports: That Tortoise Hill,

【Ditto】

tears welling, backbone hunched,

怎似蟠山气郁葱？

蟠龙冈呵，

他有三千粉黛，
八百烟花，
更那十二屏风。
鸣环动佩应雌雄，
辞楼下殿交鸾凤。
怎贪他不住的游龟，
倒抛除了活动的真龙？

（内介）令旨：依驸马所奏。着武成侯择日备仪仗、羽葆、鼓吹，赐葬顺义公主于蟠龙冈。叩头谢恩。

（生谢介）千岁千千岁。（起介）

（右）恭喜了。爱者是真龙，蟠龙冈十二分贵地哩。驸马，可知周弁也疽背而死，其子护丧归国了？

（生哭介）伤哉！故人。

（右）呀，朝房下有列位老国公王亲的酒到。

【卜算子】

（众扮国公酒席上）

纨裤插金貂，
日近天颜笑。
日边红杏倚云高，
锦绣生成妙。

can scarcely match Dragon Hill´s verdant rise.

Oh, Dragon Hill!

It has three thousand beauties all around,
and flowers of eight hundred types,
let alone the painted screens of twelve cliffs.
The bubbling jewel springs echo clanking mail;
its steep descent curves like the phoenix tail.
How can we choose a tortoise on the waves[5]
instead of a real dragon full of life?[6]

VOICE WITHIN: Hark His Majesty´s decree: The royal son-in-law´s suggestion is accepted. The Marquis of Martial Feats shall decide on an auspicious date, and see to it that the honor guard and musicians, hearse and canopy are well prepared. The Princess of Righteousness shall be buried at Dragon Hill. Kowtow to thank His Majesty.

CHUNYU (kowtows): May Your Majesty live thousands and thousands of years! (He rises to his feet)

PREMIER: Congratulations! The real dragon is extremely benevolent! Dragon Hill is the most auspicious place. By the way, has Your Excellency heard that Zhou Bian died of a deep-rooted ulcer on his back? His son has accompanied his remains back to the capital.

CHUNYU (bursting into tears): Oh, heavens! My dearest friend!

PREMIER: Look, the lords and nobles are waiting for you in the side hall with wine.

(Enter lords and nobles with wine and food)

【The Fortuneteller】

L & N:

Clad in silk and wearing gold,
he receives the brightest beams
like a blooming apricot near the sun
— a lustrous picture on brocade.

（见介）驸马拜揖。

（生）列位老国公、老王亲拜揖。

（众）右相国拜揖。

（右）不敢。

（众）驸马远归，愚亲们都在二十里之外迎接。今蚤到公主府上香，知驸马谢恩出朝，故此相候。

（生）多劳列位老国公、老王亲，我淳于棼有何德能？

（众）二十年间，每劳驸马盛礼，时节难忘。今日拜相而回，某等权此公酒迎贺。（酒介）

【八声甘州】

闲身未老，喜乘龙拜相驸马还朝。

（生）

玉人何处？

肠断暮云秋草。

（众）驸马、公主同往南柯之时，老夫们都在荣饯。

（生）便是。

南柯去时有凤箫，

北渚归来无鹊桥。（泣介）

（合）

临鸾照，

怕何郎粉泪淹消。

(They greet Chunyu) Our respects to the royal son-in-law.

CHUNYU: My respects to you all, you lords and nobles.

L & N: Our respects to you, Right-hand Premier.

PREMIER: Respects to you, too.

L & N (to Chunyu): The day you returned to the capital, wee all went ten miles out of town to welcome you. And this morning wee went to offer incense at the princess´ mansion. Then wee learned you were attending a royal reception. So here wee are waiting for you.

CHUNYU: Thank you very much for taking the trouble to come. My humble self isn´t worthy of such attentions.

L & N: Wee are much obliged to you for all the gifts you bestowed on us at the various festivals during the past twenty years. Now that you´re back at Court and promoted to the rank of premier, wee would like to take this opportunity to offer you our collective congratulations. (They offer wine)

【Eight Tunes From Ganzhou】

Congratulations on your promotion and return,
while in the prime of life.

CHUNYU:

But where´s my darling wife?
The autumn grass wilts and wrings my heart.

L & N: When you and the princess set out for Southern Bough, our old selves were all present at the royal send-off.

CHUNYU: I certainly remember.

My phoenix sweetheart then was at my side;
the magpies now no longer span the sky.[7]
(He weeps)

ALL (refrain):

Avoid the mirror,
for fear of seeing a face etched by tears.

【前腔】

（生叹介）

有谁看着红锦袍？
叹凄然系玉，
瘦损围腰。

（众）

俺朝班戚畹，
还让你人才一表。
香风簇锦云汉高，
夜月穿花宫漏遥。（合前）

（众）驸马，今有请书启知：一来恭贺驸马拜相之喜；二来解闷；三来洗尘。老夫忝为国公之长，先请驸马少叙。其余国戚王亲，以次轮请。便请右相国相陪。

（生）老国公，王亲可也多着。

（众）驸马，天人也，人所尊敬，愿无弃嫌。

（生）领命了。

权重股肱相，
恩光肺腑亲。
满朝相造请，
何日不醺醺？（下）

【Ditto】

CHUNYU (sighs):

Who cares about a crimson robe of silk?[8]
Though a jade belt still engirdles,
the waist has shrunk and waned.

L & N:

Of all courtiers and royal kin
you are the most admired and gifted one.
A fragrant wind escorts you up the sky,
but in the moon´s brightness the night grows long.
(All sing the refrain)

ONE LORD: Your Excellency, allow me to cordially invite you to my humble abode, firstly to congratulate you on your promotion to premier, secondly to offer you some solace and thirdly to welcome you back to the capital. Since my humble self is the most senior in years, I hope I can have the honor of being the first to invite you. My peers will then take their turns. I also hope Your Excellency, the right-hand premier, will honor us with your presence.

CHUNYU: But there are so many of you!

L & N: You´re revered by every one of us. Please don´t snub us.

CHUNYU: Well, I think I have to accept your invitations.

Once you become the right-hand man,
You are admired by all the clan.
The whole Court competes to invite;
No day can pass not being tight.

(Exeunt Chunyu, lords and nobles)

（右相吊场）看驸马相待各位老国公、王亲，气势盛矣。（叹介）且自由他。

冷眼看螃蟹，

横行到几时。（下）

(Manet Premier)

PREMIER: Look, how snobbishly he treats those lords and nobles! (Sighs) Well, for the moment, let him have his day.

Detachedly I watch the crab.

How much longer can it sidewise crawl?[p]

(Exit)

第三十七出　粲　　诱

【忆秦娥前】

（贴引宫女上）

宫眉样，
秋山淡翠闲凝望。
闲凝望，
秦楼梦断，
凤笙罗帐。

〔唐多令〕

何处合成愁？
人儿心上秋。
大槐宫叶雨初收，
唱道晚凉天气好，
问谁上
小琼楼？

自家郡主琼英是也。妹子瑶芳，嫁与淳于驸马，出守南柯，入为丞相，当朝无比。不料妹子过世，举国哀伤，敕葬龙山，威仪甚盛。昨日驸马还朝，俺王素重南柯之威名，加以中宫之宠信，出入无间，权势非常。满国中王亲国戚，那一家不攀附他，朝歌暮筵，春花秋月。则俺和仙姑、国嫂三家寡妇，出了公礼，不曾私请得他。

Scene 37 Inviting Lures

(Enter Duchess Qiongying with maids)

【The Qin Maiden, first half】

QIONGYING:

The painted brows conceal
a pair of eyes like autumn´s limpid pools.
Limpid pools,
in which reflects a dream
about the bliss of love.

Where does woe reside?
There in the heart it hides.
A shower has just bathed the Sophora leaves;
A coolness suffuses the crystal sky.
Who´s climbing up
My boudoir tower?

I´m Duchess Qiongying. My cousin Yaofang was married to Chunyu, who left the Court to govern Southern Bough and is now returning with unmatched celebrity as the premier. Unfortunately, my cousin expired early. The whole kingdom grieved at her death, and by royal permission she was buried on Dragon Hill with a grand funeral service. Yesterday, the royal son-in-law made his first appearance at Court since his return. As the King thinks highly of his achievement in Southern Bough and the Queen dotes on him, he has attained unrivaled power and can enter the inner palace any time he likes. The lords and nobles are vying to fawn on him. Parties and feasts last from morning till night. Spring´s full blooms and autumn´s full moon, the best of everything! Priestess Itty, Lady Truffle and I, wee three widows, chipped in with the collective banquet, but so far wee haven´t been able to invite him to a private party. His handsome

想起驸马一表人才，十分雄势，俺好不爱他，好不重他。

【金落索】

当初呵，

娟娟姊妹行，

出听西明讲。

绣佛堂前，

惹下姻缘相。

秋波选郎，

配瑶芳，

十五盈盈天一方。

瑶台贵婿真无两，

恰好翠袖风流少一双。

非吾想，

倘其间有便得相当，

迤逗他忘怀醉乡，

伤心洞房，

取情儿我再把这宫花放。

昨日约了灵芝夫人、上真子，早晚公主处上香，回来过此，必有讲谈也。

【忆秦娥后】

（老旦同小旦道装上）

彩云淡荡临风泱，

世间好物琉璃相。

琉璃相，

figure always haunts my eyes. How manly he looks! And how I admire him! How I love him!

【Golden Lacework】

Once upon a time,
wee cousins trickled out the cave
to attend lectures by Qixuan.
Before the altar, however,
I felt a surge of natural drive.
With batting eyes
I picked him for Yaofang,
who traveled to earth´s end at age fifteen.
The marble palace prized a well-matched pair;
at Court wee missed a couple of congenial youths.
I often mused,
what if there´s a chance to be close to him
and drown him in a sea of tenderness.
In the heat of a tryst
his new virility will make me bloom again.

Yesterday Lady Truffle and Priestess Itty invited me to go with them to offer incense at the princess´ mansion. I´m sure they´ll drop in for a chat on their way back.

(Enter Lady Truffle, and Priestess Itty in a Taoist habit)

【The Qin Maiden, second half】

TRUFFLE, ITTY:

Fabulous clouds disperse before the wind;
beautiful things are always frail as glass.
Frail as glass.
Where is the belle of jade?
Only the beau remains.

玉人何处？
粉郎无恙。

(见介)琼英姐，闲坐闷愁，怎的不去公主府烧香耍子？好少的人儿也。

(贴)怎生行礼？

(老)俺国中王子王孙一起，侯伯王亲一起，文武官员一起，举监生员一起，僧道一起；父老儿男过了一起，然后命妇逐班而进，又是军民妻女；过了本国，是他南柯进香，依样文武吏民分班而哭；过了南柯，方才各路各府差人以次而进；便是檀萝国也差官来进紫檀香一千二百斤。看他银山帛海，好不富贵也！

【金落索】

朱丝碧琐窗，
生帛连心帐。
八尺金炉，
日夜烧檀降。
是人来进香，
似同昌，
公主哀荣不可当。
敲残玉磬归天响，
摆下鸾旌拂地长。
偷凝望，
可怜辜负好淳郎。
据着他为人儿纪纲，
言词儿栋梁，
堪他永远为丞相。

(They greet Qiongying) Cousin Qiongying, why didn´t you go to the princess´ mansion to offer incense? It would be good fun, much better than sitting here alone. And there were so many young men!

QIONGYING: How did the ceremony go?

TRUFFLE: Wee paid tribute by turns. First, the princes and their sons; next, the dukes and marquises; then the civil officials and military officers, the scholars and students, the priests and monks, the town elders and men; and then the ladies with titles and womenfolk. After that, came people from Southern Bough, also in groups according to rank and status. And finally it was representatives from the other provinces and prefectures. There were even special envoys from Rattan Sandalwood who paid a tribute of one thousand two hundred pounds of red sandalwood joss sticks. Silver was piled mountain high and silk spread like the sea. It was really an eyeful of wealth!

【Golden Lacework】

Thin gauze veiled the green window frames;
raw cloth shrouded the mourning tent.
A golden burner eight feet tall
cremated joss sticks dawn to dusk.
Thousands and thousands thronged the place,
a grandeur that surpassed
the most beloved princess in history.
The jade chimes struck up a heavenly tune;
magic banners floated and hung to ground.
I stole a glance at Chunyu,
Who, pitiably, stood apart from the crowd.
He has to bear and shoulder state affairs,
he, a master of ardent words.
May he forever be the premier!

（老）不论他为人，则二十年中，我们王亲贵族，那一年不生受他问安、贺生、庆节之礼？如今须得逐家还礼才是。

【刘泼帽】

南柯太守多情况，
感年年礼节风光。

（小旦）

如今又做了头厅相。

（贴）

须与他解闷浇惆怅。

（老旦笑介）琼英姐，你要与他解闷，你我三人，都是寡居，到要驸马来做个解闷儿哩。

（小旦）我是道情人哩。

【前腔】

拼今生不看见男儿相，
怕粘连到惹动情肠。

（老）兴到了也不由的你。

（合）

倘三杯醉后能疏放，
把主人见爱难谦让。

（老）讲定了，向后请驸马，三人轮流取乐，不许偏背。

驸马兼为相，
新来主丧亡。
既然连国戚，
相爱不相妨。

No matter what one thinks of him, simply judging by the gifts he gave to us and to the lords and nobles on festivals and on birthdays over the past twenty years, wee owe him a great deal. It´d only be proper that wee return his generosity one after another.

【Pomao Liu】

The Taishou was scrupulous in detail;
on every festival he sent us gifts.

ITTY:

And now he takes charge of affairs of state,

QIONGYING:

wee should console him for his loss of mate.

TRUFFLE (chuckles): Cousin Qiongying, you want to give him some consolation? Don´t forget that wee three are all widowed. Perhaps he´ll be the one who´s going to offer some consolation.

ITTY: Don´t include me. I´m a Taoist nun.

【Ditto】

In this life I swear not to look at men,
for fear that they may stir and hook my soul.

TRUFFLE: Well, given the chance, you may not be able to hold your ground.

ALL:

If three cups of sweet wine shall make us loose,
he may offer something wee can´t refuse.

TRUFFLE: Let´s make it clear that wee take turns entertaining the royal son-in-law. No secrecy behind the others´ back.

The premier is the son-in-law,
And he recently lost his spouse.
Since wee are kindred of one house,
It won´t matter if love is pawed.

第三十八出　生　　恣

【懒画眉】

（生冠带引众行上）

则为紫鸾烟驾不同朝，
便有万片宫花总寂寥，
可怜他金钿秋尽雁书遥。
看朝衣泪点风前落，
抵多少肠断东风为玉箫。

（众）禀老爷：到府了。

（生叹介）我连下马通忘记了。

〔集唐〕这

夹道疏槐出老根，
金屋无人见泪痕。
戚里旧知何驸马，
清晨犹为到西园。

俺淳于生，自公主亡后，孤闷悠悠。所喜君王、国母，宠爱转深；入殿穿宫，言无不听。以此权门贵戚，无不趋迎；乐以忘忧，夜而继日。今日晚朝，看见宫娥命妇，齐整喧哗，则不见俺的公主妻也。

（末）报，报，报，有女官到。

（生）快请。

Scene 38 Reckless Abandon

(Enter Chunyu in a ceremonial robe, attended)

【The Lazy Thrush】

CHUNYU:

Too bad that lovers cannot in the same world live,
hers too remote for even the wild geese to reach.
One feels deserted though amidst a thousand blooms;
tears fall and stain my ceremonial robe
that no number of jolly tunes can wipe away.

ATTENDANTS: Sir, wee are home.

CHUNYU (sighs): I even forgot to dismount!

The old roadside trees with their roots exposed,
The empty house where only tears remain,
Have watched the royal in-law many years,
Who saunters to the garden every dawn.

To me, Chunyu Fen, life became depressing and lonely after the death of my dear wife the princess. However, the king and queen never stopped pampering me with favors. They gladly listen to my advice and allow me to enter the palace freely. And that makes me the most sought-after figure with the nobles and social-climbers, inviting me to parties and banquets that last night after day. That brings temporary relief to my melancholy. At this afternoon´s Court session I saw a happy gaggle of Court ladies and maids, but my dear wife was not among them.

FOOTMAN (enters): Report, report, report. A woman palace officer is at the gate.

CHUNYU: Please send her in immediately.

(Enter a woman palace officer holding a letter)

【不是路】

（旦扮女官持书上）

莲步轻跷，

翠插乌纱双步摇。（见介）

（生）

因何报？

多应娘娘懿旨下鸾霄。

（旦）不是。

洗尘劳，

琼英郡主和皇姑嫂，

良夜里开筵把驸马邀。

（生喜介）

承尊召，

等闲外客难轻造。

即忙来到，

即忙来到。

（旦）这等，

青禽传报去，

驸马一鞭来。（下）（内响道介）

（生）许时不见女人，使人形神枯槁。今夜女主同筵，可以一醉也。正是：

遇饮酒时须饮酒，

不风流处也风流。（下）

【No Passage Here】

OFFICER:

My tiny feet skip forward;
pheasant plumes quiver on my office hat.
(She greets Chunyu)

CHUNYU:

What´s brought you here?
Are you bearing an edict from the queen?

OFFICER: No.

To welcome you,
Duchess Qiongying and royal womenfolk
cordially invite you to a nocturnal feast.

CHUNYU (beaming):

I gladly accept
that invitation to the exclusive place.
I´ll come at once.
I´ll come at once.

OFFICER: Then I´ll hurry back to make a report.

The blue bird takes off with the news;
The royal in-law soon alights.

(Exit Officer)

(Fanfare within)

CHUNYU: Having been away from woman for so long one really feels parched. Tonight, I can drink my fill with the hostess, just as the old saying has it:

When you can drink make sure you drink your fill;
When you can catch romance don´t drop the catch.

(Exeunt)

(Enter Duchess Qiongying with women palace officers)

【鹊桥仙】

（贴引女官上）

恹恹睡损，

无人偎傍，

有客今宵临况。

（老、小旦上）

几年不见俊儿郎，

叨陪侍玉楼欢唱。（见介）

（老）

日暮风吹，

叶落依枝。

丹心寸意，

愁君未知。

（小旦）今夜琼英姐作主，与淳郎洗尘解闷，俺二人叨陪。客还未到，闲商量一会。闻的淳郎雅量，三人之量，谁可对付？

（贴）灵芝嫂有量。

（老）三人同灌醉了他要子便了。

（丑上）驸马到。

【前腔】

（生上）

金鞭马上，

玉楼莺里，

一片彩云凝望。（笑介）

【The Magpie Bridge】

QIONGYING:

Drowsy sleep makes me tired
with no one at my side,
but this night I have a guest for a feast.

(Enter Lady Truffle and Priestess Itty)

TRUFFLE, ITTY:

Lone years have passed without a handsome man.
Tonight wee come to sing and dance with one.
(They greet Qiongying)

TRUFFLE:

Shed by a sunset breeze,
The leaf still hugs the tree.
Can he possibly guess
The yearning in my chest?

ITTY: Tonight, Cousin Qiongying is to play hostess to Chunyu. Wee two are to make up the company. Since our guest hasn´t arrived yet, wee can make some arrangements. I hear Chunyu is a heavy drinker. Which one of us can be his match?

QIONGYING: Cousin Truffle has a good capacity.

TRUFFLE: Together wee three can booze him up and have fun.

MAID (enters): Here comes the royal son-in-law.

(Reenter Chunyu)

【Ditto】

CHUNYU:

I whip my sweating steed
toward the sunny perch
— a puff of fiery cloud there beckons me.
(With a grin)

聊抛旧恨展新眉，
清夜红颜索向。

〔西江月〕

（生）（拜介）
自别琼英贵主，
年年想像风姿。
（贴）
劳承驸马费心期，
今夜一杯尘洗。
（老）
每恨淳郎新寡，
（小旦）
可怜公主差池。
（生）
原来是上真仙子和灵芝，
（合）
且喜一家无二。

（生）小生回朝，已蒙诸王亲公礼相请，何劳专设此筵？
（贴）驸马不知，此筵有三意：一来洗远归之尘；二来贺拜相之喜；三来解孤凄之闷。前几日为众王亲国公占了贵客，俺三人商量，上真姑是道情人，灵芝夫人与妾双寡，更无以次之人可以为主，只得俺三人落后，轮班置酒相敬。今日妾身为主，他二人相陪。
（生）小生领爱了。
（贴）内侍们看酒。
（内使女官持酒上）
驸马多年骑五马，
客星今夜对三星。
酒到。

Brushing aside old pains to hug new love,
in this crystal night I seek rosy cheeks.

CHUNYU (greets Qiongying):

Despite the years I was away from Court,
Your image is imprinted on my mind.

QIONGYING:

It's so sweet of you to remember me.
Allow me please to entertain you now.

TRUFFLE:

Your recent widowed state is our concern.

ITTY:

It's a sad thing the princess died so young.

CHUNYU: So it's

You Lady Truffle and Priestess Itty.

ALL:

Happily wee are of one family.

CHUNYU: After my return to Court, you and the lords and nobles have all chipped in to treat me. Why take this special trouble?

QIONGYING: Your Highness, there are three reasons for tonight's dinner party. First, it's to welcome you back after your long stay in Southern Bough. Second, it's to congratulate you on your promotion to premier. Third, wee wish to help you forget your loneliness. Wee would have liked to invite you earlier, but for days you were engaged by the lords and nobles. As Priestess Itty is a Taoist nun, Lady Truffle and I are both widowed, wee couldn't compete with them in playing host. So wee decided to wait until they had all had their turns, and then wee three would take turns treating you. Tonight I'll play hostess, and these two will make up the company.

CHUNYU: I'm most obliged to you.

QIONGYING (to palace officers): Bring us wine.

【解三醒犯】

（贴众把酒介）

二十年有万千情况，
今日的重见淳郎，
和你会真楼下同欢赏。
依亲故
为卿相，姊妹行家打做这一行。
虽不是无端美艳妆，
休嫌让，
捧金杯笑眼斟量。

【前腔】

（生把酒介）

则为那汉宫春那人生打当，
似咱这迤逗多娇粉面郎。
用尽心儿想，
用尽心儿想，
瞑然沉睡倚纱窗。
闲打忙
小宫鸦把咱叫的情悒怏。
羞带酒，懒添香，
则这恨天长
来暂借佳人锦瑟傍。
无承望，
酒盏儿擎着仔细端详。

OFFICERS (reentering with wine):

The royal in-law rides a fine tall steed;
A nova now invades the trio stars.

Here comes wine.

【Three Tries to Sober Up, Combined】

THE THREE LADIES (proposing a toast):

Many things happened in the twenty years,
and today wee finally meet again
— upon the primrose tower wee celebrate.
Since by royal link,
you to premier rose,
wee cousins may stoop to being professionals.
Though wee no longer boast of gorgeous looks,
don´t hesitate.
Raise your gold cup to be a smiling judge.

【Ditto】

CHUNYU (proposing a toast):

I have long envisioned a life in fairyland
with lovely beauties waiting on my handsome self.
How often I schemed!
How often I dreamed
that I dozed off against the windowsill!
Nothing came, however,
except that raven caws disturbed my sleep.
With liquor´s help,
I had life ignored.
To kill the long and empty days
I took shelter by the singers´ lute.
Who could have guessed

【前腔】

(贴众)

则道上秦楼多受享，
则道上秦楼多受享。
恰咱风吹断凤管声残，
怎得玉人无恙？
今何世？
此消详，
这是翠拥红遮锦绣乡。

(生背介)

盼艳娇，
灯下恍，
则见笑歌成阵，
来来往往，
颠倒为甚，
不那色眼荒唐？

(贴)月上了。驸马宽怀进酒。(贴、老旦、小旦奉酒介)

【蛮儿犯】

(贴众)

半盏琼浆，
且自加怀巨量。

(贴背介)

听他独自温存，
话儿挨挨好不情长。

(回介)

芳心一点，
做了八眉相向，
又蚤阑干月上。

I´d one day face fairies over a cup of wine.

【Ditto】

THE THREE LADIES:

Wee thought jubilance filled the palace tower,
wee thought jubilance filled the palace tower,
but a gust sucked out the tenuous wind from our flute.
Who can warrant a lasting spouse?!
What place is this?
By appearance,
it´s no less than a trysting nest of green and red.

CHUNYU (aside):

The fairies I dreamed of
appear by candlelight.
Their songs and laughter rise and fall
as they flicker in and out.
Is it a scene crooked by mist?
Is it because my eyes are color-stained?

QIONGYING: The moon is up. Sir, please remove your coat and drink more.

【Southern Shorties, Combined】

THE THREE LADIES (offering wine):
Don´t leave your cup unfilled;
please have another brimming bowl.

QIONGYING (aside):

Listen to his soliloquy.
What a trickle of fond and sensuous coos!
(Turns around to face Chunyu)
A single word can touch the heart;
eloquence flows from eye to eye.

（合）

画堂中几般清朗。（小旦奉酒介）

【前腔】

（生）

幽情细讲，

对面何妨？

演煞宫娥侍长。

旧家姊妹俨成行，

就月笼灯衫袖张。（合前）（贴再奉酒介）

【前腔】

（贴众）

风摇翠幌，

月转回廊，

露滴宫槐叶响。

好秋光风景不寻常，

人带幽姿花暗香。（合前）（生回奉酒介）

【前腔】

（生）

把金钗夜访，

玉枕生凉，

辜负年深兴广。

三星照户显残妆，

好不留人今夜长。（合前）

（生睡介）醉矣。

（贴）早已安排纱厨枕帐了。

The moon has climbed above the balustrade.
(Refrain)
The hall is filled with Luna´s crystal light.

【Ditto】
CHUNYU (offering wine):
Do elaborate, please
and say it face to face,
since it is pent up in your heart.
See what a lovely group you cousins form;
the moon shines through your spread of filmy sleeves.
(Refrain)

(Qiongying offers wine)
【Ditto】
THE THREE LADIES:
The breeze fills the screens;
the moon wheels her beams;
dewdrops clink on Sophora leaves.
What an autumn night of unusual sight,
lithe bodies float amidst the fragrant blooms!
(Refrain)

【Ditto】
CHUNYU (offering them wine in return):
An evening trip to the boudoir
has led me to yearning pillows
and accumulated years of craze.
The shining stars reveal a burning face;
in such company night is never long.
(Refrain)

(生)难道主人不陪?

(小旦)怕没这样规矩?

(老)驸马见爱，一同陪伴罢了。

(贴笑介)这等，我三人鱼贯而入。

【鹅鸭满渡船】

(众)

怕争夫体势忙，
敬色心情嚷。
蝶戏香，
鱼穿浪，
逗的人多饷。
则见香肌褪，
望夫石都衬迭床儿上。
以后尽情随欢畅，
今宵试做团圞相。

【尾声】

(生)

满床娇不下得梅红帐，
看姊妹花开向月光。

(合)俺四人呵，

做一个嘴儿休要讲。

乱惹春娇醉欲痴，
三花一笑喜何其?
人人久旱逢甘雨，
夜夜他乡遇故知。

CHUNYU (yawning): I´m drunk.

QIONGYING: The mosquito net is set up and the bed is made.

CHUNYU: Isn´t the hostess joining me?

ITTY: I´m afraid there isn´t such a practice.

TRUFFLE: If that´s the royal son-in-law´s wish, why shouldn´t wee all comply?

QIONGYING (smiling): Well, let´s enter one after another.

【A Ferry Full of Geese and Ducks】

THE THREE LADIES:

Wee scramble legs and arms for the man,
with bursting outcries in the heart.
Like butterflies sucking blooms,
fish swimming in and out of waves,
the ecstasy makes us drool.
Soon wee are stripped to the skin;
our bodies anxiously he sprawled out on the bed.
With complete abandon our spirits soar;
wee twist and twine into a carnal ball.

【Coda】

CHUNYU:

The plum-red net cannot contain a bed of buds,
which swelled and burst open toward the moon.

ALL: The four of us,

as one mouth, must not let this secret out.

The swelling blossoms make one drunk with glee.
Or why do the flower trio spread their lips?
Like saturating rain for long-parched fields,
Every night wee meet in exotic land.

第三十九出　象　谴

【菊花新】

（右相上）

玉阶秋影曙光迟，
露冷青槐荫御扉。
低首整朝衣，
咽不断铜龙漏水。

我右相段功，同心共政，与我王立下这大槐安国土，正好规模。不料俺王招请扬州酒汉淳于棼为驸马，久任南柯，威名颇盛，下官每有树大根摇之虑。且喜公主亡化，钦取回朝，却又尊居左相，位在吾上；国母以爱婿之故，时时召入宫闱，但有请求，无不如意；这也不在话下。兼以南柯丰富，二十年间，但是王亲贵戚，无不赂遗，因此昨日回朝之后，势要勋戚都与交欢，其势如炎，其门如市。勋戚到也罢了，还有那琼英郡主、灵芝夫人，连那上真仙姑，

Scene 39 Heavenly Signs

(Enter Right-hand Premier)

【Fresh Chrysanthemums】

PREMIER:

Autumn dawn breaks late on the palace steps;
cold dew lingers on the Sophora leaves.
I smooth my robe for early Court;
clepsydra´s dragon mouth forever drips.

I´m Duan Gong, the right-hand premier. With diligence and loyalty, I helped His Majesty establish this Great Sophora Kingdom, and have managed to expand it to its present size. But inadvertently, His Majesty summoned a drunkard named Chunyu Fen from the city of Yangzhou, and married his daughter to him. In addition, he appointed him Taishou of Southern Bough Prefecture. During the past twenty years that Chunyu has gained a threatening popularity. That alarms me because an oversized bough could shake the whole tree. By a stroke of luck, the princess died, so he was recalled to Court. But who knew he would be promoted over my head to the position of left-hand premier. The queen dotes on him so much that he´s frequently summoned to the inner palace, and he can get whatever he asks for. Apart from that, armed with the riches of Southern Bough, he bought the hearts of the nobles and lords during his long tenure as Taishou. That´s why as soon as he returned to Court all those aristocrats were so eager to befriend him. He´s like a blazing fire drawing moths toward him, and the street in front of his house is crowded like a bazaar, with traffic from every corner of the kingdom and people of all imaginable trades. You can´t blame those nobles and lords — but those royal ladies, such as Duchess Qiongying, Lady Truffle, and even that Priestess

都轮流设宴，男女混淆，昼夜无度。果然感动上天，客星犯于牛、女、虚、危之次，待要奏知此事，又恐疏不间亲。打听的昨日国中，有人上书，倘然吾王问及，不免相机而言。老天，非是俺段功妒心，此乃社稷之忧也。吾王驾来，朝班伺候。

【前腔】

（扮内臣传呼拥王上）

根蟠国土势崔嵬，
朝罢千官满路归。
一事俺心疑，
甚槐安感动的白榆星气？

（右相参介）右相武成侯段功叩头，千岁千岁。

（王）右相平身。卿可闻的国中有人上书否？

（右）不知。

（王）书上说的凶，他说："玄象谪见，国有大恐，都邑迁徙，宗庙崩坏。"他说玄象，是何星象也？

（右）正要奏知，有太史令奏，客星犯于牛、女、虚、危之次。

Itty! One after another, they invite him to house banquets, women mixing with men, and turning night into day! Their dissoluteness and dissipation must have incurred the wrath of heaven, for a nova has appeared in the region of Altair and Vega. I ought to report this to the king, but the old saying that "the unrelated shouldn´t come between those related by blood" has given me second thoughts. I learned, however, that yesterday a countryman presented to the throne a memorial on this astronomical phenomenon. If the king happens to ask about it, I can act on the occasion. Heaven above! It´s not that I´m jealous; it´s a matter of the national interest. Here comes His Majesty. I shall attend him.

(Enter King, with eunuchs announcing his approach)

【Ditto】

KING:

The ancient roots strike deep, the crown strikes awe.
A thousand officers have filled the Court,
yet one misgiving bothers me:
What has disturbed the stars above our head?

PREMIER (greeting King): Duan Gong, Marquis of Martial Feats and Right-hand Premier kowtows to Your Majesty. May you live thousands and thousands of years!

KING: Please rise. Have you heard that someone has submitted a memorial?

PREMIER: No, I haven´t.

KING: It sounds very serious, for it claims that astronomical observations show bad omens. Our kingdom is to suffer a major disaster in the form of the collapse of our ancestral temple, and the capital has to be relocated. What astronomical phenomenon does this refer to?

PREMIER: That´s what I was going to report on. The chief astrologer reported that a nova has appeared in the region of Altair and Vega.

（王）那书中后面，又说："衅起他族，事在萧墙。"好令俺疑惑。

（右）是这国中，别无他族了；便是他族，亦不近于萧墙。大王试思之。

（王）别无人了，则淳于驸马，非我族类。

（右）臣不敢言。

（王）将有国家大变，右相岂得无言。

（右）启奏俺王：

【琐窗郎】

客星占牛、女、虚、危，

正值乘槎客子归。

虚危主都邑宗庙之事，牛女值公主驸马之星。近来驸马贵盛无比：

他雄藩久镇，

把中朝馈遗；

豪门贵党，

日夜游戏。

（王）一至于此？

（右）还有不可言之处，

把皇亲闺门无忌。

（合）

感天知，

萧墙衅起再有谁？

（泪介）

可怜故国迁移。

（王恼介）淳于棼自罢郡还朝，出入无度，宾从交游，威福日盛，寡人

KING: The memorial goes on to say that the trouble is caused by an alien being from within the palace. That really puzzles me.

PREMIER: In our kingdom there´s no other alien. Even if there is, it couldn´t get into the palace. Doesn´t that mean something to Your Majesty?

KING: Except for my son-in-law Chunyu, who else is an alien?

PREMIER: My humble self is not in a position to discuss this.

KING: In face of such a dire national disaster, how can you, my right-hand premier, say nothing?!

PREMIER: Your Majesty:

【Man at the Window】

The nova that invades Altair and Vega
coincides with the man´s return to Court.

Those constellations govern the fate of our ancestral temple and our capital. Vega and Altair symbolize the princess and her husband, who is enjoying unprecedented popularity nowadays.

He´s long ruled a prosperous place,
and sent lavish gifts to the lords.
From house to noble house,
he revels day and night.

KING: Is it really that serious?

PREMIER: And there are even worse things.

He mixes too with royal womenfolk.
(Refrain)
Heaven above!
Who else can wreak havoc in palace halls?!
(Sobbing)
Alas, the kingdom has to move away!

KING (enraged): That Chunyu Fen, since I released him from his duties at Southern Bough and recalled him to Court, he has abused my trust to

意已疑惮之。今如右相所言，乱法如此，可恶！可恶！

【前腔】

他平常僭侈堪疑，
不道他宣淫任所为。
怪的穿朝度阙，
出入无时。
中宫宠婿，
所言如意，
把威福移山转势。

罢了！非俺族类，其心必异。(泪介)(合前)

(右跪介)臣谨奏：语云：“当断不断，反受其乱。”驸马事已至此，千岁作何处分？

(王)听旨：

【意不尽】

且夺了淳于棼侍卫，
禁随朝只许他居私第。

(右)依臣愚意，遣他还乡为是。

(王)不消再说，
少不的唤醒他痴迷还故里。(王下)

weave himself a power net. Even my royal self begins to feel the threat of his omnipresence. And according to what you´ve said, he could even be so regardless of propriety! If that isn´t outrageous, what is?!

【Ditto】

I did notice that he abused his power,
but didn´t expect incest in the house.
No wonder he so often enters private halls,
disrespectful of day and night.
The queen´s pampered son-in-law,
who easily gets what he wants,
has turned our favors to mischievous ends.

Well, you can never expect an alien to be of one heart and one mind with you. (He weeps)

(Refrain)

PREMIER (kneels): Your Majesty, the ancients said: "Make a quick decision, or suffer a sure affliction." Bad as the situation already is, what is Your Majesty´s decision?

KING: Hark my edict:

【Coda】

First strip him off his guards and lock him home,
also forbid him from attending Court.

PREMIER: In my humble opinion, wee´d better send him back to his native place.

KING: I know what to do.

Wee shall wake him from his trance and dispatch him home.

(Exit King)

（右叹介）可矣，可矣。虽则淳于禁锢，奈国土有危。正是：

上天如圆盖，
下地似棋局。
淳于梦中人，
安知荣与辱。

PREMIER (sighs): Well, let it be so. Although wee may place him under house arrest, wee can´t evade the national disaster.

Like a dome heaven curves above;
Like a chessboard the earth spreads flat.
Chunyu in his tumultuous dream,
Can he tell glory from disgrace?

第四十出 疑 惧

（生素服愁容上）

太行之路能摧车，
若比君心是坦途。
黄河之水能覆舟，
若比君心是安流。
君不见大槐淳于尚主时，
连柯并蒂作门楣？
珊瑚叶上鸳鸯鸟，
凤凰窠里鹓雏儿。
叶碎柯残坐消歇，
宝镜无光履声绝。
千岁红颜何足论？
一朝负谴辞丹阙。

自家淳于棼，久为国王贵婿，近因公主销亡，辞郡而归，同朝甚喜。不知半月之内，忽动天威，禁俺私室之中，绝其朝请。天呵！公主生天几日，俺淳于入地无门。若止如此，已自忧能伤人；再有其他，咳，真个生为寄客。天呵，淳于棼有何罪过也？

【胜如花】

无明事可奈何？
恰是今朝结果。

Scene 40 Pending Threat

(Enter Chunyu in plain clothes and looking worried)

CHUNYU:

Compared to serving the royal house,
Smooth are the Taihang Mountains' rugged paths;
Compared to serving His Majesty,
Safe are the Yellow River's swift whirpools.
Not long ago, when I married the princess,
He prized me as a new arch for his door.
We were mandarin ducks on a coral tree,
A pair of fledglings in a phoenix nest.
The coral is smashed and the bough hewn off;
The mirror is tarnished and footsteps hushed.
A royal son-in-law is no big deal;
Once favor shifts, you're driven out of Court.

I'm Chunyu Fen, the king's celebrated son-in-law for many years. Recently, I gave up the office of Taishou and returned to the capital because of the death of my dear wife. At first I was warmly received by my peers, but in less than a fortnight heaven turned its face away from me. Now I'm put under house arrest and forbidden to attend Court. Oh, heavens! The princess has just left this world, and now I can't even find a foothold in it! Such an adverse turn of fortune is enough to crush any man. But, what if the worst is yet to come? Alack! That must be the fate of one living under the roof of others. Oh, heaven, what could I have done to offend you?

【Nicer Than Flowers】

It's hard to tackle shadowed plans.
The consequence is all you see:

不许俺侍从随朝，
又禁俺交游宴贺，
只教俺私家里住坐。
这其中纷然事多，
这其间知他为何？
有甚差讹？
一句分明道破，
就里好教人无那。
莫非他疑俺在南柯也？
并不曾坏了他的南柯。

不要说人，便是这老槐树枝，生意已尽。树犹如此，人何以堪？今日要再到南柯，不可得矣。罢了，罢了。向公主灵位前，俺打觉一会。公主呵！

【金蕉叶】

（贴扮公子泣上）

家那国那，
两下里泪珠弹破。（见生哭倒介）
原来俺爹爹在此打磨陀，
冷清清独对着俺亲娘的灵座。

（生泣介）我儿，起来，起来。

〔长相思〕

有来由，
没来由，
不许随朝不许游，
要禁人白头。

I´m strictly banned now from attending Court;
I´m forbidden to party with old friends;
nothing can I do but sit idly home!
Of the myriad happenings through the years,
who knows which one could have incurred this blame?
What wrong did I do?
Why doesn´t His Majesty make it clear,
rather than keep me groping in the dark?
Is he suspicious of my exploits in Southern Bough?
Honestly, I did nothing to hurt the branch.

Such is the fickleness of life. Look at this ancient Sophora tree. The long years have almost exhausted its vitality. If there´s no permanency to speak of for a tree, what can there be for a mere human? Judging by this state of affairs, even if I wished to, I would never again be able to return to Southern Bough. Forget that. Forget that. Just let me sit for a while before my dear wife´s memorial tablet. Oh, dear princess!

(Enter Son, weeping)

【Golden Palm Leaves】

SON:

Oh, my family, my country!
Tears unrestrained are shed for both of them.
(Collapses as he sees Chunyu)
So Daddy is consuming his days in this way,
talking to Mom´s memorial tablet in the cold.

CHUNYU (weeping): Get up, my son. Get up.

There may be reasons,
There may be none,
Banning me from Court and from fun,
Turning me into a white skeleton.

（贴）

好干休，

恶干休，

偷向椿庭暗泪流，

亡萱相对愁。

（生）儿，前日父子朝见，国王悲喜不胜。半月之间，便成此衅，却是因何？

（贴）天大是非，爹爹还不知？

（生）你兄弟俱在宫中，俺亲朋禁止来往，教俺何处打听？

（贴）爹呵，这等，细细听儿报禀：

【三换头】

无根祸芽，

半天抛下。

客星一夜，

犯虚危汉槎。

（生）国主何从得知？

（贴）有国人上书，说："玄象谪见，国有大恐，都邑迁徙，宗庙崩坏。"

（生）这等凶却何干俺事？

（贴）他书后明说着："衅生他族，变起萧墙。"

（生）是那一个国人，这等胆大！便是他族，何知是俺？

（贴）右相段功就中谗谮了，说虚危者，宗庙也；客星犯牛女者，宫闱事也。

SON:

Good outcome,

Bad outcome,

There in private tears you succumb

In the comfort of my departed Mom.

CHUNYU: Son, the other day when we met the king, he seemed immensely pleased to see us. How did it come about that he could do such an about-face in less than a fortnight?

SON: The reason is as obvious as the sky. How can you not know?

CHUNYU: You brothers and sisters are all kept in the palace, and I´m not allowed to see anyone. How can I know?

SON: Dad, let me tell you then.

【Three Change of Tune】

A rootless reproach
fell out of the sky.
A nova one night
intruded upon Vega and Altair.

CHUNYU: How did His Majesty learn of that?

SON: A countryman handed in a memorial, saying that "astronomical observations show bad omens. Our kingdom is to suffer a major disaster in the form of the collapse of our ancestral temple, and the capital has to be relocated."

CHUNYU: What has that to do with me?

SON: The memorial made it clear that "the trouble is caused by an alien being from within the palace."

CHUNYU: Who is that countryman? How dare he? If an alien is to blame, why point at me?

SON: Duan Gong, the right-hand premier, inserted some ugly words. He said that the two constellations are the governing stars of our ancestral temple and the capital; a nova intruding upon Vega and Altair indicates an

(生)牛女，俺和你母亲就是了。

(贴泣介)他全不指着母亲。

(生)再有谁？

(贴)

说琼、芝新寡，

三杯后有甚么风流话靶。

(生)呀！段君何谗人至此？

(贴)国王甚恼，说驸马弄权结党，不可容矣。

(生)国母怎生劝解。

(贴)

说到萧墙话，

中宫怎劝他？

(生)儿，不怨国人，不怨右相，则怨天；天，你好好的要见那客星怎的？

(贴)

那星宿冤家，

着甚胡缠害我的爹？

【前腔】

(生)

流言乱加，

君王明察。

亲儿驸马，

偏然客星是他？

总来被你母亲看着了。他病危之时，叫俺回朝谨慎，怕人情不同了。今日果中其言。

affair in the palace.

CHUNYU: That´s nothing anomalous. Altair and Vega refer to me and your mother.

SON (sobbing): He said Vega doesn´t stand for Mom at all.

CHUNYU: Who else could it stand for?

SON:

He meant the widowed Qiongying and Truffle.
Three cups of liquor led to some indecency.

CHUNYU: What! How can Lord Duan so slander me?!

SON: The king was very angry. He said that you abused your power to form a clique, and that cannot be tolerated!

CHUNYU: Didn´t the queen try to put in a word for me?

SON:

On an issue as grave as that,
how could she venture to intrude?

CHUNYU: Son, I won´t blame that countryman; neither will I blame the right-hand premier. There´s only heaven to blame. Oh, heaven! Why do you have to let that nova appear?

SON:

How could that damned astrologer
fabricate such nonsense to frame my Dad?

【Ditto】

CHUNYU:

As rumors fly about,
the king must keep alert.
How can the nova
be his beloved son-in-law?

Things have really turned out as your mother predicted. On her deathbed, she warned me that when I came back to Court I had to be very cautious, for public sentiments might not be the same. How insightful she was! (He weeps)

（泣介）

你娘亲曾话，
到如今少不得埋怨自家。
瘦尽风流样，
腰围带眼差。

（贴）爹爹，“风流”二字，再也休题。

（合）

说甚繁华，
泣向金枝恨落花。

【入赚】

（扮紫衣官上）

走马东华，
来到淳于驸马家。

（生）

堪惊诧，
他陡从官里来寒舍。
有何宣达？

（紫）

令旨随朝下，
特来宣召咱。

（生对贴慌介）

猛然心里动，
敢有甚吉凶话？

（紫）

俺看见天颜喜洽，
多则是中宫记挂，
这几日不曾行踏。

Having been forewarned by your Mom,
today I only have my wretched self to blame.
Gone are my days of high romance,
now I languish and pine away.

SON: Daddy, please don´t mention the word "romance" again.

BOTH:

Forget the glory that is gone.
Just shed your tears beneath the Golden Bough.

(Enter a palace officer in a purple robe)

【A Fresh Start】

OFFICER:

Riding toward the east,
I´ve reached the house of the royal son-in-law.

CHUNYU:

What a surprise!
He descends from the palace to my humble place.
What message does he bring?

OFFICER:

An edict issued by the king
is summoning you to the Court.

CHUNYU (in a flurry, to Son):

My poor heart fluttered with a start.
Do good or evil prospects lie ahead?

OFFICER:

His Majesty seemed in a genial mood.
It might be that the queen is missing you;
of late you have been absent from the Court.

CHUNYU:

No time for me to seek an oracle.
Is it solely about the queen´s concern?

OFFICER:

（生）

急切里难求卦，

是中宫可的无他？

（紫）

惊心怎么？

你须是当今驸马。

（生）紫衣官，这是右相呵，

他弄威权要把江山霸，

甚醉汉淳郎独当了星变考察？

（贴）爹爹，

且暂时喑哑，

恁般时有的伤他。

（紫辞介）

你斟量回答，

俺紫衣人先去也。（下）

（生）儿，此去如何？

（贴）或是好意，亦未可知。（响道介）

夫子常独立，

鲤趋而过庭。

一闻君命召，

不俟驾而行。

Why are you so alarmed?
You´re still the honored royal son-in-law.
CHUNYU: Sir, it´s the right-hand premier.
It´s his insidious design to usurp the throne.
Who will believe that a drunkard has caused the stars to change?
SON: Daddy,
would you please pipe down for a while?
Why do you have to provoke that man?
OFFICER (taking his leave):
Mind what you say before the king.
I must hurry back to the palace now.

(Exit Officer)

CHUNYU: Son, what do you think is awaiting me?
SON: Maybe it´s some good news. But I can´t guess.
(Fanfare within)

The sage once stood there lost in thought
When his son came across the yard.
Soon as the sovereign had him called,
He didn´t even need a cart.

第四十一出　遣　　生

【金鸡叫】

（王引内使上）

王气余霄汉，

伤心玄象，

为谁凌乱？

（老上）

非关女死郎情断，

（叹介）

意外包弹，

就中离间。

（见介）（老）大王千岁。

（王）梓童免礼。

〔鹧鸪天〕

（老）千岁，

默坐长秋心暗焦，

这些时宫闱不见粉郎朝。

（王笑介）

你不知他凭依贵势干天象，

俺处置他空房入地牢。

（老泣介）原来这等了。天呵！

Scene 41 Sent Home

(Enter King, attended)

【The Golden Rooster】

KING:

My royalty is heaven blessed,
but ill signs there appear.
Who caused such an anomaly?

QUEEN (enters):

Of course it was not our girl nor her spouse.
(Sighs)
It´s some sinister plot,
aiming to sow discord.

(She greets King) May Your Majesty live a thousand years!

KING: Don´t stand on ceremony.

QUEEN: Your Majesty,

I sat absently in my palace hall;
For many days I haven´t seen our son-in-law.

KING (chuckles): Don´t you know that he

Abused our trust to alter heaven´s way?
I've therefore had him locked up in his empty house.

QUEEN (weeping): So that´s why I don´t see him any more. Oh, heavens!

I thought he was

A happy-go-lucky,
Who seeks high company.
And now he´s spending lone days tediously.

KING (angrily):

You only care about those petty household things.
Don´t you know he has ruined my royal base?

则说他能笑散，

美游遨，

怎知他于家为国苦无聊？

（王恼介）

笑你区区儿女寻常事，

败坏王基悔怎消？

（老）千岁，一个女婿，怎么会败了你王基？

（王）你深宫不知，有国人上书：星象告变，社稷崩移；祸起萧墙，衅生他族。他族，不是他，再有谁？

（老）难道驸马会占了你江山么？

（王）你怎知小小江山，也全亏一个“法”字？他坏法多端哩！

（老）他不过噇些酒儿。

（王）噇些酒儿？连琼英侄儿、灵芝、上真，都着他噇去了！

（老）谁见来？

（王恼介）你要他乱了宫才为证见么？今日设酒，遣他回去。你把那些外孙收养了，不许多言。

（老旦泣介）老天呵！不看女儿一面！

（报介）驸马午门外朝见。

（王）传旨着他进来。（内擂鼓介）

【逍遥乐】

（生朝衣上）

款曲趋朝重见，

宫庭盈泪眼。

（叹介）

盼朱衣只在殿中间。

恨远芳容，

QUEEN: Your Majesty, how can your son-in-law ruin your royal base?

KING: Since you stay in the inner palace most of the time, you may not have heard that a countryman has submitted a memorial. It says there are astronomical signs that our ancestral temple will collapse because of an alien being within the palace. If by "alien being" the report doesn´t allude to Chunyu, who else can it mean?

QUEEN: Do you really think your son-in-law would grab your land and take your kingdom away from you?

KING: What do you know? Small as my kingdom is, it´s established on the foundation of law. And he´s transgressed the law on numerous occasions.

QUEEN: His weakness is simply his love of the cup.

KING: Love of the cup? He´s made love to my niece Qiongying, and Truffle, as well as Itty.

QUEEN: Is there a witness?

KING (angrily): What witness? Won´t you believe it unless it happens to you yourself? I´ll give him a farewell banquet today and send him home. You take care of the grandchildren and keep quiet.

QUEEN (sobbing): Oh, heavens! For pity´s sake, or at least for the sake of our deceased daughter, don´t be harsh with him.

EUNUCH (enters to report): The royal son-in-law is waiting for an audience outside the palace gate.

KING: Send him in. (Drums beat within)

(Enter Chunyu in a ceremonial robe)

【Happily Free】

CHUNYU:

Obediently I return to Court,
poignant tears brimming in my eyes.
(Sighs)
I hope to find good luck awaiting me.
If my wife were alive,

惊承严谴，
暗恃慈颜。

一日不朝，其间容刀。我战兢兢行到宫门之内，礼当俯伏吞声。

(见介)罪臣驸马都尉左丞相淳于棼叩头，俺王、国母千岁千千岁。

(内使)请驸马平身，上殿。(生应千岁起躬介)

(王)寡人偶以烦言，因而简礼，谅之，谅之。

(老看生哭介)呀！驸马何瘦之甚也？

(生躬介)是。臣蒙天谴，幽臣私室。自思以公主之助，守郡多年，曾无败政。流言怨悖，委实伤心！

(王)已设有酒，为卿排闷。

(末持酒上)

冷落杯中蚁，
孤凄镜里鸾。

酒到。

(王)今日之酒，亲把一杯。

【皂罗袍】

堪叹吾家贵坦，
记关南饯别，
对影鸣銮。(生跪饮介)

(王)再斟酒。(生跪饮介)

I wouldn´t be so accused.
But the queen may help.

One day´s absence from Court, and a razor-sharp split cracks open. Trembling from head to foot I shuffle in. Here I must prostrate myself. (Kowtowing) Your Majesty´s condemned servant, the royal son-in-law and left-hand premier Chunyu Fen kowtows. May Your Majesty and Your Ladyship live thousands and thousands of years!

EUNUCH: Rise and come forward into the palace hall.

(Chunyu shouts "long live" and rises, keeping his back bent)

KING: The other day I said things in a fit of anger, and in consequence you suffered some inhospitality. I hope you won´t take it to heart.

QUEEN (weeps as she examines Chunyu): How can my son-in-law have grown so thin?

CHUNYU (making a deep bow): How could it be otherwise? I was condemned by heaven and placed under house arrest. My heart bleeds as I review the past. How successfully I, with assistance from the princess, discharged my duties at Southern Bough, and for so many years! But all of a sudden I was targeted and brought down by a rumor.

KING: I´ve prepared a wine banquet to cheer you up.

EUNUCH (enters with wine):

Let emmet spirits buoy you up,
A lone figure in the mirror.

Here comes wine.

KING: Today, I´ll personally offer you a cup.

【The Black Robe】

My honored son-in-law, remember you
the send-off party south of town,
the two of you a happy pair?
(Chunyu kneels to receive the cup of wine)

(老)内侍，连斟驸马数行。

止因淑女便摧残，

看承君子多疏慢。

(生叩头起介)

臣饮过三爵，

心愁万端。

客星何处，

天恩见宽？

(合)

风光顷刻堪肠断。

(生背介)怎说到“风光顷刻堪肠断”？

(王)驸马沉吟，知吾意乎？幸托姻亲，二十余年，不幸小女夭化，不得与君偕老，良用痛伤！

(生)公主仙逝，有臣在此，可以少奉寒温。

(王)这不消说了。则是卿离家多时，亦须暂归本里，一见亲族。

(生)此乃臣之家矣，更归何处？

(王笑介)卿本人间，家非在此。(生作昏立不语介)

(老)淳郎忽若昏睡懵然矣。

(生作醒介)呀！是了。俺家在人间，因何在此？(放声大哭介)哎哟！臣忽思家，寸心如割，不能久侍大王、国母矣。

Have another cup. (Chunyu accepts and drinks)

QUEEN: You servants, fill the cup for the royal son-in-law.

Distressed by our daughter´s untimely death,
wee have regretfully neglected you.

CHUNYU (kowtows and rises):

Thank you for the three cups of wine,
which evoke a host of woes.
Does this new favor mean
the nova was removed?

KING (refrain):

All that is but a moment to recall.

CHUNYU (aside): What does he mean by "All that is but a moment to recall"?

KING: Think hard, my son-in-law. You know what I mean, don´t you? Wee do appreciate your marrying our daughter and having been with us for twenty years. It´s most unfortunate that our daughter died early and couldn´t accompany you into old age. How that grieves us!

CHUNYU: Though the princess passed on, I´m still here. I can offer you some filial consolation.

KING: Thank you for saying that, but you´ve been away from home for a very long time. I think for the time being you ought to go back to your native place and see your folks.

CHUNYU: This is my home. Where do you want me to go?

KING (laughing): You belong to the human world. This isn´t your native place.

(Chunyu stands motionlessly in a stupor)

QUEEN: He seems to have dozed off.

CHUNYU (suddenly recovering his senses): Yes, that´s right! My home is in the human world. Why am I here? (He bursts out crying) Alas! Your humble servant has suddenly become homesick. There seem to be a thousand knives piercing my heart. I´m sorry I can´t wait on Your Majesty

(王)叫紫衣官送淳郎起程。
(生)外孙三四，俱在宫中，还请一见。
(王)诸孙留此宫中，自能抚育，无以为念。
(生哭介)这等，苦煞俺也！
(老)不用苦伤，但要淳郎留意，便有相见之期。
(生拜介)拜辞了。

【前腔】

忽忆乡园在眼，
向迷中发悟，
有泪阑珊。

(王)

因风好去到人间，
三杯酒尽笙歌散。

(老泣介)驸马，你真个去也呵，

归心顿起，
攀留大难。
几年恩爱，
你将如等闲。(合前)

【意不尽】

(生)

向尊前流涕锦衣还，
二十载恩光无限。

(王、老)淳郎，淳郎，

则怕俺宗庙崩移你长在眼。

and Your Ladyship any longer.

KING: I´ll order the purple-robe palace officers to send you home immediately.

CHUNYU: My children are in the palace. May I see them before I leave?

KING: Don´t worry about them. They´ll be raised in the palace and taken good care of.

CHUNYU (sobbing): Oh, it pains me to part from them!

QUEEN: Don´t be so sad. As long as you remember us, wee shall meet again.

CHUNYU (bows): Farewell.

【Ditto】

My hometown suddenly flashed back,
awakening me from a trance.
Welling tears blind my eyes.

KING:

Wish you plain sailing to the human world.
After three cups of wine the banquet ends.

QUEEN (weeping): My son-in-law, are you going to leave us like this?

Your heart is pulled homeward;
it cannot be detained.
Those happy years of love,
will they be swept clean from your mind?
(Refrain)

【Coda】

CHUNYU:

Tears overflow the cup as I depart,
after a glorious twenty-year career.

KING, QUEEN: Chunyu, Chunyu,

you´ll witness the collapsing of our royal house.

酒尽难留客，
叶落自归山。
惟馀离别泪，
相送到人间。

The guest won't stay when wine is gone;
A falling leaf returns to ground.
Nothing except our rolling tears
Follow you to the human sphere.

第四十二出　寻　　寤

(二紫衣上)事不三思，终有后悔。我大槐安国王生下公主，当初只在本国中招选驸马便了，却去人间请了个淳于棼来尚主；出守南柯大郡，富贵二十余年；公主薨逝，拜相还朝；专权乱政，谪见于天，国主忧疑，着我二人仍以牛车一乘，送他回去。(笑介)淳于棼、淳于棼，好不颓气人也！正是：

　　王门一闭深如海，
　　从此萧郎是路人。

(生朝衣上)

　　忽悟家何在，
　　潸然泪满衣。
　　旧恩抛未得，
　　肠断故乡归。

我淳于棼，暂尔思家，恩还昼锦。思妻恋阙，能不依依。(泣介)(见紫衣介)请了。便是二十年前迎取我的紫衣官么？(紫懒应介)

(生)想车马都在宫门之外了？

Scene 42 The Realization

(Enter two palace officers in purple robes)

OFFICERS: If one doesn´t think twice, he´ll surely regret what he´s done. Take for example the king of our Great Sophora Kingdom. If he´d only looked for a son-in-law within the kingdom! But he had to summon that Chunyu Fen from the human world for his daughter. What´s more, he appointed him Taishou of Southern Bough Prefecture, and allowed him to enjoy twenty years of wealth and fame. At the death of the princess he was recalled and promoted to premier, but he monopolized power and created such chaos that even heaven showed signs of displeasure. It was only then that our king began to worry and commanded us to take him back in the ox cart in which wee had brought him here. (They laugh) Chunyu Fen, Chunyu Fen, what an underdog you are now! It´s said:

Once the palace gates shut behind your back,
You´re nothing but a stranger on the street.

(Enter Chunyu in a ceremonial robe)

CHUNYU:

All at once I remembered home;
Down poured my tears that soaked my robe.
On the one hand, old glory drags,
On the other, my hometown pulls.

I, Chunyu Fen, suddenly suffered a pang of homesickness, and His Majesty kindly permitted me to go back to my native place. But I can´t help feeling miserable now that I´m actually tearing myself away from the royal life and the place where my wife lies. (He weeps. Greets Officers) Nice to meet you. Aren´t you the two who brought me here twenty years ago? (Officers mumble a reply) My coach and my attendants are waiting outside the palace gate, I suppose.

（紫）着。（行介）

【绣带儿】

（生）

才提醒，

趁着这绿暗红稀出凤城。

出了朝门，

心中猛然自惊。

我左右之人都在那里？前面一辆秃牛单车，岂是我乘坐的？咳！

怎亲随一个都无？

又怎生有这陋劣车乘？

难明。

想起来，我去后可能再到这朝门之下，

向宫庭回首无限情。

公主妻呵，

忍不住宫袍泪迸。

看来今日我乘坐的车儿，便只是这等了。待我再迟回几步。呀！便是这座金字城楼了。怎军民人等见我都不站起？咳！

还乡定出了这一座大城，

宛是我昔年东来之径。

少不得更衣上车而行了。（更衣介）

〔长相思〕

着朝衣，

解朝衣，

故衣犹在御香微，

回头宫殿低。

意迟迟，

OFFICERS: Yeah.
(They walk)

【The Embroidered Ribbon】
CHUNYU:
Jolted awake,
I quit the palace in autumn´s decaying green.
Once outside the palace gate,
my heart skips a beat to perceive:
My attendants are nowhere in sight, and there´s only a balding old ox and a shabby cart waiting out there. That´s certainly not for me! Oh!
Why don´t I see my valets and footmen?
How is it there is only such a broken cart?
That puzzles me.
Once I leave this place, I wonder if I may ever enter the palace gate again.
Feelings surge as I glance back one more time.
Oh, my dear wife!
Bitter tears drip onto my palace robe.
Well, it seems this cart is my lot today. Let me take a last look around. That´s the multi-storied gate tower with the four huge characters in gold. Why don´t the people in the streets stand to attention when they see me? Ah!
A home-bound ride transports me out of town.
The road seems unchanged since the time I came.

Now I must take off my palace robe before I get onto the cart. (He changes into plain clothes)
I donned a robe,
Then took it off;
It still retains the smell of palace scent.
The distance makes the palace small.
My mind lingers,

步迟迟，

肠断恩私双泪垂，

（叹介）

回朝知几时？

（紫）上车快走。（紫随意行走做不畏生打歌介）

一个呆子呆又呆，

大窟弄里去不去，

小窟弄里来不来，

你道呆不子也呆？

（鞭牛走介）畜生！不走？

（生）便缓行些么？

【前腔】

消停，

看山川依然旧景，

争些儿旧日人情。

（紫衣急鞭牛走介）（生恼介）看这使者，甚无威势，真可为怏怏如也。（紫鞭牛走介）（生）紫衣官，我且问你，广陵郡何时可到？（紫不应笑歌走介）（生恼介）咳，我好问他，他则不应。难道我再没有回朝之日了？便不然，谢恩本也写上得几句哩。（紫衣笑介）

（生）

他那里死气淘声，

怎知我心急摇旌？

销凝。

也则索小心再问他。紫衣官，广陵郡几时可到？

My steps loiter,
Two lines of tears for state and private thoughts.
(He sighs)
Which year may I return to Court?

OFFICERS: Hurry up and jump in! (They walk sluggishly in spite of Chunyu´s urging, and sing a ditty)
How can you tell which fellow is a fool?
Into a big hole he´d refuse to go;
Into a tiny hole he´d push and drool.
Isn´t that noodle-head the biggest fool?
(Whipping the ox) Faster, you beast!

CHUNYU: Let him take his time.

【Ditto】

No need for haste.
Just let me take in the familiar view
to recall and relish the happy times.

(Officers whip the ox to hasten the pace. Chunyu angrily) Look at these two, sulky and sullen, as if they were doing a humiliating job. (Officers keep whipping the ox) Officers, may I ask how long it´ll take to reach the city of Yangzhou? (Officers simply ignore his question. They laugh and chant the ditty without slowing down. Chunyu angrily) Damn! I asked them politely and they wouldn´t even answer! Are they so sure I´ll never have a chance to return to Court? I can do them a favor by putting in a good word when I present a memorial to the king. (Officers laugh disdainfully)

They keep on making those annoying grunts,
while pressing questions crowd and fill my head
— obsessive thoughts.

Well, let me ask again. This time more humbly. Sirs, when can we reach the city of Yangzhou?

（紫）霎时到了。（鞭牛走介）

（生望介）呀，像是广陵城了。

渺茫中遥望见江外影，

这穴道也是我前来路径。

（又走介）呀，便是我家门巷了。

（泣介）

还傒幸依然户庭，

泪伤心，

怎这般呵夕阳人静？

（紫）到门了，下车。（生下车入门介）

（紫）升阶。

（生升阶介、望见榻作惊介）不要近前，我怕也！

（紫高叫介）淳于棼！（叫三次生不应、紫推生就榻、生仍前作睡介）

（紫）槐国人何在？淳郎快醒来。我们去也。（急下）

（生惊介、醒做声介）使者，使者。

（丑持酒上）甚么使者？则我山鹧。

（溜、沙上）淳于兄醒了。我二人正洗上脚来。

（生）日色到那里？

（丑）日西哩。

（生）窗儿下甚么子？

（溜）余酒尚温。

（生）呀！斜日未隐于西垣，余樽尚湛于东牖，我梦中倏忽，如度一世矣。

OFFICERS: In a moment. (They continue to whip the ox)

CHUNYU (peering ahead): Ah, that seems to be Yangzhou.

I see the city walls looming up far ahead.
This is the tunnel through which I came years ago.

(They walk) Ah, this street leads to my house. (He weeps)

I wonder if my house still stands intact.
Tears flow uncontrolled.
And why is this late afternoon so quiet?

OFFICERS: Here wee are. Get off! (Chunyu gets off the cart and enters the gate) Ascend the steps.

CHUNYU (mounts the steps and stops short as he sees his couch): No, I can´t go forward. It frightens me.

OFFICERS (calling out aloud): Chunyu Fen! (Thus three times. Chunyu makes no response. They push him onto the couch. Chunyu sleeps on the couch as before) No more of the Sophora. Wake up, Chunyu. Wee are leaving.

(Exeunt Officers in a hurry)

CHUNYU (startled, wakes up): Sir! Sir!

(Enter Partridge with wine)

PARTRIDGE: What sir? It´s me, Partridge.

(Enter Liu Second and Sha Third)

LIU, SHA: So you´re awake, Brother Chunyu. We´ve just washed our feet.

CHUNYU: What time of the day is it?

PARTRIDGE: The sun is setting in the west.

CHUNYU: What´s that on the windowsill?

LIU: That´s the half cup of wine you left. It´s still warm.

CHUNYU: Ah! The declining sun still hangs above the western wall, and my half-empty cup still sits limpid on the eastern windowsill, but in my dream I´ve lived a whole lifetime.

(沙、溜)做甚梦来?

(生作想介)取杯热茶来。(丑取茶上介)

(生)再用茶，待我醒一醒。(丑又取茶上介)

(生饮介)呀，溜兄、沙兄，好不富贵的所在也！我的公主妻呵。

(丑)甚么公主妻？你不做了驸马？

(生)是做了驸马。

(溜)那一朝里驸马?

(生)这话长，扶我起来讲。(溜、沙扶起生介)你们都不曾见那使者穿紫的?

(沙)我三人并不曾见。

(生)奇怪！奇怪！听我讲来：

【宜春令】

堂东庑，

睡正清，

有几个紫衣人轩车叩迎。

你说从那里去?

槐根窟里，

有个大槐安国主女娉婷。

那公主小名，我还记的，唤做瑶芳，招我为驸马；曾侍猎于国西灵龟山。

(丑)后来怎的?

(生)这国之南，有个南柯郡，槐安国主把我做了二十年南柯太守。

(溜、沙)享用哩。后来呢?

(生)公主养了二男二女，不料为檀萝小贼惊恐，一病而亡，归葬于国东蟠龙冈上。

LIU, SHA: What did you dream of?

CHUNYU (trying to recall): Fetch me a cup of hot tea. (Partridge goes off and reenters with tea) Another cup, please. I´m not fully awake yet. (Partridge fetches another cup) (Sipping tea) Ah, Brother Liu and Brother Sha, it was a wonderful place! And my princess wife!

PARTRIDGE: What princess wife? You dreamed you married a king´s daughter?

CHUNYU: That´s right.

LIU: Which dynasty was that?

CHUNYU: It´s a long story. But first help me up. (Liu and Sha help Chunyu sit up) Didn´t you see two envoys in purple robes just now?

SHA: No, we three didn´t see anyone like that.

CHUNYU: That´s strange. Well, let me tell you about it.

【Spring Time Minitune】

On the verandah,
I was deep in sleep
when two in purple bowed and helped me to a coach.
Where do you think they led me?
Into a hole at the Sophora´s foot.
There was a kingdom there whose monarch had a girl.

I even remember her maiden name. She was called Yaofang. I married her and became the son-in-law of the king, and later went hunting with him at Tortoise Hill west of the capital.

PARTRIDGE: And?

CHUNYU: There was a prefecture called Southern Bough in the south of the kingdom, and the king made me its Taishou. So there I stayed for twenty years.

LIU, SHA: Wow! You must have had a good time. What happened next?

CHUNYU: The princess gave birth to two sons and two daughters, but unfortunately bandits from Rattan Sandalwood gave her a terrible shock. She fell ill and died. And I buried her on Dragon Hill east of the capital.

(丑哭介)哎也！可怜，可怜，我的院主。

(生)

猎龟山他为防备守檀萝，

葬龙冈我凄惶煞了鸾镜。

(沙)后来呢？

(生)自公主亡化，虽则回朝拜相，人情不同了。

势难行，

我情愿乞还乡境。

那国王、国母见我思归，无奈许我暂回。适才送我的使者二人，他都是紫衣一品。

(丑)哎呀，不曾待的他茶哩。

(生)二兄，你道这是怎的？

(溜)不知呢。

(沙)我也不知。

(生)怎生槐穴里去？

(沙、溜)敢是老槐成精了。

【前腔】

花狐媚，

木客精，

山鹧儿，

备锹锄看槐根影形。

(丑取锹上介)东人，东人，你常在这大槐树下醉了睡，着手了。

(生)也说得是。且同你瞧去。(行瞧介)

PARTRIDGE (sobs): Alas! My poor lady of the house!

CHUNYU:

The hunting was a war game against Sandalwood;
the passing of my wife induced an adverse change.

SHA: So what happened next?

CHUNYU: After the death of the princess, I returned to Court. Although I was promoted to premier, public sentiments had changed.

As enmity rose,
I begged to return to my native place.

When the king and queen saw that I was so determined to go, they reluctantly granted me permission. The two envoys who accompanied me back just now were top-ranking officers privileged to wear purple robes.

PARTRIDGE: Too bad I didn´t have a chance to offer them tea.

CHUNYU: Brother Liu and Brother Sha, do you have any idea what brought on that dream?

LIU: It beats me.

SHA: Beats me too.

CHUNYU: How could I have gotten into a tree hole?

LIU, SHA: Maybe that old tree has acquired a spirit through its long years of existence.

【Ditto】

Foxes can bewitch,
and trees can gain souls.

Partridge,

bring spades and hoes to the Sophora´s root.

PARTRIDGE (goes off and reenters with a spade): Master, since you´ve so often gotten drunk and slept under that tree, maybe you were possessed.

CHUNYU: You said it! Let´s go over and have a look.

(They walk over and inspect the tree)

(溜)这槐树下不是个大窟栊？(掘介)有蚁，有蚁。

寻原洞穴，

怎只见树皮中有蚁穿成路径？

(溜)向高头锹了去。

(众惊介)呀！你看穴之两旁，广可一丈；这穴中也一丈有余，洞然明朗。

(沙)原来树根之上堆积土壤，但是一层城郭，便起一层楼台，奇哉！奇哉！

(丑惊介)哎也！有蚁儿数斛，隐聚其中，怕人！怕人！

(生)不要惊他。

嵌空中楼郭层城，

怎中央有绛台深迴？

(沙)这台子土色是红些。(觑介)单这两个大蚁儿并着在此，你看他素翼红冠，长可三寸，有数十大蚁左右辅从，余蚁不敢相近。

(生叹介)想是槐安国王宫殿了。

(溜)这两个蚁蛘，便是令岳丈、岳母哩。

(生泣介)

好关情，

也受尽了两人恭敬。

(溜)再南上掘去。呀，你看南枝之上，可宽四丈有余，也像土城一般，上面也有小楼子，群蚁穴处其中。呀，见了淳于兄来，都一个个有举头相向的，又有点头俯伏的，得非所云南柯郡乎？

(沙)是贵治了。

LIU: Look! There´s a big hole at the bottom of the tree. (He digs) Ants! Ants!

Searching for their nest,
we´ve come upon a web of ant-bored trails beneath the bark.

Let´s scrape off the bark further up.

ALL (in astonishment): Look! The cave is almost ten feet in breadth and ten in depth, and it´s quite bright inside!

SHA: So they´ve laid dirt on the roots, one tier of earth followed by one terrace of housing. That´s really amazing!

PARTRIDGE (appalled): Oh, my! There must be several bushels of ants living in here. That´s scary!

CHUNYU: Don´t alarm them.

Tiers of castles hang in the empty space.
Why lies there a red platform in its depth?

SHA: This platform of earth does seem redder than elsewhere. (He takes a closer look) There are two giant ants on the platform, each about three inches long. Look, they have translucent wings and red crowns. They´re protected by a ring of several dozen large ants, and ordinary ones dare not even go near them.

CHUNYU (sighs): That must be the king´s palace.

LIU: And these two giants are your parents-in-law!

CHUNYU (weeps):

Emotions overflow,
for they treated me like an honored guest.

LIU: Let´s dig south following this big bough. Look here! Near its tip, some forty feet apart, is another mound of cave town. The terraced caves are all occupied by ants. Brother Chunyu, look! When they see you, some raise their heads to salute you, and some drop their heads as if bowing. Isn´t this the Southern Bough Prefecture you talked about?

SHA: This must be your old jurisdiction.

【前腔】

南枝偃，

好路平，

小重楼多则是南柯郡城？

(生)像是了。(叹介)我在此二十年太守，好不费心，谁道则是些蝼蚁百姓？便是他们记下有七千二百条德政碑、生祠记，通不见了，只这长亭路一道沙堤还在。

有何德政？

也亏他二十载赤子们相支应。

(丑)西头掘将去。

(沙)呀，西去二丈，一穴外高中空，看是何物？(觑介)原来是败龟板，其大如斗，积雨之后，蔓草丛生。既在槐西，得非所猎灵龟山乎？

(生)是了，是了。可惜田秀才一篇《龟山大猎赋》，

好文章埋没龟亭，

空壳落做他形胜。

(沙)掘向东去丈余，又有一穴，古根盘曲，

似龙形，

莫不是你葬金枝蟠龙冈影？

(生细看哭介)是了。你看中有蚁冢尺余，是吾妻也。我的公主呵！

【前腔】

人如见，

泪似倾，

【Ditto】

The bough stretches south;
roads extend.
That terraced construction must be your major town.

CHUNYU: It does look like it. (Sighs) For twenty years I governed that place to the best of my ability, and my people turned out to be no more than ants! The stelae they raised in my honor with as many as seventy-two hundred records of my good deeds and the eulogy to my exploits are all gone now. Only the sand bank is still discernible.

What good did I do
that they should have praised and supported me for twenty years?

PARTRIDGE: Let´s dig westward.

SHA: Ah! Twenty feet to the west there´s a dome-shaped thing in a hollow. Let´s see what it is. (He peers) So it´s a rotten tortoise shell as large as a hat. Soaked in rain water, weeds flourish on top of it. Since it´s west of the tree, it must be Tortoise Hill where you hunted with the king.

CHUNYU: So it is. It´s funny to think that Scholar Tian penned a eulogy to such a thing.

A eulogy was wasted on a rotten bone;
a hollow shell was hailed as a historic site.

SHA: There´s another cavity ten feet to the east. It´s threaded by winding old roots.

Curling like a dragon,
isn´t it here where you entombed your Golden Bough?

CHUNYU (inspects the place carefully and bursts into tears): This is the place! Look at the foot-tall mound there. It´s my wife´s tomb! Oh, my dear princess!

【Ditto】

Again we meet;
tears cascade.

叫芳卿恨不同棺共茔。

为国王临并，

受凄凉叫不的你芳名应。

二兄，我当初葬公主时，为些小儿女，与右相段君争辩风水，他说："此中怕有风蚁。"我硬说："纵然蚁聚何妨？"如今看来，蚁子到是有的了。

争风水有甚蟠龙？

公主曾说来，

他说为我把蝼蚁前驱真正。(内风起介)

(丑)好大风雨来了，这一科蚁子都坏了他罢。

(生慌介)

莫伤情，再为他绕门儿把宫槐遮定。(盖介)

(丑)盖好了，躲雨去。

(众)

不自逃龙雨，

因谁为蚁封？(下)

(内叫介)雨住了。

(丑上笑介)好笑，好笑，孩儿天，快雨快晴。(瞧介)哎呀，相公快来。

(生、沙、溜急上)(丑)你看这些蚁穴，都不知那里去了？

How I wish to lie with you in this very grave!

Distrusted by His Majesty,

I called your name but you no longer came to help.

Brother Liu and Brother Sha, as I recall it now, I´ve had an argument with the right-hand premier on the *fengshui* of the burial ground in relation to the prosperity of my posterity. He contended that the place might be plagued by ants. And I insisted that there was no need at all to worry about an ant infestation. As it now turns out, it indeed is occupied by ants.

What good luck did the curling dragon bring?

I remember the princess said

she´d wait for me underground as a cricket or an ant.

(Sound of rising wind within)

PARTRIDGE: A heavy rainstorm is coming up. We´d better destroy this nest of ants.

CHUNYU (emotionally):

Don´t hurt them.

Let´s take the trouble to board up this big Sophora hole.

(They cover the hole)

PARTRIDGE: It´s covered up. Let´s seek shelter ourselves.

ALL:

Who doesn't flee the dragon rain

But shields an ant hole in its stead?

(Exeunt all)

VOICE WITHIN: The rain has stopped.

(Reenter Partridge, laughing)

PARTRIDGE: What weather — now rain, now shine! Like a baby, smiling one moment and crying the next. (Looking around) Alas! Master, come here quickly! (Reenter Chunyu, Liu and Sha hurriedly) Look at these caves. The ants are all gone!

(众惊介)真个灵圣哩。

(生)也是前定了。他国中先有星变，流言国有大恐，都邑迁徙，此其验乎？

【太师引】

一星星，

有的多灵圣，

也是他不合招邀我客星。

(沙)

可知道沧海桑田，

也则为漏泄了春光武陵？

(生)步影寻踪，旨如所梦。还有檀萝堑江一事可疑。

(丑想介)有了，有了。宅东长堑古溪之上，有紫檀一株，藤萝缠拥，不见天日。我长在那里歇昼，见有大群赤蚁往来，想是此物。

(生)着了。此所谓全萝道赤剥军也。

但些小精灵能厮挺，

险气煞周郎残命。

(溜)那个周郎？

(生)是周弁为将，他和田子华都在南柯哩。

(丑)有这等事！

(生)连老老爷都讨得他平安书来，约丁丑年和我相见。

(溜)今年太岁丁丑了。

(生)这是怎的？可疑，可疑。

胡厮胫，

和亡人住程，

怕不是我身厢有甚么缠魂不定？

ALL (surprised): Unbelievable!

CHUNYU: That must have been predestined. First they saw a nova, then rumors spread that there would be a catastrophe and the capital would have to be relocated. Isn´t this proof?

【The Chancellor´s Interlude】

Tiny as they are,
they by divine permission live.
They shouldn´t have brought an intruder to their cave.

SHA:

How many times have sea and land switched hands!
Was that caused by unwitting outbursts of romance?

CHUNYU: Bit by bit, our search has traced and confirmed my dream. Only the part about Gorgeville and Rattan Sandalwood remains unproved.

PARTRIDGE (thinking): I´ve got it! There´s a red sandalwood tree by the old brook to the east of our house. It´s a huge tree with rattan clinging all over its trunk. I often nap under it, and I remember seeing hordes of red ants crawling about. It must be that tree.

CHUNYU: Yeah, they must be the so-called red-breasted soldiers of Rattan Sandalwood.

Those teeny beings were awfully brave,
for they almost caught and killed Mr. Zhou.

LIU: Which Mr. Zhou?

CHUNYU: Zhou Bian, of course. Both he and Tian Zihua were with me in Southern Bough.

PARTRIDGE: Really?!

CHUNYU: Believe it or not, the king even managed to fetch me a letter from my father. In his letter he said he´d meet me in the year of *ding-chou*.

LIU: Why! This year is the year of *ding-chou*.

CHUNYU: Indeed! Is that a prophecy?

That´s ridiculous.
How could I´ve communed with the dead?

(沙)亡人的事，要问个明眼禅师。

(丑)有，有，有。刚才一个和尚在门首躲雨。

(生)快请来。(丑出请介)

【前腔】

(扮小僧上)

行脚僧，谁见请?

(见介)

原来是淳于君有何事情?

(生)师兄从何而来?

(僧)我从六合县来。

(生)正要相问，六合县有个文士田子华、武举周弁二人可会他?

(僧)是有此二人，平生至交，同日无病而死。

(生惊介)这等，一发诧异了。

(僧)这中庭槐树掘倒因何?

(生)小生正待请教。这槐穴中有蚁数斛，小生昼卧东廊，只见此中有紫衣人相请小生，去为国王眷属。一混二十余年，醒来一梦，中间有他周、田二人在内。今闻师兄言说，知是他死后游魂，这也罢了。却又得先府君一书，约今丁丑年相见，小子十分忧疑。

Was I possessed by an evil spirit of some kind?

SHA: About the afterlife, you have to consult an insightful Chan master.

PARTRIDGE: Wait! Just now there was a monk taking shelter at our gate during the storm.

CHUNYU: Send for him immediately.

(Exit Partridge to find the monk)

(Enter a monk)

【Ditto】

MONK:

I´m a roving monk.

Who is seeking me?

(He greets Chunyu)

So, Mr. Chunyu, what can I do for you?

CHUNYU: Where did Your Reverence come from?

MONK: I´ve just come from Liuhe County.

CHUNYU: I happen to have a couple of friends there, a scholar named Tian Zihua and a martial arts master Zhou Bian. Did you see them?

MONK: I know them both. They were bosom friends, and they died on the very same day without suffering any obvious illness.

CHUNYU (taken aback): What?! That´s amazing!

MONK: Why are you digging up this Sophora tree?

CHUNYU: That was what I intended to ask you about. There were several bushels of ants living in the hole in the tree. While I was napping on the eastern verandah this afternoon, two envoys in purple robes emerged from the hole and invited me to their kingdom. I became their king´s son-in-law, staying there twenty years. When I woke up, I found it had been nothing but a dream. Strange to say, Mr. Zhou and Mr. Tian were there too. What you said just now seems to explain it. It could´ve been their souls roaming after their death. But what´s even more incredible is that I received a letter from my deceased father. In his letter he made an

敢有甚嫌三怕九？

恰今年遇丑逢丁。

(僧)这等，恰好契玄本师择日广做水陆道场，你何不写下一疏，向无遮会上问此情缘？老师父呵，

破空虚照映一切影，

把公案及期参证。

(生揖介)

承师命，

似盂兰听经，

又感动我竹枝残兴。

(僧)这功德不比盂兰小会，要清斋闭关七七四十九日，一日一夜念佛三万六千声；到期燃指为香，写成一疏，七日七夜哀祷佛前；才有些儿影响。

(生)领教。则未审禅师能将大槐安国土眷属，普度生天？

(僧)使得。

【尾声】

(生)

尽吾生有尽供无尽，

但普度的无情似有情，

我待把割不断的无明向契玄禅师位下请。

appointment with me for the year of *ding-chou*, and that's this year! That's really unsettling.

Am I in an ill set of numbers trapped?

Ding comes across *chou* in this very year.

MONK: It just happens that Master Qixuan is going to conduct a grand Buddhist ritual. Why don't you write a petition and present it to him on that occasion. The master,

his insight sees through shadows and disguise;

he can reveal the cause and effect of life.

CHUNYU (raises his clasped hands in salutation):

Thank you for your advice.

Like Ullambana once again,

I may find new luck at the bamboo grove.

MONK: This time it's quite a different matter from attending the Ullambana ceremony. You must fast reclusively for seven seven-days, and chant Buddha's name thirty-six thousand times every day and night. Only after that can you write the petition while burning your fingertips as if they were joss sticks. Then pray another seven days and seven nights before Buddha's statue. In that way your piety may accomplish results.

CHUNYU: Thank you for your teachings. By the way, can the Master enable all my relatives in the Great Sophora Kingdom to transmigrate to heaven as well?

MONK: He certainly can.

【Coda】

CHUNYU:

I devote my bounded life to the boundless cause

to transmigrate the insensate from endless woes.

To the seat of Master Qixuan I'll present my haunting qualms.

空色色非空，
还谁天眼通？
移将竹林寺，
度却大槐宫。

Rūpa śūnya, śūnya rūpa,
Who has eyes of divinity?
To the world of eternity
He transports the Great Sophora.

第四十三出　转　　情

【浪淘沙】

（僧持幡上）

顶礼大南无，
击鼓吹螺，
天歌梵放了紧那罗。
昼夜灯幡长续命，
照满娑婆。

【前腔】

（僧持磬上）

人在欲天多，
怕煞阎罗。
新生天里有愁么？
次第风轮都坏却，
甚么娑婆？

【前腔】

（生捧香炉上）

弟子有丝萝，
曾出守南柯。

Scene 43　　Love Extended

(Enter a monk, holding a banner)

【Washing off Sand】

MONK:

Before Buddha we lie prostrate.
Beating drums and blowing shells,
we hum and chorus the religious tunes.
Our magic banners and eternal lamps
irradiate the world.

(Enter a second monk, holding a bell)

【Ditto】

SECOND MONK:

Born into the world of desires,
man is afraid of death.
Will he be happy in the upper spheres?
The wheel of fate soon plunges him to hell
— a worse place than this world.

(Enter Chunyu, holding an incense burner)

【Ditto】

CHUNYU:

I once enjoyed the marriage tie,
and governed Southern Bough.
What are things like in the heavenly spheres?
If only love can last forever there,
I can endure this world.

光音天里事如何？
但是有情那尽得，
年少也娑婆。

(生放香炉礼佛介)(合掌向众介)弟子稽首。

(众)一切众生，顶礼如来威光，凭仗禅师法力。有精心的檀越，戒行的沙弥，呗赞者百千万人，海潮音如雷震沸；拜祈者四十九日，河沙泪似雨滂沱。果然无碍无遮，必当有诚有感。只待法师慧剑遥指，务令众生以次生天。

(生稽首介)凡诸有情，普同慈愿。

【北仙吕点绛唇】

(净扮契玄老僧威容上)

奏发科宣，
诸天灿烂，
琉璃殿。
梦境因缘，
佛境里参承遍。

(生向净稽首介)弟子淳于棼稽首。(众稽首介)

(净)老僧修行到九十一岁，才做下这坛水陆无边道场；也亏了先生们虔心，斋了七七四十九日，拜了这七日七夜。这几夜，河路广破暗之灯，焰口饱清凉之食；虔求恳至，誓愿弘通。今夜道场告终，

(He puts down the incense burner, salutes the statue of Buddha and the monks) My respects to you all.

MONKS: The omnipotence of the great Buddha, evinced through the master´s magic powers, commands the respect of all beings. Gathered here are both secular devotees and devout ascetics. The hundreds of thousands of throats hymning in chorus reverberate like thunder over a boiling sea. For forty-nine days they have prayed. Their tears have fallen in torrents and washed off myriads of grains of dirt; their sincerity and dedication have opened them up to Buddha. At the command of the master´s magic sword, they are to be reborn in heaven.

CHUNYU (raises his clasped hands before his chest in salutation): May all beings be gratified.

(Enter Qixuan, venerable and dignified)

【Painting Cherry Lips, Northern Style】

QIXUAN:

Up go the prayers
to heaven´s splendor
— all is crystal clear.
The karma in a dream
can be clarified by the Buddhist beam.

CHUNYU (salutes Qixuan): Your disciple Chunyu Fen here pays respects to the master.

(Monks salute Qixuan)

QIXUAN: Thanks to my life-long diligence in practicing Buddhism, at the age of ninety-one I´m finally able to administer this grand ritual of infinite beneficence. Your piety, which you´ve demonstrated by fasting seven seven-days and praying another seven, is also a contributing factor to this success. These nights, floating lamps spread and sparkle over streams and ponds; sacrifices and offerings satiate the hungry souls in hell. Your fervent prayers have enabled you to look forward to attaining your wishes.

先生可有甚祈请？替你铺宣。

(生)小生第一要看见父亲生天；第二要见瑶芳妻子生天；第三愿尽槐安一国普度生天。

(净)好大愿心。你可便燃指为香，替你铺陈情疏。倘有奇验，以报虔诚。(众发擂吹介)(生膜拜三拜介)

【混江龙】

(净)

这淮南卑贱，
淳于棼扑地礼诸天。(生烧指介)

(净)

则他恨不的皮剳烛点，
则这些指顶香燃。
为他久亡过的老椿堂葬朔边，
和他新眷属大槐宫变了桑田。

他老亲呵，
鱼雁信暗寄与九重泉。

他眷属呵，
怎蝼蚁情显豁在三摩殿？
仗福力如来立地，
和他度情缘一众生天。

(净)祈请已过，待我杨枝洒水，布散香花。

【油葫芦】

(净众杨枝洒水介)

我待手洒杨枝有千百转，

On this final night of the ritual, is there any wish you´d like to have fulfilled? I´ll help you obtain it.

CHUNYU: Firstly, I wish to see my father rise to heaven; secondly, I wish to see my dear wife Yaofang rise to heaven; thirdly, I wish to see all beings of the Sophora Kingdom rise to heaven.

QIXUAN: Those are no small wishes! You may now burn a fingertip to serve as a joss stick while I convey your wishes to Buddha. Your piety may be amply rewarded.

(Monks beat drums and blow conches. Chunyu makes three kowtows)

【A Roiling Dragon】

QIXUAN:

Chunyu Fen from the south of Huai,
prostrates himself before the heavens high.
(Chunyu burns a finger)
He´d rather sacrifice his skin and flesh
to make candles of his fingertips
for his father who died long ago on the northern front,
and his lately acquired Sophora kindred who were drowned.
His father
wrote and sent him a letter from the springs of hell;
his wife
revealed her maiden love before your holy seat.
Great Buddha, please give him your blessings now,
and bring his loved ones into the celestial spheres.

I´ve prayed for you. Now let me sprinkle holy water with this willow twig and scatter these fragrant petals. (Qixuan and Monks sprinkle water with willow twigs)

【The Glib Cricket】

My willow twig has made a thousand twists and turns

洗尘心把甘露显。

（散花介）

香风台殿雨花天，
人天玉女持花献，
花光水色如空旋。
仗如来水月观，
把世界花开现。
水珠儿撒地虫儿咽，
纥哩子吐红莲。

（净）多时分了？

（众）月待中哩。

（净）大众一路行香，绕此天坛之下；则老僧与先生登于坛上，看望诸天中有甚么景象也？（众应介）

（净）

欲穷他化路，
须待净居天。（同生下）（内鼓吹唱介）

（众）

散花林，
花气深。
如来佛，
观世音。
诸天眼，
众生心。
三明度，
九幽沉。

that purge the heart of all its earthly dirt.
(He scatters petals)
Fragrant petals are borne down from the skies,
which fairies have collected with soft hands.
The hues of drops and petals whirl around,
real as the moon´s reflection on the pond,
yet in its center blooms the world.
The insects lick and gulp the fallen drops;
in their innocent heart a lotus sprouts.

What time is it now?

MONKS: The moon has almost reached the zenith.

QIXUAN: Now all of you, circle this sacrificial altar and offer joss sticks. Mr. Chunyu and I shall ascend it to see what view we may find in the heavens. (Monks respond in chorus)

To reach the worlds of emptiness,
One has to get beyond desires.

(Exeunt Qixuan and Chunyu)

(Music within)

MONKS (chanting):

Flowers fly;
sweet smells rise.
Buddha wise,
Guanyin nice.
Heavens´ eyes
see three lives;
hearty cries,
hellish hives.

(Exeunt Monks)

【天下乐】

(净持剑引生上)呀！

蹬上了天坛月正圆。

天也么天，

真乃是七宝悬，

闪星光高寒露气鲜。

(生)这天坛之上，怎生带宝剑来？

(净)

这剑呵，

坏天风几劫缘，

断天魔即世缠，

恰才个步天罡今夜演。

(生叹介)小生最苦是我父亲许下丁丑年相见，则除是今夜生天相见也。

【那吒令】

(净)待见呵，

不怕几重泉，

则要你孝意坚；

不怕几重天，

则要你敬意虔；

不怕几重缘，

则要你道意专。

这点心黑钻钻地孔穿，

明晃晃天坛现，

敢盼着你老爷爷月下星前。

(Reenter Qixuan with a sword in one hand, Chunyu following)

【Universal Happiness】

QIXUAN: Oh,

up on heaven´s altar the moon is round.
What a nocturnal sky
with the seven gems[1] hanging there
and the stars sparkling in the crisp fresh air!

CHUNYU: Why have you brought a sword to this sacred place?

QIXUAN:

This sword
can break the cycle of persistent love,
and cut the evil tangles in this life.
This very night I shall perform the magic steps.

CHUNYU (sighs): Poor father! Unless he´s rising to heaven tonight, he has no other way to keep his appointment with me for the year of *ding-chou*.

【Nalakūvara Minitune】

QIXUAN: If you want to meet with him,

as long as you are filial,
fear not the depths of nether springs;
as long as you are pious,
fear not the heights of lofty skies;
as long as you are resolved,
fear not the cycle of life´s turns.
Devotion can bore a hole through the pitch-black earth;
on the altar heaven reveals itself.
Your father may appear beside the moon and stars.

CHUNYU: It wasn´t utterly inconceivable to hear from my father, but how could ants have turned into human beings?

QIXUAN: They have it in their karma. It was merely a change of outward

(生问介)老爷儿罢了，蝼蚁怎生变了人？
(净)他自有他的因果，这是改头换面。
(生)小生青天白日被虫蚁扯去作眷属，却是因何？
(净)彼诸有情，皆由一点情，暗增上騃痴受生边处。先生情障，以致如斯。
(生)几曾与虫蚁有情来？
(净)先生记的孝感寺听法之时，我说先生为何带眷属而来？当有二女持献宝钗金盒，即其人也。

【寄生草】

则为情边见，
生身儿住一边。
你灵虫到住了虫宫院，
那騃虫到做了人宅眷，
甚微虫引到的禅州县？
但是他小虫虫凑着好姻缘，
难道老天天不与人行方便。

(生)咳，小生全不知他是蝼蚁，大师怎生不早道破也？
(净)我分明叫白鹦鹉说来，蚁子转身，你硬认是女子转身。
(生)是小生曾听来。
(净)便是你问三声烦恼，我将半偈暗藏春色：头一句“秋槐落尽空宫里”，可不是槐安国？第二句“只因栖隐恋乔柯”，是你因妻子得这南柯也。第三句“惟有梦魂南去日，故乡山水路依稀”，此是梦

appearance.

CHUNYU: How could I´ve been carried off in broad daylight to become their relative?

QIXUAN: It was all because they have feelings, and since love is the strongest of all feelings, it was not surprising that they became infatuated with you. On your part, you also happen to be the type that is susceptible to an infatuation. The consequence was only natural then.

CHUNYU: I don´t think I ever had any feelings for such insects as ants.

QIXUAN: Sir, don´t you remember the time you attended my sermons at the Temple of Filial Force? I asked you why you´d brought your family along. There were two young women there offering a pair of gold hairpins and a rhino-horn jewel case to Buddha. They were ants.

【Parasitic Grass】

In order that you find your love,
you left your corporeal self behind
and moved into the palace chambers of insects,
thus making them family members of a man,
all because fate once led you to the temple yard.
Since those tiny insects have captured such felicity,
why should heaven deny them their unordinary luck?

CHUNYU: Ah, I didn´t have the least idea they were ants. Why didn´t Your Reverence give me a hint?

QIXUAN: I made the white parrot squawk "ants turned around," but you took it as "Aunts, turn around."

CHUNYU: Well, I did hear the parrot say that.

QIXUAN: When you asked me about kleśa, I also gave you clear clues in the verse. The first line is "Autumn leaves cast from the Sophora tree." Isn´t that referring to the Sophora Kingdom? The next sentence says "You stay fast wedlocked to an arbor branch." That implies you secured the position of Taishou through a wedlock. The last sentence is "When

醒时节，依然故乡也。

（生）小生是曾沉吟这话来。

（净背介）便待指与他诸色皆空，万法惟识，他犹然未醒，怎能信及？待再幻一个景儿，要他亲疏眷属生天之时，一一显现，等他再起一个情障，苦恼之际，我一剑分开，收了此人为佛门弟子，亦不枉也。（回介）淳于生，当初留情，不知他是蚁子；如今知道了，还有情于他么？

（生）识破了，又讨甚情来？

（净笑介）你道没有情，怎生又要他生天？呀！金光一道，天门开了也。

（生看惊介）是也。

【么】

（净）

一道光如电，
知他是那界的天？
莫非是宝城开看见天宫院？
宝楼开放入天宅眷？
宝云开散作天州县？

（生）呀！天上甚么声响？

（内风起介）

知他世界几由延？
却怎生风声响处星河变？

（内作奏乐、报介）忉利天门开。

the sunny dream quits the southern bough, You will return along the homebound route." That means when you wake up from the dream you´ll find yourself still in your own house.

CHUNYU: I did mull over those lines.

QIXUAN (aside): I´ve made it clear to him that all things he sees are empty, and all assumptions are just for perception. But he´s not yet awakened and still in doubts. I´ll produce another illusion so that he can see his kinfolk ascending into heaven. When he falls into yet another infatuation, I´ll dissever his entanglement with one quick stroke of my sword. It´ll be worth my while if I can have him converted. (To Chunyu) Mr. Chunyu, when you first fell in love with her, you didn´t know she was an ant. Now that you know it, do you still love her?

CHUNYU: Since I´ve seen through all this, how can there be any more soft feelings?

QIXUAN (laughing): If you don´t love her any more, why are you praying for her rebirth in heaven? Look! A golden flash! Heaven´s gate is opened.

CHUNYU (astonished): Indeed!

【Ditto】

QIXUAN:

It flashes like a thunderbolt.
Just guess the gate to which sky is unlocked?
Is it revealing heaven´s most forbidden halls?
Is it opening to receive the latest guests?
Or the clouds are formatting into ether towns?

CHUNYU: Ah, what sound is that in heaven?
(Sound of rising wind within)
I wonder how far it is from our place.
How´s it that the wind is causing the stars to move?

(Music within)

VOICE WITHIN (announces): Gate to the second sky is open. The thirty-

(又报介)檀萝国蝼蚁三万四千户生天。

(净作惊介)是忉利天门报声，檀萝国蝼蚁三万四千户生天。你看纷纷如雨，上去了也。

(生)哎！檀萝国是我之冤仇，我这一坛功德，颠倒替他生天，怎了？怎了？(净笑介)

【赚煞】

则你有那答里冤，
这答里缘，
那蠢诸天他有何分辩？

(生)檀萝杀了南柯多少人马？多少业报？

(净)

恁虫豸儿杀害是前生怨，
但回头也普地生天。

(生哭介)则要见我的亲爷，我的公主妻也。

(净)跟我下了天坛，向三十三诸天位下，再烧一个指顶如何？

(生)疼也！

(净)哎！

打捱着指轮圆，
为满门良贱，
点肉香心火透诸天。
等一个星儿转，
步天坛你再看天面。
那时节敢爷儿相见，
重会玉天仙。

(净扯生下介)(众上鼓吹唱前“散花林”云云下)

four thousand households of ants from the Kingdom of Rattan Sandalwood now rise to heaven.

QIXUAN (excitedly): An announcement from the gate to the second sky! The thirty-four thousand households of the Rattan Sandalwood Kingdom are rising up to heaven. See how they go, like raindrops pulled upward!

CHUNYU: Why! The Rattan Sandalwoods are my enemy. How is it that my prayers have sent them up to heaven?! How´s that?!

【Coda】

QIXUAN (laughing):

Though you may bear a hatred to that one,
or cherish a love for this one,
what difference does that make to the senseless skies?

CHUNYU: The Sandalwoods killed so many of my Southern Bough soldiers that they should be punished through many cycles of lives.

QIXUAN:

The cause of killing was laid in their previous lives.
Once they repent they can to heaven rise.

CHUNYU (bursts out crying): But I want to see my father! I want to see my princess wife!

QIXUAN: Follow me down the altar and pray to the tablet of the thirty-three skies. It might be necessary that you burn another fingertip.

CHUNYU: It hurts terribly!

QIXUAN: Ah,

what if you have to burn them all?
It´s for the old and young of your clan;
the smoke from your scorching flesh will reach the skies.
When the Dipper turns another notch,
we can ascend the altar once again.
Then you may be able to see your dad,
and see again your fairy wife.

(Qixuan pulls Chunyu off stage. Reenter Monks from one stage door, singing "Flowers fly..." and off through the other door)

第四十四出　情　　尽

(生作指疼上)哎也!

　　焚烧十指连心痛,

　　图得三生见面圆。

小生虽是将种,皮毛上着不得个炮火星儿。今为无边功德,烧了一个大指顶,到度了檀萝生天。如今老法师引我三十三天位下,又烧了这一个大指顶,重上天坛,专候我爹爹、公主生天也。(内风起、生惊介)天门开了。(望介)又在说天话了。

(内报介)大槐安国军民蝼蚁五万户口同时生天。

(生喜介)好了,好了,分明说大槐安国军民蝼蚁五万户口生天,咱南柯百姓都在了。则不见爹爹和公主的影响,苦了这坛功德也。

【香柳娘】

　　谢诸天可怜,

　　谢诸天可怜,

　　则我爷儿不见,

　　又朦胧隔着多娇面。

　　展天坛近天,

　　展天坛近天,

Scene 44 Love Ended

(Enter Chunyu, holding a painful finger)

CHUNYU: Ouch!

A pain in the finger sends pangs to heart,
all for a perfect union with loved ones.

Although I´m a born soldier, my skin can´t even stand the burn of a tiny spark. Yet in order to achieve an infinitely benevolent deed, I burned a fingertip. But that only sent the Rattan Sandalwoods to heaven! The master then led me before the tablet to the sphere of Trāyastrinśa,[1] and there I scorched another finger. Now we´re back on the altar, waiting to see my dad and my wife rise up to heaven. (Wind rises within. Excitedly) Heaven´s gate is open once more! (He looks up) Here it speaks again.

VOICE WITHIN: The fifty thousand households of worker and soldier ants from the Great Sophora Kingdom now rise to heaven.

CHUNYU (happily): Hear! Hear! The announcement has made it clear that all the fifty thousand households of the Great Sophora Kingdom have risen to heaven. That includes my people in Southern Bough. But, why can´t I see my dad and my princess wife? What a disappointment it is for all my pains!

【Fragrant Willow Dame】

Oh, heavens, take pity on me!
Oh, heavens, take pity on me!
I haven´t seen my missing dad,
nor the pretty face of my lovely wife.
The altar leads me to your side.
The altar leads me to your side.
(He kowtows)
I´m praying here with all my heart;

（拜介）

　　拜的我心虔，

　　有灵须活现。

　　盼云端悄然，

　　盼云端悄然，

好了，好了，

　　那北上有云烟，

　　似前灵变。

呀！天门又开了。（内风起介）

（外扮老将上）淳于棼我儿，你父亲来了。

（生跪哭介）是我的爹。

【前腔】

（外）

　　叹游魂几年，

　　叹游魂几年，

　　你孝心平善，

　　果然丁丑重相面。

（生）爹爹，儿子生不能事，死不能葬，罔极之罪也。母亲同来么？

（外）你母亲久生人世了。

　　则我坟茔蚁穿，

　　我坟茔蚁穿，

　　却得这因缘，

　　爷儿巧方便。

我去也。

（生哭介）爹爹，那里去？

please grant my prayers if you can hear.
Up at the clouds I look and stare.
Up at the clouds I look and stare.
Look, look!
A cloud is approaching from the north,
an omen of some sort.

Ah, heaven´s gate is open again. (Wind rises within. Enter his father, an old general)
FATHER: Fen, my son! Your father´s here!
CHUNYU (kneeling and weeping): Oh, Father, is it really you?

【Ditto】
FATHER:
Oh, my soul has roamed many years!
Oh, my soul has roamed many years!
Thanks to your filiality,
we meet now in the year of *ding* and *chou*.
CHUNYU: Dad, as a son I feel extremely guilty, for I wasn´t able to attend on you while you were alive, nor was I able to give you a proper burial when you died. By the way, is my mother with you there?
FATHER: No. She´s been reborn on earth for quite some time now.
Ants had intruded on my grave.
Ants had intruded on my grave.
But by a curious turn of fate
I gained this lucky chance to rise.
Farewell.
CHUNYU (weeping): Dad, where are you going?
FATHER (refrain):
It´s sheer bliss to rise to heaven!
It´s sheer bliss to rise to heaven!
Let´s pray both in sky and on earth

（合）

喜超生在天，

喜超生在天，

两下修行，

和你人天重见。

（生哭介）亲爹，你也下来，待儿子摩你一摩儿。

【前腔】

痛亲爹几年，

痛亲爹几年，

梦魂长见，

那些儿孝意频追荐。

（外）我都鉴受了。我儿，你今后作何生活？

（生）依然投军拜将。

（外）快不要做他，犯了杀戒。

再休题将权，

再休题将权，

我为将玉皇边，

还怕修罗有征战。

天程有限，我去也。（合前）（外下）（生哭介）

（右相、周、田三人如前扮上）淳于公请起，休得苦伤。

（生起望介）原来是段相国、周、田二君。

（众）是也。

（生）右相，一向谗间小生，却是为何？

（右笑介）淳于公，蟠龙冈风水在那里？

（周）淳于公，我被你气死也！

so that we can in heaven meet.

CHUNYU (crying): Dear father, come down here so that I can touch you.

【Ditto】

For years I cried over your death.

For years I cried over your death.

In dreams we often met;

only there could I vent my filial thoughts.

FATHER: I´ve received them all. My son, what plans do you have for the future?

CHUNYU: I guess I´ll join the army again.

FATHER: No, don´t do that. That means you´ll have to commit killing.

Never again seek army ranks.

Never again seek army ranks.

As a general in the upper world,

it irks me to think of the war of gods.

I must be leaving you now, since in heaven we can´t delay.

(Refrain)

(Exit Father)

(Chunyu continues to weep. Enter Right-hand Premier, Zhou Bian and Tian Zihua, dressed as before)

PREMIER, ZHOU, TIAN: Lord Chunyu, please get up. Don´t let sorrow get the better of you.

CHUNYU (rises to his feet and looks up): So it´s you, Premier Duan, Mr. Zhou and Mr. Tian!

PREMIER, ZHOU, TIAN: Yes, it is.

CHUNYU: Premier Duan, why did you always slander me?

PREMIER (chuckles): Lord Chunyu, how did the *fengshui* of Dragon Hill turn out?

ZHOU: Lord Chunyu, just think how unfairly you treated me, and that sent me to my grave!

（生）我廿载威名，都被你所损哩。

（田）则我田子华，始终得老堂尊培植。

（右笑介）这恩怨都罢了。如今则感淳于公发这大愿，我们生天。

【前腔】

（右众）

是同朝几年，
是同朝几年，
苦留恩怨，
也只似南柯功德和那檀萝战。
弄精灵鬼缠，
弄精灵鬼缠，
识破枉徒然，
有何善非善？（内鼓吹介）

（众）请了。国王、国母将到。（合前）（下）

（生）是国王、国母模样也。（跪迎介）

【前腔】

（王同老旦众掌扇拥上）

立江山几年，
立江山几年。（见介）

（生）前大槐安国左丞相驸马都尉臣淳于棼叩头迎驾。

（王）淳郎，淳郎，生受你了。

CHUNYU: My impeccable reputation of twenty years was ruined by you!

TIAN: Only I basked in Your Excellency´s favor all the time.

PREMIER (laughing): Let´s forget personal grievances. We should all thank Lord Chunyu for praying for our rebirth in heaven.

【Ditto】

PREMIER, ZHOU, TIAN:

We´d been colleagues for many years.
We´d been colleagues for many years.
Grievance or gratitude,
were as real as the war with Sandalwood or feats in Southern Bough.
All is a phantom haunting you.
All is a phantom haunting you.
As soon as you see through the mist,
there is no longer good or bad.

(Music within) The king and queen are coming. Farewell.

(Refrain)

(Exeunt Premier, Zhou and Tian)

CHUNYU: Sure enough, they are the king and queen. (He kneels in welcome)

(Enter King and Queen with attendants holding fans)

【Ditto】

KING, QUEEN:

For years we ruled a piece of land.
For years we ruled a piece of land.

CHUNYU (greeting King and Queen): Your humble servant, the former left-hand premier of the Great Sophora Kingdom and your son-in-law, Chunyu Fen, here kowtows.

KING: Mr. Chunyu, we thank you.

（老旦）淳郎，别时曾说来，你若垂情，自有相见之期。那些外甥子通跑上天去了，你可见？

（生）不曾见哩。

（老旦）都做天男天女了。

咱一门良贱，

为天眷属非魔眷。

（生）敢问此去生天，比大槐宫何如？

（王）

去三千大千，

去三千大千，

不似小千般，

如沙细宫殿。

淳郎，我去也。公主和宫眷们后面来。（合前）（下）

（生叩头送起介）公主将到，小生竦身以俟。算来二十载南柯，许多恩爱。（望介）还不见，怎的？（又望介）云头上几个宫娥彩女来也。

【前腔】

（小旦道扮同老旦、贴上）

误烟花几年，

误烟花几年，

寂寥宫院。

QUEEN: Mr. Chunyu, do you remember at the time we parted I said as long as you remembered us, we should meet again? Just now your sons and daughters have skipped up to heaven. Did you see them?

CHUNYU: Really? I didn´t see them.

QUEEN: They´ve become celestial boys and maidens.

The old and young of all our clan
have risen to join the heavenly throng.

CHUNYU: May I ask, how does heaven compare to the Sophora Kingdom?

KING:

The universe of three thousand worlds,
the universe of three thousand worlds
is quite unlike the earthly one,
where towers are merely piles of sand.

Mr. Chunyu, we´re leaving. The princess and other royal womenfolk are coming.

(Refrain)

(Exeunt King, Queen and attendants)

(Chunyu kowtows to them as they leave and then rises to his feet)

CHUNYU: The princess is about to arrive. Just think how lovingly we lived during those twenty years in Southern Bough! I´m craning my neck in expectation. (He looks into the distance) What is keeping her so long? (He stares harder) There are several palace maids in colorful clothes coming on a puff of cloud.

(Enter Priestess Itty, Lady Truffle and Duchess Qiongying)

【Ditto】

THE THREE LADIES:

For years we missed the joy of love,
for years we missed the joy of love,
and led a lonely life.

(生)又不是公主，是上真仙姑、灵芝夫人和琼英姐。

(老众笑介)

那淳于郎子风流面。(见介)

(生)三位天仙请了。

(老旦叹介)淳郎，淳郎，我四个人滚的正好，被那个国人的狗才打断了我们的恩爱。

(生)那里是国人？便是那不知趣的右丞相。

(小旦)如今这话休题了。

(生)三位天仙下来，我有话讲哩。

(贴)我们是天身了，怎下的来？

(老)便下的来，你人身臭，也不中用。

最人身可怜，

最人身可怜，

我天上有好因缘，

你痴人怎相缠？

(贴)去也。公主来了。(合前)(下)

(内风起介)(生)这阵风好不香哩！(听介)你听，云霄隐隐环佩之声，的是公主到也。(拱望三次还叹，风起介)

【北新水令】

CHUNYU: It´s not the princess but Priestess Itty, Lady Truffle and cousin Qiongying.

THE THREE LADIES (laughing):

That handsome Chunyu is a gallant man.

(They greet Chunyu)

CHUNYU: It´s nice to see you three again. You look like fairies.

TRUFFLE (sighs): Oh, Mr. Chunyu, we four were having such a gluey time when that damned countryman interrupted our romance.

CHUNYU: What countryman? It was none other than that old bore, the right-hand premier.

ITTY: What is past is past. Don´t mention it any more.

CHUNYU: Come down, please, my fairy ladies. I´ve got a lot to say to you.

QIONGYING: We´ve already gained celestial bodies. How can we come down?

TRUFFLE: Even if we could, your human body smells, and you won´t be able to do it any more.

A poor carcass of human flesh!
A poor carcass of human flesh!
In heaven we live in congenial pairs.
Who´d get entangled with an earthly fool!

QIONGYING: The princess is coming. Farewell.

(Refrain)

(Exeunt the three ladies)

(Wind rises within)

CHUNYU: What a fragrant breeze! Listen, do you hear the clinking of jewelry in the clouds? This time it must be the princess. (He looks up, raises his clasped hands three times and sighs. Sound of wind again)

(Enter Princess)

【Minitune from River Xin, Northern Style】

(旦扮公主上)

则那睡龙山高处彩鸾飞，
这又是一程天地。
金莲云上踹，
宝扇月中移。
辗破琉璃，
我这里顺天风响霞帔。

(生哭介)兀那天上走动的，莫非是我妻瑶芳公主么？
(旦)是我，淳郎夫也。久别夫君，奴在这云端稽首了。我
为妻不了误夫君，
(生)
廿载南柯恩爱分。
(旦)
今夕相逢多少恨，
(合)
万层心事一层云。
(生叩头介)公主，感恩不尽了。你去后我受多少磨折，你可不知。
(旦)都知道了。

【南步步娇】

(生)

受不尽百千般东君气，
和你二十载南柯里，
无端两拆离。
则一答龙冈，
到把天重会。
恰些时弄影彩云西，
还只似瑶台立着多娇媚。

PRINCESS:

Rising from sleeping Dragon Hill upon a crane,
I have covered another span of life.
My feet now on a puffy cloud,
my fan moves across Luna´s face
as it rolls past the glassy sky.
The wind fills and flutters my rainbow shawl.

CHUNYU (sobbing): You there, walking on the clouds — aren´t you my dear wife, Princess Yaofang?

PRINCESS: Yes, my lord. It´s been a long time since we parted. Please accept my curtsey from the clouds. As your wife,

I failed to keep you lifelong company,

CHUNYU:

For death cut short our twenty years of love.

PRINCESS:

At this moment there is a lot to say,

BOTH:

But we are separated by a cloud.

CHUNYU (kowtows): Dear princess, I´m most indebted to you. But, do you know how much I suffered after your death?

PRINCESS: Yes, I do.

【Coy Steps, Southern Style】

CHUNYU:

I suffered sundry injustices at Duan´s hand!
For twenty years we enjoyed Southern Bough,
but were suddenly torn apart,
with you entombed on Dragon Hill.
Now you reappear in the sky,
riding upon a puff of rosy cloud.
You look the same as you had on the marble tower.

(生)公主妻呵，快下来有话说。

(旦)我下不来。

(生)怎下不来也？妻。

【北折桂令】

(旦)

我如今乘坐的是云车，
走的是云程，
站的是云堆。
则和你云影相窥，
云头打话，
把云意相陪。

(生)自公主去后，我好不长夜孤凄。

(旦)你孤凄么？

可知你一生奇遇，
亏了那三女争夫，
我临终数语因谁？

(生)知罪了。公主，也则是一时无奈，结个干姊妹儿。

(旦)

你则知道一霎时酒肉上朋情姊妹，
蚤忘了二十载花头下儿女夫妻。

(生)你如今做了天仙，想这些小事，都也不在怀了。则是我常想你的恩情不尽，还要与你重做夫妻。

【南江儿水】

我日夜情如醉，
相思再不衰。

公主，

Dear wife, come down please. I´ve got so much to tell you.
PRINCESS: I can´t.
CHUNYU: Why can´t you, dear wife?

【Laurel Crown Minitune, Northern Style】
PRINCESS:
Now I´m riding aboard a coach of cloud,
covering miles of cloud-paved roads.
Standing upon a turf of cloud,
I see you only through a cloudy mist,
and from a cloudy booth
I try to impart my cloudy thoughts.
CHUNYU: After you passed away, I became very lonely during those long cold nights.
PRINCESS: Lonely?
You really are a marvel of a man!
What about the three women fighting for one swain?
How could you´ve forgotten my parting words!
CHUNYU: I know I was wrong. Darling, I just couldn´t stand the loneliness. I felt like seeking some company.
PRINCESS:
You only cared about a moment´s spree with drinking friends,
and cast aside your wife of twenty years who raised your kids.

CHUNYU: Now that you´re a celestial being, I should have thought you wouldn´t mind such trivial matters. In fact I often think of our love and wish we could continue as man and wife.

【River Water, Southern Style】
Day and night I was drunk with love,
the force of which did not abate.
Dear princess,

我怕你生天可去重寻配？
你升天可带我重为赘？
你归天可到这重相会？
三件事你端详传示。
(哭介)你便不然呵，
有甚么天上希奇，
也吊下咱人间为记。

(旦)淳郎，你既有此心，我则在忉利天依旧等你为夫。则要你加意修行。

(生)天上夫妻交会，可似人间？

(旦)忉利天夫妻，就是人间，则是空来，并无云雨。若到以上几层天去，那夫妻都不交体了，情起之时，或是抱一抱儿，或笑一笑儿，或嗅一嗅儿。夫呵，此外便只是离恨天了。(叹介)天呵！

【北雁儿落带得胜令】
但和你莲花须坐一回，
恰便似线穿珠滚盘内。
便做到色界天和你调笑咦，
则休把离恨天胡乱踹。
(生)看了芳卿在云端，就是嫦娥。
(旦)你不知嫦娥，也就是人间常蚁，化作蛾儿，飞上天去。则他在桂树下，奴家在大槐宫，
都一般宫苑不低微。

will you, I hate to think, find a new spouse up there?
Can´t you take me to heaven as your mate?
Or return to earth so that we can reunite?
Those three questions I´d like you to explain.
(He bursts into tears) At least,
will you throw down a token from the sky,
something I can keep as a souvenir?

PRINCESS: Chunyu, my dear, if you really love me that much, I´ll wait for you in Trāyastrimśa to come, so that you can be my husband again. For that purpose you must be more diligent in practicing Buddhism.

CHUNYU: By the way, how do man and wife entwine in heaven? Is it done the same as we do it on earth?

PRINCESS: Couples in this sphere do it the same way as humans do, except that there´s action without effect. In the higher spheres though, there´s no more intercourse between man and wife. When desire burns, a hugging will do, or a look at each other and a smile, or simply a sniff. When one reaches the highest sphere of heaven, my lord, there are no more desires. (She sighs) Oh, heavens!

【A Wild Goose Alights with Triumph Minitune, Northern Style】
If you and I were to sit on a lotus seat,
it´d shoot and break like a string of pearls on a plate.
Suppose we do it in the higher spheres with flirting smiles,
watch out you don´t kick and puncture the lower vault.

CHUNYU: Standing on that cloud you look very much like the Luna goddess Chang Er.

PRINCESS: Hasn´t it ever occurred to you that, as her name Chang Er suggests, she´d been no more than an *earth* worm? It was only later when she´d *changed* into a moth that she was able to fly up into the sky. She now lives under a laurel tree, while I lived under a Sophora tree, both in palaces of eminent rank.

你登科向大槐，
比应举攀丹桂，
都一样上天梯。

（叹介）

你便宜，
见天女无回避。
伤悲，
怎的俺这俏云头渐渐低？（旦做坠下、生抱介）

（旦）呀！怎的吊下来？

（生）我的妻呵！

（旦）人天气候不同，靠远些儿也，哥。

（生）你怎生叫我哥？

（旦）你也曾在此寺中叫我一声妹子。

（生想介）是曾叫来。

（旦）你前说要个表记儿，这观音座下所供金凤钗、小犀盒儿，此非淳郎一见留情之物乎？

（生想介）是也。

（旦稽首佛前取金钗、犀盒与生接介）淳郎，淳郎，记取犀盒、金钗，我去也。

（生接钗盒扯旦跪哭介）

【南侥侥令】

我入地里还寻觅，
你升天肯放伊？
我扯着你留仙裙带儿拖到里，
少不得蚁上天时我则央及蚁。

Making a name in the Sophora world
is as good as winning the laurel crown[2]
— both serve as ladders to ascend the sky.
(Sighs)
Lucky are you,
who can meet a fairy face to face.
Oh, my!
Why is my cloud mount slowly sinking to the ground?

(Chunyu catches her as she falls down)

PRINCESS: Wow! How did I fall off the cloud?

CHUNYU: My dear wife!

PRINCESS: The climate in heaven is quite different from that on earth. You´d better keep your distance, Brother.

CHUNYU: Why call me brother?

PRINCESS: You once called me sister in this very temple.

CHUNYU (thinking): Indeed I did.

PRINCESS: Just now you said you´d like to have a souvenir. Aren´t the rhino-horn jewel case and gold phoenix hairpins at the foot of Guanyin´s statue the things that first caught your eye?

CHUNYU (thinking): Yes.

PRINCESS (bowing to the statue, she picks up the hairpins and jewel case and hands them to Chunyu): Darling, remember me by this pair of hairpins and the jewel case. I must be leaving you now.

(Chunyu accepts the pins and case. He kneels and clings to Princess)

【Colorful Flags Minitune, Southern Style】

CHUNYU (sobbing):

Since I ventured underground to seek you out,
how can I give up now you in heaven live?
I´ll obstinately clasp the ribbons of your skirt,
and beseech you ant you ain´t leaving me behind.

（旦）你还上不的天也，我的夫呵。

（生）我定要跟你上天。（生、旦扯哭介）（净猛持剑上砍开唱呀字后，旦急下，生骇跌倒介）

【北望江南】

（净）呀！

你则道拔地生天是你的妻，

猛抬头在那里？

你说识破他是蝼蚁，那讨情来？怎生又是这般缠恋？

（叹介）

你睁着眼大槐宫里睡多时，

纸捻儿还不曾打喷涕。

你痴也么痴，么痴，

你则看犀盒内金钗怎的提？

（生醒起看介）呀！金钗是槐枝，小盒是槐荚子。啐！要他何用？（掷弃钗盒介）我淳于棼，这才是醒了。人间君臣眷属，蝼蚁何殊？一切苦乐兴衰，南柯无二。等为梦境，何处生天？小生一向痴迷也。

【南园林好】

咱为人被虫蚁儿面欺，

一点情千场影戏，

做的来无明无记。

都则是起处起，

PRINCESS: My lord, it´s not your time to come to heaven yet.

CHUNYU: I will go up to heaven with you!

(Chunyu clings to Princess and weeps. Qixuan rushes on stage, separates them with a flourish of his sword and a protracted "Ah —." Princess hurries off stage, and Chunyu drops to the floor in a stupor)

【Recovering the South, Northern Style】

QIXUAN:

You think she´s your wife who rose from the earth to sky,
but raise your eyes and tell me where she is.

You said once you realized she was merely an ant, your affection for her had been swept away. How come you´re still so sentimental? (He sighs)

You dreamed wide-eyed in the Sophora palace many years,
which took less time than puffing up a paper spill.
Aren´t you the biggest fool of fools?
Why don´t you take a second look at those pins in the case?

CHUNYU (coming out of his stupor, stands up and looks): Why! The gold hairpins are but twigs from a Sophora branch, and the case is nothing but a seed pod from the tree. Bah! What´s the use of them! (He throws them away) I, Chunyu Fen, am really awakened this time. Isn´t the hierarchy of royalty and subjects the same as that of ants? The ups and downs of life are no different than what happened in the Sophora Kingdom! All is a dream, even going up to heaven! I´ve been living in a dream until this very moment!

【The Lovely Garden, Southern Style】

As a human I was deceived by tiny ants.
A spark of love spawned many shadow scenes,
in which I lost my sense of time and place.
All things are started by a cause,

教何处立因依？

(净)你待怎的？

(生)我待怎的？求众生身不可得，求天身不可得，便是求佛身也不可得，一切皆空了。

(净喝住介)空个甚么？(生拍手笑介，合掌立定不语介)

【北沽美酒带太平令】

(净)

众生佛无自体，
一切相不真实，(指生介)
马蚁儿倒是你善知识。
你梦醒迟，
断送人生三不归。
可为甚斩眼儿还则痴？
有甚的金钗槐叶儿？
谁教你孔儿中做下得家资？
横枝儿上立些形势？
早则白鹦哥泄漏天机，
从今把梦蝴蝶掐了羽翅。

我呵，

也是三生遇奇，
还了他当元时塔锥，
有这些生天蚁儿。

呀，

要你众生们看见了普世间因缘如是。

but how can I hold to a proper course?

QIXUAN: What do you want now?

CHUNYU: What do I want now? Vain is it to seek a human form. Also vain is it to seek a celestial form. It´s even vain to seek a Buddha´s form. All is empty.

QIXUAN (shouts): What´s empty?

(Chunyu claps his hands and laughs. Then he raises his hands palm to palm before his chest and stands silent and stiff)

【Shopping for Sweet Wine with Peaceful Minitune, Northern Style】

QIXUAN:

Buddha is not contained in any form;
no shape whatever can be real.
(He points at Chunyu)
An ant could have become your bosom friend.
Due to your protracted dream,
you´ve lost your foothold in the human world.
But why were you still dreaming when you´d woken up?
What of gold hairpins or Sophora twigs?
What about the wealth you accumulated in a hole?
What about your prominence on a bough?
The white parrot had given you an obvious hint.
From now on your wings of butterfly dreams are clipped.

Oh, my!

I´ve come across a rare event,
through which I paid off my pagoda debt
by sending these ants to the world above.

Ah,

I hope that show of karma has shed new light on the truth of life.

(Enter monks, holding joss sticks, banners and musical instruments)

（众香幡乐器上，同净大叫介）淳于生立地成佛也。（行介）

【清江引】

笑空花眼角无根系，
梦境将人殢。
长梦不多时，
短梦无碑记。
普天下梦南柯人似蚁。

（众拜介）万事无常，一佛圆满。

春梦无心只似云，
一灵今用戒香熏。
不须看尽鱼龙戏，
浮世纷纷蚁子群。

QIXUAN, MONKS (shout): Chunyu Fen has become a Buddha. (They walk around)

【River Qing Interlude】

How strange that the flower we see does not exist!
It´s a dreamland that haunts the mind.
A long dream doesn´t take much time;
a short dream won´t be noted down.
People are like ants dreaming on the Southern Bough.

(They salute the statue of Buddha) Nothing is constant, only Buddha is omnipresent.

A man may float high in a cloud-like dream
Until it's punctured by the incense smoke.
Just now you've seen a play of various scenes;
This bustling world's the same as that of ants.

NOTES

Scene 1

[1] MO: one of the seven major role types of a *chuanqi* play. The others are SHENG, DAN, JING, CHOU, WAI and TIE. It is usually MO´s function to give a brief introduction to the story at the beginning of a *chuanqi* play.

[2] Camellia Hall: the name Tang Xianzu gave to his study.

[3] Checkrein Bower: a small structure close by Tang´s study. The name implies that he´ll no longer leave home to seek an official career.

Scene 2

[1] In Chinese, the family name precedes the given name.

[2] Yangzhou: a major city on the northern bank of the Yangtze River, about 150 miles upstream from Shanghai.

[3] Dongping County: in the western part of Shandong Province.

[4] Chunyu Kun: a celebrated jester of the Warring States Period (475-221 B.C.).

[5] Chunyu Yi: a famous doctor of the Han Dynasty (206 B.C.-A.D.220). His daughter was lauded as an example of filiality, for she volunteered to be a serving maid in the palace in exchange for her father´s release from prison.

[6] Liuhe County: about 40 miles to the west of Yangzhou City.

[7] Zhenyuan reign: a period title of the Tang Dynasty (618-907). The seventh year of that reign was 791. In feudal times, each emperor gave a name (or sometimes more than one name) to his reign.He might change the name with the idea of starting things afresh.

[8] Yingchuan County: in present-day Henan Province.

[9] Pingyi County: in present-day Shaanxi Province.

[10] The repeated lines of a refrain are usually omitted from the drama script when the wording is the same.

[11] The Huai: a river between and parallel to the Yellow and Yangtze rivers.

Scene 3

[1] "May someone live long" is a common salutation in Chinese, but the number of years thus expressed depends on the receiver´s social status. To the emperor, it is ten thousand years; to a king or a prince, it is a thousand years; to ordinary elders, it is one hundred years.

[2] Mount Tai: in present-day Shandong Province, and one of China´s five sacred mountains.

[3] This and the following lines in this speech are collected citations from the classics which make reference to the Sophora tree.

[4] To differentiate *court* from its other meanings, the initial letter is capitalized when it refers either to the place where the king holds office or to the royal government.

[5] Duan Gong in Chinese puns on a homophone "(to) ruin (someone´s) career." His title "Marquis of Martial Feats" also carries implied irony, for we´ll later learn that martial feats are what he has never accomplished.

[6] It was a custom to sprinkle clean sand on the streets leading from a new premier´s residence to the Court.

[7] Liu Bei: the king of Shu during the period of the Three Kingdoms (220-280). It is said that there was an exceptionally tall mulberry tree standing in his parents´ courtyard.

[8] Chen Sheng: a rebel leader who overthrew the Qin Dynasty (221-206 B.C.). Legend has it that he was prompted to lead the rebellion after hearing a prophesy uttered by a fox in a willow grove.

Scene 4

[1] Tianjian reign of the Liang Dynasty: 502-519.

[2] Zhenjiang: a city on the southern bank of the Yangtze River opposite Yangzhou.

[3] Yangzhou was an affluent place in the Tang Dynasty, famous for beautiful women and flowers, while Zhenjiang was renowned for its Buddhist temples, Sweet Dew Temple among them.

[4] A combination of solid and broken lines that forms 64 hexagrams as expounded in *The Book of Changes (I Ching).*

[5] An analogy to the bell and drum towers in front of the main hall of a Buddhist temple.

Scene 5

[1] The Books refer to the four fundamental works of Confucianism, namely, *The*

Analects of Confucius, The Great Learning, The Doctrine of the Mean and *Mencius*. History refers to the Five Classics, which consist of *The Book of History, The Spring and Autumn Annals, The Book of Rites, The Book of Changes* and *The Book of Poetry*. These were the rudiments of learning, popularly known as The Four Books and Five Classics.

[2] According to *The Book of Rites*, "three months before a woman is to be married ... she should be taught the four virtues of a wife." (Ch. 44 "Marriage Rites")

[3] This line refers to the Yuan Dynasty (1271-1368) play *Mr. Zhang Boils the Sea*, in which Zhang boils sea water in a magic silver pot to force the dragon king to allow him to marry his daughter.

The following line refers to a well-known story of the ancient philosopher Zhuang Zi (Chuang-tzu), who once dreamed of himself changed into a butterfly. Upon waking, he could not decide whether it was he who had dreamed of being a butterfly or he was actually a butterfly dreaming of being a man.

[4] Throughout the play, the author deliberately chooses words with reference to tiny insects, such as fleas and mosquitoes, to remind the audience of events taking place in the ant world. In this case "sting" is used in place of "stick/cling," and "***ant***knowledge" instead of "acknowledge."

[5] Guanyin: a very popular Bodhisattva in China, named Avalokiteśvara in Sanskrit, and a personification of benevolence and beauty.

Scene 6

[1] Han Xin (?-196 B.C.): a renowned general of the Han Dynasty. In his early life he was very poor and lived in obscurity.

[2] Qu Yuan (340-278 B.C.): a great poet and a minister of the State of Chu during the Warring States Period. Disillusioned by his fatuous ruler, he drowned himself in the Miluo River in present-day Hunan Province.

Scene 7

[1] Within: i.e. behind the backdrop, a partitioned off area of the stage which serves as a tiring room.

Scene 8

[1] Sumeru: the name of a sacred mountain in Indian mythology as well as in Buddhism, believed to be the center of the universe.

[2] śūnya: a Buddhist term in Sanskrit which means the entitylessness of things. Its Chinese translation borrows the word *kong*, which carries such meanings as emptiness,

nothingness.

Rūpa: a paired term with Śūnya, which means the concept of things. In Chinese it borrows the word *se* (color), which carries a derived sense "sex."

The quote could also be translated into: Emptiness is colorful. Or more plainly: Nothingness is something we can see.

[3] To replace the Sanskrit transliteration with English words, the translation would roughly be: Color is empty. Or more plainly: Why are the things we see nonexisting?

[4] Dharma: roughly speaking, the governing rules of Buddhism.

[5] Sarigha: a monk.

[6] Mūlakleśa: a Buddhist term in Sanskrit, meaning the primary causes of life´s anxieties and miseries.

[7] Upakleśa: the secondary causes of life´s anxieties and miseries.

[8] Refer to the coda in Scene 4.

[9] The name of the sutra in Sanskrit is Saddharmapuṇḍarīkasūtra.

[10] Song Yu: a poet of the Warring States Period. In one of his odes, he praised the beauty of his east-side neighbor´s daughter, but insisted that despite her leering at him over the wall for three years, he remained unmoved.

[11] Bridal stand: According to folklore, a rich family might select a son-in-law by building a high platform at a thoroughfare. The maiden daughter would sit on it and seek a suitable spouse from among the passers-by. When she located a desirable man, she would throw a silk ball at him. The person hit was to be the bridegroom.

Scene 9

[1] Bow-arched shoes: tiny shoes, usually embroidered, worn by women who had bound feet.

Scene 10

[1] Ruan Ji: one of the seven eccentric scholars of the Wei and Jin dynasties and a follower of the Taoist sage Zhuang Zi. A recluse, he took refuge in wine.

[2] Liu Ling: another of the seven eccentric scholars. It is said that he told his servant to attend him with a spade as he drank, and bury him on the spot wherever he should fall down dead.

[3] A bed in the east chamber alludes to a son-in-law.

[4] This is a wordplay on the names of two historical figures, both of whose names include the Chinese word *guo*, which means "country." Translated literally, the surname *dou*

means "sinus," and *kong* means "hole." The middle name *guang* means "vast," and *an* means "peaceful."

[5] A sign erected at the gate of a noble family, usually with the authority of a special decree from the emperor as a kind of honor, requiring passers-by to get off their horses and walk past.

[6] The fifth drum: an ancient unit for measuring night time, indicated by a number of drumbeats sounded from the town's drum tower. Starting from nightfall, a night was divided into five "drums," at about two-hour intervals. The fifth drum was therefore at daybreak.

Scene 11

[1] A Yellow Gate Herald: a palace officer in charge of sending in reports to the emperor and announcing the emperor's decrees. The position was usually filled by eunuchs. Yellow Gate refers to the main palace gate.

[2] Cracking whips: special whips were cracked at the commencement of a royal audience to call for attention and silence.

Scene 12

[1] *The Book of Rites* specifies the wild goose as a betrothal gift because it was believed to keep to a single mate throughout its life.

[2] Altair and Vega: in fairy tales they are personified as the herd-boy and weaving-girl respectively.

[3] Heaven's son: a literal translation of *tianzi*, namely, the emperor, who claimed to be the son of heaven.

[4] Ruan: Ruan Zhao, a farmer who went to collect medicinal herbs in the Tiantai (heaven's stage) Mountains, where he met and married a fairy maiden. In less than a year, however, he became so homesick that the fairy had to send him back home.

[5] A traditional way of greeting is to raise one's clasped hands in front of the chest and move them up and down.

[6] These two lines are from *The Book of Poetry*.

[7] For Song Yu, refer to Scene 8, Note 10.

Scene 13

[1] Jade boy: a handsome young gentleman.

[2] See Scene 8, Note 11.

[3] As part of a traditional wedding ceremony, the bride and groom would drink wine

from a pair of gourd cups which were prepared by splitting a dried gourd into halves. The two halves symbolize a perfect match, and the golden color of the gourd suggests prosperity.

[4] Gold flappers: ornaments on official hats, symbolic of the wearer´s social status.

[5] Nong Yu: the name of a princess of the State of Qin in the Spring and Autumn Period (770-476 B.C.). She had a keen interest in playing the flute, and fell in love with a master flute who was able to imitate the calls of phoenixes and attract them. Then one day the couple flew off on the back of two of the legendary birds.

[6] In literary works a woman´s painted eyebrows are often compared to the distant hills into Chinese traditional painting.

[7] Clouds and rain: In Chinese literature, when "clouds" and "rain" are juxtaposed, it often carries a subtle implication of sexual intercourse.

Scene 16

[1] Mount Wu: a mountain on the upper reaches of the Yangtze River, famous for its kaleidoscopic clouds and unpredictable rains. It may also refer to the goddess of the mountain. In literary works it, as well as the Gaotang Temple on it, is often employed as a euphemism for a love affair. Hence the expression "clouds and rain." (See Scene 13, Note 7)

Scene 17

[1] An indication that the sun is high.

[2] Taishou: the title of the chief executive of a prefecture.

Scene 18

[1] See Scene 13, Note 5.

[2] An ancient way to calculate the years before the Christian era was introduced into China was to permute and combine the ten heavenly stems (*tian gan*) and the twelve earthly branches (*di zhi*) into a cycle of sixty years. Used together with the period titles of the emperors the year can be easily fixed. *Ding* is the fourth of the heavenly stems, corresponding to the element of fire, and *chou* is the second of the earthly branches, represented by the ox.

[3] Chunyu and Princess do not perform a kowtow to the palace officer but to the imperial edict which embodies the presence of the king. The officer switches back to his own personal identity as soon as the reading is finished, and therefore as one of lower status he must kowtow to the royal son-in-law and princess.

Scene 19

[1] The royal walk: the central lane of the pavement in the palace courtyard, which was reserved for royal use. At an audience, the military officers and civil officials used to stand on opposite sides of the walk, and a person who had a report to make would step out onto the walk.

Scene 21

[1] This is a deliberate anachronism meant to be comical, as the story is set in the Tang Dynasty. (See Scene 2)

Scene 22

[1] There seems to be a problem with the original stage direction, for the text gives no indication as to when the singers have come onstage.

Scene 23

[1] A short form of Mahāmaudgalyāyana, one of the ten chief disciples of Śākyamuni.

Scene 25

[1] Chang Er: the goddess of the moon.

[2] Legend has it that Chang Er stole and drank up the longevity elixir her husband, the great archer Yi who shot down nine of the ten suns in the sky, had begged from the Queen of the West, and was thus able to fly to the moon and live forever there.

Scene 26

[1] A rattle-drum: a small drum with a handle and two wood strikers attached by a piece of string to each side. One twists the handle to make clear consecutive beats. Originally a toy, it is used by street hawkers to attract attention.

Scene 27

[1] A jargon used in mahjongg games. "South Wind" is one of the pieces.

Scene 28

[1] The poem tells of a military expedition to the east.

Scene 29

[1] Badur: a Mongolian word for "brave man."

Scene 30

[1] Nanking: This could be a deliberate anachronism, for the city of Nanking didn´t assume its present name until the year 1441. At the time the story is set in, i.e. the Tang Dynasty, the southern capital, which Nanking literally means, referred to the present city of Chengdu, Sichuan Province.

[2] Guan Yu: a famous army general of Shu in the Three Kingdoms Period. On stage he is always portrayed in a red face. One story of his bravery and martial skill is that he killed the celebrated general from the other camp, Hua Xiong, with just one stroke of his broadsword. When he returned to his own camp his cup of wine was still warm. (The Chinese prefer to drink warmed wine, especially if it is low-proof rice wine.)

Scene 31

[1] In the face of the advancing troops of Jin, King Fu Jian (reigned A.D. 357-385) was so terrified that even the trees on the opposite hills looked like enemy soldiers to him; hence the proverb: On the Bagong Mountain, every tree and grass becomes an enemy.

[2] In this scene the tunes alternate between the northern style and the southern style. Northern tunes are usually more stentorious while southern ones are softer.

[3] This refers to two lines from Du Fu´s poem:

Boats west of Yellow Straw Gorge don´t return;
Few travelers venture past the Red Rock Cliff.

[4] Liu refers to Liu Bei (see Scene 3, Note 7). Together with Guan Yu (see Note 2 in the previous scene) and Zhang Fei, they are known as the "three sworn brothers." Zhang Fei was an intrepid but hot-tempered army general.

[5] Most rivers in China flow west to east owing to the Plateau of Tibet.

[6] Fan Kuai: one of Liu Bang´s most renowned generals. His bravery saved Liu Bang, the first emperor of the Han Dynasty, from an assassination attempt during a banquet at a place called Hongmen.

[7] Zhou Yu: the military chief of Wu in the Three Kingdoms Period. He was not known as a drinker, but that his colleagues compared his charisma to drinking the most conquering wine.

Scene 33

[1] In Chinese literature, the cry of the cuckoo is often associated with sadness.

Scene 34

[1] *Fengshui*: literally "wind (and) water," is an old belief in the geographical and architectural influence on the fortunes of the residents.

[2] See Scene 3, Note 6.

[3] This puns on a drinking jargon "to fight one´s way through many mountain passes," which means one drinks a bottoms-up with each and every guest at the party — in succession. The elders here imply that it would be most difficult for them to have their voices heard by heaven, i.e. the king.

Scene 36

[1] A brilliant, or promising, statesman is figuratively called "the pillar of the state." The "one pillar" here refers to Premier Duan himself.

[2] A court-tablet: a strip of polished ivory, wood or bamboo, which officials held in their hand when received in audience by the emperor, on which they could note down the key points of their intended report.

[3] The dialogue between Chunyu and Right-hand Premier centers around the *fengshui* of the locations. It was believed that the nose of the dragon is an auspicious place, while the lips incur war and death.

[4] As is explained in *fengshui*, if the location takes the shape of a tortoise, it should have a lowered head; if it takes the shape of a dragon, it should be winding. It would be inauspicious otherwise.

[5] According to *fengshui*, if a location has the configuration of a tortoise, it should look stable, while that of a dragon should show momentum. The contrary will be most inauspicious.

[6] The preference of the "real dragon," which was a title reserved for the emperor, reveals how ambitious Chunyu is. The two tunes of "The Calla Lily" pun on jargons of *fengshui* and a personification of the hills.

[7] This refers to a legend that on the seventh day of the seventh lunar month, all magpies will gather in heaven to form a bridge across the Milky Way to facilitate the annual union of the separated lovers, Altair the herd-boy and Vega the weaving-girl.

[8] Crimson robe and jade(-studded) belt were the symbolic costume of high officials.

[9] The sidewise movement of the crab is used figuratively to depict the swaggering arrogance of a bully.

Scene 43

[1] The seven gems here refer to the moon, which was believed to be composed of seven kinds of precious stones.

Scene 44

[1] In Buddhist belief heaven is divided into 28 spheres, of which Trāyastrimśa (popularly known as "the 33 skies") is the second lowest. With its main palace on the top of the fabulous Mount Sumeru, it is the highest sphere with any connection to earth.

[2] This refers to winning the first place in the imperial examinations.

TRANSLATOR´S POSTSCRIPT

A Dream Under the Southern Bough was written in 1600 by Tang Xianzu, two years after he had written *The Peony Pavilion*. The author, then 51, had retired to his hometown following an unsuccessful official career.

In this play, the dream, which is pivotal in *The Peony Pavilion*, has expanded to almost the length of the play. In fact, the play is about a dream, in which the hero, a discharged army officer named Chunyu Fen, dreams that he enters an ant hole, and ends up marrying the daughter of the king of the ants. The king of the ants appoints Chunyu Fen to a high position in his administration. For some 20 years, he pursues an illustrious career, until, following the death of his wife, his downfall is engineered by a political rival. The king of the ants has Chunyu Fen arrested and expelled from his realm.

He wakes up to find that the glories and disgraces he has experienced so acutely were no more than a dream during his afternoon nap. His curiosity, however, leads him to the discovery of a huge colony of ants nesting in a hole in an ancient Sophora tree in his courtyard, under which he often feasts. Mystified, he seeks help from a Chan master Qixuan, who brings him to the realization that all is empty and meaningless.

Because of that nihilistic conclusion and the copious allusions to and quotations from Buddhist scriptures throughout the play, some critics suggest that the play reveals Tang´s conformity to Buddhism and the dulling of his social criticism in his late years.

A more careful examination reveals that Tang has woven many satirical episodes and a great deal of pungent criticism into the play. The incompetence and greediness of the chief of staff (Scene 21) can be seen as typical of local Ming Dynasty officials. In the prefectural office, there isn´t even a copy of the laws. Nepotism and factionalism are rife, and Chunyu himself bluntly admits that he has been appointed to "a nepotic position." (Scene 16) The officers he in turn selects re his drinking cronies. His rivalry with the right-hand premier is a reflection of the bitter power struggle in the imperial court. His criticism touches the highest level when he says:

Compared to serving the royal house,
Smooth are the Taihang Mountains´ rugged paths;
Compared to serving His Majesty,
Safe are the Yellow River´s swift whirpools.

(Scene 40)

Despite the pervasion of Buddhism in the play, we may also detect some disquiet with the way the religion was practiced. For instance, a monk named Five Don´ts sings:

We worship Buddha day and night,
who sits aloft on a flesh—colored lotus seat.
Not averse to wine and women,
we´re subject to fortune, fate and face.
One can´t escape from the iron girdle round the world.

(Scene 7)

To him, Buddha´s lotus seat is nothing but a pile of human flesh. Just like the chief of staff, who proclaims, "Without silver, what´s the good of being an officer?" (Scene 21) the Buddhist deities in heaven would not refuse such a gift as "a necklace of precious jewels, which is worth hundreds of thousands of ounces of pure gold." (Scene 8) And although Master Qixuan has promised that chanting the *Blood Pool Sutra* can guarantee a long and healthy life (Scene 23), it in no way helps the princess avert her misfortune. With these layers of complication, the play offers scope for diverse interpretations to generation after generation of readers.

This play may remind one of Franz Kafka´s novel *The Metamorphosis*

(1915), in which "When Gregor Samsa woke up one morning from unsettling dreams, he found himself changed in his bed into a monstrous vermin." (Translated by Stanley Corngold, Bantam Books) Just as Gregor´s metamorphosis from human into a vermin helps us see better the alienation of human beings in the society of Kafka´s time, Chunyu´s dream of entering the ant world throws light on the social problems of the late Ming Dynasty.

It is interesting to note that both writers choose to have their protagonists transformed into insects. While Kafka writes about a single insect, Tang portrays a whole colony. As we all know, ants live in societies with a queen and males and a social division of labor, a fact that adds a more vivid human touch to the story. And that is a point the play intends to make: Except for their outward appearance there is not much difference between humans and ants.

There are other points of contrast between Kafka´s story and Tang´s play. In *The Metamorphosis*, the story takes place only after Gregor wakes from a dream, and develops in the human world with Gregor in the degraded form of a vermin. But the main body of Chunyu´s story evolves in a dream as he moves into an alien world of insects, where he is "upgraded" to a member of the royal family. The readers of the novel and the audience of the play are thus led to view the world from two contrasting angles.

The Metamorphosis leaves us in no doubt as to what Gregor looks like, as we see him through the eyes of his parents, sister and others. In Tang´s play, however, the change does not occur at a physical level. Although Chunyu tells us that he dreams of himself living in the ant world, on stage, he, and all the ant characters, actually appear as human beings. The ant king offers a popularly-accepted reason in his entrance poem:

A thousand years make animals human,
So here wee appear as king and subjects.(Scene 3)

This kind of self-awareness on the part of the actors is one of the pronounced characteristics of the traditional Chinese stage.

To constantly remind the readers of this double identity, Tang makes full use of an intriguing language phenomenon by choosing the word "flea" instead of "early." The two words happen to be homophones in Chinese, pronounced as *zao*. In the ancient classics as well as in the Yuan and Ming Dynasty plays, the Chinese character *zao* (flea) can be used in place of *zao* (early), so this is not unique to this play or to Tang. But what is noteworthy in this play is that *zao* (flea) is disproportionately adopted where *zao* (early) should have been used. Of the 36 instances of the use of *zao*, 27 use the character for "flea," and are mainly associated with the ants. Though there seems to be a slight lack of consistency, every time the word is used by the princess, it takes the form of "flea." Flea in its broad sense may refer to any insect of small size.

This ingenious use of Chinese words presents a challenge to any translation attempt. To compensate for the loss, a different pair of English homophones has been selected, namely "we" and "wee" — the latter happens to carry the same implication of tininess as "flea." By using "wee" instead of "we" whenever an ant character sings or speaks, the translation hopes to preserve the subtle implication and achieve the same literary effect.

In this translation I carried on my experiment with the irregular verse lines in order to reflect the rhythm and tempo of the original, an experiment started with my revised version of *The Peony Pavilion*. Since Chinese classical drama is mainly sung rather than spoken, the above two elements are essential to the mood of the play. The basic pattern is to use iambic tetrameters to reflect the five-word lines and pentameters for the seven-word lines. Other line patterns vary accordingly, but not rigidly. For instance, iambic dimeters for three-word lines, trimeters for four-word lines, and hexameters for ten-word lines.

Generally speaking, the iambic foot is desirable, with variations occurring mostly in the first foot. Rhyming is not meticulously attempted, though in the original text each scene keeps to a mono-rhyme. And assonance rhyming is explored to enhance the musicality of the verse. For more details, readers may refer to the prefaces to *The Peony Pavilion*.

In this translation, the layout intends to exhibit the difference between the songs, the spoken parts and the intoned poems in the original text. The songs are indented 0.75 cm from the left in separate lines, while the spoken parts are indented 0.25 cm and in continuous lines. The intoned poems, which usually accompany a character on and off stage, are put in italics and indented 0.5 cm.

The translation is based on Prof. Qian Nanyang's annotated text published by The People's Literature Publishing House in 1981, with reference to Prof. Qian's proofread version in *The Collected Plays of Tang Xianzu* published by The Shanghai Classics Press in 1978 and Mao Jin's punctuated text in *The Sixty Plays*.

Zhang Guangqian

ABOUT THE TRANSLATOR

Zhang Guangqian, Professor of English at the University of Science and Technology of China. Graduated from the Department of Foreign Languages, Anhui University, in 1976, and the postgraduate Research and Study Program in English Language and Literature, Beijing Institute of Foreign Languages, in 1985. His major translations include:

2006 ***Selected Plays from the Yuan Dynasty.***
Beijing: Foreign Languages Press

2003 ***A Dream Under the Southern Bough.***
Beijing Foreign Languages Press.

2001 ***The Peony Pavilion (revised).***
Beijing: Foreign Languages Press.

1998 ***Into the Porcelain Pillow — 101 Tales from Records of the Taiping Era.***
Beijing: Foreign Languages Press.

1994 ***The Peony Pavilion.***
Beijing: Tourism Education Press.

图书在版编目（CIP）数据
南柯记／（明）汤显祖 著；张光前 译.
–北京：外文出版社，2006
（大中华文库）
ISBN 978-7-119-04165-0
Ⅰ. 南…　Ⅱ. ①汤…　②张…　Ⅲ. 英语–对照读物，戏剧–汉、英
Ⅳ. H319. 4：I
中国版本图书馆 CIP 数据核字（2005）第 079106 号

出版策划：徐明强　胡开敏
责任编辑：杨春燕　胡开敏
重印修订：刘奎娟
重印编辑：杨春燕　刘倩雯
重印监制：冯　浩

大中华文库
南　柯　记
〔明〕汤显祖　著
张光前　译

出 版 人：徐　步
出版发行：
外文出版社
（中国北京百万庄大街 24 号）
邮政编码 100037
http://www.flp.com.cn
电话：008610–68320579（总编室）
008610–68995852（发行部）
008610–68327750（版权部）
制 版：北京维诺传媒文化有限公司
印 刷：深圳市碧兰星印务有限公司
开 本：960mm × 640mm　1/16　　**印 张：**39. 25
2006 年第 1 版第 1 次印刷
2020 年第 1 版第 2 次印刷
（汉英）
ISBN 978-7-119-04165-0
（精装）
定 价：120. 00 元